Expanding Therapeutic Possibilities

Expanding Therapeutic Possibilities

Getting Results in Brief Psychotherapy

By

Steven Friedman

and

Margot Taylor Fanger
Harvard Community Health Plan

Lexington Books
D.C. Heath and Company/Lexington, Massachusetts/Toronto

Illustrations by Sarah Friedman

Library of Congress Cataloging-in-Publication Data

Friedman, Steven, 1945–
    Expanding therapeutic possibilities : getting results in brief
psychothrapy / by Steven Friedman and Margot Taylor Fanger.
      p.   cm.
    Includes bibliographical references and index.
    ISBN 0-669-24451-1 (alk. paper)
    1. Brief psychotherapy.   I. Fanger, Margot Taylor.   II. Title
    [DNLM: 1. Psychotherapy, Brief—methods.   WM 420 F9113e]
RC480.55.F75   1991
616.89'14—dc20
DNLM/DLC
for Library of Congress   90-13712
                                      CIP

Published simultaneously in Canada
Printed in the United States of America
International Standard Book Number: 0–669–24451–1
Library of Congress Catalog Card Number: 90-13712

The paper used in this publication meets the minimum requirements of
American National Standard for Information Sciences—Permanence of
Paper for Printed Library Materials, ANSI Z39.48-1984. ∞™

  92 93 94 95 8 7 6 5 4 3 2

To Donna, my most dependable source of constructive ideas and loving communications . . . and to Sarah, whose enthusiasm and love of life are a continual source of inspiration. —S.F.

To my companion on trips to Mexico . . .
and our offspring, Steffen, Ross, and
Katharine. —M.F.

Psychotherapy is sought not primarily for enlightenment about the unchangeable past but because of dissatisfaction with the present and a desire to better the future.

—Milton H. Erickson

Contents

Figures and Tables

Figures

Tables

Preface

This book has emerged from our desire to offer to other therapists an approach designed to increase the effectiveness of psychotherapy in general, brief therapy in particular. Over a number of years, we each found ourselves generating and synthesizing therapeutic skills that enabled us to meet creatively the demands of practice in a managed health care setting (the Harvard Community Health Plan, an HMO). We developed not only particular skills, but also a specific point of view that we have found enormously useful in directing clients toward the results they want. We call that point of view the *possiblity paradigm*.

Writing a book demanded even more synthesis and creativity. We found that our different backgrounds (Steven's in experimental psychology, developmental research, and clinical psychology; Margot's in social work) and our combined forty-nine years of clinical practice gave us a richly diverse pool of experience upon which to draw. Steven became aware of Margot's reputation for innovative therapeutic approaches shortly after he joined the mental health staff of the Braintree Center of the Harvard Community Health Plan. Margot, working at the Cambridge Center, was delighted to discover a colleague whose basic outlook and therapeutic techniques were much the same as hers. We both emphasize client's competencies and resources rather than deficits and pathology; we both consider language the critical instrument of change; we both structure our interventions around the goals of the client.

Several years after our first meeting, Steven began to think about writing a book that presented a positive, health-oriented model for effective therapy. Margot enthusiastically accepted his invitation to join in his project. This book is the result.

We have been greatly influenced not only by family systems therapists, especially Virginia Satir, but also by Milton Erickson and his continuators, most notably Jay Haley, Paul Watzlawick, Bill

O'Hanlon, Ernest Rossi, Steve deShazer and the neurolinguistic pro-
grammers, Richard Bandler, John Grinder and Leslie Cameron-Bandler.

However, our experiences working in a health maintenance organization for many years are the basis for the development of our own
special "brand" of time-effective psychotherapy. Although the model
presented here is not the only one that might be useful in a specific
situation, it is one with which we both have experienced significant
success.

This book outlines a set of "wellness" strategies that we have
found useful in helping clients shift their views of reality, thereby opening up options for change and growth. The strategies are "systemic"
and "eclectic." They are systemic in that they assist the client to find
the resources necessary for personal growth and change in the social
environment in which he or she lives and relates. They are eclectic in
that they are based on the integration of various models of brief psychotherapy into a framework for the time-effective treatment of clients
with a diverse array of complaints.

Over time, therapists tend to develop a "tool box" of clinical
intervention strategies to use with clients. The fewer the tools, the
greater the danger that the therapist will try to "fix" multifold difficulties with limited resources (Haley 1969). While therapists who rely on
a single technique may be successful sometimes, they can also cause
much unnecessary wear and tear on both themselves and their clients.
A therapist who relies on a single technique must accept only a select
group of clients for whom this specialized tool will work. Some brief
therapists fall in this latter catergory (Mann 1973; Sifneos 1972) and
are able to work effectively with a small and select number of people.
A large majority of those seeking help, however, are excluded from
participating in these therapies, since they fall outside such a therapist's
preset therapy criteria.

We believe in a tool box with a wide variety of "implements" to
deal efficiently and effectively with all requests for help. We hope that
other therapists will consider the ideas discussed here as well as experiment with them in their own practices.

We strive to avoid complex assumptions about a situation when
simple assumptions leading to simple interventions will be effective. We
search for the simplest, least drastic, least intrusive, least stigmatizing
methods that will sucessfully reach the *client's* goal. Only when the
most economical approach has been tried without success, do we then
move to the next level of complexity.

As possiblity-oriented therapists, we aim to maximize our effectiveness with clients by making initial contacts count. We have found that
most significant change in psychotherapy is likely to happen early in
the therapy process when the therapist is least "captured" by the cli-

ent's view of reality and most able to engage the client with outside perspective. By "hitting the ground running" we increase our leverage in the change process. A therapist who becomes involved with the client over a long period may be inducted into the client's reality to such an extent that another level of intervention such as consultation with a colleague or the use of a therapy team becomes necessary.

Rather than focusing on the "DSM" or the "dark side of man", we take a perspective emphasizing the "BSM" or "bright side of man" (Shulem 1988). It is our intention to share this perspective and illustrate its utility and efficacy in dealing with a variety of clinical situations. A story will help to illustrate the benefits we see of a "wellness" model in contrast to one that focuses on deficits, limitations, and dysfunction (Barker 1985: xiv).

> Several decades ago, a group of men at the University of Wisconsin started a serious writers' group. Calling themselves *The Stranglers*, they were merciless in criticism. Not to be outdone, a group of women, who named themselves *The Wranglers*, set up a corresponding group. But their idea was to accentuate the positive, to look for the good in their colleagues' work, to be encouraging and gentle in their criticism.
>
> Twenty years later, the university, curious as to what had happened to the two groups, made a survey. Each group had had equal talent; only their approaches differed. And what had happened? Not one of the men had amounted to anything as a writer. But of the women's group, half a dozen were notably successful.

Part I of this book provides the conceptual map for the clinical journey. Here, we compare the *possiblity paradigm*, a pragmatic, resource-oriented model for effective clinical intervention, with a more traditional view of the change process and discuss the physiological benefits of creating a climate of positive expectancy. We also outline our assumptions in a possibility-oriented therapy and present a schedule of intervention for working with clients in a time-effective manner.

Part II concentrates on the treatment process. We focus on how one can maximize the effectiveness of the first contact with the client in the "crucial initial interview" and discuss the keystone of our therapy, the concept of "reframing."

Part III explores a set of clinical strategies for intervening effectively with individuals, couples, and families. We also speak to some complex, and often ignored, clinical issues such as psychiatric hospitalization and the use of psychotropic medications and substance abuse, and discuss the application of the possibility paradigm in therapeutic consultations and team collaborations.

Part IV presents several full-length clinical examples to demonstrate the application of the possibility paradigm over time. The final chapter is a summary of our thinking about change and the therapy process.

Throughout the book, we emphasize the practical application of brief therapy methods with individuals, couples, and families. The clinical material is presented to give the reader as close a view of the therapeutic process as possible in hope that the methods and principles we describe will come to life in a practical and useful way.

Acknowledgments

A book is a uniquely personal production and a composite of the influence of many people. We have been fortunate to have had many supervisors, colleagues, and students who have nurtured and amplified our thinking about the process of psychotherapy and have, over the years, offered us their own valuable ideas and input. To these people we are especially grateful: Michael Bennett, Sally Brecher, Matthew Budd, Simon Budman, Richard Caplan, James Donovan, Richard Fitzpatrick, Katherine Grimes, James Harburger, Hyman Kempler, Marjorie Lavin, Cynthia Mittelmeier, David Mirsky, Sally Pettus, James Sabin, Robert Schneider, Sylvia Skinner, Ronnie Tilles, Bennett Tittler, David Van Buskirk, and April Westfall.

Many of the ideas presented in this book germinated in the fertile soil of Harvard Community Health Plan, a comprehensive health maintenance organization that has provided quality, mental health treatment for over twenty years. It has been a privilege to work in this supportive setting. Margot wants to especially thank the HCHP Teaching Center and its director, Gordon Moore, for his support and encouragement over the past fifteen years. In addition, she is most grateful for the HCHP Foundation's support in providing the opportunity to pursue her explication of effective therapeutic methods. To our colleagues in mental health, internal medicine, and pediatrics at Harvard Community Health Plan, who have supported us in numerous ways, we offer our appreciation.

Genevieve Carpenter, Gerald Stechler, and Peter Vietze were major influences in Steven's early thinking and research on developmental processes and human competence, and to them he owes special thanks. Instrumental in the development of Margot's skills as a therapist have been Lydia Rapoport, Virginia Satir, Leslie Cameron-Bandler, John Grinder, David Kantor, Barry Dym, and Richard Chasin; she offers warm thanks to them all. She would also like to recognize the signal role of her writing coaches in her ongoing learning of that skill.

The authors would like to give special thanks to Sarah Friedman who created the illustrations for this book.

Last, but certainly not least, we thank the hundreds of clients who have taught us so much about what is possible.

Some of the clinical examples in this book have been published elsewhere in somewhat different form, and have been adapted with permission from S. Friedman (1990), Towards a model of time-effective psychotherapy: A view from a Health Maintenance Organization, *Journal of Family Psychotherapy* 1(2):1–28 copyright 1990, Haworth Press; S. Friedman (1989), Child mental health in an HMO: A family systems view, *HMO Practice* 3:52–59 copyright 1989, JB Lippincott Co.; S. Friedman (1989), Brief systemic psychotherapy in a health maintenance organization, *Family Therapy* 16:133–144 copyright 1989, Libra Publishers, Inc.; S. Friedman, (1989), Strategic reframing in a case of delusional jealousy, *Journal of Strategic and Systemic Therapies* 8:1–4 copyright 1989, Don Efron; and S. Friedman and S. Pettus (1985), Brief strategic interventions with families of adolescents, *Family Therapy* 12:197–210 copyright 1985, Libra Publishers, Inc.

Identifying information in the clinical illustrations has been changed to protect the privacy of the clients involved.

Part I
Fundamentals: Mapping the Journey

Part 1
Fundamentals: Mapping
the Journey

1
Introduction

A Story

Long ago, in a faraway village by the sea, the people lived together in harmony and happiness. In this village, at the foot of the mountains, lived two sisters, Anna and Kata, born of the Liza family. These sisters viewed the world in very different ways. The older, Anna, was a penetrating thinker, who was always looking beneath the surface of things; she enjoyed taking objects apart and trying to put them back together. Anna would spend many hours studying the relationship of one thing to another to understand how they worked. She had a special capacity for analyzing the world around her. Appearances were never accepted at face value but had multiple meanings that required active effort to gain necessary understanding. Her ability to understand and analyze situations was much admired by the people of the village.

Her younger sister, Kata, was also very curious about the world. In contrast to her older sister, Kata focused her attention on the beauty of the world. She would enjoy spending a day in the forest watching the behavior of the animals and immersed in the beauty around her. She treasured that beauty and actively avoided interfering with the flow of nature. Kata tried to understand the world by asking questions and observing. Her optimism, astuteness about the natural order of things, and positive view of the world were much appreciated and valued by the people of the village.

As life grew more complicated, the villagers sought out Anna and Kata for their wisdom and good sense. They came with the hope that these wise sisters could help them deal with the confusions, daily irritations, and worries in their lives. However, Anna and Kata, as you might imagine, had very different ideas about the human condition.

Anna Liza, the older sister, believed that only through a long and arduous process of self-reflection and introspection could you understand and so overcome the past negative influences that created your problem. She believed that deep, dark forces lurked beneath the calm exteriors of the people she saw. The metaphor she would use to describe this process involved the volcanic mountain that rose to great heights beside her village. Beneath its usual calm exterior there was tremendous tension and volatile energy. Anna would relate the present difficulties of the people she saw with childhood events that were usually unsavory or painful or both.

Anna generally met with people on a very regular basis over a period of several years. The people she saw would become very dependent on her, and found themselves unable to make life decisions without her. Anna viewed their regular contacts with her as the most important hour in their week. At certain points Anna would refer, in her notes, to someone, as "defensive" and "resistant." She would then make "interpretations" that were attempts to "break through" these "resistances." Anna was committed both to the "growth" of the people she saw and to "being there" as these changes occurred.

Kata Liza, on the other hand, viewed people as healthy, resourceful, and open to change. She influenced people by planting the seeds of ideas for change. Kata saw people on an "intermittent" basis, with meetings sometimes many weeks or even months apart. She might see people once or twice but also might be involved with them over many years. She focused on, and took seriously, what changes the person wanted. Kata was interested in whether the people she saw were satisfied with the progress they were making in dealing with their original request for help, and she kept track of their progress in meeting that goal.

Kata focused on the present and the future rather than on the past; she believed that it was through a focus on a future of expanded possibilities of effective action that one could begin to establish a vision for change. She viewed what people did outside their meetings with her as more important than the meetings themselves. The people she saw generally did not develop strong feelings of dependency on Kata, although they respected and liked her, and they often came to her reporting changes they'd made on their own. Kata viewed people as open and motivated to change and matched and tailored her interventions to their world views. Her notes contained comments like: "How can this client expand his resources?" or "Suggest a visit to the cemetery to help Mary deal with the loss of her sister." Kata's favorite metaphor was the natural flow of the river that meandered its way through her village. The continuity and flow of the river implied movement, change, and self-direction.

Over time, each sister took on apprentices who went out into the world bringing their different philosophies to the many people in the community who were unhappy. The authors of this book are disciples of Kata Liza (and her daughter, Norma Liza). Although trained in the philosophies of Anna Liza, we believe that change can be facilitated ("catalyzed") more effectively by capitalizing on the client's strengths, resources, and energy for change. We take the view that an optimistic, future-oriented perspective is most effective in amplifying the client's abilities and capacities in moving toward change and taking effective action. We view people as capable and motivated and so construct interventions that build on our clients' world views. This approach emphasizes not limitations, deficits, and pathology, but possibilities, strengths, and health (Masterpaqua 1989; Seeman 1989). "This model is very compatible with the theory of continuous improvement in industry (Berwick 1989) in which focus is placed on *processes which need to be further improved* rather than on individual defects or deficiencies" (Friedman 1990: 24). We assume that "people are doing the best they can" and it is our job as therapists to help build on the strengths and resources that already exist.

We address the creation of a context for change for people who want to be more effective in their lives. We have developed our approach working in a setting that emphasizes high-quality, time- and cost-effective mental health treatment. Although developed in a specialized health care setting, the principal ideas are relevant and applicable to other settings where clinicians want to add a useful, effective, and action-oriented philosophy of therapeutic change to the various skills they already have.

When people come to see a therapist, they are usually interested in developing new coping skills and tend to remain in psychotherapy for between only four and eight sessions (Budman & Gurman 1988). The constraints set by medical insurance companies also play a part in limiting the number of mental health visits. In addition, current economic conditions have forced many state and local human service agencies to limit their services to the many people requesting them. Therapists must maximize the time they have with clients to produce change in a time-effective manner. The pragmatic, time-sensitive framework offered here will guide the therapist in working effectively and economically with a diverse array of clients. It is oriented toward measurable and observable behavioral change.

The principles and ideas discussed in this book are not an attempt to compress models of traditional long-term therapy into a short-term format. Rather, our orientation reflects *a radical departure from traditional models of psychotherapy* (a "paradigm shift"). This is evident in the way we think about possibilities for change, in the solution-oriented way we approach clients, in the way we and our clients co-construct solution-oriented interventions, and in the way that we emphasize *action as the basis for new learning*. The creation of *new action possibilities* is our primary focus. Our goal becomes freeing clients to see multiple options and alternatives, to view reality in new ways, and to use these new perspectives as a means to move on in their lives with increased choices of behavior.

In addition, we view our work as *systems consultation* (Wynne, McDaniel & Weber 1986, 1987). In collaboration with the client, our job becomes one of facilitating and catalyzing a process of change that will become self-sustaining and maintainable in the client's everyday life. "The consultant takes a comprehensive 'meta' view of the consultee's concern . . . bringing a fresh viewpoint to a clinical problem" (Wynne, McDaniel & Weber 1986: 9). Since we view learning and change as a *nonlinear* or *discontinuous* process, we see the possibility for major life or behavior changes with minimal therapeutic input. We will make the case that the history of a difficulty is not necessarily correlated with the need for intensive and/or open-ended therapy. We believe that even longstanding difficulties can be successfully dealt with using a brief treatment framework.

Our Philosophic Assumptions

A Developmental Model

A developmental model accepts change as a natural, normal, and expected part of living. We believe individuals, couples, and families arrive for therapy when they are in life-stage transitions. At these transition points, when they must accommodate to changing needs, difficulties may often arise. These "snag" points require the client to "recalibrate" or revise old structures, rules, and expectations in making the transition to the next stage (Budman and Gurman 1988; Carter and McGoldrick 1988; Haley 1973). With that in mind, we anticipate periods of active involvement in treatment (when these developmental issues are paramount) separated by periods of no contact while the client is "out in the world," practicing what he or she has learned.

Since we view *change as an inevitable part of living,* we expect the people we work with to be changing in the course of their daily living outside our offices. This belief is based on the assumption that, given time, people are generally resourceful enough to generate creative solutions to life problems.

The therapeutic process encompasses more than our minimal contacts with the client. Traditionally, "the patient [was] viewed as relatively inert . . . [and as continuing] in his or her current state in the absence of intervention. [This is] out of keeping with our current thinking about adult life. [The traditional view overestimates] the healing power of psychotherapy while underestimating other change inducing forces in the patient's life" (Bennett 1984: 173).

Since change is inevitable, much of our work involves facilitating movement through the normal transitions of life. This may involve gently nudging our clients to modify old rules and expectations and/or normalizing their plight in such a way that they become more open to experimenting with some variations on an old pattern or theme.

By seeing people intermittently (with two to four weeks between contacts) we demonstrate our expectation that clients are capable of *experimenting* on their own with distinct ways of dealing with their predicament. This notion of experimentation is a vital one in our work. It is through such a process that new ideas and solutions can be generated and supported. "Giving time allows the [client] to reinvent their own map and do something original" (Cecchin, in Boscolo et al. 1987: 237).

The Power of Expectations

We are all familiar with the powerful effect that expectations have on our behavior. Studies have been conducted (Rosenthal and Jacobson 1968) demonstrating how one's expectancies about people's abilities, for example, which children in a classroom will do well and which will do poorly, influence the outcome. These "self-fulfilling prophecies" (Watzlawick 1984) play a major role in the therapeutic process and can be used to create a context that supports change. An example of the power of positive expectations is summarized by Watzlawick (1984: 109) from a case originally reported by Gordon Allport:

> In a provincial Austrian hospital, a man lay gravely ill—in fact at death's door. The medical staff had told him frankly that they could not diagnose his disease, but that if they knew the diagnosis they could probably cure him. They told him further that a famous diagnostician was soon to visit the hospital and that he could spot the trouble. Within a few days the diagnostician arrived and proceeded to make the rounds. Coming to this man's bed, he merely glanced at the patient, murmured *"moribundus,"* and went on.
>
> Some years later, the patient called on the diagnostician and said 'I've been wanting to thank you for your diagnosis. They told me that if you could diagnose me I'd get well, and so the minute you said *moribundus* I knew I'd recover.

The power of expectations is documented in the classic study by Rosenhan (1973) in which he instructed several relatively well functioning "confederates" to portray themselves as "mentally ill" in order to gain admission to several psychiatric inpatient units. Once these confederates were admitted they were then instructed to return to behaving "normally." In spite of this, the hospital staff continued to interpret their behavior as reflective of mental illness and kept them hospitalized for extended periods of time. The psychiatric labels applied became static categorizations of the "patients" and the perceptions of the staff were determined by these original diagnostic impressions. No matter how the "patient" behaved, the staff would distort these data to fit their original diagnoses.

This study illustrates both the negative spiral of self-fulfilling prophecies as well as the stigmatizing impact of accepting a one-time judgment of reality as "the continuing truth." In addition, it points up the need for the therapist to be wary of static diagnostic formulations whose very language may determine and guide one's view of the person as a static being. As we can see, people develop a presuppositional frame based on their initial impressions that then serves as a structure for organizing and explaining new input. By using a language of options and possibilities that generate hope for change, rather than static diagnostic categories, we expand perspectives rather than constrict them.

The Language of Possibility

H. Anderson and H. A. Goolishian assert that "Change is the evolution of new meaning through dialogue" (1988: 372). It is clear that our "capacity for language [serves] to crystallize and stabilize [our] knowledge of [ourselves] and others" (Berger & Luckmann 1966: 36). How we, as therapists, talk with the client about the original complaint to a large extent determines the direction in which therapy will move. Our participation in the therapeutic process helps both to define the client's concerns and to create potential solutions.

The language of the therapist is most effective when it is the language of change, of optimism, of positive expectations, and of normal growth. By participating in a conversation that amplifies options and positive outcomes, the therapist provides a context for the client to both see and act on new possibilities. The therapist, by using the language of possibilities rather than that of limitations, of strengths rather than deficits, of successes rather than failures, provides a positive foundation for successful solutions. The questions we ask and the words we use to talk about clients' situations influence the responses we get (see figure 1–1).

Tomm (1987) has developed a method of interventive interviewing that uses questions as a means to induce positive expectations about outcome. For example, the therapist might ask a parent, "How much progress do you think she [your child] actually will make in the next month . . . in six months? Who will be the most surprised by her progress?" (Tomm 1987: 173) or, as a way to generate hope or optimism, "When [not if] she does [become capable of ———], who will

Figure 1–1.   "The way in which a question is asked determines the way in which an answer may be found" (H. von Foerster, in P. Watzlawick's **The Invented Reality**, page 46). Drawing by Shanahan; © 1988, The New Yorker Magazine, Inc.

be the first to notice? In what way will your relief or [happiness] show? How will it improve your relationship? Who would be the first to suggest the change be celebrated?" (Tomm 1987: 174). Through questions of this type, the therapist enables positive change.

We shall provide clinical illustrations of the power of language to effect change and the role of the therapist as a "participant manager of the therapeutic conversation" (Anderson & Goolishian 1988). We will also see that the specific words the therapist uses to talk to the client significantly shapes not only the definition of the desired change, but also how the client views it, which is an initial step toward creating that change.

"Kairos" or the Crucial Moment

"Most simply stated . . . a single drastic therapeutic experience can bring sudden relief or start one on the road to health" (Alexander, in Alexander and French 1946: 163). The concept of *kairos* (Kelman 1969), a Greek word meaning "opportunity" or "turning-point," is critical in our work. "*Kairos* implies a right time in the course of events to do certain things that will favor a crucial happening . . . an opportunity which must be immediately recognized and seized upon" or the possibility will disappear (Kelman 1969: 80). We view *"time as an ally"* (Hobbs 1966) in that events in time (whether fortuitous or planned) may serve to improve the situation. The therapist makes an effort to build on those fortuitous happenings in the life of the client to effect change.

For example, Victor Hugo in his novel *Les Miserables* (discussed in Alexander and French 1946: 68–69; and in Watzlawick 1987: 93) shows us, in the example of Jean Valjean (a hardened criminal), how a totally unexpected act on the part of the bishop (his treating Valjean with kindness, after Valjean had stolen silver from the church) had a major impact on changing his life. Rather than asking for the silver to be returned, the bishop turns the situation around such that Valjean must change. Hugo puts it this way:

> Jean Valjean was trembling in every limb. . . . "Now," said the bishop, "go in peace." . . . Jean Valjean felt like a man who is just about to faint. The bishop approached him, and said, in a low voice: "Forget not, never forget that you have promised me to use this silver to become an honest man." Jean Valjean, *who had no recollection of this promise*, [author's emphasis] stood confounded.
>
> He [Valjean] felt indistinctly that the priest's forgiveness was the most formidable assualt by which he had yet been shaken. . . . One thing which he did not suspect is certain, . . . that he was no longer the same man; all changed in him, and it was no longer in his power to get rid of the fact that the bishop had spoken to him and taken his hand.

We have all probably experienced or witnessed such one-trial learning in our work with clients. It may be that an unexpected or even tragic event such as a death or illness precipitates a dramatic shift in the client's reality. In these situations, change is *discontinuous* rather than gradual. As therapists, we can look for the *kairos*, the moment that must be seized, in creating a context for change.

As Gleick (1987), in his book *Chaos*, points out, small changes or oscillations in natural systems can create large, unpredictable changes. This so-called butterfly effect[1] is very common in nature and provides a useful analogy for our clinical work. For Gleick, and other "chaos" scientists, natural processes are viewed as unpredictable and constantly changing. However, there is a certain degree of order within these seemingly chaotic events. When a small fluctuation occurs in one part of the system, the whole system reverberates. Following such perturbations, the system rearranges itself into a new pattern. This idea is inherent in the therapist's use of "pattern interventions," which attempt to create a perturbation in an existing pattern or process and by so doing open up new possibilities (deShazer 1985; O'Hanlon and Weiner-Davis 1989; O'Hanlon and Wilk 1987).

The Social Construction of Reality

"The experiencing consciousness creates structure in the flow of its experience, and this structure is what conscious, cognitive organisms experience as 'reality' " (von Glaserfeld 1984: 38). Carlos Castaneda in *The Journey to Ixtlan* (1972: ix) talks about don Juan's view of reality: "For don Juan, . . . the reality of our day to day life consists of an endless flow of perceptual interpretations which we, the individuals who share a specific membership, have learned to make in common." It is these common assumptions that generally guide and influence our thinking in a linear, cause-and-effect manner.

However, our views of reality and causality vary significantly depending on our vantage point. This is brought home rather dramatically in the Japanese film, *Rashomon*, in which four people describe the same incident through their varied lenses. As the stories unfold, what "happens" becomes dramatically different. The great impressionist artist, Claude Monet, painted dozens of works looking at the same scene at different times of the day. For him, each scene, with its unique lighting and shading, represented a different, and equally authentic, view of a constantly shifting reality. His goal was to paint "sensation," that fleeting sense of change which defines reality. With this in mind, we take the position that there is no one "Truth" but only the subjective realities each of us experience as "the truth."

Although we have learned to "punctuate" the world in linear or cause-and-effect terms, the world we experience is complex and multi-determined. Many of the concerns people bring to therapy have to do with differences in how events in time are "punctuated." An example is the alcoholic who says he drinks because his wife nags him, and the spouse who says she nags him because he drinks. Where does "truth" lie? Our goal is not to determine truth but rather to help the client out of the trap of linear thinking.

This process of linear thinking is also evident in other spheres. For example a child's grades drop and the guidance counselor says "we're concerned that the child's feelings about her lack of a father are responsible for the drop in her academic performance". Since these two events may have no connection whatever, the counselor is making an assumption about reality. As we will see in chapter 3, the therapist can actualize change more rapidly by avoiding complex assumptions.

Constructivism is a school of thought that emphasizes the subjective nature of reality. This means that as humans we construct our own versions of events in the world. These constructions are neither right nor wrong, but serve to influence our thoughts, feelings, and actions in a situation (Watzlawick 1984). As Kreilkamp points out "we never know the whole story . . . the essential struggle is not . . . to arrive at the truth, but rather to make a difference, to try something new and see what happens, to persuade the patient that there are other ways to live and other possibilities" (1989: 151).

Since reality is arbitrarily "punctuated" depending on our vantage point, we strive to accept the individual's view of the world, *and working within that context* or frame of reference, to facilitate the change process. "The more the therapist understands the client's reality, the more he/she can co-create with the client a new reality that facilitates changes in a manner acceptable to the client" (Coale 1989: 10).

Mind as a Social Phenomenon

"Mind is immanent in the larger system—man *plus* environment," (Bateson 1972: 317). The idea of "mind" is one that goes beyond the brain of the individual and reflects an interactional process between the individual and the environment (Bateson 1972). The evolving system (or "mind" in Bateson's terms) is comprised of our actions and the feedback produced by our actions in a continuing cycle of self-correction and change. The concept of "paranoia" can be used to illustrate this cybernetic process.

To diagnosis someone, in the traditional way, as "paranoid" implies that the paranoia is *in the person*. A cybernetic position sees "paranoia" as developing as an interactional process in which a pattern of suspicions is built up based on that person's interactions with others in the environment. This interactional patterning then becomes internalized and the person presents with paranoid ideas. You can diagnose someone as paranoid and then make an attempt to control the behavior or you can try to understand the interactional patterning that supports the development of the paranoid process and work to modify those patterns in generating a new internalized reality (Tomm 1989).

Minuchin (1974: 11–12) provides an example of how our ideology about paranoia affects our treatment approach. In this example, you can see how "a paranoid community" developed supporting a client's belief system; and then how a cybernetic approach, which views the person with the environment as part of a greater whole, led to a successful outcome.

> An Italian widow in her late sixties, who had lived in the same apartment for twenty-five years, came home one day to find her apartment robbed. She decided to move and called a moving company. It was the beginning of a nightmare. As she described it, the people who came to move her things tried to control where she went. When they moved her belongings, they purposely misplaced and lost precious possessions. They left sinister markings—cryptograms—on her furni-

ture. When she went outside people followed her, secretly signaling to each other.

She went to a psychiatrist, who gave her tranquilizers, but her experiences did not change. She was then referred to an inpatient unit where another psychiatrist interviewed her. He purposely left bottles on the table. Although she did not know what they were, they appeared clearly dangerous to her. He recommended hospitalization but she refused. She went to see another therapist, whose interventions were based on an ecological understanding of the old and lonely. He explained to the woman that she had lost her shell—the previous home where she had known each object, the neighborhood, and the people in the neighborhood. At this point, like any crustacean that lost its shell, she was vulnerable. *Reality had a different experiential effect.* These problems would disappear, he assured her, when she grew a new shell. They discussed how to shorten the time this would take. She was to unpack all her belongings, hang up the pictures that had decorated her previous apartment, put the books on the shelves, and organize the apartment so it was familiar. All her movements were to be routinized. She was to get up at a certain time, shop at a certain time, go to the same stores . . . and so on. She was not to try to make new friends in the neighborhood for two weeks. She was to go back and visit her old friends.

As Minuchin (1974: 12) points out: "The frightening experience of unfamiliarity with new circumstances had been interpreted . . . as a conspiracy against her. In the very measure by which she tried to communicate her experiences, *her environmental feedback had amplified her experience of being abnormal and psychotic.* Her relatives and friends had become frightened for her and had in turn frightened her by their conspiracy of secrecy." In this situation, one might say that "mind" is represented by this woman's interaction with her environment. Her "paranoid" behavior was constrained and influenced by environmental input.

As this case illustrates, our behavior is influenced by the context in which it is embedded. Since language is a significant part of our basic human structure (Maturana and Varela 1987), our evolving knowledge of ourselves and the world is colored and amplified by our linguistic interactions with others. In the therapy process, two or more people engage in a linguistic dance in which ideas are co-constructed and negotiated such that *new* versions of reality evolve. Each participant's ideas serve to "perturb" the other in a continuous, circular process. These perturbations allow each participant to re-calibrate their views of, and actions in, the world.

Therapists cannot separate themselves from the therapeutic equation. "It is a mistake to describe the therapist or client as unilaterally steering ('manipulating') the interactional dance in which they partici-pate" (Keeney and Sprenkle 1982: 15). As distinct from a first-order cybernetic view in which therapists place themselves apart from clients and try to objectively "tinker" with a process (as a mechanic works on a car), a second-order view assumes that the therapist is an active contributing member of the client's ecology. As such, the therapist is positioned *within* rather than outside the system (Hoffman 1985). In practice, the therapist sometimes takes a more "pragmatic" (first-order) stance and sometimes acts as a "participant-facilitator" in the therapy process (Real 1990).

An Ecological Perspective

On a global scale we are all part of a larger social matrix or network in which there is a state of mutual dependency and interdependence (Bateson 1972). In this larger ecosystem, changes in one part influence and impact on the others. A person using a spray can containing CFCs in New York City is affecting the atmospheric ozone levels in Singa-pore. A nuclear accident is not a local phenomenon but has implica-tions and repercussions for the global health and well-being of billions of people. Our tampering with the ecological balance by either intro-ducing new elements to it (toxins; air pollutants) or by destroying already existing parts of it (destruction of entire species or biomes) is fraught with great peril for the whole.

In the summer of 1988 Yellowstone National Park experienced a series of very intense fires, which spread over forty percent of the park area.[2] The fires in Yellowstone, although frightening in terms of poten-tial damage to humans and their structures, did in the end serve as a reminder that there is some logic to natural evolutionary processes. What the fires created was *increased diversity* in the ecosystem by providing more varied environmental/ecological niches, which encour-aged species proliferation. Survival depends on a wide variety of op-tions and a flexible menu of choices. With the clients we treat, there are also natural evolving processes that call for great respect on the part of the therapist. It is our job to promote increased diversity of functioning by not imposing our own values or beliefs, but by accept-ing the client's own unique evolutionary development.

Our involvement with the smaller systems that comprise our clini-cal domain also require an *ecological perspective*. We must avoid upset-ting the client ecosystem, which has within it the resources to solve its own problems. Milton Erickson (in Gordon and Meyers-Anderson 1981: 6) tells a story that emphasizes the above points[3]:

> I was returning from high school one day and a runaway horse with a
> bridle on sped past a group of us into a farmer's yard looking for a

drink of water. The horse was perspiring heavily. And the farmer didn't recognize it so we cornered it. I hopped on the horse's back. Since it had a bridle on, I took hold of the tick rein and said, "giddy-up." He headed for the highway. I knew the horse would turn in the right direction. I didn't know what the right direction was. And then the horse trotted and galloped along. Now and then he would forget he was on the highway and start into a field. So I would pull on him a bit and call his attention to the fact that the highway was where he was *supposed* to be. And finally about four miles from where I boarded him, he turned into a farmyard and the farmer said, "Where did you find him?" About four miles from here. "How did you know you should come here?" I said "I didn't know. The *horse* knew. All I did was keep his attention on the road." I think that's the way you do psychotherapy.

With Erickson, we view the therapist as a guide who takes his cues from the client and relies on the client's natural momentum towards movement and change. The therapist needs to have faith in the healing power contained within the client's natural ecology.

An ecological perspective assumes that the client, *in his system*, has the resources to create change (Friedman 1984; Friedman and Friedman 1982; Haley 1976). It is not the therapist's job to dictate how the system should look, but only to serve as a guide or facilitator (a catalyst) in the quest for change. As Dunst, Trivette, and Deal (1988: 163) point out "help-giving efforts are empowering if they strengthen normal socializing agents (relatives, neighbors, the church, etc.) and enhance a sense of community that emphasizes the promotion of . . . competence."

In promoting competence and change, we attempt to involve aspects of the client's natural social network in the treatment process. We also encourage client participation in self-help groups (AA, Al-Anon, OA, parent support groups, and so on), which provide a useful therapeutic function for many people (Jacobs and Goodman 1989). By activating client support systems (siblings, friends), we minimize the long-term dependency of the client on institutional resources and encourage and facilitate the building of a natural network of relationships that can be activated in times of crisis. An ecological view also includes a person's biological functioning. As we will see in chapter 8, the biologic component (as in children with attentional problems) can be effectively incorporated into the therapist's systemic thinking.

Sometimes our own institutional systems place constraints on behavior that distort people's competencies. This process can be seen in the nursing home context. As a consultant to several nursing homes, one of us [SF] found it illuminating to see how elderly residents labeled as "senile" and viewed as incompetent, confused, and disoriented could function very well outside the nursing home context. One dramatic example (Friedman and Ryan 1986) involved a woman who was abruptly transferred to a nursing home from her apartment where she had lived for most of her life. The nursing staff viewed her as confused and disoriented and diagnosed her as suffering from "senile dementia." One day she secretly left the nursing home and returned to her own neighborhood, a distance of over thirty miles! This woman, who had been abruptly cut off from her friends and community, was seeking to reconnect with the environment she knew. While showing confusion in getting around the nursing home setting, she had no problem navigating on more familiar terrain.

As therapists we need to be sensitive to the impact of environmental constraints on behavior and appreciative of the complex interplay of person and environment. By so doing, we can work to better structure those aspects of the client's natural ecology that will help support and maintain positive coping skills.

Learning in Action

"Like the adage 'nothing succeeds like success' there is no more powerful therapeutic factor than the performance of activities which were formerly . . . impaired or inhibited. No insight, no emotional discharge, no recollection, can be as reassuring as accomplishment in the actual life situation in which the individual failed" (Alexander and French 1946: 40).

In a series of experiments using kittens as subjects, Held and Hein (1963) demonstrated that active, self-produced movement in the sensory environment facilitated learning.[4] The brief, possibility-oriented therapist must require that the client actively negotiate his environment in such a way that new information is acquired and new learning is accomplished.

Robert White (1959), in his classic paper on the development of competence, discusses the idea of "effectance motivation" (that is, the natural tendency to act on the environment to produce an effect) and the "feelings of efficacy" that go with such exploratory behavior. The infant's play consists of miniature "experiments" that provide him with useful information about how the world works (see Piaget 1952; Sherrod, Vietze, and Friedman 1978). Groos (see White 1959) refers to the "joy in being a cause" that an infant experiences as he begins to experiment with his ability to have an impact on objects and people in the world. Such "experiments" allow the infant to gain understanding about the world, and these active efforts to gain new information is what learning is all about.

Action leads to new understandings of ourselves and our social environment. The cybernetician, Heinz von Foerster (1984: 61) articulates this idea with the following "imperative": "If you desire to see, learn how to act."[5]

Therapy, like learning, requires action and interaction in the world. Feelings are part of our humanness and need to be accepted, acknowledged, and respected; however, the *proper focus of treatment is not feeling but action* in the world. In our work, the future takes precedence over the past. While, at times, encouraging the expression of feelings about past hurts, the therapist focuses his or her attention on actions that will move the person past these feelings and into a new state.

An *orientation to the future* avoids, both for the client and the therapist, a position of absorption in the self-pitying morass of client guilt, shame, and failure. The therapist, while acknowledging the past hurts of the client, empowers him or her to gain a renewed sense of competence, control, and mastery. We request that the client specify the behaviors he or she wants in the future, but doesn't have now. Next, we help the client identify those steps needed to make that image a reality. These active efforts toward change, in contrast to a passive stance, contribute significantly to the client's learning and ultimate success. As a fortune cookie recently informed one of us, "the first step to better times is to imagine them."

Expanding Possibilities

Variation-seeking behavior is a biological imperative (Fiske & Maddi 1961). Humans are "wired" to seek information, explore their environments, and search for differences (see Friedman 1975).[6] "Observation of play behaviors attests to the biologic importance of variation-seeking and novel experiences . . . unless play and exploration have appropriate structure in the environment to operate upon, significant learning will not be generated" (Chase 1969: 269).[7] In fact, when exploration is not permitted, people begin to engage in bizarre behavior (see Friedman and Ryan 1986).

Much of the therapist's job is to help the client expand his or her abilities and create solutions that expand horizons. Part of the therapist's job is to enlarge the client's perceptions of options and to create a context in which the client can experience increased variety. Possibility-oriented therapists must help clients get past the rigid mind-sets they have developed that have prevented or inhibited problem resolution. Seeing a situation only one way is a form of stimulus deprivation, with the client moving down blind alleys. By presenting the client with information in a novel manner (for example, via reframing) or in a provocative way (Farrelly and Brandsma 1974; Napier and Whitaker

1978) the therapist can disrupt these patterns and facilitate flexible frames of reference.

The reader is invited to try the following experiment, which illustrates the concepts discussed above. Your task is to "plant" ten trees in five straight rows with four trees in each row (Erickson and Rossi 1979: 341–42; see figure 1–2 for solution).

As you can see, to solve this problem, you must avoid a "boxed-in" perceptual set. All too often we succumb to self-imposed limits. As therapists, we need to think outside of preconceived sets and help our clients envision possibilities not limited by their prior assumptions. At times, we also need to help our clients become more sensitive to information and cues in the environment that will afford new perspectives.

"A [person] hurrying to an important business meeting is likely to perceive only the cues that help him get there faster, whereas a [person] taking a stroll after lunch is likely to pick up a substantial amount of casual information" (White 1959: 327). The possibility-oriented therapist needs to provide opportunities for "casual" learning. The client may be focusing so hard on the difficulty that he or she becomes entrenched in a "more of the same cycle" (Watzlawick, Weakland & Fisch 1974). Milton Erickson (see Haley 1973) had an exceptional talent for getting people to engage in casual activities as a way of allowing them to discover their own solutions. For example, he might instruct a client to hike up to Squaw Peak, and try to discover Erickson's reason for sending him there.

These tasks of "ambiguous function" (Lankton & Lankton 1986) involve the assignment of a specific activity the goal of which is ambiguous and undefined. One such assignment described by Lankton and Lankton (1986: 24) was used with a depressed man who said that

> he had no feelings and felt like he was behind an "invisible shield."
> . . . He didn't share his feelings with anyone or rely on anyone for support. . . . Carol [one of the therapists] presented him with a dozen roses and the instruction that he was to give them away, one at a time to whomever he selected, as long as three of them were given to men. Carol suggested some places he might go and told him to say to the person as he gave each rose, "I'm not feeling too good myself but I hope this brightens your day."

The man got very positive responses from people for his actions and increased his connectedness to others, including his wife and daughter from whom he initially reported feeling very remote.

By creating an atmosphere that supports client experimentation, shifts can be triggered in the client's self-perception behavior. As Varela (1989: 22) points out, "to let go of a fixed viewpoint. . . . is the key to human sanity." As therapists, we must be ready to introduce opportunities for unfamiliarity and "differentness" in pointing our clients toward new learning. We can capitalize on the biologic imperative to variation-seeking by engaging the client in "experiments" (homework) that provides useful feedback and new ideas.

However, in assigning a task or homework assignment or presenting a new idea, the therapist needs to consider what the client is ready and able to hear and assimilate. The idea or task needs to be noticeably different from what the client has experienced before, yet not so different that it will be rejected out of hand. By presenting ideas that are slightly different (or incongruent) from the client's level of expectation, we increase the possibility the client will acknowledge and make use of this information, rather than reject it.[8] This principle is an important one in helping the therapist develop effective interventions and will be discussed again.

Playfulness, Humor and the Use of Metaphor

"The patient, it might be said, suffers from gravity. For him life is a burden. . . . Eventually he must find laughter in the midst of his accustomed tears and glimpse his own absurdity. Without irreverency, both he and the therapist stay mired in earnestness" (Fisher 1970: 54). The therapist, by demonstrating a playful attitude, models for the client that life is not to be taken so seriously. Whitaker (1976: 160) talks about the usefulness of play in helping the therapist maintain perspective. By modeling playfulness the therapist serves to free the client from a deadly seriousness that may be contributing to the mood of anxiety and hopelessness. The use of metaphor, in addition, allows the client to experience images that offer views of an alternative future with the problem solved.

Erickson (see Haley 1973, 1985) was a master of metaphoric communication. By telling stories and anecdotes, Erickson would seed ideas for needed therapeutic work or make indirect points that might otherwise be rejected. For example (discussed in Lankton and Lankton 1986), one day Erickson's father was trying to get the cow into the barn before a storm. He was pulling on the head of the recalcitrant cow without success. Erickson came along and had another idea. He went behind the cow and pulled on its tail. The cow quickly ran into the barn! Such anecdotes provide a humorous way to introduce ideas and expand perspectives. Humor has a positive effect, both on client mood and client physiology.

Psychotherapy, like play, depends on the "manipulation of frames" (Bateson 1972: 191). In therapy, the participants step outside their accustomed realities and engage in a dialogue that has a special set of rules. In contrast to a game with a rigid set of rules, therapy is an evolving process in which the therapist uses language as a means to

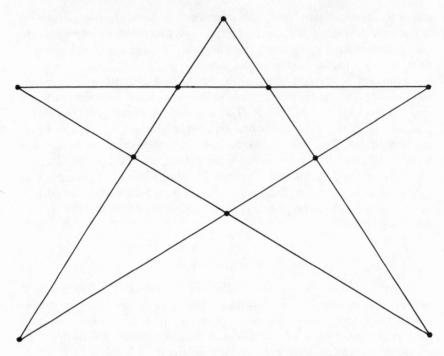

Figure 1–2. Solution to the "Tree" Problem.

influence the client. "Before therapy, the patient thinks and operates in terms of a certain set of rules for the making and understanding of messages. After successful therapy, he operates in terms of a different set of such rules" (Bateson 1972: 191). Through dialogue, the therapist creates a context in which the client's previously accepted rules (or views of reality) are shifted and options are developed for new, evolving interactions with the environment.

Prologue

Recently, one of us went on a whitewater rafting trip in Colorado. I had been on several other trips but never on such a wild and potentially dangerous stretch of river as the one on which we were about to embark. When they handed out helmets, my anxiety level went up another notch. It would be me, my wife, three other "high-rollers" and the guide, who fortunately had over ten years experience riding this river.

I sat on the right side of the boat, my wife across from me on the left. Since we had to paddle, it was necessary to stay balanced on the edge of the raft (otherwise we could easily find ourselves out of the raft, in the frightening rough water in the middle of the river). In addition, we needed to be ready to shift paddle operations at a moment's notice, to make a right or left turn or to slow the raft. Although the guide had some control over the raft, it was up to the combined team work of the paddlers to implement his directions in finding smooth passage in the turbulent river.

Small shifts in paddling could make a large difference in whether the boat proceeded downriver intact or flipped over dumping all or some of us into the river. Occasionally we would come up against difficult stretches with "reverse hydraulics" that could easily flip the boat; in these instances we had to work extra hard to avoid "going in the hole". At other times it worked best to try to hit the oncoming wave head-on, maintaining control through constant paddling in moving through the river.

After this trip, I realized how much the experience was like doing brief therapy. The therapist, just like the river rafter, must use the client's momentum to progress, must quickly seize the moment when the currents are just right to alter course, must keep flexible and loose while maintaining balance. By riding the natural currents in the river, the rafter is able to reach his goal. The rafter must know when to hit the wave head-on and when to find safe passage in another part of the river. Later, there will be time to relax in a quiet pool on the side of the river.

Notes

1. The "butterfly effect" was named by Edward Lorenz, who half-facetiously said that a butterfly moving its wings in Singapore today could effect the weather in New York several weeks later (Gleick 1987).

2. Although there has been much debate over whether it would have been better to contain the fires or allow the forests to burn, the burned-off land itself has already begun a new cycle of growth. In fact, some plants (such as aspen trees and firewood shrubs) are thriving there, and some birds (such as bluebirds and woodpeckers) actually gravitate toward these burned areas. One additional benefit of the 1988 Yellowstone fire was to reduce the potential for future fires by consuming areas of dead wood. The ashes of Yellowstone provide fertile ground for new growth.

3. From *Phoenix: Therapeutic patterns of Milton H. Erickson* by Gordon and Meyers-Anderson (1981). Reprinted by permission of the author and publisher, Meta Publications, P.O. Box 565, Cupertino, Calif.

4. Held and Hein (1963) placed pairs of infant kittens, initially reared in darkness, in a patterned environment. One of the kittens passively moved

through the environment by being placed in a "gondola" that rotated around the cylindrical apparatus. The other kitten actively moved through the environment. When the active kitten walked around the cyclindrical environment, the passive kitten's gondola moved also. Both kittens had free movement of their heads. After spending three hours a day over several days in the apparatus, each kitten was tested on a series of visual discrimination tasks. The kittens who actively moved through the environment and had control over that movement, demonstrated success more rapidly on the visual tasks than the kittens who passively experienced the environment. These results support the idea that learning requires active involvement and autonomous movement.

5. Castaneda in his book *Tales of Power* (1974: 24) comments: "That's the flaw with words, . . . they always force us to feel enlightened, but when we turn around to face the world they always fail us and we end up facing the world as we always have, without enlightenment. For this reason, a sorcerer seeks to act rather than to talk and to this effect, he gets a new description of the world—a new description where talking is not that important, and where new acts have new reflections."

6. Differences and their elaboration are the information bits that form the basis for changed perceptions (Bateson 1972). The human is "programmed" from birth to seek differences in the environment (Haith 1976). The newborn infant is capable of detecting small differences in its visual environment (Friedman, Bruno and Vietze 1974; Friedman 1975; Salapatek and Kessen 1966). Neurophysiological studies (Hubel and Weisel 1962) suggest the organism has a built-in need for stimulation (specific cortical cells that are responsive to certain kinds of stimuli such as lines, angles, and edges). These data support the idea that the human organism is "wired" to detect differences.

What we mean by information—the elementary unit of information—is *a difference which makes a difference . . . idea* in its most elementary sense, is synonymous with 'difference' " (Bateson 1972: 453). The therapist facilitates or catalyzes the development of new ideas by creating increased diversity and variety in the world view of the clients. By the helping the client to "see" and acknowledge new information (differences), a new view of "reality" can be constructed. In addition, the therapist can help the client detect and acknowledge the significant, small positive steps made toward the goal. In chapter 3, an example is given of how this may be accomplished.

7. When repeatedly exposed to the same visual pattern, infants, even in the first days of life, will reduce their attentiveness, returning to investigate and visually explore, when the pattern is shifted and a "novel" one is introduced in its place (Friedman 1972; Friedman and Vietze 1975). "Interest seems to require elements of unfamiliarity: of something still to be found out and of learning still to be done" (White 1959: 304).

A number of early experiments in the psychology of learning demonstrated how humans become disadvantaged when they become "set" or "fixed" on a particular mode of problem resolution. This "functional fixity" as Duncker (see Woodworth and Schlossberg 1954) referred to it, is a common impediment in problem solving. Infants have also shown a tendency to become "stimulus bound" (Friedman 1975; Stechler and Latz 1966), "hypnotized" by one aspect of the environment, and to have great difficulty shifting focus to another part of the visual field. As adults we also can develop "tunnel vision" such that we become immune to seeing alternatives (differences) around us.

After dealing successfully with a series of problems requiring a common set of strategies, we have all probably experienced finding outselves confused and at a loss when confronted with some variation in what is needed for solving the problem. We become "rigid" in our thinking and our previous successes impede or inhibit our ability to think creatively. In fact, Luchins (see Woodworth and Schlossberg 1954) found that when a much simpler solution to a problem was possible his subjects would revert to more cumbersome (less economical) procedures that had been learned in sucessfully solving earlier problems.

8. Research has indicated that humans and other animals respond positively to small changes and find large changes overwhelming or distressing (Berlyne 1960; Hunt 1965). "Small discrepancies from an adaptation level are experienced as more pleasurable than are larger discrepancies" (K.E. Weick 1984: 45). Several studies have demonstrated that unexpected information is met with increased arousal and upset and has a disorganizing effect on behavior (Carpenter et al. 1970; Hebb 1946). In the same way, the therapist needs to consider the client's readiness to assimilate new information. When the therapist offers an unfamiliar perspective, the client is activated.

2
Paradigm Shift: From Problem to Possibility

> *What* is the matter with Mary Jane?
> She's crying with all her might and main,
> And she won't eat her dinner—rice pudding again—
> What *is* the matter with Mary Jane?
> —A.A. Milne[1]

How many clients as they enter into therapy feel like Mary Jane? Do clients want to be forced to eat rice pudding or to be asked what they want for dessert? Does the idea of recounting all of their problems, weaknesses, and failures have special innate appeal, or are they willing to do this because there is something *else* that they want or hope for? It is our contention that clients surrender themselves to therapy because they hope that their lives will be more satisfying if they are able to change certain actions, if they increase their sphere of competencies. So why not first find out what new actions and competencies they **want?** In so doing, the shape of the entire therapy takes on a different, positive contour. *Working unremittingly under positive auspices is the essence of the paradigm shift from problem to possibility.*

Do not be deceived by the apparent simplicity of this statement. The change is profound. Possibility is **not** the opposite of problem; the possibility paradigm is rather *an entirely different frame of reference.* The shift proposed here is the difference between first- and second-order change. In first-order change, solutions are sought by doing more of the original problem-solving behavior, "more of the same." In the problem paradigm, that involves a detailed discussion of *what is wrong* in an attempt to understand the causes and so to "right" or "cure" it. The shift to the possibility frame injects the discontinuity and logical leap of a second-order change when the therapist asks *what is wanted,* rather than exploring "the problem." Thus, it puts the initial interaction in an entirely new light by offering "something entirely different."[1] In the problem paradigm the therapist stays in the client's frame of reference by asking him or her to describe in detail the cause of the anxiety or upset, what he or she wants *to get away from;* in other words, *more of the same.* In the possibility paradigm, the therapist asks

---

[1]Milne, A.A., *When We Were Very Young.* New York: E.P. Dutton, 1924. Reprinted with permission.

the client *something completely different:* what does the client want *to go toward,* what he or she thinks will transform life for the better. When you make this logical leap of asking the client what he or she *wants,* you interrupt the old pattern of thinking, challenge the old assumptions and move the client into a new and hopeful perspective.

We use "paradigm" here to mean a frame of reference or a mental set consisting of complementary or interlocking assumptions. The paradigms of therapy in which we operate both shape our views of what constitutes effective therapy and direct our actions in the conduct of such therapy. The paradigm shift to possibility that we propose here changes both the goals of treatment to realizing future desires (rather than curing past ills) and the strategies for reaching those goals. Strategies in the possibility frame emphasize interrupting current dysfunctional behavior patterns rather than searching in the past for causes. The client is afforded a treatment experience of a different order, one which concentrates on developing the resources to get what he or she wants. We believe that learning to be the person you want to be is not only very different from learning why you are the way you are, learning to be the person you want to be *does not require understanding why you are the way you are.*

A more detailed comparison of these two treatment paradigms leads directly to an understanding of the central importance of language to possibility. The deliberate use of the language of possibility augments the psychophysiological resources of both client and therapist as it generates hope. Since humor also enhances psychophysiology, teach the client both to hope and laugh. All of these elements, hope, humor, and the expectation of success, support the generation of effective therapy, which is the attaining of the observable results requested by the client.

Comparing Treatment Paradigms

How are the problem paradigm and the possibility paradigm completely different? In the possibility frame of reference the therapist immediately engages the client to project the future desired and makes it clear that the client has the responsibility for making those changes. You show that you will be a resource-catalyst for the client, helping the client, to mobilize his or her own particular abilities in the process. You immediately start demonstrating your method of feedback responsiveness by adjusting your behavior to the client's words and behaviors in the initial encounter. You guide the client to be a partner in charge of what happens. Whereas in the problem frame, the therapist emphasizes a detailed search into past history to find the causes of current upset, assuming that insight into causes will produce desired change.

Also, in the problem frame of reference, the client is expected to follow the lead of the "expert", learning the therapist's language and model of change. If the client does not follow this regimen, he or she is considered "resistant" or not ready for treatment.

Many theories of diagnosis and psychotherapy emphasize what is "wrong" with people (English and Finch 1954; Noyes and Kolb 1963; DSM-III-R 1987). What are their weaknesses? Who or what is to blame for their problems, that is, what are the *causes?* Therapists have been taught to look into the client's past in an effort to understand the causes of the present difficulties; in the belief that insight per se would automatically change the situation for the better. But human beings are more complex than this, as Ann Weick states: "Human interaction is acausal; the attempt to assign blame is meaningless because to do so artificially isolates one thread in a multicolored tapestry. The pattern is only apprehended when one stands back and looks at the whole" (1984: 21).

The possibility paradigm focuses not on causes, but on connections and cybernetic interrelationships or feedback loops. In possibility-oriented therapy, the immediate first step toward a solution in asking the client what he or she *wants* in specific behavioral terms. This asks the client to focus attention on the part of the "multi-colored tapestry" to be changed. In other words, both you and the client look at the present patterns to define together particular new actions that may enhance the client's life in the future. In asking the client what he or she wants—rather than what the problem might be—you shift the conversation into a different frame and at the same time *shift responsibility for change to the client*. This shift mobilizes the client's strengths. As Norman Cousins says, "Activity, no less than confidence, is deeply connected to the environment of restoration" (1989: 162). Clients are immediately engaged in their own healing process as they discover that their wishes will shape the therapeutic interaction. This immediately reverses the more traditional view that the therapist will decide what is needed and then "fix" the client. It further implies that clients will be able to attain their desired goals; this engenders hope and expectation, essential ingredients in effective therapy.

In psychotherapy's traditional problem frame, therapists have often assumed responsibility for changes the clients make while in treatment. When clients improved, therapists claimed credit for the success; if the therapy failed, therapists often labeled the clients as "resistant" or "unready for treatment." In the possibility frame, the therapist and the client immediately become partners in identifying the desired goals. The therapist is the catalyst who promotes the client's movement toward the desired change—not the analyst who determines causes (Bennett 1989). In possibility-oriented therapy difficult or "resistant" behaviors in a client are viewed as useful interpersonal feedback. As Erickson and Rossi say:

> We believe that most so-called resistances have some reasonable basis within the patient's own frame of reference. *Resistance is usually an expression of the patient's individuality!* The therapist's task is to understand, accept, and utilize that individuality to help patients bypass their learned limitations and to achieve their own goals. (1979: 68)

The client's "resistance," therefore, provides a rich source of information about that client's uniqueness that can be used in shaping therapeutic interactions as well as in designing treatment strategies. Employing this paradigm shift, then, has the added advantage of precluding "failure" on the part of either you or the client. For the possibility-oriented therapist there is only feedback. If the first treatment strategy does not produce the desired result, then feedback permits you and the client to modify further strategies, recursively, until the client achieves the changes desired.

While the emphasis is always on future solutions, you, as a possibility-oriented therapist, elicit the client's past history sparingly, examining only the specific occurrences that place stumbling blocks on the path to achieving the client's own goals. After establishing what a

Table 2–1.
Paradigm Change: From Problem to Possibility

Problem Frame	Possibility Frame
Problem/what's wrong	Outcome/what's wanted
Explores history & limitations to discover cause	Explores strengths & resources to design strategies
Cure/failure: gets better or lives with limitations, resistant, or not ready for treatment.	Feedback: gets outcome or recycle to achieve outcome, utilizes client's individuality
Techniques: free association, reflect back, passive listening, interpretation, etc.	Strategies (techniques): tasks, change history, reframing, paradox, etc.
Goal: insight	Goal: specific behavior change
Questions Asked	
What's the problem?	What do you want?
Why is it happening?	In what context?
How does that limit you?	How would you know if you got it?
Who/what is to blame?	What stops you?

Note: problem frame moves *away from anxiety*, possibility frame *moves toward hope*; notice the difference in internal body response.

client wants, you then probe for obstacles: what is it that stops the client from having what he or she wants right now? It is at this point that past difficulties and/or present problems may be explored. Crucial, however, is the purpose of that historical exploration—the gathering of information to move the client toward the possibility of new effective action. How historical material is sought and used will be discussed later, in chapter 5 on the treatment process.

Enhancing Mind/Body Resources

The problem-to-possibility shift, activated by the language of possibility, contributes to significant positive physiological sequelae as well, for *both* client *and* therapist. The conceptual split between body and mind is increasingly recognized as artificial; the evidence of reciprocal interplay between psyche and soma is accumulating. Norman Cousins states:

> At one time, a compartmentalized view of the human body was generally accepted. Recent knowledge of the anatomical and functional links between brain and body point in a different direction. Brain researchers now believe that what happens in the body can affect the brain, and what happens in the brain can affect the body. Hope, purpose, and determination are not merely mental states. They have electrochemical connections that play a large part in the workings of the immune system and, indeed, in the entire economy of the total human organism. (1989: 73)

Language serves as a primary mediator in mind/body reciprocity. The words we use in conversation compel experience in the listener— be the listener ourself or another. We blush when we hear a compliment; our heart rate increases and mood changes upon hearing threats or insults; we may laugh or cry while reading a book. Since words evoke both psychological and physiological states, we need to choose our words with care to generate in our clients the mood and physiology that we consider to be advantageous for their therapy. Through the language that we use we can create optimistic moods that foster restorative psychophysiological change.

Language creates a psychophysiological response in us whether we are actually having the experience, or whether we are just pretending to have it. "Experience" here means an effect on both physiology and mood. There are studies that show that mental imagery of emotional states, induced by instructions for reliving these states, or by arranging facial muscles in specific ways, produce the same physiological states as spontaneous emotions (Schwartz, Weinberger and Singer 1981; Ekman,

Levenson and Friesen 1983; Locke and Colligan 1987; Norris 1988). Ekman, Levenson, and Freisen elaborated their findings to include not only autonomic nervous system changes among the various emotions, but also differing responses among negative emotions. They reported that while anger yielded increases in both hand temperature and heart rate, fear produced an increase in heart rate but a decrease in hand temperature. Most notably, however, happiness was characterized by low rises in both hand temperature and heart rate (1983). Further, the feedback linkage between mental attitude—or mood—and physiology has been established. As Rossi states: *"Mind modulates the biochemical functions within the cells of all the major organ systems and tissues of the body via the autonomic nervous system"* (1986: 108).

> In the language of communication theory, the hypothalamus functions as a *transducer;* it converts the neural impulses of the "mind" into the hormonal "messenger molecules" of the body. This is not speculation; this is fact that we can see under the microscope. . . . Stress and emotions experienced on the level of mind are transduced into body processes by the hypothalamus-pituitary-endocrine-system route. (Rossi, in Zeig 1985: 373 and 376)

So if we change our mood, our physiology changes, and if we change our physiology, our mood changes.

> Positive emotional arousal may reduce our vulnerability to . . . destructive processes. Adequate periods of serenity and elation produce hormonal changes that are the opposite of those produced by anger, fear, and depression. They provide restorative changes countering the emotional reactions to threatening stimuli. They also act as psychological defenses preventing responses to threat by allowing the individual to perceive the situation as controllable. (Henry 1989: 60)

Henry goes on to say that the kind of support found in a therapeutic relationship can be decisive in maintaining immunocompetence during distressing events, for it "has been shown to be associated with reduced levels of serum cholesterol and uric acid and greater immunity, including higher lymphocyte counts and mitogen responses" (Henry 1989: 61). This feedback loop has powerful implications for dealing with the stress that clients bring to therapy.

> One way of defining stress in scientific terms is "any challenge to homeostasis." Homeostasis describes the balance or stability of the body in its internal enviroment. Essentially, we can define stress as any experience that perturbs the body, or threatens to perturb it, from this state of balance. Of course, the body's job is to try to redress that

balance and it does so through a variety of means, including the use of hormones. (McEwen 1990: 50).

This has further significance for the kind of therapeutic environment and interaction that we aim to provide, for what he goes on to say is that "What a human being experiences . . . can affect the output of hormones . . . these hormones can act back on the brain and the body. . . . *What we experience in our environment can actually change the very make up of our bodies and our brains*" (McEwen 1990: 51). [Emphasis added.] Our contention is, therefore, that providing the positive experience of the possibility paradigm potentiates healing changes.

Clients generally seek therapy when they encounter stress in their lives, be it anxiety, depression, or both. Both of these moods decrease immunocompetence (Kiecolt-Glaser et al. 1984, 1985; Rossi 1986; Locke and Colligan 1987; Norris 1988; Cousins 1989; and Solomon 1990). It is important to distinguish between what might be called negative stress (anxiety, depression) and positive stress or *eustress* (life-enhancing challenge), for in both of these states the sympathetic nervous system is innervated. However, in eustress, immunocompetence does not decrease.[2] Immunocompetence, therefore, can be used as a physiological index of the stress that inspires requests for therapy. And therapy, with its built-in "intimate, confiding relationship," is an optimal context in which to deliberately evoke positive and resourceful physiological states. So when clients arrive with the stressors of depression and anxiety, we need to help them change their mood and balance their autonomic nervous system, to enable them to view their life situation as an immunoenhancing challenge.[3] Therapists must teach or access coping skills to help clients meet their life challenges. And how do we start? By using the language of possibility.

The language of possibility interrupts the client's cycle of distress and creates the possibility of hope, change, and a new view of life. *Such language does so simply by asking what the client wants rather than what's wrong.* Taking the client into the realm of hope changes his or her physiology as well and makes him or her more resourceful, right down to the immune-cell level. When the client first appears in your office, you will either join—and so reinforce—the client in her cycle of psychophysiological distress by asking what's wrong, or you will shift the client into a new psychophysiological resourcefulness by asking what the client wants. In the problem frame, the historical questions about the client's limitations and where the causal blame lies, can increase the bleakness of the initial mood. These deficits, difficulties, and despairs are what clients want to get away from (they trigger the fight-or-flight sympathetic nervous system stress response). In

possibility-oriented therapy, interrupting the client's depressed or anxious mood with the question about what is wanted, followed by an
exploration of what here-and-now behaviors need changing, give the
client the immediate experience of an optimistic mood-shift (which triggers the beginning of the beneficial balancing of the autonomic nervous
system). *Language that promotes more positive physiological states is
the essence of the possibility frame,* and this same physiology can
engender the more resourceful mood of hope. Kent et al. say "benefits
in health may accrue from being in a positive emotional state" (1989:
68), and we would emphasize that this means *both* physical *and* mental
health, since humans are but one system. Using this language highlights
the difference between the client's seeing him- or herself as recovering
rather than as ill.

Possibility-orientation expands the dimensions of what constitutes
effective therapy by attending specifically to the body/mind unity and
by deliberately using language to mobilize body/mind resources. *"When
the 'mind' is in a context, the 'body' is necessarily also in that context.
To achieve a different physiological state, sometimes what we need to
do is to place the mind in another context"* (Langer 1989: 177). And
the language of possibility and hope creates that context, for both you
and the client. Not only does this inclusive body/mind approach benefit
clients, but therapists report that they themselves feel less physically
depleted and more hopeful when working in the possibility paradigm.[4]

This is not surprising since we therapists are, of course, subject to
the same psychophysiological feedback systems as our clients; and
therefore, could be subject to the development of non-positive moods
while working in the problem frame. Hence our contention that the use
of the language of possibility, including humor, enhances the psychophysiological well-being of both client and therapist, enabling both
to be more hopeful and resourceful.

Humoring the Client

> A merry heart doeth good like a medicine; but a broken spirit
> drieth the bones.
> —King Solomon

> Humor is one of the truly elegant defenses in the human repertoire.
> Few would deny that the capacity for humor, like hope, is one of
> mankind's most potent antidotes for the woes of Pandora's box.
> —George E. Vaillant

The mind/body wisdom of King Solomon is now being demonstrated in
the laboratory; humor and laughter produce a positive psychophysiolo-

gical state.[5] William Fry, a longtime researcher on the effects of laughter, says:

> Laboratory evidence demonstrates that mirth and particularly mirthful laughter have an impact on most physiological systems. . . . The general pattern is one of stimulation followed by relaxation. For example, the heart rate increases during laughter. After the stimulating behavior has diminished, the heart rate drops below its normal level. This pattern of stimulation and relaxation is pretty well correlated with the psychological features of arousal and catharsis. (1990: 6)

Since the mind and body are one continuous feedback system, it follows that the positive physiological events mentioned above also produce a more positive mood. As David Bresler, an expert on pain management, says: "Laughter is good for both body and mind. It eliminates nervous tensions which upset body functions and it clears the mind of annoyance and resentments. . . . Laughter leaves a feeling of well-being, of personal satisfaction, and of contentment" (1981: 311). Freud suggests that "humor is a means of obtaining pleasure in spite of the distressing affects that interfere with it" (in Vaillant 1977: 117). There is significant support for the view that the ability to see stressors from a humorous vantage point significantly moderates the effect of stressful moods (Martin and Lefcourt 1983). Humor pervades the fabric of possibility-oriented therapy, you continuously look for chances to elicit smiles and laughter from your client. This is not because the you do not take the client's situation seriously, but, on the contrary, exactly *because* you are quite earnest about the work of therapy; and you hold the belief that *humor potentiates the therapeutic context of hope and possibility.*

As Allen Klein says in *The Healing Power of Humor* (1989), "Humor gives us power and new perspective. . . . In laughter, we transcend our predicaments. We are lifted above our feelings of fear, discouragement, and despair. People who can laugh at their setbacks no longer feel sorry for themselves. They feel uplifted, encouraged, and empowered" (1989: 3–4). There is even a study that demonstrates that positive affect, including humor, improved problem-solving abilities (Isen, Daubmon, and Nowieki 1987). The humorous mood, then, may open the client to seeing the new possibilities needed to make the changes he or she wants. And, of course, the therapists who join in the laughter are "uplifted, encouraged, and empowered" themselves. Even smiling can yield positive effects,[6] including enhancing the immune system.[7] "Smiling can help us take the first half-step away from our physical and psychological pain. It is only a part of an overall picture, but when we can smile in spite of our pain, we begin to focus away from our discomforts" (Bresler, in Klein 1989: 96).

Smiling and laughing are also specific antidotes to anxiety, fear, and rage.[8] Tears stemming from emotions, either pain or joy, are also truly cleansing, removing from the body harmful elements caused by stress.[9] Laughter helps increase inventiveness and openness to new learning while making the process lighter and more pleasant for both client and therapist. Therefore, in the service of intentional and effective therapy, the therapist does well to cultivate assiduously his or her own particular style of humor.

Hoping for the Best

"If . . . depression and certain other emotional states seem to retard healing, it seems reasonable to assume that hope could enhance it," so says Jerome Frank in his classic work *Persuasion and Healing*. He goes on to say: "Anxiety and despair can be lethal; confidence and hope, life-giving" and further "it is doubtful that any form of therapy can succeed unless it . . . mobilizes the patient's hopes" (1973: 75–76, 164). The importance of hope, along with what is now known about its biological substrate, makes it imperative for you to actively engender a mood of hope in your clients. Virginia Satir believed that "by putting the emphasis on hope, people enter the process of therapy with a positive feeling, whereas a primary orientation on . . . problems is perceived negatively and is depressing to the individuals in treatment as well as to the therapist" (Satir and Baldwin 1983: 185). Possibility-oriented therapy builds in a focus on hope by asking the client what he or she wants in the future. The emphasis on the future, rather than on the past, is one of the signal characteristics of possibility-oriented therapy. "Unconcerned with the ambiguity of past experience, hope implies a process; it is an adventure, a going forward, a confident search . . . hope fires hope" (Menninger 1959: 484, 486). Hope also fires the client's expectations—expectations of getting the needed and desired results. Hope and expectation are indissolubly intertwined. The role of hope in generating effective treatment cannot be overestimated.

Much is made of the importance of clients' positive expectations; it is almost universally hailed (Frank 1973). Freud said "Expectation colored by hope and faith is an effective force with which we all have to reckon . . . in *all* our attempts at treatment and cure" (Freud, in Frank 1973: 137). *Expectation* can be considered the activating energy of hope. "Favorable expectations generate feelings of optimism, energy, and well-being and may actually promote healing, especially of those illnesses with a large psychological or emotional component" (Frank 1973: 136). It is equally important for you to be hopeful and to expect the treatment that you offer will be effective. As Malan says, "The *therapist's enthusiasm* ... has a direct bearing on the process and outcome of therapy since it brings with it a corresponding heightened excitement in the patient" (1975: 13). Therapists who undertake brief therapy from "bitter practical necessity" (Fenichel and Rapaport 1954: 243), and tell themselves that open-ended therapy would be better, may well be standing in the way of their own best therapeutic results. Therapists need to genuinely embrace limited goals *and see the possibilities in them* (Rapoport, in Katz 1975; Budman and Gurman 1988). Therapists who are unaware of their biases may inadvertently sabotage the brief therapy process.[10] As psychiatrist James Harburger said, "When I was learning to practice brief therapy, before I believed a patient could surface relevant early material in the first few sessions, it never happened."[11]

Brief therapists need not only to *expect* but also to *intend* to succeed in brief therapy. Your anticipation of effective brief work directly supports the *intentional design* of such therapy. Such expectations and intentions fuel not only the patient's hope, but also the therapist's, which, in turn enhances the potency of the work. As Frank says: "Expectations of patient and therapist seem to affect duration and outcome of treatment, . . . [so] that the more congruent these are, the better the outcome of treatment should be" (1973: 159). Therapy conducted without such expectation and intention is less apt to produce the desired results (Weakland et al. 1974). Therapy is likely to be undermined by any assumption of the therapist, conscious or unconscious, that brief treatment is a second-class option, and that open-ended therapy is still the treatment of choice (Budman and Gurman 1988). On occasion, a longer therapy may be necessary when brief therapy has not yielded the hoped-for results. Brief therapist Bill O'Hanlon says: "I begin therapy with new clients assuming that it will be brief, and I let my clients teach me how long it will be" (1990: 49). [It is also important to distinguish between long-term weekly therapy and open-ended intermittent therapy in which the therapy relationship is long, but the number of sessions are relatively few. This will be discussed further in later chapters.]

We have made the argument that placing the therapist's mental set about therapy squarely in the possibility paradigm will benefit both the client and the therapist, not only in the more efficacious generation of effective therapy, but also in augmented psychophysiological health for both. We see the use of positive language as central to this endeavor, not only in asking clients what they want, but also in constantly pointing them in the direction of new—and expanded—views of possible effective actions in their lives. Thus, the therapist challenges the client's negative assumptions. This paradigm offers the "something entirely different" perspective of second-order change, with verbal reframing and humor as handmaidens to support optimism about the future as well as to aid in the beneficial balancing of the autonomic nervous system. This approach emphasizes the transformation of *stress* into *challenge* by focusing the client's attention not on what to leave in the past, but rather on what to go toward in the future.

Notes

1. *Change: Principles of Problem Formation and Problem Resolution* (1974) by Watzlawick, Weakland, and Fisch elucidates these distinctions in more detail.

2. "[Hans] Selye differentiated between the type of stress that caused illness and the type of stress—'eustress'—that was life-enhancing. . . . The psychobiological basis of this distinction between negative and positive emotions in response to stress has recently been investigated by a number of researchers. . . . They found a significant difference in the body's response to 'threat' (stress) and 'challenge' (eustress). Threat is associated with two factors: (1) an increase in the blood level of catecholamines (epinephrine and norepinephrine, secreted from the adrenal *medulla* in response to sympathetic stimulation described earlier as the alarm response of the autonomic nervous system); and (2) the release of cortisol into the bloodstream by the adrenal *cortex* (signaled by the pituitary gland sending ACTH to the adrenal cortex. . . . Challenge, on the other hand, is associated only with an elevation in catecholamine levels" (Rossi 1986: 119).

3. In the Ongoing Research News section of *Advances* (1990) it was reported that Dr. Richard Dienstbier, in talking about "the toughness response, cites various studies on behavior which conclude that sufficiently extended stressful situations can lead to depletion of catecholamines. However, perceiving a situation as challenging prevents both high cortisol levels and catecholamine exhaustion. He cites other studies showing that high cortisol baseline rates are associated with anorexia, depression anxiety, and neuroticism" (*Advances* 7, no.1:6). Suzanne C. Ouellette Kobasa writes (1990: 219–30) about the "stress-resistant personality," citing the essential ingredients of commitment, control, and challenge.

4. Both authors have received positive feedback about using the possibility frame from colleagues and students. Typical responses include "I felt lighter," "the problem felt manageable, not so overwhelming," "comforting to feel that I didn't have to have the whole answer, more of a partnership," "I felt more in control and more focussed, didn't join the client's depression," "more purposeful, building on the client's point of view," "it was more hopeful, I had more energy."

5. "Positive emotions appear to have specific biochemical correlates, which in turn have specific effects on tissues and diseases" (Melnechuck, in Rossi 1986: 109). Lee S. Berk also reports positive physiological effects from laughter: Humor reduces . . . negative consequences of classical stress (distress) . . . cortisol levels . . . also decreased significantly. . . . Cortisol is involved with the

immune system. For example, we know that increases in the level of cortisol can suppress the immune system. It appears that by lowering cortisol levels humor may positively impact immunomodulation (What are the physiological effects of laughter? *Mind-Body-Health Digest* 4, no. 2 [1990]: 6).

6. "According to a study done by psychologist James Laird of Clark University, facial expressions can trigger our mood by returning us to happier memories. Laird found that students remembered happier thoughts when they were smiling; conversely, grim stories were more easily remembered when they were frowning. In other words, if you are anxious asking for a raise, making a business call, or even telling a joke, try smiling; it can help you recall a time when things went well" (in Klein 1989: 95). " 'It now seems clear,' says social psychologist Fritz Strack, 'that facial expressions are an integral part of emotional experiences.' Strack, who conducted similar reasearch to Laird's, found that his subjects' reactions to cartoons were enhanced when he forced them to smile by having them hold a pen in their mouth. Both these researchers agree that it does not matter if you are smiling for real or faking it. A phony smile can trigger happy thoughts just as easily as a genuine one. 'So if you really want to appreciate humor,' notes Strack, 'it's important that you smile—even if you have to fake it a bit' " (in Klein 1989: 95–96).

7. "Dr. John Diamond believes in smiling, or even looking at a smile . . . gives us what he calls 'life energy.' 'We have always known,' says Diamond, 'how beautiful and beneficial a smile is. Now we can show—actually demonstrate—the therapeutic value of smiling.' . . . he states that smiling helps strengthen the thymus gland, an important contributor to a healthy immune system, because the zygomaticus major (those smile muscles) and the thymus gland are closely linked" (in Klein 1989: 97).

8. In the *Mind-Body-Health Digest* article "Performance anxiety: a mind-body approach," Diane Nichols, a clinical social worker at the Miller Health Care Institute for Performing Artists in New York City specializing in helping performers overcome their anxiety, is quoted as saying "The first step is to smile. It's been shown that, physiologically, you can't smile and experience fear at the same time" (*Mind-Body-Health Digest* 4, no. 1: 3). "Fear and rage are two emotions that have been associated with heart attacks. Stanford University psychiatrist Dr. William Fry, Jr., who has done extensive research documenting the physiological benefits of laughter as well as other aspects of the humor story, notes that these emotions are countered and alleviated by humor. Fry says that humor can play a major role in maintaining a healthy heart. 'Humor acts to relieve fear,' he states. 'Rage is impossible when mirth prevails' " (in Klein 1989: 9).

9. "Tears of sorrow and tears of joy seem to be related too. Dr. Wm. Frey, II, a biochemist . . . has found that emotional tears contain a greater concentration of protein than tears that are produced by other means, such as from cutting an onion. Frey believes that tears resulting from sadness play an important part in removing harmful substances that are produced by stress. He also speculates that the tears of laughter serve the same function as the tears of sorrow. In other words, laughter's tears may also carry away harmful toxins from the body, and the suppression of them, as in the suppression of emotional tears, increases our susceptibility to stress-related disorders. But in spite of all

the similarities, there is one big difference between laughter and crying: Laughter helps us transcend our suffering; crying does not" (in Klein 1989: 20–21).

10. For a fuller discussion of unconscious influence and the role of expectation, see the chapters on "Experimental Studies of Persuasion" and "Placebo Effect and the Role of Expectations" in Frank (1973).

11. Personal communication.

3
The Therapist's Assumptions

What is the first thing a pianist does before beginning to play? What is the first thing a baseball player does before swinging at the oncoming pitch? At what does the Tai Chi master work the hardest? In these situations as well as many others in life, one develops an opening posture or stance, a pattern of readiness that serves as a foundation for action. The pianist pulls the piano bench into position, sits upright facing the piano, gets his fingers over the keyboard, positions his feet under the piano, and gets ready to play. The baseball player gets into a highly stylized stance in the batters box in readiness for the oncoming pitch. The Tai Chi master works hardest at developing the proper balance or stance for engaging in a series of ritualized exercises.

In the same way, the possibility-oriented therapist adopts an attitude, posture, or set of expectations about change. The therapist thinks about the psychotherapy change process, not as a sort of reconstructive surgery, but as an attempt to catalyze the client or client system to use his (or their) resources to identify and reach a well-specified goal. This requires a paradigm shift from a traditional and pathological causal model of change to a constructivist model based on "wellness" and strengths. What follows is a description of those therapist "postures" or "attitudes" that we have found most helpful in applying a "wellness" model.

Approach the Client with a Naive, Curious, Open, Inquisitive Mind

Hoffman (1985) makes the case that the therapist should approach the client as if he were "E.T.—the extraterrestrial." In so doing we put aside our assumptions and biases, and approach the client with an open mind. The therapist joins with the client's view of reality without attempting to impose a set of assumptions based on his or her own reality. "If your mind is empty, it is always ready for anything; it is open to everything. In the beginner's mind there are many possibilities; in the expert's mind, there are few" (Suzuki, in Patterson 1987: 252). Rather than making assumptions and judgments about the client to diagnose dysfunction, the therapist frees himself of such assumptions and becomes open to listening carefully to the client's story.

A useful therapeutic posture is one of free-floating attention, openness, flexibility, and a readiness to respond to cues and behaviors that are in the direction of solutions. By developing skill at being "distracted by important information" (Hill 1986), the therapist approaches the client from a naive, curious, inquisitive point of view. "Being naive simply means that we reject received wisdom that something is a problem; . . . to be naive is to start with fewer preconceptions . . . naive beliefs favor optimism" (K.E. Weick 1984: 47).

The clients engage in circular and repetitive patterns over time. These recursive cycles make up the client's reality. The therapist's posture is one of curiosity and exploration, gently introducing (exploring) ideas that will serve to disrupt these cycles and patterns.

Respect the Client and the Client's Resources and Creativity

People are doing the best they can under the circumstances. With that in mind it is important to normalize and praise past and present successes and positive actions. By assuming good intentions the therapist builds an alliance with the client based on respect and understanding. By accepting and trusting that people have a good reason for seeking treatment and that they have a good sense of their own needs the therapist accept them on their own terms. By viewing the client as the expert on his or her experience, the therapist avoids imposing his or her own reality on the client's. One way to show respect for the client is by "normalizing" concerns and issues. "Normalizing is a way of conveying to a [client or] family that they are not unique or alone in their struggles but that these are part of the human condition" (Wells 1980: 86).

In one clinical situation, a woman had changed therapists, since she got the message from her first therapist that she was capable of dealing with her issues on her own and didn't require therapy. She felt that her concerns had not been acknowledged. In addition to acknowledging and normalizing her concerns (she was in the process of getting a divorce) I [SF] also allowed her to regulate the frequency of appointments, which she did in a thoughtful manner. By letting her make appointments as she needed them, I was giving her the message that I respected her ability to make these decisions. This served to foster her own sense of independence and autonomy. One day she came in and said "I don't think I need this anymore" and we ended our sessions. She has since come back for several one session "consults."

It is important not to lose sight of the fact that the therapist is also a human being. As Greenson (1972) puts it, "civility towards the patient, compassion for his plight, respect for him as a human being, and the acknowledgement of our own lapses . . . are vital ingredients for a productive [therapeutic] atmosphere" (217). The therapist is a human participant in a structured conversation. A well-timed apology will go a long way towards shoring up a tenuous alliance, while a confrontative ("You're being defensive") posture will only serve to create distance and distrust. If there is a "contest" between the therapist and the client, nobody wins. The therapist must accept the fact that he is a fallible human being, or as Milton Erickson put it "just another bozo on the road of life" (in Zeig, 1985). The basic position taken here is that the therapist is always on the client's "side." As Patterson so articulately points out, "the . . . therapist views the [client] with such respect that he or she simply cooperates with the [client's] efforts to heal [him] self" (1987: 246).

Too often, external systems attempt to impose their philosophy, values, and expectations for change on the client or client system. In many cases institutions and agencies take over the functions of the client system in ways that undermine the system's capacity for self-healing and self-regulation.

In one situation, a fourteen-year-old boy, Fred, was being evaluated at a local hospital after displaying some behavioral difficulties in his school setting. Fred had a history of learning disabilities and epilepsy and was living with his single-parent mother and two older brothers. During the testing, Fred made some comments that the tester interpreted as reflecting "clear suicidal ideation" and recommended that Fred be hospitalized immediately. When the mother was told about this, she tried to explain to the tester that her son sometimes made comments that could be misunderstood and that she did not see the need for him to be put into a psychiatric hospital. The tester decided to notify the Department of Social Services, saying that the mother was demonstrating neglect for her son. Fred was taken out of his school and hospitalized for a two-week period.

After the hospitalization I met with Fred and his family. I focused on empowering the mother as the expert on her son and empathizing with her over how she was treated by the hospital. Over time, we developed a good relationship in which our contacts around her son always included her input, perspective, and active involvement.

Through her efforts, Fred gained better control over his behavior and began to demonstrate increased maturity in his social relations. My approach focused on *what the mother and son were doing well* and not on limitations or deficits. Our work continues as a team effort in helping Fred gain increased control over his tendency for impulsive behavior.

In many instances the client or client system has already taken steps in the direction of resolving the presenting difficulty. The therapist merely serves to facilitate, amplify, and support solution-generating processes already underway. The following clinical situation demonstrates the strength of the system to solve its own problems. Here, I [SF] empower the father to deal with his daughter around an issue familiar to both of them. The natural healing capabilities of the family are supported and facilitated.

A thirteen-year-old twin girl, Joy, was referred for being "depressed" by her pediatric neurologist, who was treating her for a seizure disorder. A meeting with Joy, her twin sister, her older sister (age 15), and her parents revealed that over the past three to four weeks, Joy was fighting more with her older sister and was expressing ideas of "feeling different" from others. She would sometimes say "I'm going crazy." In the meeting, other family members described Joy as "very perceptive and sensitive . . . and good at expressing feelings." Her mother viewed the fighting at home as reflecting the fact that Joy "is not feeling good about herself."

In the course of the initial interview I discovered that the father had a twenty-five-year history of epilepsy. After being symptom-free on medication for twenty years, he recently had a grand-mal seizure at home and cracked three vertebrae. Following that episode he described a loss of short-term memory, a problem with motor coordination, and sleep difficulties. It was apparent that for a period of time father was seriously ill and nonfunctional. As we discussed father's illness, the family became very sad and tearful. During the period of father's illness the family had not openly shared their fears and worries with each other or with him.

I framed Joy's recent behavioral changes and the fighting between her and her older sister as reflecting her need to express for the whole family their worry and upset over father's condition. Now that the father's health crisis was over, the family was dealing with the emotional aftereffects, which Joy was delegated to express. I encouraged family members, in the session, to share with father their concerns and love for him, which they were able to do quite effectively. In addition, I instructed the father to spend some time with Joy over the next two weeks in educating her about epilepsy and sharing with her his own experiences of "feeling different" as a function of his condition.

The family returned two weeks later and reported that the fighting between the siblings had decreased significantly; that the father had talked with Joy as discussed; that Joy had a better understanding of her condition; and that the family found the previous meeting useful in "getting us connected again."

By allowing them time to carry out a "homework" assignment, I had placed the client/client system in a position to assume increased responsibility for change. At the same time, I avoided "getting in the way of the normal restorative-processes of life" (Hobbs 1966).

> Weekly psychotherapy [seems] neither ideal nor well suited to the majority of people seeking help for problems in living. Families have self-healing capabilities, which can be nurtured by use of less intervention or more selective intervention which more fully acknowledges and respects the families' natural capacities for solution development. (Friedman 1990: 11)

In one family I [SF] was seeing, the son had a difficult time letting his parents know when he was feeling under pressure about school. Between family meetings the mother and son developed a plan in which the boy, when he was feeling under pressure, would remove the bracelet he wears on his arm. The mother would notice this and initiate a discussion with him about school.

In another situation, a woman described a creative way to help herself stay calm at work and feel more positive when she was beginning to feel "down." She would begin singing out loud. Soon others in the area where she worked joined in and the mood of the whole work environment improved!

The mother of a two-year-old girl sought consultation in preparing her daughter for her anticipated two-week absence (The mother was going to be traveling outside the country.) When I [SF] asked what she had been thinking of doing, she described the following: During the previous few weeks she had been tape-recording herself reading stories with her daughter before the child went to sleep. She planned to ask her husband to play a different story for the daughter each night while she was away. In addition, she had prepared little gifts that her daughter could open each day while her mother was gone. In light of the mother's expertise, my job as therapist was simply to affirm her creative plan and wish her well on her trip.

Respect the Client's Request

The therapist should view the client's predicament as a bridge to solution development and change. By respecting the client's current functioning and behavior, the therapist sends the message that he or she understands the situation and will work with the client's request. (Clinical examples in later chapters will illustrate the forms that such respect takes and how the therapist's respectful approach serves to engage the client or family in a process leading to successful mastery of the presenting difficulty.) The therapist works to develop an intervention strategy that both matches the client's belief system and is effective in persuading the client to take a small step toward modifying the distressing behavior.

"Resistance" is not a useful concept (deShazer 1985). Since there is comfort in the familiar, the client or client system holds onto what it knows best. As Hoffman says, "resistance is an artifact of the way therapists present themselves rather than a trait of a mule-like [client or] family" (1990: 7). Thinking in terms of a "resistant" client implies that there is something internal to the client and the client system that "intends" to oppose the therapist or sabotage change. Such a stance does not lend itself to a partnership or team approach in which therapist and client work together toward solution development. When therapeutic interventions are not successful, it means that the therapist has not yet listened closely enough to what the client wants. The intervention must be revised to better match the client's belief system. We prefer to think about "challenging therapeutic encounters" rather than difficult clients.

See Capacity: Generate an Optimistic Stance Regarding Change

Milton Erickson welcomed "symptoms" and incorporated them into his creative interventions. One very dramatic example is described by Haley (1973: 28):

> When Erickson was on the staff of Worcester State Hospital, there was a young patient who called himself Jesus. He paraded around as the Messiah, wore a sheet draped around him, and attempted to impose Christianity on people. Erickson approached him on the hospital grounds and said "I understand you have had experience as a carpenter?" The patient could only reply that he had. Erickson involved the young man in a special project of building a bookcase and shifted him to productive labor.

The focus of therapy is in "bringing about change and expanding the person's world, not upon educating him about his inadequacies" (Haley 1973: 67). The possibility-oriented therapist supports and builds on the client's current strengths, assets, and resources and is future oriented, and assumes that the client's present situation contains within it the necessary resources to generate an effective solution.

Therapists need to be wary of initial impressions. We sometimes see people at their worst (under the most trying conditions) and therefore need to be tolerant, respectful and nonjudgmental in our approach. Several years ago, one of us [SF] was talking by phone with the maternal grandmother and guardian of a teenage girl who was being referred to the mental health department. My initial impression of the guardian, based on this phone conversation, was that she was tangential, had a thought disorder of some kind, and was possibly psychotic. In meeting her several days later, I found out that she had a significant hearing impairment, which accounted for her behavior on the phone.

In another situation, I [SF] had read a report on a family seen in therapy at another agency. The report was very negative and judgmental about the family and portrayed a picture of a seriously emotionally disturbed child whose parents were both inept and unsupportive of treatment. They were described as needing intensive treatment and were viewed as unlikely to change (the previous agency had been unsuccessful in helping them). In my first family meeting with them I was ready to see "pathology" and was puzzled by their refusal to acknowledge the significant problems, which I "knew" they had. I was struck by the level of "denial" displayed by this family, which added to my concern.

I finally realized that I was stuck in a negative set about this family, and this negative set would have the effect of creating a "self-fulfilling prophecy" (in essence, I would probably also fail with this family). Before the second session I made up my mind to "forget" the report I had read and to approach this session from a fresh and naive position. I found myself better able to form an alliance with the parents and over a sixth-month period of therapy twice a month, created a context in which change occurred.

See Crises as Opportunities

There is a Japanese concept known as "kaizan," "every defect is a treasure." This idea is very Ericksonian, seeing each problem as containing the seeds for its solution. A recent newspaper article described a program in which teenagers who had been painting subway cars with graffiti were now being paid to put their work on canvas and selling them to earn money. In this very creative program, the talents of these teenagers, rather being discouraged (and the teenagers defined as "bad" or "delinquent") were utilized and channeled into a productive and worthwhile venture. This is an excellent example of turning a difficulty into an asset.

One day, two colleagues were discussing a woman who had called in during a crisis. She was very tearful, upset, and unable to function at work. One of these clinicians had noted my name [SF] on the medical record and involved me in the discussion (I had seen her with her husband and son two years earlier). While agreeing with my colleagues that this woman was clearly in crisis, I encouraged them to view the crisis as having a useful and positive function in allowing her to experience the full impact of some of her actions. The clinicians had been thinking of giving her some anti-anxiety medication to help her calm down and feel more in control. On the other hand, I was viewing this as an opportunity for this woman, who had, in the past, avoided responsibility for her own behavior, to have to confront some of the issues she had been so effectively avoiding for so long.

I agreed to meet with her on an emergency basis, at which time I told her that I knew that some useful learning would come out of the pain she was obviously experiencing. We discussed what goals she might have for therapy based on her current situation and developed a plan for getting support from the extended-family members she was planning to see over the coming week. She did raise the issue of medication, which I told her might be worth discussing at the next session about two weeks later. When she came in for this meeting, she was much more in control, had obviously and successfully weathered the crisis with family support, and had some perspective on her behavior.

In another clinical situation, in which a crisis became an opportunity for change, a couple came to therapy after the wife had gone on a shopping spree and charged significant sums of money on their joint credit cards. The husband was very angry with his wife and wanted an explanation for her "erratic" and "impulsive" behavior. We discussed their roles regarding finances, and it became clear that the husband was the financial manager and tended to be very "future-oriented," working to save money for some future time. The wife, on the other hand, was secretly upset and resentful about the husband's tight rein over the purse strings. The husband was described as "blowing up" when the wife would ask for money and would give her lectures about being careful with her spending. The wife's overspending now left the couple having to rethink their financial roles, as they planned how to pay off these large debts.

I [SF] discussed this "financial crisis" as a real opportunity for change and framed the wife's behavior as creating a crisis that would require the couple to have to renegotiate their roles and attitudes toward finances. They would need to make adjustments to what had become a very rigid and constraining structure (with the husband feeling burdened by financial responsibilities and the wife by her husband's rigidity about money). We discussed ways for husband to "let go" of his anger and to see this as an opportunity to "re-calibrate" their roles around finances. The wife's overspending was also a metaphor for the couple's focus on material aspects of their life together at the expense of other aspects of their relationship. The crisis led directly to helping this couple to reestablish intimacy.

In contrast to situations, like the one above, where a crisis is the basis for therapeutic contact, the therapist sometimes needs to precipitate a crisis in the session, in order to provide the client(s) an opportunity for movement and change. Minuchin and Fishman (1981) talk about "increasing the intensity" of the interaction in destabilizing old unproductive "routines" and in allowing new options to evolve. By doing so, the therapist shows respect for the ability of client (or system) to go beyond its usual operating style.

With one family, with whom I [SF] was working, the parents were both intensely focused on the children who served as "steam release valves" drawing their parents' focus whenever tension between the spouses began to rise. The oldest child, a ten-year old boy, understood my metaphor of the family as a "pressure cooker" and agreed that he sometimes would "help" the family by creating "trouble." The parents had gotten comfortable using the children to avoid intimacy and closeness. In one session, after asking the children to leave the room, I had the parents sit face to face and have a discussion. When the discussion became heated, I continued to push them to go beyond their usual distancing operations. As a result, some unaired issues were exposed. It became clear that the couple was "asking" me to help them overcome their usual impasse, and my doing so created an opportunity for reestablishing a more satisfying level of intimacy. By showing them that I respected their capacity to move on in their lives, I allowed them to risk being more vulnerable and open.

Set Limited and Achievable Goals
(Think Small)

In the words of the well-known Chinese proverb "a journey of a thousand miles begins with a single step." Daniel Patrick Moynihan (now a senator from New York) was in charge of federal funding for cities in the late 1960s. At that time the mayors of large cities were calling, asking for help, and talking about how overwhelming their needs were, and how they therefore deserved support. What Moynihan did was to let them know that money was not going to go to cities where the problems were overwhelming but rather to cities where specific problems could be identified and specific goals delineated. After speaking with several mayors in this way, word got around and soon they were calling and telling Moynihan that the problems were no longer overwhelming but were manageable, particularly with some support from the federal government. As K.E. Weick points out "people define . . . problems in ways that overwhelm their ability to do anything about them. Changing the scale of a problem can change the quality of resources that are directed at it" (1984: 48).

It is of paramount importance that the therapist collaborate and negotiate with the client (family) in specifying a reachable goal (Fisch, Weakland and Segal 1982; Haley 1976; O'Hanlon and Wilk 1987; K.E. Weick 1984). Families, in particular, can seem like a "three ring circus", where there is so much going on that the therapist must work at focusing on one aspect of the situation. Fogarty (1983) has compared therapy to cleaning a house in order to emphasize the importance of working on "one room at a time."

Goal setting is important in keeping the focus on the original request and its resolution (deShazer 1985; Fisch, Weakland & Segal 1982; Haley 1976; O'Hanlon and Wilk 1987; K.E. Weick 1984). Barker (1985) compares the process of psychotherapy to "traveling through a jungle. . . . You need to know where you want to end up— otherwise you will wander aimlessly until you die of starvation or some creature eats you" (69). Groups such as Alcoholics Anonymous are successful because they talk about "stay[ing] sober one day or one hour at a time. . . . The impossibility of lifetime abstinence is scaled down to the more workable task of not taking a drink for the next twenty-four hours" (K.E. Weick 1984: 42). As Weick says

> a small win is a concrete, complete, implemented outcome of moderate importance . . . small wins are . . . opportunities that produce visible results. . . . Once a small win has been accomplished, forces are set in motion that favor another small win. . . . Much of the artfulness in working with small wins lies in identifying, gathering, and labeling several small changes that are present but unnoticed. (43–44)

On a recent vacation to the mountains of northwest Wyoming, I [SF] was impressed by how much I could notice ("see") in the mountains, streams, trails, and forests around me when a trained guide with especially acute sensitivity to the environment was leading the trip—in contrast to when I was without such assistance. By looking with such guided sensitivity I could make out the outline of the tan and white antelope against a background of earth tones and green shrubs. The therapist, similarly, can be such a guide for the client by accentuating and elaborating on small differences or variations in the client's problem-focused world. By accentuating those positive aspects of the client's situation that blend in and are ignored or easily overlooked, the therapist, just as the guide, can help create a more diverse reality containing new information (a new set of distinctions) that may lead to increased options for action and change.

People generally tend to ignore or overlook small but significant changes and need the therapist to point out these positive steps. In some situations, for example, parents may not notice when the child has made some progress toward the goals set.

Recently, I [SF] saw a mother and father who were coming in with concerns regarding the behavior of their eleven-year-old son. Their son refused to sleep under the covers of his bed and would sleep without wearing a pajama top. This upset the parents very much. The parents believed that because of this sleeping arrangement he was not getting a good night's sleep and was tossing and turning for much of the night. They also reported that he was "always intruding" into his younger sisters' activities and was viewed as generally irritable and noncooperative around the house, repeatedly tuning-out their requests. After my first contact with the family, several goals were explicitly discussed, namely that progress would be reflected in the child sleeping under his covers, wearing pajamas to bed, interfering less with his sisters' activities, and helping some around the house in a way that could be seen as cooperative (for example, feeding the dog).

I requested that the parents watch very closely for things that their son "does well" over the next two weeks and make a special effort to acknowledge this to him (something they had not been doing). The parents and child agreed that a negative cycle had developed, and they all expressed a desire to try to break this cycle. When they came in for the second session, the parents began complaining again about the boy's behavior.

I inquired about the specific issues we had discussed in the initial session. The mother reported that the boy was sleeping under the covers at night, was wearing his pajamas, and had made some attempts to cooperate at home. I emphasized the significance of these changes (the concern about the son's sleeping habits had been ongoing for over two years!). By punctuating these changes as significant I was able to get the parents to acknowledge the progress they had made and compliment them and their son on their successes.

By the third session the parents had "noticed" the progress more clearly and had acknowledged the changes their son had made. A positive cycle had been established. The son, who could see the changes in himself and his parents volunteered "my parents are nicer now," a comment which surprised his parents who never expected to hear anything positive from their "noncooperative" son.

Bowen (1978: 443–44)[1] provides the following illustration emphasizing the usefulness of defining goals in behavioral terms:

A hospitalized mental patient was permitted a town pass. En route back to the hospital, hallucinated voices resulted in his becoming immobile as he tried to board a busy bus. The bus company complained about the hospital permitting "sick" patients in town. A usual psychiatric approach would have been to tell the patient that he was "too sick" to go to town and passes would be suspended until he was "better." Instead, this patient was told that town passes were being suspended until he learned to behave himself in public. He practiced hard trying to learn to act normally in spite of the voices.

Within a week he asked for a town pass. The town trip was uneventful and within another week he was out of the hospital and back at work supporting his family, with some voices still present. The voices disappeared after a brief period of outpatient therapy. If told the passes were suspended because of "sickness" until he was "better" he would have been confronted with two conditions out of his control. When put in terms of behavior that offended others, he had a situation he could control, and he did. Confronted with "sickness" and "better" he could have gone into chronic illness, passively waiting to get better. . . . Most people are put in mental hospitals because of odd or uncontrollable behavior. Hospitalization has been markedly shorter for those put there for "unacceptable behavior" than similar patients hospitalized for "sickness."

Keeping Our Assumptions Simple

In figure 3–1 the authors have outlined a *continuum of assumptions* to guide the actions of the therapist in *finding the simplest and most direct strategy* for creating a context for change. The therapist tries simple interventions based on simple assumptions before proceeding to more complex analyses of the situation. Four sets of assumptions are outlined, starting with the most direct and empowering (that is, solution-oriented) and going to the least economical and most complex (psychodynamic). Our primary goal is to use the least intrusive, least pathologizing, most empowering methods and the most economical set of assumptions about the client's predicament in creating a context for

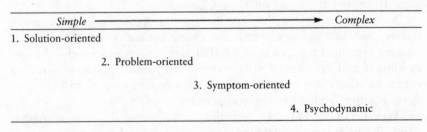

Figure 3–1. A Continuum of Intervention Assumptions

change. The most economical approach being the one that requires the least amount of theoretical preconception and hypothesis generation. For example, the psychodyamic approach requires an elaborate set of assumptions about the etiology of behavior and defines change as requiring "insight" and exploration into past determinants of current behavior. The client's problem is seen as the manifest content of a deeper and more covert issue usually requiring "intensive" psychotherapy.

On the other hand, a *solution-oriented approach* accepts the client's request and uses this as a bridge to solution development (deShazer 1985; 1988; O'Hanlon & Wilk 1987; O'Hanlon & Weiner-Davis 1989). The request for change is accepted as a "gift" (Ritterman 1983) from the client, one that provides direction and focus to the therapeutic endeavor.

The *problem-oriented approach* is based on the work of the Mental Research Institute and attempts to understand and alter those interactional patterns that sustain the problem. The *symptom-oriented* approach looks for the "function of the symptom" in the larger system and uses strategic directives to create change.

The first three approaches (solution-, problem-, and symptom-oriented) are based on models derived from the work of Milton Erickson. Below, we outline each of these three models and their commonalities and differences. As the reader will see in clinical material to be presented, each approach can be a useful means for creating a context for change. As was discussed earlier, many varied approaches can be effective and there is no one "right way." The therapist's job is to draw on an economical set of assumptions that will most rapidly liberate the client from the problem.

Below is an example that may help clarify the differences among these models. The reader is encouraged to think about varied treatment approaches in effectively managing this situation: How would you approach this situation? What additional information would you need to develop an intervention? What assumptions are you making in generating your intervention ideas?

A pediatric nurse practitioner referred a thirteen-year-old girl (Mary) who was described as "setting fires . . . [her] mother has found evidence of fires set in patient's room and patient has admitted to setting fires . . . [her] mother requests mental health referral." For the initial session, Mary arrived with her mother. I [SF] inquired into Mary's fire-setting behavior. Mary described setting fire to small pieces of paper in her room on a fairly regular basis over a two-year period. She would light the paper and observe it burning and then put it out in her trash basket. One day the paper she had lit was not fully put out and ended up catching the trash basket on fire. Mary put out this fire but her mother noticed the charred basket and questioned her about her behavior. This led to the request for a referral. I asked both Mary and her mother if there were any other issues that concerned them at this time. Both said "no."

Table (3–1) outlines the assumptions that each approach (identified in Figure 3–1) might make in dealing with the above situation.

Table 3–1.
The Continuum of Intervention Assumptions as Applied to a Clinical Situation

Presenting Complaint. Thirteen-year-old, setting fires in room over two-year period.

Simple

Solution-oriented. Assess pattern of occurrence; client request for change acknowledged and accepted; therapist requests variation in behavior, building on client-generated resources [e.g., "What do you do when you resist the temptation to set a fire"?].

Problem-oriented. What maintains habit or behavior pattern? Assume behavior is maintained by influence of others in the system; try to introduce variation in pattern [e.g., "What alterations in the problem-maintaining cycle need to be made to solve this problem?].

Symptom-oriented. Assume behavior has meaning in the family system; prescribe necessity for symptom maintenance [e.g., "What function does symptom serve for the family?" Is Mary trying to detour attention away from, or call attention to, problems in her parents' relationship?].

Psychodynamic. Assume behavior has symbolic meaning requiring exploration and insight; see patient individually to deal with internal conflicts [e.g., Mary's behavior is symptomatic of deeply rooted, intrapsychic conflicts that require exploration and analysis].

Complex

The Intervention

I asked Mary if there were times when she felt the urge to light a fire but resisted the temptation to do so. She said that this did happen on occasion. I then asked what she did when she avoided the urge to light a fire. She then named several things she would do instead of lighting a fire (examples included calling a friend on the phone; exercising; riding her bicycle; writing a song; going downstairs to be with one or another family member; working on her homework; and cleaning her room). I encouraged her to make a list of all those things she does that are successful in helping her resist the urge to light a fire. When next she feels the urge, she is to do one or more things on her list. The mother removed all matches from the house as a precaution, and it was clear that Mary knew how to put out a fire should one occur. Both mother and Mary seemed to accept this plan, and a second appointment was set for ten days later, with the mother and Mary to call me should the need arise.

At this second meeting Mary reported that she had not set a fire during the past ten days. On five occasions she reported feeling the urge to light some paper but did "something else" on her list which she had posted on her refrigerator. Mary described the urge to light a fire as "not that hard to resist." Her mother had noticed that Mary was spending more time out of her room and with the family than previously and was participating more in family activities. I supported the good work of Mary and her mother and scheduled another appointment in three weeks. I also asked Mary to call me in ten days with an update on her progress. Ten days later, as planned, Mary called and informed me that she had continued resisting the urge to light fires. She reported "feeling the urge" only once during this period and most of the time she "forgot all about it." I spoke with Mary's mother who felt satisfied with Mary's progress. We decided to cancel a scheduled appointment we had made for two weeks later. A follow-up contact, almost three months after our last meeting, indicated that Mary had set no fires over this period.

In the above clinical example, the most economical approach was used to overcome the complaint. I neither inquired into past hisory nor tried to hypothesize about the cause or meaning of the behavior (from a psychodynamic point of view). I did not define the behavior as serving some function within the family system (such as detouring attention onto herself and off a marital problem) nor did I make assumptions about what was maintaining the behavior (the Palo Alto Mental Research Institute approach). I simply directed the client to engage in a set of self-generated behaviors that helped her resist the urge to light fires.

Before turning to other clinical examples, a brief description is given of each of the Ericksonian-based approaches noted above.

Solution-Oriented Approach

Steve deShazer, of the Brief Family Therapy Center in Milwaukee (1985, 1988) and William O'Hanlon of the Hudsen Institute in Omaha (O'Hanlon & Wilk 1987; O'Hanlon and Weiner-Davis 1989) have each developed models to look beyond problems. Rather than a focus on problem-maintaining behaviors, the solution-oriented school focuses instead on acknowledging and supporting those things that the client or family are already doing that are in the direction of solving the presenting problem.

Little attention is given to the past, and then only to a discussion of past *successes* that the client has experienced. Therapist and client cooperation is paramount, and the therapist takes the initiative to create that atmosphere of cooperation. Therapy is defined as a cooperative venture in which the therapist assumes that change is inevitable and works to positively connote the client's situation. The language of change is used in conveying to the client an expectation of solving the problem (for example, instead of "*if* things change," the therapist says "*when* things change").

The goal of the therapy is to construct a viable solution to the presenting complaint. This is done by focusing attention on "exceptions" to the problem (times when the problem is *not* happening). deShazer (1985, 1988) emphasizes the importance of building on what the client is doing that is successful rather than on what is not. These ideas have been further adapted and applied in couples treatment using psychodramatic techniques (Chasin, Roth and Bograd 1989).

Rather than using a traditional focus on problems, the solution-oriented model attempts to create a vision or picture of how things will be without the presenting complaint. The idea is to encourage a future orientation in which the therapist builds on the client's picture of a future without the complaint. The therapist pays attention to the client's strengths and resources rather than his limitations or deficits. deShazer (1988: 5) asks clients the "miracle" question: "Suppose that one night while you were asleep, there was a miracle and this problem was solved. How would you know? What would be different?" In this way he begins therapy by looking at the endpoint (the positive outcome) and then helps the client to build on previous successes in moving toward that goal.

The solution-oriented therapist (1) has the client provide the description of how life will be *when* the difficulty is resolved; (2) "utilizes" what the client brings to the problem-solving effort (as a way of gaining client cooperation); (3) builds on the client's strengths and assets (supporting what the client is already doing that works); and (4) develops interventions that are effective in getting the client to "do something different" in creating a small but noticeable change. The therapist's goal is to alter the client's view of the complaint and/or encourage the client to vary the usual mode of thinking about the situation.

In many clinical settings a client may have to wait several weeks for an initial appointment. Over this waiting period, the client may have already taken steps (made changes) in the direction of solution development that can be built on and supported (Davis, deShazer and Gingerich 1987). For example, one of us [SF] was seeing a divorced couple who were coming for treatment at the request of the court. There had been a history of "communication problems" between the couple concerning their two children. When they arrived at my office, a number of positive steps had already been taken and the communication between them was described as "significantly improved." Rather than investigating past difficulties, I merely asked them to tell me what they were each doing that moved things to this new positive level. We then discussed what it would take to maintain this improved level of communication. We met several more times over a period of two months. At each of these sessions I supported and complimented each of them on their efforts to maintain a civil and cooperative posture with the other. Each was able to report about things the other one was doing differently that served to make them more comfortable ("listening without being critical," "continuing to inform the other about school related happenings," and so forth). Therapy proceeded this way until they both felt comfortable continuing on their own.

Problem-Oriented Approach

The problem-oriented approach is exemplified by the work of the Mental Research Institute (MRI) in Palo Alto, California (Jackson, Fisch, Watzlawick, and Weakland). In their publications (Fisch, Weakland, and Segal 1982; Watzawick, Weakland, and Fisch 1974; Weakland et al. 1974) they emphasize that "problems [are] primarily an outcome of everyday difficulties . . . that have been mishandled by the parties involved. When ordinary life difficulties are handled badly, unresolved problems tend increasingly to involve other life activities and relationships in impasses or crises, and symptom formation results" (Weakland et al. 1974: 147).

Difficulties are seen as arising around the normal developmental transitions of life—marriage, birth, adolescent separation, and death—which provide opportunities for the development of vicious cycles in which the very attempt to solve a "problem" may in fact exacerbate the situation, leading to attempts at "more of the same" solutions. The MRI interventions "involve deliberate attempts to prevent the oc- curence of problem-maintaining behavior" (Watzlawick and Coyne 1980: 13). Their therapy is goal-oriented and problem-focused with the therapist assuming responsibility for helping the client (and/or those around him) resolve the presenting complaint.

For example, family members who are actively trying to cheer up a person who has become depressed and inactive may find themselves becoming frustrated and upset. The more effort they put into trying to activate the person the more depressed and apathetic the person may get. A cycle is created in which the person remains "depressed" while others around him are actively working to "help" him. The more energy they put in the less he seems to do, and they become caught in an endless downward spiral.

The MRI therapist looks for a way to disrupt this cycle and end the "game." One way to do this is to get the people most motivated for change together and work out a plan in which they are to pretend, for example, to be more "depressed" and incapacitated than the "de- pressed" person is. For example, the man's spouse could fail to engage in the kind of usual behaviors her husband has come to expect (such as "forgetting" to cook dinner). The hope is that the man will become activated to take increased responsibility and will come out of his "depression."

The MRI therapists usually take a "one-down" position vis-a-vis the client, and may restrain change, or use techniques of reframing and paradox in moving the client (who may not be the "symptomatic" person) to take action in disrupting the pattern or cycle in which the presenting complaint is embedded (see Watzlawick and Coyne 1980). The goal is to work with the most motivated person or persons in the social system to encourage a small change that will establish a new pattern or cycle in dealing with the problematic behavior.

The utility of MRI's problem-focused approach is evident in the following example involving a four-and-a-half-year-old boy, Mark, re- ferred by his pediatrician after being hit by a car. Mark was described as "ok physically" but having "nightly night terrors" requiring multiple attempts to calm him down. The accident occurred while the maternal grandmother (MGM) was visiting. MGM and Mark were sharing the same bedroom. I [SF] met with the mother, MGM, and Mark for an initial meeting one week following the accident. The mother described the specifics of Mark's behavior: he would go to bed at 8:30 P.M. and at about 11:30 P.M. would wake up and begin "crying and fidgeting" and would be generally unresponsive to attempts by both his mother and MGM to calm him down. These episodes would last for about one hour, after which he would go back to sleep on his own. MGM described herself as "very close to Mark." It became clear in the course of this meeting that his mother and MGM were both vying to be the one who would be successful in calming Mark down at night.

I framed Mark's night awakenings as a natural outcome of the trauma he had experienced and something that would resolve itself in time. It was clear that the dedicated attempts of his mother and MGM to minister to Mark simultaneously were only serving to exacerbate the difficulties. My goal was to reduce the problem-maintaining behavior by getting his mother and MGM to stop working so hard on Mark's behalf. I decided to give both the mother and MGM a task: his mother was to spend fifteen to twenty minutes each day desensitizing Mark to crossing the street (since he was also displaying some fear in this area); MGM was asked to take charge of dealing with Mark at night "for the next three nights" (at which time she would be returning home). This was framed as a way for her to help her daughter get a few good nights sleep before MGM left. The mother and MGM agreed to their tasks.

Eight days later a meeting was held with Mark and his parents. His mother reported that she had not gotten up on the three nights that MGM was available and that, beginning after our last session, Mark had shown a significant decrease in the amount of time he was awake at night. She reported that it worked better for her to do less when Mark did wake up since he was able to get himself back to sleep without help. She continued to take Mark on walks as agreed, although these fears had decreased markedly as well. She was commended on her successful efforts. No further contacts were requested.

Symptom-Oriented Approach

The creative work of Jay Haley (1976) and Chloe Madanes (1981) (Co-Directors of the Family Institute of Washington, D.C.) exemplify the symptom-oriented approach. They assume that symptoms are "contracts" between people and are therefore adaptive in relationships. Symptoms develop within a social system such that the symptomatic behavior becomes a communicational metaphor for some unresolved issue in the system. "A problem is defined as a type of behavior that is part of a sequence of acts between several people. The repeating sequence of behavior is the focus of therapy" (Haley 1976: 2).

The symptomatic behavior serves some useful function for the social network in either drawing attention in an indirect manner to some issue in the system (metaphoric function) or in stabilizing an unbalanced system (social function). An example of the metaphoric function of the symptom is a boy who has been aggressive and violent. The therapist tries to understand how this behavior reflects ongoing issues and problems in that child's social system. One hypothesis would be that the boy is living in a family in which there are problems with control of impulses and that the boy's behavior is a metaphor for these issues in the family system.

Haley (1976: 90–93) discusses the case of a man who feared that he would die without warning from a heart attack. The strategic therapist directs his attention to what function this fear serves in the system. The therapist takes the man's comments about his heart as an analogy for some other problem (perhaps the man's fears about his heart have an important function in the marriage in that intimacy and activity with the spouse can be conveniently avoided or regulated).

Another example of the metaphoric function of the symptom is evident in a family with a nine-year-old child who was spending all his money on baseball cards. The parents were upset with this and took the boy's cards away. The next day at school the boy was upset and was seen by the guidance counselor who called the mother and suggested the need for counseling. When the family was seen, it became clear that the boy's obsession with spending money on baseball cards was a metaphor for the parents' obsession with their own financial distress due to father's recent job loss. The boy's behavior was a metaphor for the parents' distress.

A symptom serves a social function when it detours attention away from some other issue and onto the symptomatic person. For example, a child who continually acts up in school and draws increased focus and attention from his mother may be making a "benevolent sacrifice" in protecting mother from focusing on her own unhappiness with some element in her own life. This symptom serves to stabilize the social system and in so doing protects some other issue from surfacing. In a sense, the symptom is an attempted solution to a systems dilemma and reflects the family's creative efforts to work out a compromise in solving a systems problem. The problem of the "identified patient" functions as a protective act with benevolent chararacteristics (and is sometimes framed as such).

In common with the other therapeutic models discussed, the presenting problem is respected and taken as the main focus for therapy. The strategic therapist develops idiosyncratic interventions based on the needs of the particular clinical situation. The therapist is goal-oriented and takes responsibility for developing effective intervention strategies that will solve the presenting problem. Psychiatric diagnoses are avoided, and problems are framed in nonpathological terms that empower and activate members of the system to deal successfully with the presenting complaint. Therapy is planned in stages; direct interventions, paradoxical prescriptions, "ordeals" (Haley 1984), and the use of "pretend" techniques (Madanes 1981) are some of the intervention strategies used.

Before looking at a clinical illustration of this approach, it is important to reiterate a point made in the Introduction, namely, that since we function in a world of diverse realities, we can never know the "Truth." With that in mind, the therapist does not accept the symptom's "function" as an ultimate truth, but rather only as a useful leverage point for change (a form of "reframing") that will be discussed in more detail in a later section.

A seventeen-year-old girl, Laura, was referred to the mental health department following an episode in which she passed out after drinking a significant amount of alcohol. In addition, in the previous three months she had stayed out all night on several occasions and had not informed her parents of her whereabouts. She had been absent from school a great deal and her grades had dropped as well. Laura is the older of two children (her brother is fourteen). In my [SF] initial meeting with the family, the mother volunteered that her husband had an acknowledged drinking problem. Laura indicated that before coming home in the evening she would generally call her mother to find out if her father had been drinking. If he had, she preferred not to come home.

Both parents were very concerned about their daughter's behavior and especially the most recent episode in which she drank herself semiconscious. Laura's behavior was a metaphor for how out of control she and the rest of the family were feeling. I framed Laura's behavior as a "sacrifice she is making for the family" in drawing attention to father's alcohol problem while at the same time detouring attention away from him and onto herself. I told Laura that I saw her as acting in a benevolent manner in caring about her family. Her father seemed taken by the idea that his daughter, about whom he cared a great deal, was going to such lengths to show her worry and care about him. He acknowledged his excessive alcohol use, and although he refused my offer to see a substance abuse counselor in the department, he did agree to speak with a friend from work who attends AA. I encouraged the mother and the children to attend Al-Anon (and Alateen) meetings. It was clear from my contact with this family that there was a great deal of caring and love among family members. I told the family that as long as the father continued drinking Laura, as the oldest, probably would continue to worry about her parents and might try again to detour attention onto herself.

In the fourth and final meeting six weeks following our initial session, father admitted to drinking to excess on only one night, and the family could see that he had been making a concerted effort to cut down. The mood of the family was more positive. Laura had not been involved in any further drinking episodes and had resumed calling home when she expected to be late.

How does the therapist choose among the models discussed when approaching a clinical situation? While each of the three approaches outlined above can be useful in different situations, we tend to start with the most direct and economical approach (the solution-oriented method) before moving to another model. The decision to shift frameworks is usually based on the client's response to solution-oriented interventions.

In some clinical situations, a solution-oriented approach may miss the significant metaphoric function of the presenting complaint. At such times we respect the necessity for the presenting difficulty (we accept its metaphoric function) and shift to the symptom-oriented model. This process is illustrated with a case that began with a referral from a pediatric neurologist who had been treating a fifteen-year-old boy (Lee) for "chronic headaches." The referral indicated that medical treatment had not been effective and that Lee was "neurologically normal." My first session with this Chinese family consisted of seeing Lee with his mother and younger brother (age 14). When I inquired about the absence of the father, I was told that he was at home and had been very sick. He had been diagnosed with terminal cancer two years earlier and had been hospitalized several times since then. Even when the father was not in the hospital, mother bore the major caregiving responsibilities, with some help from her sons. It was clear from their description that father was in great pain and was very ill.

Lee's headaches had begun four months prior to this initial contact and were described as severe and "unpredictable." They could last from five minutes to a half hour. When I asked Lee what he had tried that was successful in helping to end the headaches sooner, he could not come up with anything specific. His mother reported "I can't get Lee to relax" and believed that he was putting himself under tremendous pressure regarding both his school work and his worry about his father.

The younger brother was more easygoing and tended to take his school work less seriously. He also spent more time with their father than his older brother. At the end of the session I asked Lee to prepare a chart of his headaches, indicating when they occurred, how long they lasted, how intense they were, and what he did that helped relieve the pain and end the headaches most quickly.

At our next meeting, two weeks later, Lee indicated that his headaches were continuing and that he'd forgotten to bring the chart as planned. His recollection of the data he had collected indicated that the headaches were continuing to occur on an almost daily basis with varying intensity and no clear effective way to stop the pain. Since it was clear that the mother and her sons were deeply troubled and saddened by the father's deteriorating medical condition, I framed Lee's headaches as "sympathy pains" for his father. I asked him in what ways, other than the headaches, could he demonstrate that he was worried about his father. He admitted that he was not as demonstrative as his younger brother in showing his feelings, and that he would, at times, actively avoid contact with his father.

Would he be willing, I asked, on those days when he experiences a headache, to spend twenty to thirty minutes with his father? On days when he did not have a headache he could choose whether or not to spend time with his father. He agreed to this and mother seemed pleased with the idea of getting some relief herself. I told Lee that "being with his father" could take many different forms and didn't necessarily require talking.

At a session ten days later, Lee reported that his headaches were continuing. As requested, he spent time with his father on a daily basis. I asked the mother if there were some other ways Lee could help her in caring for her husband. She suggested that he learn how to insert the IV line each evening. Lee was initially reluctant but finally agreeable to learn how to do this. We ended this session with my reiterating how I saw the headaches as Lee's way of sharing his father's pain. I told Lee that although the headaches were painful, they were necessary in demonstrating his caring and concern for a very important person in his life who was dying. I suggested he continue the plan we developed in the previous session. We made another appointment for ten days later.

When the family arrived, they indicated that father was again hospitalized and was dying. The mother was very tearful. Lee indicated that he had a least one headache each day over the period but the intensity was reduced. He had spent time with father as planned while he was home. I encouraged frequent visitation in the hospital in light of his father's apparent critical condition.

I received a call before the next session from a cousin in the family who informed me that the father had died and the family would be cancelling their appointment for that day. The mother called about a week later and scheduled another appointment. Lee's headaches had increased in intensity since his father's death. Since he had died at home, the whole family was present—as were other relatives and friends. I predicted that the headaches might continue for a while longer since Lee may be feeling some increased pressure and responsibilities as the oldest son. Two additional meetings were held over the next six weeks; and, for the first time, Lee reported both reduced frequency and intensity of the headaches. He was playing intramural basketball and taking increased time to relax.

We decided to stop our contacts at this point with plans made for me to follow-up. About two months later I mailed Lee a brief note inquiring about his headaches. He called me, soon after, to say the headaches were "almost all gone now" and he appreciated my interest.

It was clear that Lee's headaches, rather than a problem to be removed, were actually his way of providing an opportunity for the family to begin the grieving process for the father. According to cultural mandates, it would have been difficult for this family to directly ask for help in dealing with the anticipated loss of the father. Lee developed a concrete complaint that provided the "ticket in" to treatment. Once it was clear that an attempt to directly impact on the headaches would not be effective, I shifted my approach and began to frame the headaches as necessary and useful, although temporary. I then tried to encourage Lee to find other ways to share his caring and love for his father.

The ability to modify the therapeutic course is necessary in other situations as well. At times, by accepting the assumptions of the referring agent, the therapist can get sidetracked from a solution-oriented perspective. With the family described below I [SF] began by accepting the pediatrician's view that the client's problem of "stress incontinence" and the fact that the client "cries easily when admonished by the teacher," reflected his sadness and upset over issues in the family. Only after several sessions, did I "shift gears" and directly attend to the stress incontinence issue.

Dan (age 9) was living with his mother and two older sisters. His father and mother had divorced four years prior to the referral, with the father described as having a history of "bi-polar disorder." In our initial meeting the children revealed how much they worry about their father, who lived alone in a house trailer about an hour's drive from the family. Dan was clearly tearful when talking about his father, and the oldest daughter, after trying to put up a front that "everything is fine," finally began crying also. The whole family, including the mother, were worried about the father. He was planning to return to the Midwest in the coming month, where his family of origin resided. All agreed that the father's move would relieve them of significant worry.

Discussion in the next two meetings focused on the family's feelings of relief and loss in regard to the father's move. A meeting with Dan individually revealed a child who felt very sad and tearful about his father's "sickness." I told Dan that I admired how freely and openly he could share his feelings. During the summer following the father's leaving, Dan spent a month visiting with him. On return, Dan reported that he had "the best summer yet." His mother felt that Dan had made the "best transition home (after seeing his father) he has ever made." He would usually come back from visits feeling sad and upset. The school reported no further tearful episodes, and his mother saw Dan as "happier now."

Although these initial meetings seemed useful to the family, I wasn't sure they were impacting on the original request (to deal with Dan's stress incontinence). When I inquired about the incontinence, Dan indicated that the problem was still happening, usually at school approximately every other day. It seemed to happen most frequently when Dan was laughing, which according to mother he was doing more of now. At this point, I decided to take a more direct approach in dealing with the targeted issue. I asked Dan if he wanted to work on this problem so that he could feel more in control and more relaxed with his peers at school. He seemed to reluctant to agree to this. When I pursued him further about his thinking, he shared the feeling that "this would mean more therapy," something he didn't feel he needed. I told Dan that he would not be involved in "therapy" but rather that I would teach him a technique for gaining increased control over his sphincter. After agreeing to this, I asked Dan to keep a record of when the episodes of incontinence occurred and to bring this with him to a meeting we scheduled for two weeks later.

We met three more times (for twenty minute sessions) in which I taught him to use and practice (at home) Kegel exercises in tightening and strengthening his urethral muscle. Over a 2-month period, episodes of incontinence decreased from fifteen to five a month. Dan reported a positive change in his academic work and was not so fearful of laughing with his friends at school.

Conclusions

We have presented here some of our assumptions and beliefs about possibility-oriented therapy. As you will see in the clinical examples to follow, there is no one method and strategy for helping clients reach their goals. With that in mind, we encourage you to think about other alternative approaches that might be equally effective. In addition, we hope you find the methods and strategies discussed relevant to your own clinical practice and we encourage you to experiment with these strategies in your clinical work.

Note

1. Murray Bowen, *Family therapy in clinical practice* 443–44, copyright © 1985, 1983, 1978 by Jason Aronson, Inc. (Reprinted with permission of the publisher.)

Part II
The Process of Treatment:
A Guide to the River

4

The Crucial Evaluation Interview

> The therapist's job is . . . to create a context within which the client can generate his own possibilities, . . . taking the action he needs . . . in his own inimitable way.
> —John Weakland

What makes the initial evaluation interview crucial? This first session sets the stage for the psychotherapeutic dance to follow. It is here that the process of mutual discovery begins. Never again will so much fresh information about the client be available. Selection, which will make some of it marginal, has not yet begun. All is new, undimmed by familiarity. You are doing much more than simply forming an impression of the client. You are beginning to learn the client's reality. To enter the client's world, you must observe and respond to the client's assumptions as reflected in both verbal and nonverbal behaviors. You need to understand the client's assumptions, for these will be negotiated in the therapy to achieve the client's goals.

How do you create a context that enables a client to begin to determine those desired new possibilities? Clarity about your goals for each client is essential, for it is these goals that fashion the treatment. Implementing these goals depends on your use of language and nonverbal metalanguage. From the first encounter we find ourselves *attending to metalanguage*—the elements of nonverbal communication: rapport, calibration, and joining. Joining the client, stepping into the client's world, involves suspending our own judgmental assumptions—while retaining positive expectations—for it is the client's assumptions that guide the initial "dance." As we will see, careful attention to language is central to the process of joining; both in *using language to create experience* and in *using language to specify experience*. All of these activities aim to produce a mutually-agreed-upon, *well-constructed goal* or outcome, as well as a plan for future sessions, and perhaps a task assignment.

Before the client ever arrives you need to know what result *you* want to achieve in this session. What are the therapeutic headlines that you will use to keep the conversation on track? The leading questions in the possibility frame (see figure 4–2) are the ones that must be answered—by the client, but with your help: "What do you want?"

"How will you know when you get it?" and "What stops you from having it now?" Once sufficiently well defined answers to these questions are obtained, you have not only the client's goal described in the language of precise possibility, but also an appropriate entry point for a therapeutic strategy.

Attending to Metalanguage

The dance of therapy begins with the first handshake and ends with the last. In between, the participants learn to accommodate to subtle shifts in role; first, one leads, then the other. In this initial meeting, it is the client who must be invited to lead, so that you can observe and learn to follow his or her particular set of intricate steps. In dancing, much of learning to follow means attending to the other person's nonverbal cues; the same is true in therapy. What is in question is the development and maintenance of rapport, your ability to respond, both verbally and nonverbally, to establish a feedback loop with the client that supports continued exhange. Rapport should not be confused with liking, for while they are not mutually exclusive, workable rapport does not depend on positive regard. Rapport is rather that sense of easy connection, or being "tuned in on the same wavelength." Generally, people know when they have rapport, and when they don't, but for therapists, the critical question is: if you don't have rapport, do you know how to get it? When people are "in rapport," they are generally mirroring each other's nonverbal behavior. So the most direct way to establish rapport if you need to, is to mirror some element of the client's nonverbal behavior. And of these elements, breathing is among the most powerful—so much so that if you match the breathing of someone who is depressed, you risk developing a corresponding feeling of depression. To avoid this danger when you mirror breathing, you can practice "crossover mirroring," using an object—a swivel chair, or hand, or glasses—to echo the tempo of the client's breathing. (To establish that tempo, watch client's shoulder rather than his chest, and do this when he is listening rather than talking; when the client talks, his breathing is interrupted.) Breathing is only one nonverbal behavior to be mirrored to consolidate rapport. Posture, gesture, tone, and tempo of speech are others. Of course, to avoid the impression of mockery, mirroring must be subtle enough to keep it out of the client's conscious awareness.

Rapport is a part of the *joining* you must do in order to learn the client's "dance." Joining means starting where the client is. Jay Haley reports an example in which he asked for Milton Erickson's advice:

I had a woman who lost her voice, who couldn't speak above a whisper and there was nothing physically wrong. So, I said to Erickson, "What would you do with this woman?" Milton said, "I'd ask her if there was anything she wanted to say!" (Haley 1989: 11)

To join the client's reality, you must be a good *calibrator*; in other words, you need to develop the sensory acuity to notice both the language and body patterns that express this reality. You will find conscious training to expand your calibration skills useful in increasing your ability to notice verbal and nonverbal patterns. Noticing these patterns is useful not only in mirroring; but also in registering verbal/nonverbal incongruities, such as someone's saying yes, while shaking the head, no. With calibration you are also more aware of the nonverbal responses to questions that almost invariably appear before the verbal ones. Heightened attention to the client's nonverbal messages will help you throughout therapy.

To join the client verbally we not only reflect back the client's own words, but also notice the client's preferred sensory system as revealed in the verb forms used. For example, if a client says that "things look bleak, I just can't see my way clear," we use visual words in response; such as: "Let's focus on your situation, and see if you can you get a new perspective." In the same way that "I'm so tense that I'm touchy and irritable" or "If I have to listen to any more complaints, I think I'll scream" would call for respectively kinesthetic and auditory words in response: "So one of our goals will be to help you feel calm and relaxed" (kinesthetic); or "it sounds like you'd like to tune into another station" (auditory).[1]

As we notice the client's unique way of operating in the world, and begin to *join* with the client, we build the foundation for empathy. Empathy, or 'stepping into another person's shoes,' is essential to learning about another person's experiences and assumptions about the world. We have found it expedient to ask ourselves *"What has to be true for this person to be acting this way?"* In other words, what is the sum of this person's life experience that has shaped his or her behavioral assumptions about the world? This can be especially helpful with aggressive or challenging clients. It can direct your attention to the kind of life experiences that must have happened to the client to inspire this unpleasant behavior. In possibility-oriented therapy, you always want to find a way to utilize what clients bring—whatever it is—to help move them toward their goal. With this in mind, *all* client behaviors contain the potential for usefulness in therapy. But before you can utilize them, you have to notice them, and this can involve you in that most difficult endeavor: suspending one's own assumptions—most particularly assumptions about what constitutes "acceptable" behavior and how therapy "should" be conducted.[2]

Admittedly, this is a tall order. But suspending your basic assumptions about the world, about what constitutes moral behavior, or about how the universe should operate, means just that—shelving them for the moment, so that you can see and step into the client's assumption about reality. Remember, the client's assumptions are what need to change through therapeutic negotiation. It is necessary for the therapist to see these assumptions clearly to assist in that procedure. This kind of joining is essential to the practice of possibility-oriented therapy. When we see clients as "impossible" or "resistant," it reflects our assumptions about what that person's behavior should be, rather than what it is. We are seeing the client as not thinking or doing what we want. As Milton Erickson puts it, "The initial step in the utilization approach . . . is to accept the patients' manifest behavior and to acknowledge their personal frames of reference. This openness and acceptance of the patients' worlds facilitate a corresponding openness and acceptance of the therapist by the patients" (Erickson and Rossi 1979: 53). If a particular client tempts you to wish you didn't have to see him or her, you can then notice what your assumptions about that client are, and find ways to *appreciate* that client's individuality as a prelude to making use of it. This utilization approach can be summarized by saying that *whatever the client brings is what you wanted.*

There are, however, three assumptions that the you need to keep: (1) that it is possible for the client to reach the desired result; (2) that this result can be achieved in a small number of sessions; and, (3) that the result can be attained in an atmosphere of playfulness and humor. To be sure, it is not always the case that these assumptions are true, but if the therapist does not believe them to be possible, then they are unlikely to ever be true. Some therapists need to reevaluate their assumptions that the only way to get "lasting, deep change," is with therapy that is long-lasting, painful, and hard. We contend that the insight resulting from analysis is not only **not** the *sine qua non* of therapeutic change, but also that often it is *not* even relevant to such change. As Watzlawick states:

> Resistance to a devaluation of the *why* in favor of the *what* seems greatest in the study of human behavior. What, it is usually asked, about the undeniable fact that a person's present behavior is the result of his experiences in the past? How can an intervention that leaves past cause untouched have any lasting effect in the present? But it is these very assumptions that are most clearly contradicted by the study of actual—particularly spontaneous—changes. Everyday, not just clinical, experience shows not only that there can be change without insight, but that very few behavioral or social changes are accompa-

nied, let alone preceded, by insight into the vicissitudes of their genesis. (1974: 85–6).

The three possibility-assumptions mentioned above—that the client *can* reach his or her goal(s) in a few sessions in a playful atmosphere—form the bedrock of the therapist's belief that the therapy will succeed.

While we have been talking about rapport, calibration, empathy and joining, and suspending assumptions as separate concepts, we know that they are intimately joined—inseparable—and so occur *simultaneously* in the therapeutic process.

We now turn to those indispensable tools of talking therapy: words.

Using Language to Create Experience

> Uttering a word is like striking a note on the keyboard of the imagination.
> —Ludwig Wittgenstein

> Words are magical in the way they effect the minds of those who use them.
> —Aldous Huxley

> Words can be lethal.
> —Norman Cousins

Where would we be without language? How would we make sense of our perceptions? How would we be able to change our minds, or to decide on an action? All of these activities take place in either internal or external dialogue. Language both generates *and* symbolizes our experience; it provides a continuous feedback loop between our inner and outer worlds. Someone once said "I don't know what I think until I say it." Language creates the possibility of talking therapy. To be effective, each of us must be exquisitely sensitive to the words we use—these are the tools of our trade.

Language creates experience by calling forth personal associations to particular words. For example, imagine the aroma of one of your favorite foods cooking, next, notice the shape and color of it as it is served to you. Now imagine sinking your teeth into it, savoring the taste and texture. You can create a full experience of that food by simply reading words on a page. We fill in meanings to make sense of words we see and hear; and in this way, words compel our experience, we cannot *not* respond to them. And the experience that they elicit is either some current sensory event out of conscious awareness (for example, how does your left little toe feel at this moment?) or a representation of some occurrence in our personal history. Take the word "comfort" and discover what your personal experience is—perhaps lying on a sunny beach or curled up in front of a fire or being with a loved one. The images evoked are as various as the people who are hearing the words. So when we talk with clients it is vital to get them to specify—as closely as possible—the experience that they are representing with their words. The notion of asking for a "video description" of the event can be helpful here, in other words asking what you would see exactly as if you were watching it on videotape. Incidentally, asking for this description may also be the first step for the client to start to see his or her situation in a new light (see O'Hanlon and Wilk 1987). You must not assume that you understand even common words, for the client's "comfort" might be your "boredom." Or take the couple in Woody Allen's film *Annie Hall*, who were asked by their respective therapists how often they made love. "Hardly ever," says the man, "no more than three times a week." "Constantly," says the woman, "at least three times a week" (Langer 1989:70). In therapy, it is the client's experience you are trying to change, and so it is that experience that you must elicit accurately to promote that change.

Not only are the client's particular associations to each word important, but, equally important are the client's *actual words*. We agree emphatically with Watzlawick when he says the therapist must *"Learn and use the client's language"* (1990:87). Using the client's own language is not only part of joining the client's model of reality, but also contributes to conciseness both in shortening treatment and in excluding therapist bias. Rephrasing what the client has said in different words runs the risk of introducing extraneous muddle as the client tries to make his or her images fit your words. "One of the most basic differences between traditional psychotherapy and certain brief-therapeutic . . . procedures is the fact that in the former the patient is first taught a new 'language,' the language of the theory his therapist subscribes to. This learning process is of necessity time-consuming and greatly contributes to the length of classic therapies" (Watzlawick 1978:139).

The client's specific experiences and words are the grounding for the assumptions about what is possible in the world. For all of us, our assumptions or presuppositions about reality give our world texture, color, and sound and are the basis for our beliefs. Whatever clients say indicate their assumptions about the world. Since the core activity in therapy consists of enabling clients to expand their range of limiting assumptions about what is possible in the world; the client's presuppositions must be identified before they can be changed or expanded. For example, if the client says "I can't say no to my mother," you can respond "What would happen if you did?" If the client says "I've tried everything to get my husband to change," you could ask "Have you tried standing on your head in the bathtub whistling Yankee Doodle?" The invitation here is for you to suspend your own assumptions even as you note the client's view, so that you don't miss the meaning presented by interjecting your own. Suspending your own judgmental assumptions is a fundamental feature of effective joining. As Semrad says: "The only truth you have is your patient. And the only thing that interferes with that truth is your own perception. You may not be free to observe what there is to be observed, chiefly because it evokes feelings in you that are so troublesome that you quit looking" (in Rako and Mazer 1983:112). Another way of thinking about suspending your own assumptions is to avoid "mind-reading." The more you think that you understand, the more important it is to verify the meaning of the experience in question. If, for example, a client says "No one wants me," your question must be: "Who specifically doesn't want you?" If a client says "I don't get any appreciation," ask "How would you like to be appreciated?" As always, ask clients to be exact about their experiences.

The whole therapeutic undertaking, then, demands to be framed in what has been called *mindfulness,* in other words, "keeping one's consciousness alive to the present reality" (Nhat Hanh 1987:11). You must resist resorting to already familiar categories and instead be open to fresh information, from which you make up new categories that reflect an awareness of more than one perspective.[3] What is called for here is avoidance of old generalizations (diagnoses) that dull your awareness to the individuality of each client.

The consistent offering of *positive* language throughout the therapeutic encounter keeps new possibilities in mind. You make sure that clients state what they want, *not* what they don't want. If a client asks "to feel less anxious at work," you need to get him to say that he wants "to feel calmer at work." It is important to to school yourself to make statements in their positive form. For example, if the person giving an injection says: "This won't hurt," the patient hears and responds to "hurt." Compare this with "We'll try to keep you as comfortable as possible." In this case the patient hears and responds to "comfortable."

Many years ago Freud observed that "there are no negatives in the unconscious" (Fenichel and Rapaport 1954:144). If you want to test this, when you try to *not* think of your left little toe, notice that you first think of it. For this reason it is important for clients to state what they want, not what they don't want, for the positive language directs their experience. So with our clients (indeed in all communication, as noted in chapter 2), *when we use positive statements we enhance the experience of hope and well-being.* Toward that end we can also avoid the negations "no," "not," "nobody," "nowhere," "never," and so on. The words we choose can have a severely deleterious effect on clients. One of us [MTF] once had a client who feared requesting treatment for her panic attacks. It seems that the last therapist she had seen told her: "Your treatment will be difficult and take a long time. What's more, your panic attacks may even get worse before they get better." When the client got home, she had her worst panic attack yet. It is not enough just to avoid dire predictions, the therapist must also be supportive of whatever the client has tried, at the same time offering her hope: "You have tried a great many ways to change your situation— maybe together we can figure something else out—a new way to look at what's going on."

Clients frequently describe their situations in such a way as to make change seem impossible. Therefore, how we guide the initial conversation about what the client *wants* serves to introduce the possibility of achieving that goal. Not only in relation to the length of treatment, as mentioned above, but also in the way we point the client toward well-specified and achievable solutions. To do this, and indeed throughout our work with clients, we need to be *mindful* of the words we choose, and their implications. One can shorten or lengthen treatment; give the client hope or reinforce despair—*depending upon the specific language used*—in the initial exploration of the client's situation. The more complex, impressive, and general the ultimate goal of therapy, the longer it will take. The corollary is that it will also be longer before the client starts feeling positive and hopeful. So to give the client hope, you need to have a succinct description of positive behavior change as the stated goal.

The mindful use of language begins with the opening question. The words themselves may be simple-sounding, but it is here that you set the frame for therapy. If you ask, "What's your problem?" or "How may I help you?" the presuppositions put the client squarely in the hierarchical problem frame, the implication being that you, the therapist, are the more powerful and that the client is weaker, deficient, and helpless. If instead you inquire, "What would you like to have happen here today?" or "How would you like your life to be different as a result of therapy?" the presuppositions are those of therapist–client partnership. You have immediately included the client in the planning and decision making. The profound paradigm shift that we prescribe is contained in the deceptively simple questions that characterize the two frames: "What do you *want?*" versus "What's the problem?" Consider the presuppositions in Elvin Semrad's question: "How did you make him do that to you?" (Rako and Mazer 1983:133). This uncomplicated question challenges the client's assumptions of helplessness and provides an opening to consider a new more active view of the client's behavior.

Anticipation of success needs to be reflected in both words and questions. Rigorous monitoring of the words spoken by both you and your clients keeps the therapeutic conversation grounded in hope and action. One simple but extremely effective change is to use *when* rather than *if* when talking about desired changes. "When you are assertive with your boss, how will he respond?" conveys your certainty of a successful outcome and is quite different from the conditional "If you were assertive with your boss, how would he respond?" Another pitfall for both you and your clients lies in the words "try" or "attempt," for these are slippery non-action words. You either do something or you do not do it. We want clients to use words that will stimulate their active change, and so we demonstrate such usage with them. When asking about the present situation, mindful use of verb tenses can also convey this hopeful prospect, for example, using "will" instead of "would" or "could:" "How *will* your life be different when you get what you want?" "How *will* you respond when someone notices the changes you've made?" "What *will* you do with your new found time (or money), when *you've* stopped worrying (or smoking)?" Or, with a client who requests help overcoming writer's block, you could say "What was it like the *last* time you had it? What did it *used to be* like?" The force of the presuppositions in these questions carry the thoughts forward toward the desired goal; put the unwanted behavior in the past; and underline your expectation of mastery. Again, notice plain words, carefully chosen. In aiming at changing a client's assumptions, introducing doubt is also an effective tool. Questions such as: "What *gives you the idea* that you are unable to mobilize yourself?," "When you have had *what you call* performance anxiety, how did you know when to get anxious?" "What makes you sure?"[4] With a young graduate student in psychology who was going through some emotional turmoil, I [MTF] elicited a smile from her when, describing this as an intense learning period for her, I said, "Just think how much you can look forward to looking back on this time!"

Listening for ineffective, conditional language or speech patterns from clients can offer a chance for therapeutic intervention. One client of mine [MTF], a lawyer, came requesting help in conducting her job interviews. As I listened to her, I noticed that her complicated sentences were never completed. When I asked her about this, she said that some colleagues had complained about the vagueness of her speech. We then concentrated our efforts on helping her to complete her sentences. Another of my [MTF] clients, who requested help with making his interactions at work more effective, habitually ended his sentences with the upward tonal inflection of a question, even when they were statements. This made him sound continually uncertain. We zeroed in on his practicing inflectional changes to be able to present himself more competently. A young man who lived in a conditional world of "shoulds,"

**Figure 4–1. The Importance of Specifying Language.
"The Wizard of Id" by Brant Parker and Johnny Hart
from King Features Syndicate. Reprinted with
permission.**

"coulds" and "woulds" requested help in completing his graduate studies. Together we looked at the deleterious effect of this usage on his goal and I gave him various assignments to practice the use of "shall," "can," "want," and "will." He also made a sign to put on his desk which read "I will not *should* on myself."

Language to Specify Experience

To get clients to describe their experiences in everyday language you need to expunge the interrogative "why?" from your inquiries. "Why" implies cause and effect and so dwells in the problem frame. In possibility-oriented therapy use a cybernetic or feedback approach characterized by the question "What is going on here and now?" To manage this, use instead the interrogatives "what?" "when?" "where?" "who?" and "how?" If the client says; "I'm depressed" and you have the temerity to ask "Why?" you run the risk of hearing an entire life history. If, on the other hand, you ask: "*What's* going on that makes you think you're depressed?" or "*When* are you depressed?" or "*Where* are you depressed?" "*Who's* around when you're depressed?" "*How* do you know you're depressed?" you immediately begin to get information that is both more definite and closer to the client's experience of depression. Beware also of "What makes you?" and "How come?" since they are disguised "whys?" Another alternative, in the case of depression, to keep the inquiry in the positive frame, would be "Has there ever been a time when you weren't depressed?" This could invoke resources that point toward the possibility of recapturing a lighter mood.

Do not routinely seek a client history. Of course, on the way to identifying the specific goal, some historical material may be offered. When the client clearly wants to relate some history, then it is pursued for the sake of maintaining rapport. However, it is important to be aware that when this pursuit takes place under the umbrella of possibility, it has a different impact than when it is discussed as part of the "problem." But even when history is offered, it is an opportunity for you to keep the session focused on the goal. If, when you ask "What would you like to have happen here today?" the client responds with "I want you to get to know me," or "I want insight," you encourage them to continue "What would you like me to know about you?" or "What would you like insight about?" After joining them in this way and listening for a bit, you can then interject "Would you please tell me how you would like your life to be different as a result of my knowing you [or your getting insight], so that I can be focusing my attention to be most useful to you?" In this way, you keep your positive connection with your client, while at the same time keeping him in the possibility frame, and the conversation on track. If particular history seems germane to the design of tasks or treatment strategies, it may be pursued by asking "Where did you learn how to do that?", "Has this ever happened to you before? If so, how did you turn it around?" Here you often get the same information as you would in the problem frame, but with a signal difference, you are asking your questions under the banner of his or her desired goals, *not* his or her weaknesses (please see Figure 4–2).

How do you incorporate the mindful use of language into your conversations with clients? With deliberate and diligent practice. The

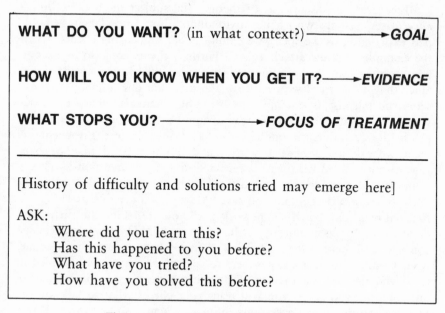

Figure 4–2. The Possibility Frame

time and energy expended in careful practice of mindful language will be repaid in therapeutic efficiency and in the pleasure of mastery of the central therapeutic tool: words. Another reward will be greater flexibility. As Watzlawick states:

> It should be immediately clear that this approach requires a significant change in a therapist's own stance. Instead of seeing himself as a firm rock in a sea of trouble, he becomes a chameleon. And it is at this point that many therapists themselves prefer to dig in behind the retort, "Anything, except that," while for others the necessity of ever new adaptations to the world images of their clients is a fascinating task. (1978:140–41)

Accentuating the positive also has an important place in statements or suggestions. For example, at the end of an initial interview in which a client flowingly expressed her depression both in words and tears, one of us [MTF] said emphatically: "Since you got yourself here, you have already started the process of change that you want, and, from now on *you will feel better!*" When the client returned for her next appointment two weeks later, she was smiling and bouncy. When asked about the marked change, she replied: "You said I would feel better and I do!" To be sure, not all clients are so responsive, but since you never know which ones will be, there is nothing to lose, and possibly much to gain in making positive statements of that kind.

Frequently in discussions of therapy the subject of therapist *influence* arises, usually with a negative connotation. Since language compels experience, as we speak we cannot avoid influencing clients (recall the example of panic attack above). Further, clients come to us exactly because they want to be influenced, otherwise they would not be there. Since that is the case, we need to make sure that our influential words serve the purpose of therapy—to help the client get what he or she wants and needs. Once more bear in mind just how much our therapeutic theory influences our client interactions; we lead the client by what we ask and by what we do and don't respond to. The bias toward open-ended treatment is reflected in a simple question like "Are Thursdays at two o'clock a good time for you?" Or if a client starts to tell you about a dream and you say, "Maybe we'll get to that later, but first tell me, how did the homework go?" you are telling the client that dreams are not as important as homework. I [MTF] have had clients come to treatment sessions and say, "Since I knew you would ask me what I wanted to have happen here today, on the way over I decided it would be . . . [and then tell me]." If you are clearly more interested in one topic than another, you will train your clients what to talk about. In other words, our expectations influence client response through the mechanism of feedback, whether we're aware of it or not. It therefore behooves us to be as certain as possible that our language reflects our intentions.[5] This responsible use of language needs to involve not only our first questions, but also all subsequent exchanges, including the formulation of the desired outcome. *"Positive and concrete formulations are preconditions of any successful influence"* (Watzlawick 1978:68) [Emphasis added].

Constructing the Outcome

> How will we know when it's time to stop meeting?
> —Bill O'Hanlon

By the end of the initial interview both client and therapist need to be clear and in agreement about what the client wants, specifically, and how the client will know when he or she gets it, described in behavioral terms. Clients will be doing either more of something or less of something or something entirely new. They may have also mentioned what stops them from being able to act this way now, but since that discussion opens the door to treatment strategies, it is not as critical at this juncture as is having a well-stated outcome. To construct this, you use the answers to the headline questions that have guided the interview. The answer to "What do you want?" gives the *treatment goal*; "How will you know when you get it?" specifies the *evidence* that will indicate the goal has been reached; while "What stops you?" points to the place where a *treatment strategy* might yield the desired outcome (again see Figure 4–2).

The work of the initial evaluation session culminates with the formulation of a *well-constructed outcome*. To be "well-constructed," the goal envisaged must be stated in positive terms—what the client *wants*, not what the client doesn't want. ("To be able to meet deadlines at work" is acceptable. "To feel less overwhelmed at work" is not.) The goal, moreover, must be a specific observable action or actions, a discrete element identified as progress toward those vaguer changes that clients often first mention. It must be stated as an action or pattern of actions that lie entirely within the client's control, ones that clients can initiate and maintain alone, without the involvement of or changes in others. You and the client together must assess the appropriateness of the request—will it be beneficial and congruent with the rest of the client's life? And while we hold the view that clients generally have the resources that they need to achieve their goals, this must also be considered. We are not suggesting to someone with an irreversible disability that we will help him or her overcome it. In such a case, you would ask "What would that give you that you don't have now?" and then explore other alternatives to seek attainment some of these desires.

Complex as all this sounds, the formulation that meets these criteria may be as simple as "I want to act more assertively with my boss." It is stated not only as something the client wants, but it would also involve an observable action, actuated by the client, and one for which the client has the necessary resources (voice and language); and it would be a positive expansion of her choices of effective action.

To summarize, a well-constructed outcome must meet five criteria:

1. It must be stated in positive language (what the client *wants*, not what he or she doesn't want).

2. It must be an observable action or behavior.

3. It must be an action that is initiated and maintained by the client.

4. It must be congruent with the rest of the client's life.

5. The necessary resources must be available to the client.

Once a well-constructed outcome has been agreed upon, it is time to plan the next step. Occasionally, a client reaches the goal in the first session, when the specific identification of the goal reveals that the client already knows how to get it. Most frequently, simply another session is scheduled, often with the statement that most likely only a few will be needed. With clients who seem to need more structure, a definite contract can be made. Treatment contracts may be for one session at a time, six sessions, three months, or whatever. A four-session, renewable contract can be particularly helpful in keeping the treatment focused. Such a contract marks the fourth session as a time for joint assessment of the treatment to date, at which time *both* client and therapist weigh the need for future therapy. Key questions for this assessment include "Are we working toward the right goal and, if not, what should it be?" "Is further treatment needed?" "Would a different form of treatment (group, or family therapy, for example) be better?" This discussion may end in different ways: in a renewal of the contract (four additional sessions) with the same or a different goal; in a shift of treatment mode; or in an interruption or ending of the treatment.

Besides making another appointment, if indicated, you may assign a task to be done between appointments. (Tasks are discussed in the chapter on treatment strategies.) Therapy sessions are typically scheduled for every other week, both because we have learned that this is a more reasonable time for task completion, and also because it emphasizes the client's ability to operate on his own. For those of us in managed-care settings, it also makes our schedules more spacious. Possibility-oriented therapy can consist either of one discrete set of treatment sessions or of a series of such sets occurring intermittently over an extended period of time. In the latter case, treatment may be thought of as "time-effective" or "time-sensitive" (Budman and Gurman 1988) rather than "brief," with a small number of therapy sessions grouped over several months or years, for instance, twenty sessions over a period of three years (Bennett 1983). (There are examples of these variants in chapters 10, 11, and 12.)

In conclusion, we offer two illustrations of initial interviews to exemplify the ideas presented in this chapter. The first, a summary of a brief treatment, with emphasis on the evaluation session, of one client and secondly, a transcription of an initial session with another.

A seventy-three-year-old retired teacher was referred by her primary care physician because she suffered from "chronic depression." In response to my [MTF] question about what she would like to have happen as a result of our talking together, she responded "To be happier." Like many general answers, it needed specifying, so I asked "How would you know if you were happier?", and she responded "My life wouldn't be on such a low level and so disorganized. I wouldn't waste so much time." When I persisted in detail-gathering, "disorganization" and "time-wasting" turned out to be "not keeping her house clean and watching too much TV." After spending some time in discussing her current living situation and daily activities, I then asked her "How would you know that you weren't disorganized and wasting time?" to which she replied, "I would be engaged in more creative activities." Those activities were identified as "spending time writing" and being more active politically. When she was questioned about "what stopped her from doing those things now," she revealed that her eyesight was deteriorating (macular degeneration). We explored at some length how her life had been influenced by this physical change. This brought out not only her sadness about the loss, but also the fact that she could no longer drive at night and found some reading difficult. At the end of the session she agreed that she would find out in more detail just what the progress of her eye condition would be, and further that she would look into finding a writing group, as well as rejoining her favorite political group. She concluded with a statement of her own "well-formed outcome" when she said "I feel better just thinking about becoming more active on my own behalf!" I saw her for five sessions over a period of four months, by which time she had taken a trip with Elder Hostel, discontinued her volunteer work with chronic patients (which she found depressing), joined both writing and political groups, and hired monthly household help. She reported an improved mood and was invited to recontact me as needed.

Here, then, is the transcription of the initial interview with a young singer with stage fright. The therapist was MTF. The annotations interspersed throughout the interview are those of SF. Notice in particular how the therapist begins the session with a future-oriented question and how she quickly joins the client in a process of mutual exploration and discovery. The therapist also requires the client to clearly define her words (such as ego) and to present her experience in specific (observable) terms.

Throughout the interview the therapist maintains a hopeful, optimistic and playful stance, even though the issue discussed is a serious matter. The therapist looks for *exceptions* to the current behavior that the client wishes to change and builds on these exceptions. She also looks for the client's *past experiences of mastery* in generating hope for change. Finally, with the client's help, the therapist creates a *task* that allows the client to shift the negative messages she gives herself to positive ones.

Therapist: Tell me what you would like to have happen as a result of our getting together.

Client: Ok, yeah, well, the reason I was referred to you was that I was seeing Betty Howard [*a nurse practitioner*], and I happened to mention to her that as a performing musician I happen to have lot of stage anxiety, and she referred me to you. I want to do something about my performance anxiety, which severely hinders my ability to perform effectively—it gets in the way of the progress of my career.

Therapist: Umm.

Client: She suggested that I see you to give me some lessons in self-hypnosis.

Therapist: So how did that grab you?

Client: It grabbed me just fine—it had never occurred to me, and it sounded like a great idea.

Therapist: When you say that it has impeded your career, what do you mean?

Client: Well. . . .

Therapist: You're a singer, right?

Client: Yeah, well in my day-to-day practicing, I work out certain ways of approaching the music, certain ways of performing, and when I'm up on stage, my heartbeat starts going real fast, and you can even hear my heartbeat in my voice when I'm real nervous [*demonstrates sound*].

Therapist: So it's in your vibrato?

Client: Right, all vibrato is not natural, some vibrato is nervous and, uh, my breath control becomes short, and I can't sing as long phrases so I have to kind of quickly replan things in the process

. . . uhh, I don't know how much you know about singing, but, the fact is that the larynx needs a certain amount of breath to keep it fluid and flexible, if you don't have the amount of breath flowing through that you're normally accustomed to, the larynx starts closing down, you lose some flexibility of sound and what the audience actually hears is not as nice as what you hear in the practice room.

Therapist: [*wryly*] So it's really just a wonderful effect!

Client: Yeah, it's fabulous, lemme tell ya—the one thing I can count on in all my performances. [*laughs*]

Therapist: Oh boy—listen though, are you sure that if you didn't have this that you would have gotten farther in your career?

Client: Pretty sure.

Therapist: It's a nasty question, but . . . you know what I mean?

Client: Yes, I know what you mean . . . well, yeah, it's affected a couple of reviews that I've gotten—reviews, you know—even though I'm skeptical about them. Everybody reads them and they really do make a difference.

Therapist: So you would like to have a full-time career singing?

Client: Yeah, right now I have a part-time job and a part-time singing career, and I'd like it to weigh more heavily on the music side.

Therapist: And has it always been like this for you?

Client: Right from my very first performance

Therapist: When you were two years old?

Client: I didn't start performing until I was seventeen.

Therapist: When you were seventeen what constituted the performance?

Client: It was in high school.

Therapist: Was it a solo?

Client: Yeah, it was a solo.

Therapist: But you had perhaps sung in other groups?

Client: Yeah, but whenever I sing where I'm not the only person on a part, it's not bad, ok, . . . since I don't feel solely responsible for the product, I don't feel so anxious. I do get sort of an adrenalin rush from the performance, and that actually helps the performance.

Therapist: Right.

Client: It's the nerves that really get in the way.

Therapist: Do you have any ideas about this? This is interesting, it depends upon how big the group is or how small—in some madrigal groups you have first and second soprano and first and second alto. . . .

Client: In fact I do have a situation similar to that now. I sing in a quartet and we all sing one person to a part, and I'm not as nervous in that situation as I would be if I were doing a solo recital, especially on pieces that present considerable vocal risks for me, stuff that I know has some particular problem spots.

Therapist: What kind of music do you sing? I'm not familiar with vocal quartet music.

Client: Well, this particular group sings madrigals, which is a Renaissance . . .

Therapist: I know what madrigals are.

Client: Oh, ok.

Therapist: I used to sing in a madrigal group.

Client: Wonderful!

Therapist: That's why I know about the different parts.

[*Notice how the therapist joins the client by sharing her knowledge of music.*]

Client: Interestingly enough I was once in a small ensemble that was a trio, and we did jazz and pop tunes, swing, and stuff like that.

Therapist: Umhumm.

Client: And that never made me nervous.

Therapist: Ahh, so it's iust classical.

Client: Yeah and also classical stuff means a lot more to me and actually that's why I stopped the pop group because it just wasn't rewarding to me.

Therapist: But you weren't nervous.

Client: No, never nervous.

Therapist: Did you sing well in that group?

Client: Yeah, I did, I was always at my best when I was on stage with that group—I related to the audience.

Therapist: But it was not satisfying.

Client: The music was not that satisfying—I mean there's a definite correlation for me between how much I get out of it and how much I've invested in it to how nervous I get.

Therapist: The more you've invested in it, the harder it is for you to sing the ways you want.

Client: [*nods and chuckles*] Talk about being set up for failure!

[*The therapist asks a question here, that actually lets that client know that this pattern that she has developed or* learned *can also be un-learned.*]

Therapist: How did you learn to do that?

Client: To be so anxious?

Therapist: No, *how did you learn to connect those two things—the more you've invested in it, the more anxious you get and the harder it is for you to sing the way you want?*

Client: Oh, uhh, I don't know, it just became such an obvious difference, performing in that pop group and doing the classical performances I'd done.

Therapist: So tell me what the differences are.

Client: Uhh, well, one thing is that in the pop group there is not a given style of singing that you have to do, not like a prescribed vocal technique that you have to do, it's much more individual, if your voice sounds a little ragged here and there, the audience attributes it to your particular style of singing, and, in fact, those ragged edges can sometimes enhance the final product, and you know in classical singing, when you go in for lessons, there's this nitpicking on every note. . . . It happens to every singer, so, you know, singers do learn to conquer this. . . . I think that most singers have more ego than I do.

[*The therapist asks the client to specify the meaning of the word "ego." She does not accept the term at face value but wants to know how this unique individual defines the term.*]

Therapist: What does that mean? Oh, that's wonderful!—What is more ego?

Client: Well, . . . maybe they don't have more ego, but their ego, let's see . . . I haven't really thought about this, that was a thrown-off statement.

Therapist: That's ok, *it has some meaning to you that's important to us,* I mean I'm responding. . . . *Everything that you have to say is important to us . . . to help us find new choices of behavior for you so that you're not subject to this,* so what do you mean by this?

Client: Ok, I guess what I mean, I see people, very successful singers, who are friends of mine, before a performance, and they're excited and exhilarated at the prospect of performing and the reason that they're excited about it is because the glory's gonna shine on them, they're going out there, they're about to do something that they're very confident that they'll do well, and they get out there and they do a great job that people love—I want people to love me that way, too.

Therapist: Umhm, of course.

Client: I guess I'm not confident that I can do that good a job— there have been instances in the past where I haven't done that good a job.

[*Here the therapist normalizes the client's experiences.*]

Therapist: I can't imagine a performer that hasn't had that experience.

Client: Yeah.

Therapist: Think about it.

Client: [*nodding*] True.

Therapist: So, tell me, you've never had this experience, of getting the glory?

Client: Well, I'm very, very self-critical, so even when my performance has been well received, and I'm standing up there smiling and accepting all the applause, inside, you know. I'm clicking through all the things that I didn't do well, god, why did I do that? You know.

Therapist: So you don't give yourself much credit when you do well, is that right?

Client: I tend not to, it's true.

Therapist: Umhum—how come? Where did you learn that?

[*The therapist sensitively tunes in to the client's discomfort as she inquires about family history. She returns to a focus on the here and now, while leaving the door open for further discussion of historical material should this be necessary. This is an intriguing intervention in that the possibility of delving into unpleasant family history becomes an added impetus for the client to rapidly master the present difficulty. This is similar to Haley's "ordeal therapy (1984).*]

Client: [*big sigh*] Well, yes. . . . Do I want to talk about this? It's something that everyone in our family has and its, well. . . .

Therapist: Who's the teacher?

Client: My father.

Therapist: We don't have to go into this . . . but there's that, which is part of. . . .

Client: I know, I know it's there . . . and I know what it is. [*She puts up her hand.*]

Therapist: And you don't want to discuss it. . . . I'm not saying we have to discuss it, at some point we may need pieces of that, but not right now if you're not ready . . . because it is possible for you to change your responses without going into your family history, I don't require that, I just got a feeling that it's such a well-entrenched pattern, and my experience tells me that we usually learn those things when we're children, not necessarily in relation to singing, but something else, so that's why I ask that question, but you don't have to answer it— maybe later or maybe never.

Client: Yeah.

Therapist: We may be able to shift this for you without ever. . . .

Client: Yeah, it is a strong enough pattern that my singing is only one small aspect of my life that is affected by that.

Therapist: Ok, what I would like to know, you said you have felt this way ever since you gave your first solo performance?

Client: [*nodding*] Um.

[*The therapist looks for exceptions to the client's difficulty and amplifies the information obtained to empower the client as a resource to herself.*]

Therapist: Has there ever been a time when it was less?

Client: There was one time, two times, when it wasn't there at all. One was for my senior recital in college, and I went in just before the recital to my voice teacher and I said please help me, I'm so nervous,

I'm afraid I'm going to fall off the stage, and he said, what are the physical manifestations of your nervousness, and I described to him the way I was feeling physically, and he sort of talked me through this routine of negating those feelings and sort of—negating isn't the right word—but trying to convince myself, even to pretend. . . .

Therapist: Neutralizing them somehow?

Client: Neutralizing them by producing opposite kinds of feelings, so I went backstage and I sat down and concentrated on those things and I knew the music so well—that that was not an issue, and by the time I walked out on stage I was perfectly calm and did perform very well. And there was another time about two years later. . . .

Therapist: I want that, but tell me an example of what another neutralizing thought was.

Client: Ok, an example was that I thought my hands were very light weight and sort of trembly and that they could go flying up at any moment, so he suggested that I feel as though my hands had great weight in them, and just, you know, that I feel very heavy and that I feel that the stage was pulling me down to it, um, and it was a very settling, you know, it was an opposing thing and it was very settling for me—the problem is that I've never been able to do this sort of thing since, I mean I've tried to think it, and for some reason it's not since worked. . . .

[*Rather than focus on the client's last comments about this technique "not working," the therapist asks for another example of successful mastery of the client's anxiety.*]

Therapist: That's great! Give me another example of what he said.

Client: My breaths were very quick and high and he said to think of bypassing the upper chest altogether, to think the breaths very deep and to realize that my body didn't need that much breath—and he actually told me to think a slower heartbeat.

Therapist: Umhmm.

Client: Which helped.

Therapist: Yes, it will.

Client: It's funny to think that one can control those things.

Therapist: Yes, but you can, when you think about it we never stop breathing, but you can also [*takes deep breath and sighs it out*], you can take intentional breaths and we can also, as you as a singer very well know, breathe from up here [*indicates chest*] or down here [*indicates belly*], you can deliberately expand your diaphragm, why not?

Client: Sure.

Therapist: It's a more obvious experience that we all have all the time, but people certainly can slow down their pulses, no question about it so, hey, why not? We're on the right track here.

Client: He was a good teacher

Therapist: I hear it! He knew just what to say didn't he?

Client: He was a very smart man.

Therapist: Anything else that he told you in this really extraordinary preparatory talk that he gave you?

Client: Those were the main things.

Therapist: Ok, great, now what was the second time?

Client: The second time was when I gave a solo recital again, a couple of years later, uh, I was working with the same pianist—one thing was that in both cases I was working with a pianist who was very capable and very reliable and in both cases we had worked on the music months and months beforehand so that the music itself, and the ways of singing it were almost second nature [*gestures into her body*], he was very calming, having him around, he was very calming before the recital, umm. . . .

Therapist: How did he do it?

Client: Well, basically by example, I was sort of running around, you know, beforehand, pacing back and forth, warming up, thinking about the music and he was sitting there with his eyes closed, and I finally went over to him and said aren't you nervous? He said "No, I know this music," and then he just closed his eyes again, and I followed his example and I just sat down and closed my eyes.

Therapist: How was that for you?

Client: It was good. I still had a lot of things running through my mind, but at least I wasn't complicating it by running back and forth and it was again, you know, a fine performance.

[*The therapist takes the material presented and lets the client know that she (the client) has the resources to master her anxiety.*]

Therapist: That's great! So what we know is that with certain kinds of preparation you have the resources to do what you want.

Client: Yes, but what has been the case in the past it took two things—one knowing the music extremely well and two having that physical preparation beforehand that's calming, and what happens nowadays is that I don't have that kind of preparation time in advance.

Therapist: You mean to learn the music?

Client: To learn it that well that, uh, that it's . . .

Therapist: It's second nature.

Client: That's right.

Therapist: So that even your father's presence couldn't knock it out of you, eh?

Client: [*laughs*]

Therapist: You say that when you have tried the kind of strategies that your music teacher in college told you, what happens, how come they don't work?

Client: They seem to be working at the time. I'll be backstage. I'll tell the other singers that I need time to myself, and I'll talk myself through some sort of relaxation routine, and I feel fine until I walk out on stage.

Therapist: What happens then?

Client: Actually, the first few measures are fine, then I begin to gradually get nervous.

Therapist: How do you know when to do that?

Client: You mean when do I get nervous?

Therapist: Umhm.

Client: I hear nervousness in other people's voiceness, I mean voices.

Therapist: "Voiceness," I hear you!

Client: [*laughs*]

Therapist: Are you sure you hear nervousness in them?

Client: Yes, in one of the singers in particular, I think that's part of it. I worry for her and for me and how the whole final product is going to come out.

Therapist: Umhmm, but you have this experience when you sing by yourself as well?

Client: Yeah.

[*Here, the therapist relabels what the client considers a defect, as a special sensitivity.*]

Therapist: So how do you do it then? You have a pattern of being able to do this in any setting? Right? [*smiles*]

Client: [*smiling*] Being able to . . . [*laughing*] I beg your pardon!

Therapist: It's true, not everybody has it.

Client: [*looking thoughtful*]

Therapist: I'm teasing you, but I'm not criticizing you, it is something you can learn.

Client: Ok.

Therapist: Therefore it is something you can relearn or unlearn, since not everybody does it. *We're looking at the particular strategy by which you get yourself to that particular result, ok?*

Client: Yeah, ok. I know one thing that happens.

Therapist: What's that?

Client: There's a different way that I hear myself when I'm in the practice room and when I'm on stage. When I'm on stage, it seems like I'm hearing much more acutely, seems like I'm hearing every heartbeat, you know, and every little diphthong that I make in the words and when I'm in the practice room I have much more of a sense of being at the beginning of a piece and working my way towards the end, it is similar on stage, but when I'm practicing that sort of terrible acuteness is not a part of my hearing.

Therapist: Umhm, ok, so what turns the terrible acuteness on?

Client: Just being in front of people, I think that suddenly I begin to hear things the ways that I think they're hearing them. I don't know.

Therapist: Anybody you're in front of? I mean when you sing for anyone?

Client: Not if I'm singing in my voice lessons where my voice teacher is the only person there. But for example we have voice classes, master classes—we're all in there together—the teacher and about a dozen students, uhh, that's very nerve-wracking and part of it is that I realize that that's my most critical audience ever.

Therapist: They're all doing the same thing.

Client: Yeah, they're all doing the same thing, and they're empathizing with what you're doing but. . . .

Therapist: Yeah, that's what we do, performing artists especially, you make comparisons.

Client: Oh yeah.

[*The therapist begins a process of "reframing" the client's difficulty and uses a particularly effective metaphor to make her point.*]

Therapist: What I'm so struck by is that on the one hand—and I think that's an excellent phrase for this—you really have an exceptional ability to observe. On the other hand, it makes you trip, if you will, and the analogy that I'm thinking of is when you first begin to walk— you probably don't remember that, but if you ever see a young person doing this, they do it with the most care, you know, they don't know how to put the foot down and what they certainly don't know is about the balance, how to make that all work and to begin with, you know, they sit down abruptly a lot more than they walk, but fortunately they're pretty close to the ground, but if I say, now, I want you to walk across the room and I want you to make sure that you put your foot down in the right way and I want you, as you're walking, to notice the sequence of all of your muscles and make sure the right ones move so that you don't fall down, can you imagine what it would be like if you attempted to walk across the room? You would most likely either be immobilized or perhaps you would fall if you could really do this to the degree I'm talking about—what muscle am I supposed to use now? Imagine! You know—well, it sounds to me like you're doing a version of that with your singing, you see.

Client: [*smiling and nodding*] That's a really good analogy.

Therapist: Which, of course, would make you trip, which in your case means hearing your heartbeat, and what do you do when you go to walk across this floor and you're uncertain, you tense, and you don't have the freedom of movement that you have when you're not thinking of it, which is the way you do it when you practice, if you just get up and walk to that door, you don't think about this. [*demonstrates*] I mean do I put the heel down first or just how do you put your foot down? This is a very complex thing that we do without thinking about it.

Client: Umhmm.

Therapist: So how come when you get up on the stage you don't know how to walk? [*Both laugh.*]

Client: Cuz I'm using a skateboard!

Therapist: But you want to use a skateboard on the stage the way that you do when you practice.

Client: Yeah.

Therapist: Ok?

Client: I can't answer that question.

[*The therapist presents a hopeful message of expected change and plants the idea that each solution can be unique.*]

Therapist: No, no, but I . . . think if you can see it that way that you can also see that *there's the real possibility of changing it.*

Client: Umhmm. [*nodding*]

Therapist: Because you have two sets of skills, one is to go for the end and to go for the flow that will get you to the end in the most graceful way that you can, using your body in the ways that is . . .

Client: Most effective.

Therapist: Yes, most effective, and the other one is your trying to figure out with each heartbeat how to do it, each breath how to do it you create and so of course it can't flow the way it does in the other one.

Client: [*laughs*]

Therapist: So don't despair, *I don't have any question but that we can do something about this,* it's just a question of what. As a matter of fact I have had good experiences with other people who have performance anxiety, but first we have to figure out just how you create it, *everybody does it differently.*

Client: Umhmm.

[*Here, the therapist asks the client to provide a detailed "video description" of her anxiety.*]

Therapist: Just trying to think about whether I want more about how you actually need this terrible acuteness. . . . What I want to know is what do you do when you're not singing in the quartet? How do you create that, because you say that what triggers you there is hearing their nervousness, but when you're singing solo you don't have that to trigger you?

Client: Well, one thing about singing in the quartet is that I generally feel pretty ok when we first get out on stage and start singing, I'm not totally responsible—I'm more responsible than in a whole choral ensemble, but I'm not the solo performer so it's pretty much a degree question there, I think what happens in a case like that is that the potential for being anxious is there already and when I hear nervousness in somebody else's voice, it turns, brings it right up to the surface.

Therapist: Sure, but when they're not there. . . .

Client: When they're not there, I think it's already there. . . .

Therapist: Something triggers it because you say that. . . .

Client: No, see. . . .

Therapist: So that's only with the quartet?

Client: The most recent solo piece I gave was an oratorio piece and there were other soloists, the soloists were sitting on stage in front of the orchestra, and there were several movements which were chorus and orchestra or the orchestra alone or other soloists with the orchestra before I had to sing anything, and I was very calm and relaxed, kind of enjoying the music, and . . . about two movements before I had to sing, I knew my turn was coming up.

Therapist: We all have these little things that we do, I don't know whether you start talking to yourself or you got a picture of yourself singing. . . .

Client: No, it's more, ok, you have to sing pretty soon, and it's that really bitchy tough aria, and it's got that horrible long phrase in it that you can barely get through even in the practice room, so how're you going to negotiate it on stage when you're nervous? [*laughs*]

Therapist: Uhuh uhuh.

Client: It's like I start focusing on the really tough parts, you know, meanwhile I'm sitting on stage just beaming down at the audience, of course. [*laughs*]

Therapist: Sure.

Client: I focus on the possible failures that I might have.

Therapist: That's right, it's wonderful, and you said you're already feeling nervous—there you are, you're going to have to sing and you're programming yourself for failure even before you stand up.

Client: Umhmm, that's right.

Therapist: And then happens? I mean we still have another movement to go, what happens next?

Client: Oh, the heartbeat starts to go, and the breath starts to get. . . .

Therapist: Right.

Client: And I say well, you know, you can do an ok job even if it's not going to be a great job. [*laughs*]

Therapist: What a friend you are!

Client: [*still laughing, throws up hands*] What can I say? Then I get up and sing, I'm usually not . . . in a case like that I almost feel that I'm not in control of what happens in that first aria and then I just. . . .

Therapist: How do you do that? How do you know you're out of control? What's your internal process in feeling out of control?

Client: I start singing, and it's one of those cases where the music is going along in spite of me, and I know I have to get through it but does not sound to my internal ear as well as I've been able to do before and yet, sometimes the acoustics of the hall throw me a little bit because suddenly there are all those people in there and it shifts the acoustics so I'm thinking in the back of my mind, oh this isn't as resonant as it was in the dress rehearsal; I may get through the long awful phrase, practically gasping at the end of it without letting anyone know. . . .

Therapist: As you're going through this . . . it's almost as if you're observing yourself singing. . . .

Client: Yeah.

Therapist: That's the flavor of it.

Client: Umhm.

Therapist: But you're observing yourself and making negative comments at the same time.

Client: Yeah, generally . . . then usually once I've gotten through that first aria and I sit down and I have other things to sing later, the other ones tend to go fine I'm not nearly as anxious for them. . . .

Therapist: That may not be the answer to the question I was just going to ask you, but with this horrifying experience, I mean what's in it for you to go through this experience?

Client: I dunno. . . . I love to sing, I love that music. It's very compelling to me, very, very compelling. . . .

[*The therapist now encourages the client to clearly specify her goal in positive terms.*]

Therapist: So, uh . . . *how would you like it to be? What's the sequence you would like?*

Client: I guess I'd like to learn to be less self-critical.

Therapist: Ok, so, could you state that in the positive rather than "less self-critical"?

Client: I would like to be able to uh, [*laughs*] this is hard! I'd like to be able to reward myself for a good performance, or an acceptable performance.

Therapist: Wow! only acceptable?!

Client: Ok, we'll change that back to good

Therapist: What would you say? "Self-critical" is more specific than rewarding self for good performance, I want something a little more specific than that, what would you say to yourself?

Client: Ok—[*laughs*]—the things I'm thinking of still have negative in them, that's why I'm taking my time, I guess I would say something like "that was a very musical performance" or, uh "Your voice has more flexibility than it has had in the past, you're improving and that's great" or things of that nature.

Therapist: Sounds nice to me. . . .

Client: [*nods*]

Therapist: When you were talking about those self-critical statements, you were quite specific about the phrasing, about not having enough breath, about not having enough breath at the end of that long passage in the aria, take one of those and see if you can say something positive about it.

Client: Ummm.

Therapist: About having run out of breath at the end of that long passage.

Client: It would be more like whew! I made it through that!

Therapist: Survival, right? [*Both laugh.*] How about, "considering how you were feeling you did a really good job with that!" Could you do something like that?

Client: Let's see—I don't know. [*long pause*] I'm certainly having a hard time with this, it's certainly something to consider. . . .

[*The therapist talks to the client about the impact of language on our inner experience and lets her know that change is not only possible but inevitable. She ends the interview by giving the client a task that allows her practice, using language "in vivo" to change her inner experience and then generalizes this task beyond the performance situation.*]

Therapist: Well, you know, *one reason that I go for these specifics, is that we really create our own experience in language, it's the only way we create experience for ourselves and we create experience not only in what other people say to us but in what we say to ourselves.*

Client: Umhm.

Therapist: As a matter of fact, I think that the majority of people who have . . . self-esteem problems keep their critical selves going by talking to themselves critically, and as you find ways to shift that—*and you will more and more since we've had this conversation*—you will find yourself asking now what would be the positive version of that? And notice the internal experience that you have as you do that. That's something I want you to do deliberately between now and the next time that I see you.

Client: Ok.

Therapist: I'd really like to get a sense of how you create this for yourself.

Client: Uhm.

Therapist: So I want you to pay attention to your negative comments to yourself deliberately taking that same item and the way you describe it and finding a way of describing it positively to yourself.

Client: Ok.

Therapist: I know you're good at that, you've done it a couple of times here—just take that same thing and turn it around and say "and you could look at it this way." Start with negative ones. And notice how you feel different in the body when you do it.

Client: Umhm, ok.

Therapist: Slows you right down, slows your heart down, slows the breathing down, truly.

Client: [*nodding*] All right.

Therapist: Ok, well let's see what we can do to shift this for you, not just about your singing, but in general, and I want you to write down a few examples so that I hear them and so that you take it seriously.

Client: Uhuh.

Therapist: Write down a few examples so you can catch yourself and you say "but one could also look at it like this." I have the sense that your unconscious is just chafing at the bit for you to change it— that you should be, you know, appreciated just as you are and be seen as you are.

Client: Ok.

By the time of the next appointment, the client was making excellent progress in observing and monitoring her own behavior. The introduction of an "observer" into her practice and performance sessions gave her a boost as she began to see that she was in charge and not merely subject to forces outside her control. While the presenting request clearly keyed back into her past experiences, we did not need to investigate those to help her attain the more relaxed performance presence that she requested. She became, with extensive encouragement, an expert in "seeing things in a new way," and this, in turn, helped her to become more self-appreciative and so more poised as a performer. As she progressed, any "slip from perfection" became fair game for the enlarged perspective of "seeing it in the larger picture." When she moved out of state, we were still addressing her acceptance of "all of herself" rather than trying to get rid of certain troublesome parts.

And so the therapist and client come to the close of their first dance, beginning to learn the particularities of each other's way of dancing. They have decided what to call their dance, and how they will know when it is time to stop. They have agreed when the dance will be resumed—and perhaps how long it will last—and further, what steps the client is to practice between now and then.

Notes

1. For further description of mirroring, matching, and calibration, see Bandler and Grinder (1979), Lankton (1980), and Cameron-Bandler (1985).

2. For a detailed discussion of suspending assumptions, see O'Hanlon and Wilk, (1987).

3. For an elaboration of the principle of mindfulness, see Langer (1989).

4. For futher examples of these kinds of questions, see O'Hanlon and Wilk (1987) and O'Hanlon and Weiner-Davis (1989).

5. For an account of experimenters' unconscious influence in psychological experiments, see Frank (1973: chap. 5).

5
The Process of Treatment

> The most important thing in treatment is to break up the patient's rigid and limiting mental sets.
> —Milton Erickson

> Psychotherapeutic treatment must aim to bring the patient to the point where his natural growth can be resumed. Treatment beyond this point . . . interferes with the natural growth potential and tempts the patient . . . to take the easy path of continuing dependency. . . . This dependency is exactly what therapy tries to overcome.
> —Franz Alexander

How does psychotherapy "break up rigid and limiting sets" so that "natural growth can be resumed"? As mentioned earlier, you the therapist must expect and intend such change. But more than that you need to have a way of understanding the process of change so that you can actively promote it. Further, clarity about your general treatment goals for each client guides you within the framework of therapeutic transactions. When you are clear about these goals, you can then direct your attention to the particular elements of an effective change process. Here again, language, the words in which you describe your goals, holds the key. If you want to solve a problem, you look for problems; if you want to increase choice of behavior, you look for desired new choices.

Unless and until you have your overarching treatment goals stated to yourself, you are a ship without a rudder, you may drift aimlessly in a sea of fascinating content-laden reefs and shoals, without knowing exactly where land lies. You are the pilot the client selects to guide the ship through what seem to be perilous waters. Your goals, like a lighthouse in the distance, keep you on the course of the client's request for a safe harbor. When the client tries to stray out of the channel, his or her digressional words, like buoy markers, warn you of losing your way. All therapists need to discover their own particular goals stated in their own particular language, for it is these words that keep the therapy "in the channel."

For us, there are three overall therapeutic goals that guide us. They are for the client to have (1) an increased choice of effective actions, (2) an enhanced ability to act autonomously, and (3) restored morale—to feel better. The first and fundamental goal—to help clients develop new choices of effective action—almost always involves the clients' taking greater charge of some aspect of their lives. Expansion of clients' practical responsibility leads to an increase in their autonomy; it fosters hope and improves morale—which in turn improves physical health. A striking example of this was reported by Judith Rodin. She designed a study

> to encourage elderly convalescent-home residents to make a greater number of choices and to have more control of day-to-day events. Immediately after the intervention and at an eighteen-month follow-up period, the group given more responsibility became more alert and active and reported feeling happier than the group of residents who were encouraged to feel the staff would care for them and try to satisfy their needs. From physicians' evaluations of the patient medical records, the "responsible" patients also showed a significantly greater improvement in health. (1986: 1273)

One of our principal jobs is to teach clients new coping skills. When clients have learned not only that there are new ways to respond to their situations, but also that *they can actually respond differently* they have gained new tools to use, and they begin to feel better. The cycle of increased choice/autonomy/morale has the potential for generalizing into other areas of their lives—picking up speed as it goes. Clients often find themselves using their new skills in other contexts as well. As Lydia Rapoport says "[There is] . . . increasing evidence that even minor modifications in functioning, values, or attitudes may serve as a nucleus for other more profound transformations in the environment, in interpersonal relations, and even in intrapsychic functioning. Improvement can become self-perpetuating, particularly if there are favorable rewards and responses" (in Katz 1975: 107).

Our aim is to help clients learn, as economically as possible, new coping skills, that will increase their sense of personal efficacy, or agency, and thus contribute to an increased sense of well-being. A corollary might be that we intend to "work ourselves out of a job" with each client as efficaciously as possible, leaving the client not only with his or her original request being fulfilled, but also with increased skills he or she can use in other life contexts, both now and in the future. To paraphrase that old adage, we solve the "problem" of hunger not by giving the person a fish, but rather by teaching him how to fish; she can then provide her own food without help from us. "Obviously one's own activities form a sounder basis for hope than reliance on the good will and competence of someone else" (Frank 1973: 137).

One further goal is to provide some experience of increased choice and agency in each session; the frame being set by the opening question "What would you like to have happen here today?"[1] Examining the presuppositions in this relatively simple question, you can see that the treatment goals are embodied in it: increased choice (some change can occur here today); expanded autonomy (the client activates the process); and improved morale (which tends to follow).[2] We teach the client to be the pilot, to successfully navigate the uncharted waters of the future and to steer clear of reefs.

Our overall goals directly support what we see as the purpose of therapy. Here we return to the difference between problem and possibility. In the problem frame, the purpose is to find a solution for the problem or a "cure" for the illness. This is often considered a discrete event, for when you are "cured," you become problem-free. In the possibility frame we offer help to those who get stuck along their evolutionary paths and this dictates our concept of therapeutic purpose: unsnarling developmental knots.

> The basic treatment model . . . should be the life model. . . . The trajectory of the life-span with its natural processes of growth, development, and eventual decline is the arena for experimentation, learning, and mastery in regard to need satisfaction and problem solving. The natural, progressive tendencies in human development are strong forces and prevail over the regressive tendencies, barring serious obstacles and obstructions. These natural growth tendencies then become our chief therapeutic ally. This concept challenges that aspect of the medical [*problem*] model which frames maladaptation and problems of living in terms of illness. . . .
> In keeping with this view, we need to abandon the concept of cure and shift to the concept of restoration and enhancement of functioning. (Rapoport, in Katz 1975: 106)

This developmental view of therapy fits well with the assumptions of the possibility-orientation in which we are constantly directing our efforts toward a judicious use of therapeutic resources to enable the client to take the next step along the natural path of personal evolution. Armed with the therapist's overall treatment goals—increased choice of behavior, amplified autonomy, and improved morale—and a conceptual framework that situates therapy as an enabling incident on a life-stage path, we are now ready to examine the specific steps of the therapeutic process.

The Process of Therapy

> Psychological problems develop when people do not permit the naturally changing circumstances of life to interrupt their old and no longer useful patterns of association and experience so that new solutions may emerge.
> —Milton Erickson

When clients come to us, they invariably want some change in their lives. This can range from wanting a happier mood or to better manage anxiety to hoping to change a relative or to satisfy some authority. They are almost universally "stuck" in some way and hope and expect that we will help them get "unstuck." As we mentioned in chapter 4 on the initial session, the first step for the therapist is always to establish rapport and to join the clients' world view in order to understand their premises. Rapport and attention to joining clients needs to be maintained throughout the therapy, and in the following discussion of treatment these will be presupposed. From the first moment of meeting you should be observing the client's behavioral, verbal, and presuppositional patterns. These characteristic patterns have led the client to the current impass. Therefore, it is just these patterns—which clients often consider unchangeable—that you will need to interrupt to open their eyes to the possibility of new effective action. This new possibility reframes their view of reality. *Reframing is the central strategy in the generation of effective therapy.* Simply stated, reframing involves producing in the client new responses to known—unwanted—stimuli; it is a negotiation of assumptions. And as we shall see, reframing also shifts internal images that support or represent these assumptions by offering an alternative image.

The critical essence, then, of reframing involves the interruption of identified dysfunctional patterns with therapeutic strategies that lead to a new perspective. This new or reframed point of view shifts or enlarges the client's existing belief system about what is possible in the world. *We often cannot control what happens or has happened to us, but we can choose or change our response to what happens—or to our memory of it.* This process of changing our response to the unchangeable circumstances of our lives is a central feature of effective therapy. Reframing enables clients to generate new reactions to old stimuli or situations and thus to discover possible new behavior choices. As Watzlawick, Weakland, and Fisch point out: "Successful reframing must lift the problem out of the 'symptom' frame and into another frame that does not carry the implication of unchangeability. Of course not just any reframe will do but only the one that is congenial to the person's way of thinking and of categorizing reality" (1974: 102–3). *Reframing is not interpretation; it neither explains nor offers insight.* Reframing simply takes the "facts" and ascribes a different, yet plausible, meaning to them. Reframing does not "produce insight but teaches a different game . . . thereby making the old one obsolete" 1974: 104).

Therapeutic verbal reframing or relabeling on the simplest level aims to create positive connotations by ascribing new meaning to the content of a situation, or by assigning an unwanted behavior to a context where it would be more appropriate. To create a *content reframe*, you need to ask, "What positive meaning could this behavior hold?" To create a *context reframe* you ask, "Is there a place where this behavior might have a positive value?" Both kinds of reframes interrupt the client's "limiting mental sets." Thus, if a client says, "I'm depressed," your response could be "That means you know what it's like to feel good" (content) or "Some things are worth feeling sad about" (context). A husband complained "I love to have my wife watch television with me, but she thinks it's a waste of time." He smiled and nodded when I [MTF] offered the content reframe, "Perhaps her physical presence provides you with comfort and love." The wife spontaneously brought out her own context reframe of "Oh, I see, like it helped me the other night to have him sitting next to me at the PTA meeting when I had to make a proposal."

While such reframes point clients to attitudinal shifts, for a reframe with more behavioral change potential, consider the case of a sixty-seven-year-old, increasingly reclusive widow. She came reluctantly to therapy at the urging of her two married daughters worried about her isolation, especially since she refused to accept their invitations to go out with them. The widow's view was that she was "being a good mother" because she didn't "add to the burden of her daughters with their little children." When I [MTF] invited her to ponder the possibility that she was being "selfish" because her daughters were so concerned about her and that she was "adding to their burdens" by not going out with them, she was startled and began considering different responses. Another example further illustrates the potential of reframing. As a thirty-seven-year-old woman who had suffered from severe migraine headaches since age twelve realized during the process of treatment that her headaches allowed her time alone to which she did not otherwise feel entitled. (The headaches were reframed by her *from* negative painful punishment *to* a positive desire for time alone.) One day, when she was riding on a bus and began to feel a headache coming on, she said "I don't need to get a headache, I'm going to take a rest when I get home!" She took the rest—to her family's surprise—and did not get the headache.

George Burns tells the story of how he had a hacking cough for several weeks and went to a number of doctors, who charged him high fees but could not cure the cough. Finally, someone recommended that he go to Dr. Ginsburg's Clinic where he waited behind about fifty people for his clinic visit, which cost only three dollars. At one point he asked the nurse to tell Dr. Ginsburg that "George Burns is sitting outside." The doctor sent back the message "Tell George Burns that Dr. Ginsburg is sitting inside." When Burns finally got his chance to see the doctor, the doctor asked him "Why are you doing it?" After which the hacking cough disappeared. In this instance, Dr. Ginsburg changed the rules—his question reframed the complaint as under Burns' control.

An excellent example of opening up options through reframing comes from a videotaped session of Virginia Satir working with a family ("A Blended Family with a Troubled Boy")[3] (also see Corrales 1989). At one point in the session, the boy's mother places a hand on the boy's knee. He quickly moves his knee away from her touch. Satir looks at the mother and asks her how she just experienced what happened. The following is the brief interaction between Satir and the mother:

Mother: He doesn't really want me to be around him.

Satir: Okay. Let's use that as a first working hypotheis. [*Notice that she does not refute the mother's comment, but accepts it as one possibility.*] Could it be that Tim at this moment doesn't know whether to trust what's going on? You think that could be? And he moves back because he doesn't know if he can trust you, not that he doesn't want you around?

Mother: Maybe.

Satir: Let's think of that as another possibility. Could we think of another possibility: that Tim also would like to participate in the choice of whether somebody would touch him or not? Is that another possibility?

And so she offers the mother two additional ways to make meaning of the son's behavior.

The Italian family therapist, Maurizio Andolfi, was dealing with a woman who engaged in "self-destructive behavior" and who described her life as very conventional and drab. She had sores and scabs all over her face as a result of scratching at her face with her fingernails. This client had previous therapy and believed that this behavior was a "neurotic symptom" that had its etiology in her early psychosexual development. Andolfi challenges this view by redefining the symptom in positive terms: "This is the first creative product of your curriculum vitae! It seems that in this sea of conformity the only creative thing you see or feel is what you have written on your face" (1979: 59). The client goes on to debate the issue with Andolfi who continues to challenge her view of her situation and the client's notion that the behavior in question is in fact a "symptom" at all. He then builds on this redefinition or reframing to interrupt his client's demoralizing set.

In another situation, a man was referred by the Department of Social Services for striking his thirteen-year-old daughter on one occasion. He defined himself as "an intense and critical person" with very high expectations. I [SF] framed his "intensity" as reflecting the depth of his caring for his daughter. Such a reframe served three purposes. First, attributing positive intent to his behavior helped me to join and empathize with him. Second, it allowed me to let him know that although I find such abusive actions unacceptable, I will not add to his already existing shame by negatively judging his behavior. Third, by reframing his behavior as caring, I communicated my assumption that he would like to show his caring in other, more appropriate ways. Since I knew the client was an avid sports enthusiast and very competitive, I also told him the following: "I'm sure you are familiar with the sport of archery. As you know, an archer who tries to hold the bow and arrow very tightly and does not allow some arc of movement, will miss the bulls-eye by a good margin. However, the archer who allows his sight to move will more likely be successful" (after Shainberg 1989). As we will see, use of such imagery can successfully bypass the logical thought processes of the left brain and provide an indirect route to influencing behavior.

Ways to relabel or reframe the presenting situation lead to ways to challenge the client's assumptions and, thus, to offer a different, positive point of view right from the start of treatment. This reframing may not only be from negative to positive, but most importantly from a situation the client cannot control to one where the client can become active on his or her own behalf. For example, to the wife who complains that her husband doesn't to talk to her enough, you can offer the idea that she wishes to find ways to be certain that her husband knows her concerns. For the father who wants his son to be more obedient, you could speak of his wish to be a more effective father. Such reframes not only look for the positive intention behind the request, but also put the responsibility for the change back in the lap of the only person who can effect the change, the client. This both restates the request in positive language, and also implies that a change can be initiated and maintained by the client. Reframing, establishing a new, possible view of a request or situation, is the critical nexus of therapeutic change, both large and small. Since we reframe principally in words, let us now look in more detail at the various ways to effect these shifts.

The Language of Change

> The power of the imagination is a great factor in medicine. It may produce diseases in man and in animals, and it may cure them.
> —Paracelsus

In his book, *The Language of Change*, Paul Watzlawick (1978) convincingly advances the intriguing theory that in order to effect therapeutic change, we have to change a person's world images. He says:

> Anybody seeking our help suffers, in one way or another, from his relation to the world. . . . He suffers from his image of the world, from the unresolved contradiction between the way things appear to him and the way they should be according to his world image. He then can choose one of two alternatives: He can intervene actively in the course of events and adapt the world more or less to his image; or, where the world cannot be changed, he can adapt his image to the unalterable facts. . . . The latter is more specifically the task and the goal of therapeutic change. (1978: 40–41)

If this is the case, then an understanding of what constitute world images is essential. According to Watzlawick, they consist of "the most comprehensive, most complex synthesis of the myriads of experiences, convictions, and influences, of their interpretations, of the resulting ascription of value and meaning to the objects of perception which an individual can muster" (1978: 43). It is his further contention that these world images reside in the brain functions of the right hemisphere. "The translation of the perceived reality, this synthesis of our experience of the world into an image, is most probably the function of the right hemisphere" (1978: 45–46).

The pivotal implication of this theory for therapists is that they need to find ways to access these right-brain images so they can be changed. There is scientific evidence to indicate that the left and right hemispheres of the brain function in fundamentally different ways.[4] The left hemisphere, in right-handed people, is dominant and processes logical language (digital communication). This leaves to the right hemisphere the imagistic (or analogical) processing. The two hemispheres represent language in quite different ways. This dissimilarity can be seen in the contrast between the two common types of clocks: digital clocks, which show time minute by minute, and analog clocks, which show time on the whole clock face. Right-hemisphere language is closer to experience, and it is the client's experience that we want to change. World images are the way we represent our experience to ourselves (and by images we mean our representations of sense, smell, sound and taste as well as sight).

So how do we access these world images from which our clients' construct their realities? One way is to use the "language of imagery" itself: stories, images, dreams, and all manner of word play—jokes, puns, aphorisms, ambiguities, and the like; indeed, whatever language that evokes mental images. Humor can play a major role in therapeutic change. In chapter 2 we discussed the physiological benefits of humor, and here we present it as a valuable means toward the end of altering the client's dysfunctional world image. Jokes can shift world images more directly exactly because the punchline violates logical, left-brain language, and so the listener must discard presumably fixed internal images to make sense of it. A shifted or expanded internal image may result.

You need to focus on what needs to be changed—*the specific image*—and *how* to change it (not why it developed or what caused it). The *what* is uncovered and described in the analogic language of the right hemisphere, the video descriptions. Translating analogic language into digital or left-hemisphere language repeats the mistake of trying to change a situation logically. When the client hears a digital-language explanation or interpretation of certain events in her life, the left hemisphere is again accessed, and her world image is not changed. "Interpretation as a form of therapeutic communication is thus a "one-way" translation, from the unconscious to the conscious, and . . . it entails a loss of that for which there are no equivalents in left-hemispheric language" (Watzlawick 1978: 47). So, besides using analogic or imagistic language, you often need to block the digital language used by the left hemisphere. This can be done through the use of confusion, double binds, paradox, illusion of choice, and relabeling—for all of these linguistic pirouettes evoke a search in our images to make sense of them. Images can also be altered by changing behaviors—as Heinz von Foerster says: "If you can do it, you know it,"[5] or "If you desire to see, learn how to act" (Watzlawick 1978: 130). In other words, if you have acted in a new way, you know it is possible. Therefore, behavioral assignments that lead the client to behave differently can change his or her world images.

Focusing, Tracking and the Need for Persistence

One of the ways we can communicate that we *know* the client *can* act differently is by persistently encouraging the client to explore alternative ways of meeting needs. By helping clients act differently we help them to change their world views about what is possible. In addition, in order to keep therapy brief, it is important to "track" and keep your attention on a targeted issue. Doing brief therapy requires that you tailor the intervention to the specific needs of the client or family (Friedman & Pettus 1985; Haley 1976). This requires that the client or family engage in relevant activities ("homework") outside the session to maximize the time-effectiveness of the therapy. In addition to generating task assignments for clients to do *outside* the therapy setting, you must also effectively track specific issues *during the session* to move the client or system toward new options and opportunities.

The following clinical example demonstrates the importance of persistent tracking of a specific issue. In this illustration, a co-therapist team [SF and Jennifer Campion, M.S.W., Psy.D.] working with a couple, aims to empower the wife to better articulate her own needs in the relationship. The wife had originally come for treatment because of her "depression." The therapist, who saw her individually, viewed her "depression" as related to her unhappiness in her marital relationship and referred her for couples' therapy. The co-therapy team that saw this couple framed the wife's "depression" as her "difficulties in asserting herself" and spent considerable time in an effort to facilitate the wife in "finding her voice." The husband (who was a salesman) was very talented at "hypnotizing'" his wife; and she, at succumbing to his hypnotic cues. He would mention something in his conversation and nonverbally cue his wife to begin talking on this particular topic. When she would report feeling angry or upset, he would minimize her feelings (for example, redefining "angry" to "slightly annoyed"). She accepted this new definition, and a level of polite interpersonal exchange was maintained.

We focused on helping the wife to articulate her own needs (that is, not be so easily "hypnotized" by her husband) and on helping the husband to gain increased comfort with his wife's more assertive behavior. Each therapist would, on occasion, take opposite positions regarding the merits and risks of change. While one would stress the risks or costs of changing (the potential for increased volatility and anger, for example), the other would stress the benefits of change (increased intimacy and closeness). Throughout the treatment (which lasted for sixteen sessions over a fifteen-month period), we worked systemically, positively connoting the "teamwork" of this couple, while working to disrupt their typical interactional routine.

In the following excerpt (from session 6), we work diligently and persistently to get the wife to assert herself and find her own voice. Notice how the husband puts responsibility for change on his wife's shoulders and how we deal with him in providing the opportunity for the wife to state her own needs. What is important in this excerpt is the idea that the therapist must be focused and persistent in moving toward the goal. This sometimes requires what Minuchin and Fishman (1981) refer to as "increasing the intensity" of the interaction. By repeating the message in many different ways, we hope to have an impact on the troublesome interactional pattern and create the basis for new, more satisfying, patterns of interaction.

Just before the segment described, we asked the husband and wife to shift their seats so that they would be facing each other directly. This was done because both husband and wife were very effective in "triangling in" one or the other of the therapists, thereby avoiding direct contact with one another. They were instructed to talk with one another about their relationship.

Wife: I guess . . . I would say I don't know what the answer is. You are working hard. Sometimes I almost feel you have a compulsion to work all the time . . . and . . .

Husband: [*Interrupts to tell his wife he has to continue to work to get sales*] . . . but that's time away. How do you balance those things out, I don't know. . . .

Wife: I don't know what the answer is.

Co-Therapist: How do you feel not having the answer?

Wife: Frustrated.[*laughs*]

Husband: What's really important to me, as I have to spend so much time working so hard, is the support you give . . . preparing the meals, picking up my suit at the cleaners, the filling up of the car with gas. If I have to take the time to do that it's even less time with the family. [*He continues to talk about his need to put time into his work . . . while the wife sits and nods her head in agreement in rhythm to his comments.*] It's hard to know what it will take to get the sale and to build up loyal clients who will stick with you.

Co-Therapist [*to Wife*]: Work hard at finding the feelings, Mary.

Wife: One of the things I really wonder is if it will be any different five years from now. And I don't have the answer to that. I have the feeling that there's always a reason, a legitimate reason, for working yourself half to death. And by working yourself half to death you don't have time for the family or to get the exercise that the doctor told you to get.

Husband: Well, for the next three Wednesday nights, I've written in big letters "SWIM." It's in my schedule. [*He then goes into his "sales pitch" about his need to get business and to work hard.*]

Wife: I guess I should be very thankful that you've blocked in the swim time on Wednesday evenings.

Therapist: Mary, you've told Harold how you care about him. I think that's clear. Now talk to him about your own needs.

[*long silence*]

    Wife: I don't know really what to say . . . [*silence*] . . . except that I need more closeness and caring than I'm getting. [*Tears are visible.*] And that doesn't mean I don't appreciate the things you do for me, because I do. But sometimes it seems like "doing for" gets substituted for "being with."

    Husband: I know you suggested two things the other day that were good. [*inaudible*] In terms of your needs, what are some of the things I can do? How can you get me to a point that I can do things "with", rather than just "for"?

[*silence*]

    Wife: I'm backed up now against the fact that you need to be out selling.

    [*laughs*]

    Therapist: Try to be a little selfish, Mary . . . Just a little.

    Wife: I wish we had time to take a walk together. I wish we had time to sit and talk.

    Husband: We talked last night from 11:30 to 12:15 . . . and then I was up at 5:20 again.

    Wife: I know, you're killing yourself.

    Husband: But it was all good stuff [*referring to the talk of the night before*], it was a good time . . . and it was time "with."

    Wife: [*smiling*] Well, maybe that's the answer, to stay up till 11:30 at night.

    Husband: I did want to share some of the things I was doing on the Jones account. That's again time "with." . . . But, what I object to is that it's not just the time "with" but the quality of the time "with." [*Wife nods in agreement.*] It's very hard to come by in this day and age. . . .

    Co-Therapist: Mary, I think your part of the responsibility that the marriage is at stake is the trouble you have being clear about what you want and how to get it . . . putting that in the forefront. It's not just Harold's responsibility . . . but the difficulty you have struggling to sustain your own voice. You give out very easily.

    Wife: I guess I do. ﹑

    Husband: But she recognizes the economic ball game, too.

    Co-Therapist: That's the latest external crisis. It's real but it functions to prevent the two of you from sustaining (the level of intimacy you both seem to want).

[*The husband then talks about his uncle who needed to "restart his marriage all over again."*]

    Wife: Maybe somewhere, somehow we need to restart ours.

    Husband: It's just very, very hard. . . . As I was saying it was going very, very well when your mother died. We had a so-called common enemy and we teamed up. It was great, terrific.

Wife: Why does it take a crisis to make us function together?

Husband: We do function together, it's just that there are some things we have to get done within our own lives.

Therapist: Mary, I'm going to give you a message, okay? I want you to be tough, because I know there's that quality in you, but you hide it somewhere. It's hidden. I want it to come out, okay? It may seem like putting demands on Harold . . . but I want you to do it. It may not be possible to work it out, but I'd like you to try . . . talking about some of those things *you* want.

Co-therapist: Borrow a sliver of your mother [*who was described in an earlier session as a "tough-minded woman"*].

Wife: [*smiling*] I'm sure it's there, too, but I don't know how to say it.

Husband: What are some other concrete things you'd like me to be doing?

Wife: I don't know. I guess I feel frustrated about this weekend . . . having company on Sunday morning and then company on Sunday lunch and then having you go off for an appointment. I guess I swallowed some nasty words when you said you had to go into the office.

Husband: I do have to go in then.

Wife: I'm glad you're not going into the office on Saturday.

Husband: Well, what are other concrete things that I can do?

Wife: We can go out to dinner to celebrate your winning the contest.

Husband: But that's a one-shot deal. What about something on a regular basis?

Therapist [*to Wife*]: Tell Harold something you know is impossible but you want.

Wife: I want to go on a cruise . . . or take a trip to Quebec.

Co-Therapist: This lady can do it!

Husband: What is a reasonable time frame in which this can happen? What do we do about the kids?

Wife: And of course, that's another problem . . . that I don't want the kids with your mother.

Husband: [*throws up hands*] See . . . it's impossible!

Co-Therapist: It was supposed to be impossible. Harold, you can be helpful to Mary as she's struggling to find a little toughness in her voice. Would you be willing to do that?

Husband: I think she should ask for more than just a cruise . . . frankly.

Co-Therapist: Are you willing to help Mary get more of her own voice?

Husband: The best time I remember her . . .

Co-Therapist: [*interrupting*] Are you willing to help, Mary?

Husband: Let me just give you a quick sample. . . .

Co-Therapist: [*interrupting again*] I don't need that. I'm sure it would be on the point and useful, but I have something else for you to do if you're willing.

Husband: Yes.

Co-Therapist: What I've noticed is that you're trying to be incredibly helpful to Mary. You are giving her cues about this, this, and this. I think, it's a little paradoxical but, what would be most helpful would be if you resist. . . instead of being so helpful. She doesn't have anything to butt up against.

Work with this couple continued, on an intermittent basis, for another year, with the wife becoming better able to find her own voice and the husband making some changes in his own behavior. As this excerpt illustrates, the therapists had to be very persistent in disrupting this couple's well-intentioned but unsatisfying "routine," and helping them reestablish new and more satisfying interactional patterns. As the wife developed her own voice, she began to experience new options both for herself and in what she expected from her relationship with her husband.

Time-Effective Therapy: Maximizing the Therapeutic Encounter

> Psychotherapeutic success depends in part on congruence between expectations a patient brings to treatment and what actually occurs; hence shaping these expectations . . . enhances the effectiveness of short-term therapy.
> —Jerome D. Frank, in *Persuasion and Healing.*

Another way of expressing this congruence is that "brief therapy is a state of mind of the therapist and of the patient [in which] the time allotted to treatment is rationed. . . . Brief treatment might be more accurately described as 'time-sensitive,' 'time-effective,' or 'cost-effective' therapy" (Budman and Gurman 1988: 10, 6). The therapist serves as a catalyst to facilitate a process of change such that the client or family can "achieve the maximum benefit with the lowest investment of therapist time and patient cost, both financial and psychological" (6).

The therapist's attitude about change and expectations and optimism about how swiftly a desired result can be obtained have significant impact on the outcome of therapy. Studies suggest that clients will comply with the therapist's expectations about the length of treatment (Frank 1973). In 'addition, no evidence exists that more therapy is "better" or leads to more enduring outcomes.[6] The creation of a positive rather than negative self-fulfilling prophecy needs to guide the therapy. This will usher the client toward the desired change.

Nicholas Hobbs (1966), who was a pioneer in the development of an innovative model for the short-term milieu treatment of troubled youngsters (Project Re-ED), reports, "The expectation of a prolonged stay in a treatment center becomes a self-validating hypothesis. A newly admitted child asks: 'How long do kids stay here?' He is told 'about two years,' and he settles down to do what is expected of him . . . [as do the] staff and parents who also 'know' that it takes two years to help a disturbed child. Myriad other constraints get established . . . [which lock-in this expectation]" (Hobbs 1966: 248–49). It is important, therefore, to approach the therapeutic process with a set of expectations that favor explicit optimism about change.

How do we maximize the time we have with the client? At many human-service agencies, resources are limited, yet the number of people requesting service continues to climb. In addition, clients do not stay in treatment very long (Budman & Gurman 1988). How then do we rapidly shape the client's expectations such that they begin to understand and accept the therapist's role as catalyst or coach in the therapeutic process and their role as an active agent of change? We can effectively reduce the client's dependency by defining our role—right from the start—as facilitative and consultative, not curative. We communicate our belief directly to clients that the paths to reaching their goals lie within their repertoire of skills and their network of resources. We do this, first, by using the possibility-frame question and, second, by pointing out examples of skills and competencies the client used in the past that will aid the client now.

From the beginning, we encourage the client to move out into the world to experiment with his or her new learnings. While we are here to help create the potential for a positive outcome, we are not here to sit with clients as they take each small step toward change. As soon as the client is able (and sometimes before the client *thinks* he or she is able), we encourage and support movement in the client's life context.

We typically see clients on an intermittent basis rather than weekly and allow them to decide when to schedule the next appointment and when to "terminate" their contacts with us. Putting scheduling under the clients' control shows respect for their judgment and their inner timetable. Many times clients opt for less frequent contact than we would have predicted. "You don't know how long the patient will need to digest the new material. It could be a day or week or whatever. So you need not see patients on a rigid schedule. It is best to let them call when they need to. A therapist should have flexibility in his schedule to accommodate the patients' needs" (Erickson and Rossi 1979: 382). In addition, we do not accept the sacredness of the fifty-minute hour, but see people for shorter or longer periods as necessary.

Client-initiated phone calls between regular sessions are also a useful medium for brief therapeutic interventions and can be incorporated into an ongoing treatment plan. Having scheduled "call-in" times allows clients to self-regulate contact while providing a known time when you will be available. Such telephone contacts can be used to support the client in managing a difficult situation and can replace a face-to-face visit. For example, during one call-in time, a client I [MTF] had seen six months before, called me, saying "Margot, I have to see you!" to which I replied, "Tell me what its about, Susan." She did, and I said, "So what questions would I ask you?" She told me and I said "So what answers would you give me?" She told me, then we both laughed and she hung up.

In possibility-oriented therapy, we prescribe the fewest number of sessions possible. These first sessions may be followed by other brief treatments, intermittently over time, if needed. The ultimate goal continues to be catalyzing the client's resources so that he or she can function well independently of the therapist. Therapy, rather than a continuous process with a fixed ending, is an open-ended process in which the client is free to return for further consultations, if needed. "Once we [abandon] cure as a goal, [we define] our problem as doing what we can to make a small social system work in a reasonably satisfactory manner" (Hobbs 1966: 246). This does presuppose clients with resources robust enough to sustain independence. There are clients for whom some kind of ongoing support is required to maintain function. With these clients, we remain available as needed, while facilitating the development of other support structures (such as continuing care groups or day treatment; see Sabin 1978).

The possibility-oriented therapist always starts with the expectation of working briefly. However, it is sometimes necessary to introduce other (adjunctive) treatment options (for example, group therapy or the judicious use of medication) and/or to be involved with a client on an intermittent basis over a longer period of time. Even in a situation where a person is actively psychotic, the possibility-oriented approach can be effective, once the psychotic process is contained. Rather than using criteria that screen people out as candidates for therapy, as some brief therapists do (Mann, Sifneos), or look for "contraindications," we always begin inclusively. By so doing, we engage the client in a way that supports, evokes, and respects the client's strengths and capabilities—irrespective of past history or current predicament.

Since life requires continuing accommodations and changes, the idea and "ideal" of termination is a myth (Budman 1990). As Frank points out, "the chances of finding therapeutic methods that will confer permanent and total immunity to life stresses are remote" (1968: 386). A colleague of ours [Richard Fitzpatrick, Ph.D.] has suggested a useful way to think about termination. He asks the client the following question: "Do you think you've learned enough how to approach the changes you want to make? Let me know if you need something else." As we will see in chapter 11, clients may need to return for "tune-ups" or "booster sessions" (Green & Herget 1989b) to help them continue the positive effects of the original treatment. In addition, with certain clients (see illustrations in chapters 10 and 12), several brief phases of therapy may be necessary in reaching the goal.

Pitfalls and Pratfalls (and Ways to Avoid Them)

While our previous experiences ground and enrich our practice, they also interfere with our abilities to do an effective possibility-oriented interview. We can find ourselves tracking some interesting hypotheses about the etiology of the problem, gathering lots of historical information, or getting very "problem-focused." In doing so, we are more likely to lose sight of or ignore the strengths and capacities of the client system for rapid change. We have outlined below ways to avoid several possible pitfalls and pratfalls that can obstruct rapid change (see Haley 1969; O'Hanlon and Wilk 1987; and O'Hanlon and Weiner-Davis 1989, for further discussion of these issues).

Define Observable Goals

Clients often have only unclear or vague ideas of what they want from therapy. We need to help the client to be quite specific in his or her wishes and hopes for treatment. Unless you and the client both know where you are headed, it is likely that you both will end up spending a great deal of time in unproductive pursuit of some vague and unspecified outcome.

It is all too easy to lose sight of both the client's request and the outcome or goal, while you focus on explanation and interpretation. "What gets reinforced and supported is the notion that openness and expression of feelings in the therapist's office—rather than movement in the real world of the client—will lead to . . . [problem resolution]"

(Friedman 1984: 24). The therapist's job is to get the client to translate his or her request into functional and behavioral terms that can be used as markers as the client moves towards attainment of his goals. We do a great injustice to our clients as well as to the profession of psychotherapy by supporting the idea of a vague, mysterious, and ineffable process that creates change. It is the brief therapist's obligation to provide a coherent structure of goals in terms that provide a clear and understandable pathway to resolution.

Developing and maintaining a clear definition of the client's request also allows us the opportunity to assess our results. At present, governmental agencies, employer groups, insurance companies, and consumers are demanding increased accountability in the utilization of mental health services. There is increased interest in the kinds of outcomes one can expect in dealing with various problems. In moving psychotherapy into the twenty-first century, we must increasingly take assessment of outcome seriously. By so doing we will be better able to examine our therapeutic endeavors, "discard[ing] approaches which are not effective and . . . elaborat[ing on] those that are" (Haley 1969: 694).

Keep Your Attention Goal-Directed

It is easy to get deflected from a specific focus as clients present many ideas and topics for discussion. However, our interaction with clients is not a social situation. Psychotherapy can easily become a voyeuristic process (Whitaker and Bumberry 1988) in which feelings and thoughts are shared by one person, who talks, while another asks questions and listens. The therapist must keep in mind that his role is not to "just make conversation" but also to structure the interaction to move it towards a specified outcome. By taking an active orientation, with a clear focus and goals for change, the therapy process is made more objective, useful, and ethically efficacious.

As we mentioned in an earlier chapter, the therapy process, at its most basic, is a "linguistic event." The therapist manages this event by helping the client move *beyond* the problem into a new realm in which the problem becomes part of the past. By keeping your focus on the goal, both you and the client are more likely to effect rapid, constructive change.

Explore Novel Alternatives and Support What Works

By finding out what your client has already tried in coping with the situation, you can gain two sources of useful information. First, you may find some rich avenues for potential solutions that can be supported and amplified; and when you do—these solutions can be attributed to the client. Second, you can track those attempts that have not worked and help the client "let go" of these to pursue other, potentially more productive pathways. By knowing what advice others have offered, you can begin to eliminate those pathways that have been tried unsuccessfully. We take special interest in the advice that significant people in the family system have given the client and how such advice has been used or not used by the client. By listening closely to the client's feelings about previously suggested ideas for change, you can expand or enlarge the client's "idea pool" of change possibilities as well as your understanding of the client's world.

Use Language Mindfully

As we discussed previously, the way we talk about a situation affects how we think and feel about that situation. If we focus on describing people in static, diagnostic terms, we may be taking part in a process of creating ("reifying") the very "pathology" we seek to transform.

Gallop, Lancee, and Garfinkel studied the impact of diagnostic labels on the "empathic" responses of a group of psychiatric nurses. When a set of hypothetical clients were diagnosed as having a "borderline personality disorder," the nurses tended to express less empathy and offered more "belittling" comments than they did to other clients. The authors concluded that by calling someone "borderline," one influences, in a rather negative way, the "helping" responses of professionals. "The diagnosis of borderline personality disorder may have become a negative stereotypic category that precedes the patient and sets the tone for subsequent interaction" (1989: 819).

Be a Clean Slate with Each New Client

In graduate school many of us learned about the importance of carefully studying previous case material and talking with previous therapists before seeing someone in treatment. It is thought that one can develop in this way a potentially valuable historical perspective. Such "historical material" can also skew your perceptions to such an extent that both the power of your entrance into the therapeutic arena and your leverage in creating change are reduced and undermined by your limiting assumptions.

Just as clients bring their unique perspectives to treatment, previous therapists also viewed reality through an assortment of lenses. While the perspectives of previous therapists may be interesting and potentially useful, you must be careful to not accept them as factual. Rather, keep in mind that each is simply a reflection of the unique viewpoint of a particular therapist. As the current therapist, you must allow yourself the opportunity to develop your own unique perspective, unencumbered (or minimally encumbered) by the "realities" of others.

Intervene Quickly to Establish Feedback

Overemphasizing historical data is one hazard, overcollecting current data is another. Do not fear intervening prematurely. The only way to find the proper start-point is to intervene and then use the client's response as feedback to formulate your next move.

One exercise that I [SF] have found useful in teaching family therapy is to instruct students, after about five minutes of information gathering with a simulated family, to begin to interact with that "family" without asking any questions. It is amazing to see how much more involved and how effective these therapists become by actively intervening in the family system without recourse to questions. While we're not suggesting that you stop asking questions, it is important not to hide behind questions as a means to avoid intervening. Tomm (1987) and others (such as Furman & Ahola 1988; Lipchik & deShazer 1986; Penn 1982) have discussed the usefulness of questions that move the family to think about reality in new ways. This is different from asking questions to gather more traditional "diagnostic" information.

In addition, too much information can feel overwhelming and may incapacitate your ability to take action. By structuring the therapeutic conversation and breaking problems down into manageable chunks, you can avoid getting lost in that garden of fascinating content that may impede your seeing the most direct paths to resolution.

A further danger in gathering masses of information lies in the temptation to try to connect such pieces of information and draw perhaps spurious conclusions. Much time can be wasted hypothesizing about past "causes" rather than focusing on a future with increased choice of actions.

The Treatment Process: An Example

The following excerpts from a series of family interviews provide a firsthand view of the possibility-oriented approach (see table 5–1 for an overview of the basic principles that guide the treatment strategies). Notice, in particular how the first interview is structured to emphasize and build on the already existing strengths and resources in the family and how the therapist works persistently to shift the parents' view of their son's behavior.

Table 5–1.
Guiding Principles and Clinical Strategies in Brief
Possibility-oriented Therapy[a]

Principles	Strategies
1. Think small.	Try simple interventions first, based on simple assumptions.
2. Complicated situations do not necessarily require complicated solutions.	Focus on solutions; what works rather than what doesn't work.
3. The client's request must be taken seriously and given primary attention.	Engage the client, and maintain a focus on the original request.
4. Cooperation and collaboration between therapist and client create a context for change.	Insist that the client be an active partner in solution development.
5. The therapist "negotiates with" the client in producing clearly defined steps to a specified goal.	Frame complaints in forms which are solvable. Be active, flexible, and focused. Use possibility language as a medium for creating change.
6. "Brief therapy is most successful when the client is persuaded to do just one thing differently."[b]	Work to get a small change going. Create a context in which novelty or playfulness can be introduced.
7. Contained within the client (family) are the seeds of solution development.	Focus on resources and strengths. Empower the client or family as change agents. Respect and support client creativity in developing solutions.
8. Change is inevitable; All clients/ families undergo developmental transitions and crises.	Normalize developmental transitions; Reframe difficulties in a developmental context.
9. Supportive client networks increase options for change.	Involve networks of support in the treatment process.
10. The therapist needs to maintain a sense of optimism, naivete and playfulness in clinical interaction.	Cultivate a sense of humor and a respect for the "benign absurdity of life."[c]

Source: [a]This table is adapted from Friedman, 1989b.
  [b]Weick, 1984, p. 45.
  [c]Whitaker, 1976, p. 164.

Initial Interview

All I [SF] knew about the family was contained in the referral form from the child's pediatrician, which said "eleven-year-old boy, rebellious, defies authority; problems have moved from home into school life; school and parents request counseling." The family consists of the parents (Jack and Jane) and their four children (Mark [4]; Janice [6]; Ben [11]; and Jim [14]). In this initial interview, all six family members are present. Notice how, right from the beginning, the therapist tries to emphasize positive change and to focus on the positive side of father's statements.

> *Therapist:* What were you hoping to accomplish by coming here today?
> *Father:* Well, . . . the school counselor identified a negative pattern . . . we met with him a few times and read a book on behavior modification . . . but it wasn't so helpful since it wasn't specific behaviors we wanted to modify, but more of an "attitude" problem that was hard to define. At any event, the idea of reinforcing the positive, . . . we thought that things would improve. He had a very positive summer in athletics.
> *Therapist:* What made it so positive?
> *Father:* We joined the track team, and Ben displayed some real talent in this.
> *Therapist [to Ben]:* You're a fast runner?
> *Ben: [nods in agreement]*
> *Father:* Ben is getting faster than me now. . . . So he did very, very well and got a lot of positive support from this . . . he is very talented at sports. He does really well at this. Academically, he's done ok . . . it's more of an attitudinal thing at school.
> *Therapist:* His grades are ok?
> *Father:* All of his grades are satisfactory with a couple of commendables.

[*When the therapist tries to focus on Ben's strengths, the parents interrupt and Ben gets defiant.*]

> *Therapist: [to Ben]:* What are you doing especially well at?
> [*The father answers*]. . . . in mathematics and in gym.
> *Ben:* No.

[*The father is the family historian, sharing background information.*]

> *Father:* Last year was a stressful year, Jane went back to work, the first time after many years and she was looking forward to it. I think it stretched her out a bit. I got very involved in a number of things outside of work, and at the end of year we both came to an agreement, mostly due to Jane's perception that we were both a bit stretched . . . so I made a commitment to reduce some of these things, and Jane left her job. We thought we would have a good shot at a good year; and after one or two months the behavior started to exhibit itself without any obvious, easily identifiable provocation, and the behavior exhibits itself in an outstanding ability to defy any authority whatever it may be, teacher, parent, coach, any area that might be directing him.
> *Therapist:* Do you have anything to add to what your husband has said?

Mother: I wanted to blame the problems on a personality clash between the teacher and Ben, but I realized there was more than that. There's some basic something that is causing this behavior.

Father: What seems apparent is that all the normal conscientious attempts have not solved the problem, so I would like to do whatever we have to and really follow through to get this resolved as much as possible. The school sees some real potential danger here. We'd like to do whatever we can now to make things better.

[*At this point, the therapist turns to the children and questions them about school and other activities. His conversation with the children serves as a way to increase their involvement in the session. He then returns to a focus on "exceptions" to the problem.*]

Therapist: Tell me about the first couple of months of school, the time you were saying things were going well; what was going well— what was working in the way you'd like things to work?

Father: Well . . . things were going well in that we weren't getting bad reports from school.

Therapist: And what about at home during that period . . . were you satisfied about how things were going?

Mother: Pretty much. We had a bad incident at the end of the summer when Ben ran away from home for a few hours . . . that upset me quite a bit. It seems to go in cycles. Things will go fairly smoothly, and then we have an incident almost out of nowhere, the last one was just before Thanksgiving.

Therapist: How would you describe what happened?

Mother: Another blowup . . . basically between Ben and myself. I got a call from Ben's teacher that he was behaving very badly in school that week and when he came home I sent him to his room . . . and then there some disagreement. [*She describes incident.*] He was very defiant to me, outrageously defiant and I threatened to punish him some more. He made some comment like "You're afraid to punish me."

Therapist: He was being very provocative.

Mother: Yes, "provocative" is the right word.

Father: Then Jane went out for a while and then came back and tried to calm herself down, but felt she had to go up and discipline him, so she has a small belt she uses . . .

Mother: Only on rare occasions . . .

Father: . . . he grabbed the belt and hit her with it.

Ben: She threw a book at me.

Mother: This was the last big incident.

[*The therapist again looks for* exceptions *to the presenting problem.*]

Therapist: How do things go between these incidents?

Mother: Fairly smoothly, . . . but there's always the undercurrent . . . always an edge. He won't conform to the family rules on a regular basis. It depends on his mood. There are days he will be anxious to please and others when he won't.

[*At this point in the interview the parents are taking the position that the "good" times are not related to their efforts or input and solely reflect Ben's "moods."*]

Therapist: [to the father]: Are there ever incidents between you and Ben?

Father: Not as frequently. Once in a while if he's in a mood he won't do what I want him to do, but usually he will know that I'm very, very serious about something he will go along with it, but I can relate to Jane's frustrations. She's with him more than I am. When I am with him for long periods and he's in a mood, and after he subtly if not directly ignores you or defies you . . . after three or four times . . . and you try to bend over backwards . . . he can get to you . . . but in general we don't get into that.

[*In the following segment the therapist brings in the notion of Ben "taking the parents seriously," another way of saying "not defying authority."*]

Therapist: So he takes you seriously?

Mother: He takes Jack much more seriously than he does me.

Therapist: What do you make of that? How do you understand that?

Mother: He's around less. I would like to think if the roles were reversed he'd give Jack as much flack as he does me . . . but I don't know that.

[*Father describes the impact of his wife's working outside the home.*]

Father: Jane likes a neat organized home, and working didn't allow her to keep to those standards . . . she didn't have as much energy . . . she was more short-tempered . . . and I was out of the house more than usual.

Mother: And that was a source of friction between the two of us. I felt like a single parent . . . many times.

Therapist: So that's now changed?

Father: I'm sure Jane would still say I'm still spending too much time out.

Mother: It's much better . . . but only after much . . . it wasn't an easy change . . . he wanted his way.

Father: I was hoping it would go away.

[*Notice how the therapist moves away from this potential marital issue but then uses the issue of mother taking father seriously in moving towards the original goal.*]

Therapist [to the mother]: Tell me, you were obviously successful with your husband regarding his involvement in all these outside activities and were able to impact on that. What do you think is getting in the way of doing this with Ben?

Mother: I wish I knew that. I wish Jack would take me more seriously at times. Yes, I was able to persuade him on that one issue. Ben is a different story. I don't understand . . . that's something I was hoping you could help us with.

Father: I've seen Ben take on his mother and create trouble after his mother has gone out of her way, on that day or the day before, doing things for him, buying things for him.

Mother: The school psychologist said he thinks there was an impartial bonding between me and Ben, at some point, which I don't understand. To my knowledge, I did the best I could with each one equally. Maybe he's right, but I don't understand it.

Father: The school psychologist sees Ben's behavior as a way of getting attention, negatively hooking people in, as a way of keeping a bonding.

[*The mother, after listening to the school psychologist, has come to accept the problem as having to do with her and Ben; something she did wrong when he was a baby. And father supports this hypothesis. The therapist rejects this thinking and redirects the interview.*]

Therapist: I don't agree with that.

Mother: You don't?

Therapist: I don't find looking at the past . . . what did or didn't happen . . . as helpful or useful. There's still a lot of old thinking around about these things, but modern thinking has rejected that. You can hypothesize and speculate forever on what might have gone wrong or whatever, without ever getting anywhere useful.

Mother: I'm glad to hear that.

Therapist: We need to start from where we are and build on some of the good things that are already happening. It's very clear to me that both of you have been very involved with the kids in their activities, in their school work, and that's had some payoff, both in their schoolwork and outside of school with their sports and other activities. So this is a circumscribed problem, not something that occurs on a daily basis, is that correct?

Mother: Yes, but there is always that undercurrent of tension that something may happen. Will he do what I ask him to do or not?

Father: I worry too, for example, that I will get a call from the rabbi that Ben is acting up.

[*The therapist again redirects the interview to when things are going well.*]

Therapist: Are there times when things go well and there are no problems at the synagogue?

Father: Yes . . . there are days that work out like that.

Therapist: Do you have a sense of what's happening on those days that makes this happen?

Father: No.

Therapist: The fact that there are those good days or times when things go well, there's something in that, that can be learned from and built on, and it's a question of trying to focus in on what's happening at those times that makes things go well.

[*The father describes Ben as "an active kid [who] likes the outdoors, doesn't like to be constrained . . . that's why school, synagogue are difficult for him."*]

Therapist: So what would tell you that things were on a more positive track? How would you know that things are just a little bit better? What would be a small positive change?

Father: Things can start off right in the morning with Ben not making his bed the way he knows how to do it . . . the first sign in the morning.

Therapist: Does that help predict his behavior for the rest of the day?

Father: No . . . we haven't been that clever yet . . . to figure this out.

In the next segment, the therapist, after complimenting the family, lays out several tasks to help the parents begin to see the positive impact of their efforts on Ben's behavior and begin to notice when things are going well at home (including when Ben takes mother seriously). The therapist prescribes a "prediction task" (after Molnar & deShazer 1987), which is described below.

Therapist: Let me tell you, I think that you've been working very hard, to get things right and do right by all the kids.

Mother: Thank you, I appreciate that.

Therapist: It's very clear, the efforts you've been putting in here. I'd like for you to think about several things between now and the next time we meet that I think will be helpful. For one, I'd like you to think about what's happening now in the family that you would like to have continue to have happen. [*I repeat this as the father writes down the instructions in a little book.*] The other thing is each evening individually make a prediction about how things will go the next day with Ben. Do this independently. And then check out what happens, does the day go well or not and how do you account for what's happening? Do this separately so we'll have two sets of predictions. For example, if you predict that Ben will have a good day, and he does have a good day, make a note on what made this possible. Also, please have the teacher and school psychologist call me.

One additional thing I would suggest for you [*to the mother*], is to keep track of times when Ben *does* take you seriously and follows through in the way you would like him to. And think about and jot down if you can what is happening at those times, what are you doing, that helps Ben take you seriously. I'll get my schedule so that we can set up another meeting.

A meeting is scheduled for two weeks later, and the parents report significant improvement in Ben's behavior, although they doubt it will last. The following excerpt is from the third meeting, four weeks after the initial session.

The Third Meeting

Therapist: It's been just about two weeks since we've met. What have you noticed? I can see you both have your notebooks. Before you look in there, can you tell me if there were any surprises?

Mother: I would say things have been pretty much on an even keel since we met last. No big surprises or disappointments.

Therapist: Are you saying that things are as they were when you were here last?

Mother: Yes.

[*Knowing how faithful the parents have been in doing their homework, the therapist teases them about being so compliant.*]

Therapist: And what have you been predicting? Or did you throw that idea out the window? You know you don't have to do everything I tell you.

[*laughs.*]

[*I turn to Ben and ask "Do you do everything that anybody tells you?*]

Ben: No.

Therapist: I didn't think so.

Mother: Once I predicted "not good" but then it turned out okay. Usually [*school*] vacation weeks—I tend to find those are more difficult.

Therapist: So you were expecting it to be more difficult and it turned out that it wasn't.

Mother: I turned out okay. I had predicted for Friday "not good" because nothing specific was planned for him [*Ben*], but it worked out.

[*In the next excerpt the therapist focuses on the positive changes that have occurred.*]

Father: They're all [*the children*] very conscious that they're coming here, and when he [*Ben*] sees us writing in our little notebooks he's very curious. He usually asks what we're writing in there.

Therapist: But you don't tell him?

Father: No.

Ben: I've tried to read his sometimes but I can't read his writing.

[*laughter all around*]

Mother: Have you tried to read mine?

Ben: I don't know where you put yours.

[*The father describes being "surprised" that things are going well for Ben in light of the fact that he has had a less successful experience in sports over the past few weeks.*]

Father: He seems to have handled that very well. He seems to have accepted that he's not the best in every sport.

Therapist: Some kind of change has happened here. Ben has done better than you were expecting, which is very good.

Father: And he had done well at synagogue.

[*Ben tells how he brings a book with him which helps him tolerate the long service.*]

Therapist: Tell me a little bit about where you think we need to go from here . . . what your thinking is at this point.

Mother: I'd like to see more communication with the school . . . to get a better idea about whether this is going to be a lasting type of thing.

Therapist: That's the big question at this point. It has been a month, which is a good period of time, but there is still the question of will things continue the way they've been going. Something has changed and we need to figure out what it is that's working so we can keep it working. What I suggest is that you look, try to come up with some ideas, about what it is that's working that you want to continue to work. So the question is what are you doing that's helping things go well. There's always going to be a bad morning, here and there . . . that's going to happen.

But more important is to keep track of those mornings that do go well and try to figure out what you're doing, what's happening that's helping things go well when people leave the house in a positive frame of mind. . . . I would also be happy to have contact with the school psychologist.

Mother: I was wondering if you looked at that report that he wrote. Those tests scores were hard to understand.

[*The therapist gets the report out of his file and reviews it; the report talks about Ben being "very angry," "impulsive", etc.; The therapist uses this as an opportunity to disqualify the negative implications of*] *the report and empower the parents as the people who know Ben best.*]

Therapist: I don't put much weight in these structured tests. They're very artificial. I find I can have a better sense of things by talking with you who really know Ben best. Those tests are set up so that you can barely come out looking okay on them.

Mother: That's very encouraging to me.

Therapist: These tests end up describing people in very negative ways and I don't find that very helpful, and it's drawing conclusions based on minimal information—I don't put much validity in all that.

Mother: Well, good . . . good. I'm glad.

Gentle Persistence

The following excerpt takes place toward the end of treatment, as the therapist tries to help the parents separate the issues they were originally concerned about from Ben's unique personality, which differs from their other three children.

Father: We were hoping we could turn him around now . . . get him in with the flow [*be like the other three children who are very compliant*].

Therapist: The one thing that will not happen is that he is not going to be like your other three kids. And he's not going to fit into the family like the other three. He's got his own unique personality. He's always going to stand out as somewhat different. That's a given. There's no way he can be made over to fit in that mold.

[*The parents talk about the potential they see for Ben to excel in his academic work rather than devoting so much energy into non–school related activities such as sports or playing with friends.*]

Therapist: He may have to find his own way, in a different way from the others. He seems more at odds with the family style. So it does require compromises on your parts, while at the same time, he does have to make some adaptations to both home and school. He's stubborn and when forced to adapt, he digs in his heels and says "I'm my own person and I won't be pushed around by this."

Father: What brought us here was the more dramatic cyclical problem and it seemed like this pretty much has been resolved. The gap between episodes is fairly large and we are focusing in the therapy on . . . that we are doing something right, let's keep doing what's right and focus on that. Although the major cyclical crisis has either stopped or they've become more distant. We still have the day-to-day rebellious attitude.

Therapist: Yes. But what you tend to overlook is that you're handling it relatively well on most occasions. Ben's wanting to run out of the house without his coat is part of his own personality style, and you are going to have to put out that extra energy and effort into containing him, in contrast to your other three who are more compliant.

Father: "Gently persistent" is the mode I try. He's got to know you'll hold the line but without getting him to dig his heels in.

Therapist: Yes.

A series of twelve meetings were held, over an eight-month period, with this family. Although still occasionally oppositional at school, Ben's behavior was no longer a major source of concern.

This material shows a therapist maintaining a positive set and complimenting the parents on their already successful efforts with their children. Building on the parents' strengths, he supports their competence to deal effectively with their son. Although the parents tend to look at the son's behavior pessimistically, the therapist persists in redirecting their focus to those aspects of the situation that are going well. He provides them with a homework assignment at the first session that enables them to begin redirecting their attention to "exceptions" to the problem. By asking them to look at these positive aspects of their son, a different view of his behavior and its meaning develops.

Conclusions

In possibility-oriented therapy the answer to the question "What do you want?" produces a statement of the goal, and the answer to "How will you know when you get it?" specifies the evidence that will herald the desired result. The question "What stops you from having that now?" pinpoints the place where the change needs to occur; where the pattern needs to be "unstuck"; the answer also gives you information for treatment strategy design. In possibility-oriented therapy, the operational definition of the process of treatment is that the therapist must (1) achieve and maintain rapport and joining; (2) not behavioral patterns; (3) strategically interrupt these patterns so that (4) the client will see the situation in a new way (shift world images), and thus (5) gain new options for effective action.

Notes

1. There are many possible opening questions within the possibility frame; for example: How would you like your life to be different as a result of therapy? What could you do to change things? If you could develop a new skill or feel different in a situation you don't enjoy now, or change some part of your behavior, what would that be? What do you want to change? What do

you need to do? What would you like to do that you can't do now? How did you decide that now is the time to change? What is your agenda?

2. Katz (1975); Rossi (1986); Masterpasqua (1989); McClelland (1989); Norris (1989); and Kobasa (1990); all cite the importance of autonomy/agency/ competence/coping skills for achieving and maintaining therapeutic change.

3. Golden Triad Films, Inc., 100 Westport Square, 4200 Pennyslvania, Kansas City, MO (R. Corrales & R. Price, Editors).

4. See discussion in chapter 2 and bibliography of *Language of Change*.

5. Heinz von Foerster, personal communication at Mental Research Institute Conference, 1985.

6. For examples, see Frank, (1973); Fisher (1980, 1984); Seeman, Tittler, and Friedman (1985); and Budman and Gurman (1988).

Part III
Strategies for Change:
Running the Rapids

Part II
Strategies for Change:
Running the Rapids

6
Clinical Strategies With Individuals, Couples and Groups

Psychotherapy can be practised in a variety of ways, from psychoanalysis, or something of that kind, to hypnotism, and so on right
down to cataplasms of honey and possets of bat's dung. Successes
can be obtained with them all. So at least it appears on a superficial view. On closer inspection, however, one realizes that the
seemingly absurd remedy was exactly the right thing, not for this
particular neurosis, but for this particular human being, whereas, in
another case it would have been the worst thing possible.
—C.G. Jung

A master gardener has many tools and skills to use in her garden;
she knows how to cultivate, nourish, support, prune, train,
water, and weed the plants in her care. She learns the nature of
each plant and plans her garden in relation to the various needs of the
many different plants. Often she tries different methods to encourage
each plant to develop its own beauty, for some need more shade and
some more sun, some more water, and some more space; she experiments until she gets the right combination to get the plant to grow,
thrive, and bloom.

Clients offer us magnificent gardens to cultivate, the gardens of
their own inner resources. These gardens, to be developed and expanded, reside in the client's imagination. What we can ask their imagination to achieve is limited only by our own flexibility and
inventiveness. When we help the client to alter internal images, the
conscious mood may also shift. A young woman came to me requesting
a change in the way that she felt when her father spoke to her. Whatever he said, she felt attacked. When I asked her to be more specific,
she said that it was "like he was machine-gunning her." She was
looking up and off in the distance as she reported this, apparently
visualizing him. She confirmed this, and then when I suggested that she

substitute pink marshmallows for the machine-gun bullets, she smiled broadly. When she returned for her second and last appointment, she described pleasant interactions with her father, ascribing the change to "seeing those pink marshmallows." This simple suggestion allowed her to reframe and so change her world image of her father such that she can smile rather than cringe when he speaks to her.

All clinical strategies are designed to reframe by changing world images.

So how do you choose your clinical strategy? By attending to what you have learned about your client as well as by responsibly conserving resources of time, energy, and money. In other words, you take all that information you gleaned by joining, calibrating, and empathizing and put it together with the client's well-constructed outcome. You continue with your own observation of his patterns noting where they need interrupting, and then choose a strategy from your collection that could most economically achieve that outcome. You look for the most succinct "cataplasm of honey" for each client, an intervention that will create an imagistic shift, so that, seeing the world in a new way, he will be able to act in new ways as well.

In the pages that follow we will take a closer look at just how you negotiate such shifts. There are two main categories of intervention that produce these transformative reframes, or *restructuring of images*. In one category you *verbally restructure* the client's images by giving directions for internal processing. This means that you change images through comparison, by using either right-brain imagistic language, as, for example, with the pink marshmallows, or by blocking left-brain language, with paradox, illusion of choice, and the like. The other category is *behavioral restructuring*, which you do by giving instructions for new external actions, often as a task assignment to be completed between sessions. Both of these categories are utilized in the illustrations throughout the rest of the chapter. All of the clinical examples come from MTF's practice, and they include individuals, couples and groups.[1]

Verbal Restructuring of Images

> Psychotherapy is fundamentally the art of changing a person's view of reality.
> —Paul Watzlawick

Clients generally *feel* their difficulties internally as they describe them.

What they need is a new perspective that can, at least momentarily, dissociate them from the situation and allow them to *see* it in a new way. Both reframing or relabeling and humor can produce this effect, as they break up the client's "rigid and limiting mental sets," if only briefly. Be constantly mindful of chances to use reframing and word-play or humor from the very beginning and throughout the therapy. When the depressed teacher mentioned in the chapter on the initial evaluation was describing her eye exam to me and complaining about the cold manner of her ophthalmalogist, the client smiled when I said, "You mean you wished she had a different 'outlook.' " With another woman who was describing a life-changing revelation that she had experienced while hiking in the mountains, I commented that it was truly a peak experience. I invariably have the goal of getting my clients to laugh during each session; and the more depressed they are, the more important this becomes.

Relabeling or reframing often has the flavor of wordplay. Here are some examples:

> I'm a perfectionist. // You can always see chances for improvement.
> I'm obsessed with food. // You have good powers of concentration.
> I'm too anxious. // Vigilance is appropriate in some places.
> I'm confused. // That gives you a chance to learn something new.
> I'm disorganized. // You see many opportunities at once.
> When he criticizes me, I feel bad. // You like others to feel good.
> When she smiles, I don't trust her. // You learn from experience.
> She's always picking men who are losers. // She's highly selective.

After demonstrating such reframes with a client, you can then begin to teach them how to do it for themselves. When they say something self-critical or "stuck," you ask "What's another way you could describe that?"

There are reframes that can be more than a simple pattern inter-ruption, and they generally involve adjusting the client's world picture by juxtaposing two values that had not been linked in the client's mind. For example, a young woman came to me requesting help in dealing with her ambivalence about getting pregnant. Her parents, who were Holocaust survivors, implied that she was not a "good daughter" because she had married a non-Jew. After discussion, she decided that to be a 'good daughter,' she should get pregnant and be happy with the life she had to live rather than dwelling on the past. As part of her redefining "good" she planned also to write a history of her family. She shifted her point of focus from the past to the future.

In another case, a shy young man who wished to be more outgoing, said, as an example of his shyness, that he was not able to ask questions at lectures; he thought it would be "selfish" of him to waste other peoples' time. When I asked him how he felt about other people asking questions at lectures, he said that was fine since he always learned something. When I then asked him if it were not "selfish" of him to deprive others of learning something new by his not asking questions, he flushed and agreed. His flush told me that the reframe had had a strong effect, for when we make associations in our area of difficulty, we often feel anxious, an indication that the sympathetic nervous system is innervated. When your reframe or wordplay has struck a chord with clients, they often show it by flushing, a sign that they have switched on their more relaxed, parasympathetic nervous system.

Another young woman requested help with smoking cessation, but was sure it would be painful. As part of her new taking control of her life she was pleased to report that she had already started to exercise regularly. Her face lit up when I offered the idea that rather than being painful, giving up smoking could give her new pleasure as she "regularly exercised" control. Yet another client, this one a young singer with performance anxiety, found a dramatic shift in this anxiety when she started using her own performance standards rather than those of her father.

Clients who have physical symptoms that they wish to change often start that change when they are able to see their symptoms as an expression of imbalance in their interaction with their environment: a signal that they need to respond to or interact differently with elements in their daily lives. This initial reframe then sets the stage for them to transform their relationship to their symptoms so that they abate or clear up naturally. Clients readily offer metaphors that can be used for reframing. One woman with stomach cramps reported that she always "swallowed" her anger. Her stomach cramps began to diminish when she started acting on the idea that she needed to "chew people out" instead. Another example is that of a fifteen-year-old girl who was referred for cheek biting. After rapport was established, the question "Who do you want to bite?" led into a conversation about her father's not wanting her to grow up.

An additional reframe, that of discovering how clients' symptoms are taking care of them, becomes a central part of the process. *Finding the positive intention either behind a symptom or behind unwanted behavior is a crucial part of possibility-oriented therapy.* When this has been disclosed, new, more positive ways of satisfying that positive intention can be found. Clients so frequently want to excise an unwanted behavior or internal response. Our job is to help them either to find new, desirable behaviors to satisfy the positive intention embedded in the old behavior, or to help them develop new responses to old stimuli. Virginia Satir uses what she calls a "Parts Party" to create a transformative reframe (Satir & Baldwin 1983). The different forms of this technique often involve a group, but it can also be used with individuals as follows: have the client choose and name six or eight "parts" of himself; half that she likes and half that she doesn't. She can then imagine them sitting around a negotiating table working on improved relations with each other. She is then asked to say what each "part" does, what is its function. Next, she is to identify the negative aspect of the positive "parts" and the positive aspect of the negative "parts." Having seen that all her "parts" have both pluses and minuses, she then finds ways to get them to work together, thus altering her view of herself and her possibilities.

For example, one thirty-five-year-old woman had a "summery, lighthearted part" that she liked and a "stern mother part" that she didn't. She realized that if she played and danced all the time as the "summery part" would like her to, that she wouldn't further her career as a lawyer; her "stern mother part" had helped her accomplish a great deal professionally. She was then able to see these two "parts" of herself as complementary rather than at odds with each other—and that the "stern mother part" could feel renewed by the occasional dance. It is important to help clients to see that there is really no "part" of themselves that they need to (or can) get rid of; the goal is simply to see the positive aspect of the "unwanted parts" so that they can add their energy to the integrated whole.

So far we have been looking at verbal reframes that evoke new images for the client to compare and learn from as the meanings of the images are negotiated. Consider also the use of a literal reframe.[2] A woman in her fifties who wanted to change her defensive responses reported being criticized by a colleague to the extent that she felt unsure about how to interact with him in the future. I asked her to recall the scene and put a baroque gold frame around it and a little museum light shining on it. What she saw then was not that the colleague was criticizing her, but rather that he was hurt. Next, I asked her to now put her picture in the style of various artists until she found one that illuminated it further. She used Seurat, then Cezanne, and finally came to Picasso, which did the trick, because seeing the two of them in Cubist parts amused her. Finally, she was able to not only let go of her defensiveness, but to look at her feelings about him so that she could decide how to interact with him in the future. Of course, when you use this, any variation of frame type or setting can be used. Putting the framed picture on a wall with other pictures, as in a museum, can also improve perspective.

Reframing often works as it alters a client's view of past experience. As Jung wrote: "The childhood experience of a neurotic is not, in itself, negative; far from it. It only becomes negative when it finds no suitable place in the life and outlook of the adult" (1966:338). The technique of revising personal history puts childhood experience into "a suitable place in the outlook of the adult." To effect this change you ask the client to change her memories by first finding a seminal historical sequence, and then by getting her to bring her present increased resourcefulness to bear on these past memories. This helps her to see her history in a new way, which, in turn, can release her from the outdated response.

It is our belief that when stresses occur, a person responds as positively as possible, given the resources available at that moment. Such responses are frequently more purposive than rational, and a limiting response becomes habituated. So, the person continues to use the restricting response even though present capabilities make it obsolete. Taking a person back in time in her internal imagery, and having her redo the old sequence with the greater resources of adulthood, often breaks up the habitual, outworn response.

For example, a young woman came requesting help in being more assertive with her boss. When I asked her how she would know if she were more assertive, she answered that she would know when she could ask her boss not to look over her shoulder while she was working at her computer. What stopped her from doing that now was a feeling of paralysis and mounting tears that overwhelmed her when he looked over her shoulder. I asked her where she had learned this response. At first she said it was just automatic, she hadn't learned it anywhere. I told her that since not everyone has that response I believed she had learned it somewhere in her earlier life. I asked her to search her memory for another time where she had those particular feelings. She complied, and was surprised to find herself in the sixth grade, having trouble with fractions. Her father was most concerned about her academic performance and would watch over her shoulder while she did her math homework. He would explode when she made a mistake, and these sessions only ended when she burst into tears and couldn't continue. Having identified this seminal scene (one which formed a limiting image), I then asked her to think about the many resources she had now that she didn't have then—most especially competence, curiosity, and the ability to relax. I said that these current resources could enable her to get a new perspective on that old situation.

To make these resources vividly present for her, I asked her to think, sequentially and in detail, of situations where she had experienced each of these resource states recently. Next, I asked her to go back and play that old scene once more in her imagination, taking with her her "older self" as a counselor. If needed, the counselor was also to give her father the internal resources he needed to be able to respond differently. This "older self" would make sure that the scenario turned out differently, helping the "younger self" to do whatever was needed to accomplish that. When she had completed this in her internal imagery (she didn't talk during the process), she opened her eyes and smiled. I asked her what she had learned from this replay. She said that all of a sudden she realized that her father's upset was fueled by his strong hope that she would get the college education that he never had. (Please note that this tactic is not about excusing the father's behavior, but rather about simply looking at it in another way.) The "older self" had also advised the father so that he could calmly offer help.

I asked her to think about the next time that the boss would look over her shoulder and to notice how she would respond to him. Another smile heralded her report that she thought she could ask him to stop. (If this had not been the case, I would have asked her what else was needed, and we would have recycled this strategy or added another one, as needed, until she felt confident that she could ask him not to watch.)

Finally, I asked her to replay the revised scene in her mind frequently, making it as vivid as the old memory. When she returned, she reported that she had asked her boss not to watch, and that he had been apologetic, adding that he enjoyed watching her work "because she did it so well"—an interpretation that had never occurred to her. Thus, her world image was shifted or reframed, and she had a new choice of effective action. In another example, while using this pattern with a reserved thirty-four-year-old librarian, she discovered an "older self," which she named Vera, who was glamourous and "always told the truth." Thereafter, when she felt uncertain about what action to take, she would consult Vera who gave her immaculate advice that led to a flowering of choices.

There is a bumper sticker that exclaims "It's never too late to have a happy childhood!" The therapeutic method to accomplish that end is simply *revising personal history*. First, identify the current behavior or response that distresses the client. Then, ask the client to recall an earlier time, or the earliest time, that she had this response. (Where did you learn that? Has this happened to you before?) If client has difficulty recalling such a time, ask her to close her eyes and "play her life backwards like a newsreel" until she encounters that same distressing feeling. If the client says she isn't able to visualize, ask her to imagine it, or *to make it up*. (Everyone has a way of recalling the past, you are just asking her to tap into that.) Ask her to find *or construct* a particular scene from her childhood memories. Next, bring her back to the here and now to be aware of resources that she currently has that she didn't have earlier (competence, relaxation, curiosity, or whatever would have been most helpful then—for example, a time when she felt really cared for and understood). Have her think of specific incidents involving each of these current resources, recalling them in enough detail to reexperience them. Next, tell her to take her present self ("the older you") back to the old scene as a counselor to help her to change that scene, either by giving her "younger self" advice or by giving the other person in the scene the resources needed to behave differently, or both. Then have the client once more close her eyes and replay the old scene with the new resources, until she learns something new, and the scene turns out differently. Get her to make this new scene as vivid and real as the old one. After that, ask her to think of the next time she will be in a situation that would ordinarily trigger the old, unwanted response, and see what happens—would her response be different? If yes, the work is complete; if no, ask what else is needed and cycle through the sequence again.

This strategy was used with a forty-year-old man who had been burdened for years by an intense fear of dying. When I asked him where he had learned it, at first he was unable to tell me, but he thought it had something to do with cancer. Asking him to concentrate on his fear and to play back the feeling in his memory, he found himself five years old watching television. He recalled this scene with great clarity, describing a room in his aunt's house, just after breakfast. He and his family were visiting his aunt because her mother (his grandmother) had just died of cancer. He was watching a public service announcement about the "seven cancer danger signals." He recalled seeing a wart on his hand that he feared was cancer. He had not recalled this event until I had asked him to follow his fear back in memory. I then reminded him of the resources that he could take back to that little boy, his "younger self," to reassure and comfort him. After he completed this process, he was quite moved as he had held the "younger self" and had reassured him that he was from this "younger self's" future and so knew that he would survive well. The imminent fear of dying disappeared, so that the first session was also the last. Telephonic follow-up several months later revealed that the change had continued. What we see in such an example is a directed catharsis, if you will; a technique that uses kinesthetic cues to go straight to an old troublesome memory that is then revised or reframed by applying the client's broadened life experience to the specific incident.

For clients with phobias or panic attacks, a similar strategy may be employed—with one vitally important difference. Since such clients are often overwhelmed with fear when recalling the initial incidents, you need to build in a *visual dissociation*. You ask clients to imagine that they are sitting in a movie theatre with you and direct them to see the start of the incident as a still snapshot on the movie screen. While this single visual dissociation may be sufficient, it is often wise to add another level of dissociation by asking them to then go into the projection booth, where they can see both the screen and the two of you sitting in the audience. Then you ask them to play the incident as a movie all the way through, until they learn something new. Following this, it is often helpful also to ask them to play the movie backwards. What typically happens in this process is that adding the actual viewing of the situation to the overwhelming sense of fear literally gives them a new perspective, thus adding a powerful sensory resource. Again you want to test your work, so you ask them to think of the next time they would expect to encounter the phobic stimulus to see if their response has altered. If not, then you find out what else is needed and use that feedback either to recycle or to undertake another strategy. A client with a flying phobia found simply discovering the dissociative technique sufficient to manage his fear. He said that when he realized that he could watch himself flying on the plane, even as he was flying, his fear disappeared.[3]

Such dissociative techniques can also be useful in treating clients with post-traumatic stress disorder. One such client, whom I saw intermittently over two years found these techniques helpful for dealing with traumatic material that we had gradually uncovered with other methods. She also found writing stories about her associations with her traumas, making them turn out differently, as well as invoking hypnotic imagery of safety, soothing, and mastery, helped her to achieve fuller integration of past experiences.

Behavioral Restructuring of Images

> You already know what is wrong; the task is to plant in mind the constructive ideas, the visualizations, which you want to realize. Eliminate defects by focusing on better procedures.
> —Elmer Green

> When learning is achieved through action, it becomes a right-brain experience and, as a result, has a much greater impact.
> —Steve Allen, Jr., M.D.

Tasks are behavioral prescriptions, or therapeutic instructions, directed to the client. Sometimes they are done in the office, but more often they are completed between sessions. They are designed to interrupt circular or stuck behavioral patterns and challenge assumptions of an individual, couple, or family. This interruption and challenge are intended to produce a new point of view, leading to new choices of effective behavior. The further benefit of enhancing clients' autonomy and self-efficacy is that they discover that they do have control over their behavior (Bennett 1985). This enhanced sense of autonomy may generalize into other areas as well. Tasks can be useful even if they are not done, because they inject the therapy into the everyday life between sessions, for clients know that they will need to explain what they need to be able to complete the task.

The idea that directed actions can change those influential world images may seem mechanistic and unfeeling to some, and to them we would pose the question, "Is it a worthwhile technique if it gets the results that the client wants?" Or as William James put it, "Action seems to follow feeling, but really action and feeling go together; and by regulating the action, which is under the more direct control of the will, we can use it to indirectly regulate the feeling, which is not" (in O'Hanlon 1987:52). For example, one client, who was requesting help overcoming her depressed mood, said that when she felt low she would automatically put on navy blue clothes. When I asked her what she wore when she was feeling fine, she immediately said "Red!" I then instructed her to dress in red and she reported an improved mood. Our experience tells us, as you can see in many of our other clinical examples as well, that, indeed, tasks can be quite useful in moving clients toward their desired goals. And while clients sometimes object to the self-conscious deliberateness of carrying out instructions, the old adage "practice makes perfect" clearly applies; for "while designing or modifying behavior . . . consciousness is needed, and in order to become conscious of deviations between the facts of behavior and the visualization of behavior, we need conscious feedback" (Green and Green 1977:25).

Basically, there are two kinds of tasks: overt and covert. In overt tasks, you tell clients what you want them to do, expecting compliance. It is well to note that these directives are not advice; advice tells the client what you think they should do, which implies judgment. A directive is designed simply to interrupt behavioral patterns, perhaps by changing their sequence, thus challenging client assumptions of powerlessness. It is generally simpler to start with overt or direct tasks. However, in situations where the interaction or habit is longstanding and/or repetitious, covert tasks can be more effective.

Covert tasks involve a paradoxical or metaphoric instruction; you expect results from either defiance or indirection. With a simple paradox you can either prescribe the symptom directly, telling the client to continue it, or perhaps ask him to schedule it at certain times or to increase it. For example, to a woman whose fear was about *"thinking about being afraid of possible panic attacks,"* I gave the instruction, "Plan to feel anxious about possible panic attacks for ten minutes in the morning from 10:00 to 10:10, and for ten minutes in the afternoon, from 3:00 to 3:10." She quickly found this tedious and gave up both the fear and the practice. "Lie in bed and don't close your eyes until you are fast asleep" (for an insomniac) or, to a perfectionist, "I want you to make a perfect mistake" are other examples. For some paradoxical instructions you need to find a positive intention for the unwanted behavior pattern so that you can congruently request its continuation. For example: in a family with a depressed mother and an acting-out teenager, the teenager might be told to continue acting-out because he is taking care of his mother by distracting her from her sadness. Paradox often moves the client into new behavior because he doesn't like being told what to do. As someone once said "Paradox is like spitting in someone's soup. He can continue eating it, but he won't enjoy it."

Indirect or metaphoric tasks are really suggestions. If you offer a story that you think may bear on the client's request, you never know just what influence it will have. You can either use relevant stories of your own experiences, or make up one that you think might point to a new direction. The stories themselves may be quite straightforward, such as telling about a client you once had with a similar request, but adding how that client saw her life differently and so got what she wanted. Or they may be more indirect, for example, talking with a client who pulls her hair out about how to garden and what plants need. (This is treated more fully in chapter 10.) Using hypnosis often enhances the effect of such stories,[4] but is not essential. I frequently ask clients to write stories about their central issues; for example, for a man who wanted to have a "meaningful job" but could not specify what that might be, I asked him to write a story about such a job. With a suitable client, you can vary this theme by asking the client to write her own story as a fairy tale, insisting that she give it a happy ending.

Task instructions need to be clearly stated in positive language, what you want the client to do, not what you want the client to avoid or stop doing. Using the carefully chosen, presuppositional language of the "illusion of choice" may forward this procedure. In this language pattern, doing the task is presupposed, it is just a question of when or how. For instance, "Do you plan to make that call about your new job on Thursday or Friday?" or "Are you going to write that letter on your computer or by hand?" Once the client has decided the "when" or the "how," he has also tacitly agreed to the task. (Parents are familiar with this technique. "Do you want to hear the story before or after your bath?")

The single most important issue in task design is to make them manageable for the particular client; tasks need to be small enough to do. While this may seem self-evident; *tasks that fail are usually too "large."* The adage "By mile it's a trial, by inch it's a cinch" applies well to task assignments. You need to check carefully both the client's understanding of the task, but also what the client feels is possible. You need to be ready to reduce the task to a size that the client agrees is feasible. A task that you would find easy to complete may seem overwhelming to the client. Besides, small changes often mobilize more general changes and still give the client a sense of control and accomplishment. I had a young man as a client who came wanting to get married: a straight-forward, well-constructed outcome. Since he had never had a date, we focused on developing his interactional skills. He worked as a receptionist in a health club and so had daily contact with many people, both club members and co-workers, most of whom were friendly and would pass the time of day with him. The task I first suggested to him was to arrange to have lunch with a co-worker. He found this much more than he thought he could handle, and asking someone to have coffee with him was only slightly less daunting. We finally settled on his offering someone a stick of (sugarless) gum, a task he thought he could do. Once more, an example of how important it is to suspend our own assumptions about what is possible and join instead the client's reality while at the same time supporting client risk taking. When the task is designed in a "do-able" size, the client's sense of self-efficacy and self-esteem are augmented.

When you want to assign a task, which one should you choose? The answer here, of course depends upon what pattern you want to interrupt and in which client. If you can design a task from the client's request, all well and good. However, there may be times when you want to assign a task, and one does not spring to mind from the subject matter at hand. For these times you may want to have a few "standard" tasks on hand that can be tailored to fit the individual in front of you. It can be useful to think of these in categories by purpose. Some such categories are decision-making, resolving "unfinished business," regulating treatment, improving communication skills, teaching reframing, and teaching stress-management techniques.

Many clients present themselves requesting help in making decisions; life decisions about school, jobs, career paths, relationships, children. A simple place to start is to have them make two lists, itemizing the pros and the cons, putting these in priority. This not only helps them to organize their thinking, but it also produces more explicit ideas. When they bring these lists to you, you can ask both what they learned from making the lists, as well as which is "heavier," which list has more high-priority items on it. If a client comes in wanting to change careers, but not knowing where to start thinking about it, you can ask him to make a "wish list" of occupations that appeal to him, *without* reference to whether or not he has the qualifications. One client in her thirties who was dissatisfied with her career in health management decided to open up a catering business with a friend, an option that had not occurred to her before making her "wish list."

For many clients, completing some unfinished interpersonal business constitutes a significant part of their agenda. These incompletions frequently have to do with losses: the death of an important person, the loss of a love relationship, moving, and the like. For others, the incompletions have to do with "leftovers" from earlier developmental stages such as still responding to parents as they did when they were children. For both types of incompletions, letter writing can be singularly helpful.

When an unresolved loss has been identified, you can give the following instructions: The client is to set aside a couple of hours where he will not be interrupted; he is to equip himself with a supply of pens, paper and kleenex; and then *without constraints* he is to write everything that he would like to be able to say to that person. He is not to edit this, since no one will see it but himself, and he is not expected to mail it. You can offer opening phrases, such as: "I am angry because. . . ," "I am sad that . . . ," "I still resent that . . . ," "I recall fondly . . . ," "I'll never forget . . . ," "You still owe me . . . ," to get him started. He is to bring the letter with him to the next session, not for you to read, but simply to see that it is done.

When the client brings the letter, don't read it unless the client insists, but rather ask the client "What's the most important thing in this letter?" and "What did you learn from writing it?" The reason for not reading his letter is simple. When you read it, you begin to associate to the content and pick out what you see as significant, which can be irrelevant. Relevance lies in your *client's* associations, not yours, for it continues to be *his* world images that you want to diversify. With clients who do insist that you read it, you can skim it and still ask the questions that elicit his associations.

If the person to whom the letter is written is still alive, a further step can be to consider sending it to that person, with or without editing. In the less common cases where the loss is of a place or object, the letter can be written as if to that place or object. It has been my experience that writing such letters is often salutory. The actual process of expressing feelings on a piece of paper seems to decrease their power; it is as if seeing the literal separation of feelings from the self— putting them "out there" on a piece of paper—brings a new and dissociated point of view.

The story of the one client illustrates the potential power of this assignment. A woman in her late twenties came to me for help with a debilitating anxiety aroused by her husband's frequent late arrivals home. While she knew that his work as a cab driver was unpredictable, she could not easily adjust to his erratic hours and spent many late nights in agony. Her sleeplessness and anxiety interfered with her own work performance, as well as with their relationship. Tracing this fear of abandonment revealed antecedents as far back as she could remember, and she connected it to the fact that her father had died suddenly six weeks before she was born. I requested that she write a letter to her father, following the instructions outlined above. When she brought it in, she described the letter writing as difficult, tearful, and draining, adding that she felt better afterwards. She learned that she had always felt there was something wrong with her since he "left her," that she was angry at her mother for being depressed for years, and that she had tried to hide these feelings from herself.

Next I asked her to write her father's reply to her letter. She was jubilant when she brought this letter in, and she insisted I read it, especially the part where he said that he always knew she "would be able to make it" and that he was "very proud of her." She was touched when he told her how sad he was not to have been there for her. She left these few therapy sessions feeling "whole in a new way" and her late-night anxiety diminished to manageable proportions. Three years later she returned reporting that she felt "ambiguous about getting pregnant." While she perhaps meant "ambivalent," confusion was indeed primary. When we uncovered her fear that if she got pregnant, her husband would die, she was able to separate old images from future ones and so consider current issues concerning pregnancy.

Another client, a woman in her late forties, requested help in her relationship with her mother. Her letter to her mother had a powerful effect on them both, enabling a limited but positive change. My client's drinking then came up as an issue. Her family were heavy drinkers, and she saw that her tendency to join them prevented her from feeling in charge of her life. She reported that her new relationship with her mother really "opened her eyes" to other changes that she wanted to make and, further, saw controlling her drinking as the first step. She then proceeded to do just that, with both my continued support and additional support from a colleague, Richard Caplan, a substance-abuse specialist. Caplan believes that the first step in recovery from abuse is just what our client experienced: seeing the possibility of positive changes occuring when the substance is abandoned.[5] Possibility-oriented therapy seems to be a natural approach with great potiential for such clients.

When a client seems to have a developmental snag, say in relating to parents, a letter of resignation can be useful. The instruction for this letter involves first identifying the specific behavior pattern the client wants to change and then writing a letter of resignation to the person who triggers this pattern. For example, a thirty-five-year-old salesman requested help in freeing himself from his mother's surveillance. She expected him to call daily and to report his activities in detail. When he deliberately omitted a day, she would call him and complain, especially if he were not home, with the implication that he was not a "good son." One of the interventions that I offered to him was to write her a letter in the following vein: "Dear Mom, After due consideration, I have decided that I do not agree with your definition of a "good son." I am now of an age where I do not think I need to call you each day to prove my rectitude and devotion. Therefore, consider this letter one of resignation from the post to which you appointed me. Sincerely." The details of the letter, of course, came from the client's own specifics and were expressed in his own words. When his letter was completed, he decided to send it to her, after we had discussed that "being a good son" might also include freeing her to pursue her own development (including an appreciation of the fact that she might not see it this way).

For some clients who want a regular therapy appointment more than a change, task assignments can be used to energize movement in treatment. There are clients who continue to come for their appointments but repeatedly fail to take any initiative for their own changes between sessions. For those clients, who seem to use therapy to continue their old patterns rather than risk new ones, connecting the making of further appointments to the completion of homework assignments can be useful. A couple who had been in marital therapy for a number of years with several different therapists seemed to want to use our sessions mainly as a forum to display their remarkably circular, vociferous, and tearful interactional patterns. Twice, I assigned them homework. Both times they returned, offhandedly saying that they had not done it, then immediately beginning to go down their well-worn verbal track. The second time, I stopped them abruptly, got them to restate their therapeutic goals, and said that I thought the homework would be a place for them to start toward these goals. I did not make another appointment, but told them I would be happy to do so after they had completed the assignment. They called back about six weeks later and then came in to talk about their homework. Each of the remaining five times that I saw them, I gave them homework and invited them to set up another appointment when they had completed it. Their penultimate assignment was to decide whether or not to separate; the last one was to write up an amicable separation agreement. The treatment lasted about nine months. Some time later the wife came in again about career issues, reporting that the separation had been liberating for them both. Thus, using task completion as a condition for future appointments helped to forward their treatment.

A special category of tasks includes activities designed to manage stress and anxiety. It seems that in our stress-prone culture almost all clients can use help with learning techniques to manage daily demands without developing panic, anxiety, or a host of other psychophysiological symptoms. In chapter 2 we discussed the positive benefits of balancing the autonomic nervous system, so it is natural to include in possibility-oriented therapy instructions in relaxation, diaphragmatic breathing, and hand warming, all of which contribute to autonomic nervous system balance and so improve psychophysiological functioning. These skills are taught in the office and then prescribed for regular practice, along with whatever form of exercise the client prefers. An important part of this discussion includes looking for the positive intention behind any physical manifestations that the client presents and linking these to the new practices.

One client, a young real estate broker and mother of two, had panic attacks and assorted vague physical symptoms in the course of a life in such rapid motion that it seemed that she never touched the ground. She was amazed to discover that she was able to meet her many obligations with more poise and balance when she created a time for daily relaxation practices. This regular practice, which she at first insisted she did not have time for, eventually enabled her to be a more serene "superwoman." The panic attacks and physical symptoms decreased markedly as she came to see them in part as a signal that she needed to take more time for herself (the positive intention). (Her panic attacks were also treated with the dissociative techniques described above.)

These techniques are often effective in helping clients manage chronic or life-threatening illness, as they can lessen both pain and anxiety, and in some instances, the body/mind effect becomes clearly evident. A forty-three-year-old client with advancing ovarian cancer, including spinal metastases, was referred by her physican to help her deal with a constant anxiety that every sensation in her body was the cancer spreading. We first concentrated on her learning relaxation techniques, which she did quite well. This seemed to free her sufficiently so that when I asked her what she would most like to do in her remaining life, she spoke of reconciling with her sister from whom she had been estranged for many years. As she began describing the historical roots of their rift, and the wrongs she felt her sister had done her many years ago, I wondered with her what would be necessary for her to forgive her sister? She was clearly ripe for this question, as she was able, over three sessions, to see that holding on to the estrangement had blighted her life more than her sister's. Then as she was able to begin a process of reconciliation with her sister, her anxieties about each bodily sensation lessened markedly. She also reported feeling more peace of mind about her own death.

Tasks or instructions that grow directly out of the client's concerns can have special impact and relevance. (There are examples in the case at the end of this chapter.) You do well, as usual, to be alert to both verbal and nonverbal messages from the client. Your acuity and flexibility are key here. For example, a counselor in her thirties came to me to sort out career issues. When we met, she looked at me directly and offered a firm handshake. But when we got settled in the office, she seemed most uncomfortable, did not make eye contact, and had difficulty talking—in marked contrast to her chattiness on the way in. When I inquired about the difference, she said that sitting in the "client" chair made her feel like a shy little girl being grilled by her teacher. I invited her to change chairs with me, and her original confident manner returned, but she felt in the "counselor" role, so could not discuss her issues. I then asked her in what situation did she feel able to talk freely and she said with a close friend. At her direction, we placed two chairs side by side, so she felt we were "equal." The balance of our sessions were conducted in this arrangement.

After you have assigned this homework and the client comes back to report about it, how do you receive or respond to it? We believe to some degree this is a matter of personal style, but that getting into a struggle with the client is counterproductive (as it is any time in therapy). He is, after all, not doing this for you, but rather for himself, to get what he wants. Again, presuppositions can support the process. For example, asking "How did it go?" or "What did you learn from it?" are open-ended and, because they assume completion, positive. Contrast those questions with "Did you do the homework?" This can be simply answered yes or no and does not presuppose task completion. If the client didn't do it, often a discussion of what got in the way can yield either modifications or new tasks, designed by or in conjunction with the client. We emphasize that the homework is for them, and is merely an action that we think might help them fulfill their original request, but it is not written in stone. Ideally, you want this to be a continuation of the therapeutic partnership.

Let us now consider taking couples to tasks.

Strategies for Couples

> Marriage is an attempt to solve together problems you never would
> have had alone.
> —Eddie Cantor

Teaching couples to improve interactional skills so that they can satisfactorily negotiate and resolve differences on their own is a central theme of most couples' therapy. Before you embark on this endeavor, however, you need to establish a *mutually agreed upon goal with the couple,* no matter how general, for unless and until you have that, you cannot fruitfully negotiate their differences, and can instead, get pulled all too easily into their dysfunctional system. One such goal might be that they both want to preserve the marriage. If one wants to save the marriage—often with magical expectations of your power—and the other does not, you have no basis on which to proceed. If one or both doubt that needed changes can happen, but would like to stay married if they can, then you can proceed; for indeed, the therapy is geared to help them make the desired changes. In many couples, the desire to preserve the marriage is understood and they want to negotiate other items such as career changes, schedule management, or child-rearing practice. Whatever their mutual goal, it must be stated in the positive, and in as much detail as they can both agree on.

When you ask what each wants, what would make it a more satisfying marriage, you need to get the specific behavioral descriptions so that each of them—and you—will know when the desired goal is reached. When you ask each for this goal, you may need to find out the positive intent of the request. For example, for the statement "I want him to show he's listening to what I say," a positive intent might be to feel that she's valued by her husband. (The husband often subscribes to this reframe as well.) You then find out what stops them from having the desired relationship *now.* Here you may need to referee to keep the conversation on track, for often couples will get right into an example of their "ritual struggle" of escalating blame and counterblame. This is often worse than fruitless, so it is good to interrupt quickly, perhaps by observing that you are sure that they do this expertly already and do not need your help to do it better. Since you have interrupted a negative pattern, you can then begin providing new models of effective interactional skills.

Toward this end, it can be helpful to state your ground rules. Often when the couple comes in, one is feeling mistreated, and therefore superior, while the other feels misunderstood and guilty. A ground rule aimed to defuse or eliminate this imbalance is that neither one of them is to blame for their difficulties, but rather it's the *relationship* that isn't working. So often one member will either speak for the other, or insist that, say, he knows what his wife is feeling better that she does. You rule that each must speak for him- or herself, and that each is the expert on his or her experience. Then, you can start to shift their habits by monitoring and correcting infractions. For instance, when a husband says "I know Mary thinks that I work too hard," you can interrupt by asking Mary if this is correct. She may answer "No, it isn't that he works too hard, it's that he's always distracted when I try to talk to him."

The therapeutic session is an excellent place to model and teach conscious observation of their current interactions as well as new ways to communicate. So you slow down the action and point to universal pitfalls, of which an outstanding example is mind reading. When partners are certain that their mind reading of each other is correct, it creates major stumbling blocks in their interactional patterns. As you teach them to monitor mind reading by asking the partner if his or her interpretation is correct, it can also serve as a reminder for you to do the same. You can help them to be more conscious obeservers of their own process in a number of ways. You can point to nonverbal sequences. For example, when she raises her voice, he slumps and looks down, and she raises it more. Slowing down such a sequence for them can help them understand how they telegraph their meanings. So you ask if they noticed it, and how they interpret it. If she says "This shows how indifferent he is—he never listens to me!" ask him what was his experience and he may answer "When she raises her voice I know I've failed again." Ask him to observe his own feelings, for instance, "How do you feel about failing again?" and he replies "Sad and hopeless," you can then ask the wife if she knew that when she raises her voice, her husband feels sad and hopeless. So in such a sequence you have then checked out her mind reading, reframed his behavior, and offered them a new interactional pattern.

Another verbal/nonverbal pattern to highlight for couples is their incongruous communication style. When a wife's body is tense and she uses rapid, high-pitched speech when she insists "But I'm glad when you go out and play basketball with the boys!" you may want to ask the husband what he understands from this. In this way you help clarify the ambiguous message she appears to be sending.

Yet another closely related hazard occurs when one partner says: "But you shouldn't have your feelings hurt, because I didn't mean to hurt you!" This statement adds proverbial insult to injury, for not only are the victim's feelings hurt, but a certain "badness" or perversity is further attached to these feelings and to the person having them. This is a prime moment to teach the couple that, in interactional terms, *the meaning of the communication is the response that you get,* and that, if you don't get the response that you intended, you need to change *your* behavior, not blame the other. As you insist that each not blame the other for the unwanted response, remind them about that other ground rule, that each is the expert on his or her experience. Several of my most common homework tasks flow directly from the above patterns: to check out mind reading, including nonverbal cues; to observe their own underlying feelings; and to practice changing *their* behavior if they don't like a response that they get.

You might say that this dangerous practice of mind reading is learned "at our mother's knee." For it is in our childhood home that we learn both how the world is and how it should be. It is here that we learn how loyalty, respect, love, and truth are expressed both verbally and behaviorally. Along with our values, we unconsciously learn what are "proper behaviors and responses" to given everyday occurrences. We store these learnings in internal images that David Kantor (1980) calls "critical foundation images." These are the very world images that we have discussed in relation to the language of change. In no therapeutic work are they more relevant and powerful than in couple's therapy where so much miscommunication is based in a clash of these images. The images themselves are often out of awareness, but can be heard in such statements as "Everyone knows this is the best way to do this" or "You can't do it that way" or "Where did you get that crazy idea?" as applied to everyday activities.

With one couple the incident that "proved" to the wife that her husband didn't love her had to do with the way he treated her when she was sick. Two weeks before, when she had had a nasty flu, he had simply drawn the shades in their bedroom and left her alone *all day*! She was certain that if he really loved her that he would behave very differently. Wanting to uncover her critical image, I asked her what it was like when she was little, and she smiled as she responded, saying "Oh, it was nice—I would be put in mother's bed, with a bell to ring if I wanted something and a TV (which I didn't have in my room) and everyone would visit me frequently and bring me my favorite ice cream and other treats—I almost didn't want to get well!" The husband listened to this with an expression of wry distaste, and when I asked him how sickness was treated in his family, he reported "Well, in my family everyone knew that when you were sick you just wanted to be left alone until you felt better, and then you'd come out." These discordant images of loving behavior around illness had produced a marital crisis.

So how do you help them resolve this discrepancy? Please note, that neither of these images is intrinsically right or wrong, but rather that some adjustment needs to occur. Each partner in the couple needs to be helped to *appreciate* the other's critical image as valid. Notice this is not asking for either agreement or substitution of images, what it does is to ask both of them to *add another image* to their original one so that, while they may continue to choose the original one, they can also respect their partner's image, and so behave differently if they choose. In this case it turned out that the wife had been upsetting her husband when he was sick by her endless fussing when he just wanted to be left alone. After the uncovering of and discussion about their critical images, they decided to do more of what the other wanted when sickness arose. In the end, they were not only more comfortable when they were sick, but also learned a valuable interactional tool that they continued to use on their own.

Furthermore, desired behaviors uncovered in critical-image exploration can then be assigned as homework. The husband in another couple complained about what he considered to be "lack of respect" from his wife. When pressed for an example, he hesitantly brought forth one that was prime but slightly embarrassing to him: his wife left the bathroom door open when she was using the toilet. And more than that, she would then proceed to tell him all the most important news of the day. While he found this disrespectful, when he pretended not to hear her, she would get angry and accuse him of indifference. She thought he was just being an "uptight fuddy-duddy." Pursuing her critical image, I asked her when she had started doing this. She reported that she grew up in a family of four girls, close in age, and that her father traveled a lot for his business. The bathroom was the family social center most days, for here the girls would gather and while bathing, fixing their nails, doing their hair, and so forth, they would share all their triumphs and disappointments. The door was often open as they and their mother wandered in and out, casually caring for their personal needs in the process. So for her, the bathroom was the place for intimate sharing. Her husband had been raised with two brothers in a house with closed doors and a mother who was "never uncovered below the neck." Respecting privacy was of prime importance, and the closed bathroom door was a mark of this as well as of consideration for others. While his wife found this rigid, she also began to get a glimmer of his point of view. I assigned her the homework of keeping the bathroom door closed, and for him—since it is always important for each to have a task—the instruction to hold her hand when they were walking or watching TV, a longstanding request of hers.

As with individuals, tasks for couples concocted from the couple's own themes can have special relevance as illustrated above, but there are some extremely efficacious routine tasks as well. At the end of the first session, if you have defined their mutual outcome and therefore are not in intense crisis, the following task can be most useful, both to discover small, more easily changed behaviors and to begin teaching them negotiation skills. You ask each one to make a list of *small* behaviors of the other person that could usefully be increased or decreased to improve the quality of their daily life. You emphasize the small size with examples such as putting the cap on the toothpaste, taking the coffee cup off the table and putting it in the sink, turning off the porch light at bedtime. They are not to show these lists to each other, but rather just bring them to you so you can decide which items to use. Frequently the items on the list are either too "large" or too "hot" to use in teaching basic negotiation techniques.

Examples of Small Items

SHE *wants him to:*	HE *wants her to:*
— decrease his look of such intense concentration when he brushes his teeth	— stop tracking large dirt particles into bed
— rinse off dishes that are not going to be washed right away	— stop looking someplace else when she hands me things
— stop wearing shorts on the weekends	— stop leaving toothpaste blobs in the sink
— pay more household bills	— stop always going to the toilet before we make love
— stop leaving notes that are terse and inexplicit	— stop complaining about cold feet while barefoot

Examples of Larger Items:

SHE *wants him to:*	HE *wants her to:*
— stop making me feel so vulnerable	— stop taking innocent remarks as criticism
— not assume I'm responsible for for all that goes wrong	— say something nice about me occasionally
— stop pushing for sex when he knows I'm tired	— share my enthusiasm about sex and Chinese food
— communicate feelings more completely and intensely	— increase trust in our family and me

While it is wise to choose one of the "small" items to teach negotiation, all of them ultimately reduce to the theme of "make me feel that you care about me and value me." Using the small items allows for a demonstration of a negotiation pattern without the risk of overwhelming emotion. One of the single most useful patterns to teach couples involves one partner asking the other how to change *one's own behavior* to get what one wants. You choose a "small" item from the prepared lists and direct the person whose item you chose to say the following to the partner: "I want X behavior from you, what can I do to get it?" For example, with an item from a wife's list, she was directed to say: "I want you to kiss me when you come home from work, what can I do to get it?" Her husband, used to hearing only demands, was momentarily stunned, but then did reply: "Well, when I get home from work, you're usually in the kitchen, so that when I have put down my briefcase and taken off my gloves and hat and scarf and coat and boots, I just don't feel like walking into the kitchen. But if you would come into the front hall, I'd be happy to kiss you." To which her response was "I don't want to do that for him!" I then pointed out that she would be doing it to get something *she* wanted, adding that she didn't have to do it, but at least now she knew how to get it. Since it is important to balance your attention to both partners, you can then choose an item from the husband's list and go through the process again. Some couples learn this quickly, and so can practice on their own, while others take many trials, as they all too easily get sidetracked into their usual "ritual struggle." The latter group needs to continue practicing with you.

While you may develop your own favorite "standard tasks,"[6] others that routinely come up are the following: for couples who never have relaxed time together, prescribe that they have a date, either to go out, or perhaps to stay home and do sexual pleasuring exercises[7]; for couples who wrangle over chores or money management, assign the making of a chore schedule or budget plan; for couples who see only the negatives in the partner, direct them to make one positive remark to the partner each day, or to do one "out of the ordinary" thing for the partner, and not tell about it. With this last task, in the next session, you can ask each what it was that the other did. They often observe more than their partners realize. Again, this is a way of having them look at their daily process in new, more positive ways.

When prescribing tasks for couples or families, it is important to take the whole system into consideration so that the member without a task does not sabotage the overall intervention. A rather dramatic example of the results of such an oversight arose with a much-hospitalized schizophrenic woman with intractable migraine, who was injected nightly with large doses of demerol by her physician-husband for pain relief. She was repeatedly detoxified in the hospital; within two weeks he would again be injecting her because "he couldn't stand her pain"; simultaneously he would warn her of the "possibility" of addiction. She was permanently detoxified only when the therapist taught the woman breathing techniques to control pain and assigned her husband the nightly task of making sure she practiced those techniques, (which maintained the structure of their marriage, the ecology of which had been gravely threatened by the detoxification alone, since that excluded her husband from her "care").[8]

Tasks don't have to be heavy or serious to be effective, a more metaphorical task can highlight differences. For example, with one couple, I asked them to describe an ideal vacation—where they would go, what they like about it, and these are the lists they produced:

She	He
—small town in New Hampshire	—Venice
—families	—shadowy, cosy
—unprotected, open	—mysterious streets
—space to live, freedom	—old wood and stone
—realness, flow, respect	—color and taste
—deep sense of belonging	—softness, nurturing
—rightful place	—enveloping, aged
—genuineness	—fun, adventure

The contrast in these lists gave them an invaluable snapshot of the disparity in their values and critical images, which, in turn, illuminated many of their unresolved issues. Indirect tasks of this kind can be playful and at the same time very effective.[9]

For couples, then, using tasks can be central in achieving desired results by teaching both negotiating skills and well-grounded observation of the partner by interrupting negative interactions with positive ones, and by regulating treatment.

Strategies for Groups

The possibility-oriented therapeutic approach is very practical when applied to short-term psychotherapy groups, for it offers a structure that keeps the clients on track, even as it monitors progress to desired results. This model of group therapy can be used with any group, but it is especially helpful with groups selected for developmental issues (leaving home, establishing relationships, midlife questions, and so forth). The group is framed in an introductory pre-group session where the approach and goals are described and discussed with eight to ten potential group members. Those who choose to participate receive a set of questions to be answered in writing and brought to the first group session. These questions are the familiar ones from the possibility or outcome frame:

> What do you want to have happen as a result of being in this group, in what way specifically do you want your life to be different at the end of the group?
>
> How will you know when you have reached your goal? (Be as explicit as possible.)
>
> What stops you from having this outcome now?

The emphasis throughout is on identifying small steps to take toward a larger goal. The eight members are told to expect occasional homework, both individual and group, as part of the fifteen weekly sessions. At the first meeting members hand in their answers. It is helpful to copy these and then return them to the members so that you can both have them for reference during and at the end of the group. Then they begin to describe what it is that each one wants while you help them specify their experience in distinct behavioral terms. Each member's telling his or her "story" gets the group process underway as members identify with each other and begin to form alliances. In this session you should be quite active in getting full group participation, as well as in helping members be as specific as possible in defining their desired goals and in identifying a first step toward these goals.

Here are two examples of this process: one is a thirty-five-year-old banker who wrote she "would like to be self-motivated. I want to enjoy my own company and to do things for myself. I want happiness not to be based on other people and what they think of me but rather on my own sense of well-being." (Her referring therapist said she was addicted to caring for others.) She said, "The first step would be for me to speak up in a group and make myself talk about me." And, indeed, this proved to be a difficult task for her.

A thirty-eight-year-old computer programmer wrote "I would like to gain a perspective on those aspects of my behavior that lead to anger and impatience." This is a good example of a statement that must be made more specific. What he was talking about was that he yelled a lot at his three-year-old. As you can easily see, with eight members, it often takes more than one session to complete this process!

As each member begins to clarify what a first step would be to advance toward his or her goal, it is often assigned as homework. Soon the sessions include reports on homework activity as well as the ongoing refinement of goals—and identification of stumbling blocks. You encourage the group to become more directly active with each other rather than expecting you to keep directing the proceedings; your aim is to increase their autonomy. Typical group transference issues may arise during this process such as feelings about the degree of leader activity, feeling unsupported, and the like.

Individual homework assignments continue as you deem appropriate, according to the feedback they give you about their progress toward the identified goals. For a woman who wanted to get over attachment to a man at work, she was to change the way her desk faced; for a musician who had a hard time limiting his girl friend's demands, he was to make practice time happen; for the computer programmer who wanted to manage his anger, he was to find a way to calmly get his daughter dressed.

Sometimes you can ask the group as a whole to do an exercise in the session, and then to continue to practice between sessions. For example: often a member will describe a difficult interaction that still bothers her, so I take her through the following sequence, at the same time inviting the other group members to choose an incident of their own to practice on, too. First, I ask her to replay the scene just as she remembers it. Next, she is to "step into the other person's shoes" and replay the scene, seeing and hearing herself from the other person's position. Then, she is to recall and play the scene from a dissociated position, seeing the two people interacting from an observer's place. When this is complete, I want to know what she has learned from this sequence. Then I will ask both her and the rest of the group to continue using this sequence with new instances that occur for them during the week and report back.

As the group continues, the leader decreases activity as part of getting the members to take responsibility for their own changes. While the leader continues to assign homework as indicated, and also reminds the group of the time limits, the group process of feedback and support among members becomes more prominent. In the last two or three sessions, the leader makes sure that each member reports on his or her progress toward the original goals. While some clients achieve one or more goal, some only begin to clearly identify what it is they want, and/or what stops them from having it now. An example of reaching more than one goal was the banker mentioned before, once she started talking in the group, she got enough courage to not only tell her parents to stop choosing a house for her, but also made plans to quit her job and travel around the world, without telling her parents first! At the end of such a group, then, at the very least, clients are clearer about what they want and how to define it, and, at best, have not only acquired new definitional skills, but also have begun to take some new effective actions.

To conclude this chapter, here is a longer account of a course of therapy. In it you will find first the client's "well-constructed outcomes" as well as verbal reframes by both therapist and client, followed by several tasks directly related to the client's twofold initial request. While task assigment and completion was principal method used, its efficacy was supported by letter writing and by a "revision of personal history" that the client found both moving and significant.

Susie Turner

Job-related difficulties moved a fifty-year-old white, divorced nurse to seek treatment. When I asked her what she wanted, she tearfully stated that she wanted restored self-confidence in dealing with her new boss and with her ex-husband. She also wanted to determine her career goals. I asked how she would know when she had reached these objectives. With some coaching, the client was able to reply that she would be able to control her tears, respond nondefensively to the boss's criticism, resolve financial issues with her ex-husband, and decide whether or not to stay in her job. The question "What stops you from doing these things now?" brought fresh tears as the client spoke of an old habit of "staying where she was not appreciated." When I asked where she had learned this, she answered immediately that her father "criticized her constantly, he had always wanted a third baseman, *not* a girl."

While the client quickly understood that her tearful response to criticism from the new boss was directly connected to that earlier training "at her father's knee," this realization did not empower her to stop the tears. The client had been newly paired with a female physician who criticized her for not consulting about all treatment recommendations. The client, an experienced nurse practitioner, had been used to a good deal of independence with her old boss and resented the new request for consultation on every decision she made. It made no difference when the boss explained her request for consultation by citing the physician's ultimate responsibility for the clients that they jointly cared for. The nurse, who had formerly seen herself as intelligent, now saw herself as "dumb." I reframed this by suggesting that the client now use her intelligence to "play dumb" by asking her boss for advice. I further suggested that the client might see the "critical boss" as the "worried or scared boss." Since the physician was overweight, the client was buoyed up by her spontaneous vision of her boss as a "Swiss chocolate balloon." I then assigned the client two tasks to complete before our next scheduled appointment. The first was to write a letter to her father that freely expressed everything she would like to be able to tell him, including a description of all her suppressed childhood feelings and the way they were tripping her up as an adult. This task aimed to develop a new perspective on these childhood experiences. The client was at the same time instructed to update her *curriculum vitae* in preparation for a possible job search.

When the client returned for her next session, she had completed both tasks, and showed me her new resumé. She reported that requesting more consultation from her boss was making the work go more smoothly. When we discussed the letter that she had written her father, she felt she had learned a lot about how much she blamed him and wanted his love, but added, tearfully, that she still felt unable to get his approval. A recent encounter with her ex-husband had also produced tears. I then focused on helping the client change her view of her past with the "revise personal history" technique. I asked her to recall either a specific or prototypical incident in her childhood where her father had criticized her and she had cried. She was then told to reenter this scene, taking her present adult abilities with her: What could she do now to help that child then? I also instructed her to give her father the personal resources he would have needed to be able to respond differently. Her task was to replay this scene until it came out more positively and she felt she had learned something new. After completing this process, she said she had gained a new appreciation of her father's positive wishes for her, as well as of his own personal struggles. I then asked her to take these new learnings and think of future contexts where she would need them: with her boss and her ex-husband. The assignments for her to complete before the next session were (1) to talk with her ex-husband about unresolved financial issues, and (2) to explore two possible new jobs.

In the two final sessions, the client reported on these assignments and continued to discuss the changes she was making at work with her boss. By the conclusion of this brief treatment (four sessions over two months), she felt good enough about her work enough to stay in her present job and had concluded the needed financial settlements with her ex-husband. The client saw new connections between her past and present difficult interactions, and felt able to behave differently in her current situation as a result. Two years later she reported that she was doing well in a new job where she had found "more independence and respect."

This illustration exemplifies the paradigm shift from problem to possibility, and the client's concomitant shift from helplessness to hopefulness, using some of the techniques described in this chapter to empower her with new choices, which increased her sense of self-efficacy and control.

Notes

1. Although we have separated clients into the categories of "individuals, couples, and groups" in chapter 6 and "children and families" in chapter 7, the approaches that we use are similar no matter who is requesting the service.

2. For the "literal reframe" and other such techniques, see Andreas and Andreas (1987).

3. The above strategies and many others are presented in books about neurolinguistic programming. See especially Bandler and Grinder (1982), Cameron-Bandler (1985), and Bandler (1985).

4. For examples of such techniques and stories, see Rosen (1982), Gordon (1978), Erickson and Rossi (1979), Grinder and Bandler (1981), and Lankton and Lankton (1989).

5. Personal communication.

6. For an elaboration of tasks, see especially deShazer (1985), O'Hanlon and Wilk (1987), and deShazer (1988).

7. Sexual pleasuring exercises are described in Kaplan (1975).

8. Reported by Nina LaFortune Prendergast, personal communication.

9. Milton Erickson was a master of indirect tasks, see especially Haley (1973) and Rosen (1982).

7

Clinical Strategies with Children and Families

> The people I worked with in New Guinea had canoes with no
> outriggers and no keel. Such a canoe is wobbly—prone to oscilla-
> tion which may become excessive and disrupt the system called
> "man-standing-in-canoe." . . . Many times "the canoe wobbled"
> and I fell into the water. . . . But most important, I had to learn
> not to be afraid of the oscillation. And the way to convince myself
> that I could control the oscillation was to cause it. If I made the
> canoe wobble with my feet, the wobbling caused by me was con-
> trollable and not frightening.
> —Gregory Bateson

Just like Bateson, the effective brief therapist must develop proactive strategies for keeping his balance in the face of strong currents that could topple the boat. In this chapter, we will present a diverse array of clinical strategies for working with families. As you will see, the strategies generated are tailored to the unique needs of the particular client system. Much of the work with families presented here focuses on an issue involving a child or adolescent.

Brief Treatment as Consultation

Sigmund Freud's well-known case of "Little Hans" (Freud 1909), provides an example of a consultative model in which the therapist carried out his treatment plan by meeting briefly with the child's father in helping Hans overcome his phobic reaction. Rather than an extensive analysis over several years, Freud took a more economical approach.

Bennett (1989) refers to the therapist's role as that of a "catalyst" in helping the client overcome obstacles in the way of his normal development. The assumption is that the client is capable and resourceful, requiring only a guide or coach who can help him draw on his resources to surmount and negotiate past obstacles on the path of life.

For therapy to be successful, the client needs to be motivated to take action. The therapist must find out who in the client system is the real "customer" (the family member most motivated for change). At times, this is not the person referred for treatment. As we will see in the clinical illustrations to follow, the therapist works with those people in the system who are most committed to change. A basic tenet that we follow is never to be the most motivated person in the room. While we are active in facilitating and catalyzing the process, ultimate responsibility for change lies with the client/client system.

In the following clinical situation, I [SF] consult with a client in dealing with her mother-in-law's intrusiveness and, working as a team, we discuss and ultimately generate an strategy for resolving this difficulty. I present several options to the client and then allow her to choose the direction she wishes to move. In addition, I involve the husband in the process as a support to his wife.

A fifty-year-old woman, whom I had seen with her family several years earlier, contacted me to discuss what she described as a "personal" issue. The woman said that her husband had had a heart attack about year ago, and that he continued to smoke and "not take good care of himself." She was both angry at him and worried about him. In addition, she described her upset with her mother-in-law who continued to treat her husband like a child and to intrude into their family life. For example, the mother-in-law would "just happen" to show up almost every day at their house when the husband was due home from work. In addition, the mother-in-law would constantly be offering to help out is some way (examples given included going to the grocery store, doing laundry, and taking the car in for an oil change). My client described resenting this intrusiveness and felt more and more alienated from both her husband and his mother.

The mother-in-law's very presence in their house would make my client feel resentful and tense. I asked her what she would most like to see happen. She answered: "To have my mother-in-law back off from interfering in my family life." I told my client that her current posture of refusing all offers might actually be serving to keep her mother-in-law involved. I suggested that her mother-in-law may be feeling shut out and unwanted and looking for some way to be useful. We discussed two other possibilities: directly tackling this issue in a face-to-face conversation with her mother-in-law, or continuing to expect that her husband would someday tell his mother to "get lost." To the idea of a direct conversation, my client decided that this would just end up leaving her mother-in-law feeling hurt and upset, something she didn't want to do. She also understood that her husband would not tell his mother to stop interfering in the way she wished.

I then suggested a strategy that I named "turning the other cheek." My client, when her mother-in-law made an offer to do something for her and her husband, was to accept this offer and in fact, ask for more. I suggested that when her mother-in-law asked if she needed something at the grocery store, she was to say yes and have a large list prepared to give her. Rather than responding defensively to her mother-in-law's offers, my client was to "turn the other cheek" and accept these offers as attempts to be helpful.

I described this approach as one in which she and her husband could work together (she was to "collude" with her husband in this plan) and that the energy of her angry feelings would be put into a constructive use. In addition, the proposed strategy would not hurt my client's relationship with her mother-in-law nor get her husband upset. I suggested she discuss these ideas with her husband and that both of them return to see me in about a week. I also suggested that each time her mother-in-law did something for her, she was to do something good for herself (for example, meeting with a friend or taking a walk).

At this next meeting, the husband indicated that he "was all for it," and that they were both prepared to say "yes" instead of "no" to the mother-in-law's offers to help. We discussed how difficult this would be to carry out and the importance of the couple supporting one another in doing a good job of encouraging the mother-in-law's involvement. I told them that by "asking for more" they would ultimately reach her limit and she, on her own, would back off. We scheduled a meeting in one month.

At this meeting, my client reported that her mother-in-law had only dropped by three times over a four-week period! My client said "I don't know what happened. She's really backed off . . . maybe she saw a therapist." When I asked if she and her husband had put the plan into effect, she responded: "Well, maybe once or twice." When questioned further, the couple mentioned that they had asked to borrow her car to drive out of state on a trip (something that they had never done before). My client reported that although her mother-in-law said yes to their request she seemed surprised. The client and I then briefly focused our attention on how she could back off from her overresponsible caretaking role vis-a-vis her husband.

The therapist works to quickly engage the family in treatment and to quickly disengage when the situation is resolved to the family's satisfaction. In this way, the client's goals are respected. The family's request is "translated" into a framework that requires the collaboration of the parents, or other significant figures in the child's life. The therapist is viewed as a "systems consultant" (Wynne, McDaniel, and Weber 1987) who translates the original request into concrete, solvable terms. Members of the client system are placed in a position of having to use their experience and expertise in grappling with the situation. Positive reframing is used to move the family's concerns out of the psychiatric realm and into a normal developmental frame, which puts the family in a responsible and competent position to find a solution.

The possibility-oriented therapist needs to engage the family in an open, playful, and curious manner. In so doing, the therapist gently "nudges" the client system to view the complaint in a new light and/or take steps to vary some aspect of the context in which the difficulty is embedded. The possibility-oriented therapist joins the family while maintaining perspective and distance and as a new member of the family system quickly engages the family around their original request while avoiding the pitfalls discussed in chapter 5.

In many clinical situations, as we discussed in an earlier chapter, the therapist must develop a persistent focus in working toward the client's or client system's goal. It is necessary at such times to avoid becoming overwhelmed with historical material. That will disrupt your focus. In the clinical vignettes to follow, the therapist becomes an active *partner* with the family in reaching a mutually agreed-upon goal and empowers family members to take steps towards that goal.

In each example, we facilitate a process that the client system then implements. The client system, in each situation, is responsible for taking action in reaching a specified goal. We tailor the tasks to fit the needs of each unique clinical situation and draw on the energy and motivation of the participants for change. When that energy level is low, we look for ways to increase it. In addition, we are careful to not move too far from the original request (such as onto a marital issue when the primary request involves the child). I [SF] remember how, in my early training, I would go rushing in to tackle an apparent marital issue, only to find myself alone in the room, the family having bolted out the door.

In the following clinical situation, I [SF] stay attuned to the mother's request about her daughters and avoid becoming overwhelmed or sidetracked by a host of other family issues. Both the natural competitiveness of the siblings and mother's frustration are used as leverage points to create a context for change.

A six-year-old girl was referred by her pediatrician for being enuretic at night for three years following a period of about one year without a problem. The relationship of the parents was uncertain; by the mother's report there had been several separations over the past three years. In addition, the five-year-old child in the family was also enuretic. According to the mother, their father refused to be involved in treatment and was a recovering alcoholic. She expressed her frustration at having had to deal with the bed-wetting problem for the past three years without success. In the initial session I asked mother to keep track of both daughters' bed-wetting behavior and suggested that she try to arrange for her husband to attend the next session, which he did not.

I realized that I needed to find a method for reducing the bed-wetting without dealing directly with what one might assume was the apparent "source of the tension"—the parents' relationship. I decided to use the natural competitiveness of the siblings in developing a task to help reduce the bed—wetting (which was occuring four to five nights per week). In the second session, I challenged each child to be the one with the most dry beds in the next week. The winner would receive a special treat from their mother. I predicted to the children in a redundant, hypnotic-like way, that "one of you will have four dry nights and the other one five dry nights." The mother was asked to keep accurate records of the bed-wetting behavior (as she had done the previous week). In addition, I encouraged her to refrain from changing the sheets in the middle of the night as she had been doing for the past three years. I asked her to call me in one week and made an appointment for two weeks later.

She called as requested to say that neither child had wet the bed for five out of seven nights, with one of them wetting herself on the way to the bathroom on one occasion but having a dry bed. Follow-up at three months indicated that neither daughter was wetting the bed any longer, except for occasional "accidents." The mother did not request further contact.

The following is another example of how you need not focus on a marital issue in order to successfully resolve a concern about a child. You can "unhook" the child issue from other issues and effectively create change. The therapist avoids distraction by maintaining a sort of "tunnel vision" and works to empower the parents to reach their goal. This view, that you can successfully deal with a situation involving a child without dealing with marital issues, is significantly different from traditional family therapy approaches (see Haley 1976; Minuchin 1974).

A three-and-a-half-year-old girl was referred for "not being toilet trained." There was no physical basis for the problem. The mother had been trying to toilet train her daughter since the girl was two, without success. Other than the enuresis and encopresis, the child was doing very well. The father refused to attend either the initial session or the second session, and a history of marital problems was evident.

At the third session, the mother was able to get the father to attend. Rather than exploring marital issues, which was *not* the primary agenda, I decided to focus on the original request. I asked the father how concerned he was about his daughter's behavior. He said that he found her behavior "upsetting and embarassing." I asked both parents if they were ready to succeed in getting their daughter over her difficulties, since what I would be suggesting would be very difficult for them to carry out. I framed the situation as one of helping their daughter make a normal developmental transition towards more independent functioning (of which she seemed clearly capable).

When they indicated that they were desperate to help their daughter and would do anything, I told them to do the following: remove all diapers from the house (except one) and do this in front of the daughter in a dramatic display (I instructed them to keep one diaper as a "memento of her babyhood"); let their daughter know that she could choose either to "make in her pants," which would leave her with an uncomfortable mess, or she could choose to use the toilet. The parents agreed, and father accepted the primary role in carrying out this plan. Four days later father called to say that the daughter had "pooped in her pants" on the first day after the diapers were removed, then she urinated in the toilet twice and on the fourth day "pooped in the potty." I communicated my congratulations for the parents' successful efforts. No further contacts were initiated by the parents.

In the next clinical vignette, I [SF] create a context for change by using the children's desire to understand and make sense out of past family confusions. The presenting concern is reframed and normalized in the light of past family history. I draw on principles of Bowen Systems Theory (Kerr and Bowen 1988) in viewing the situation in the context of the adolescent's extended family system.

A fifteen-year-old girl, Kay, was referred for mental health services after informing her mother that she had been having thoughts about killing herself ("stabbing herself with a knife"). She recently had changed schools and was having trouble entering a new peer network. Kay is the oldest of two children living with their single-parent mother, who is twice divorced.

After doing a quick genogram of the extended family system (see McGoldrick and Gerson [1985] for details on this process), a number of important "anniversary effects" became evident. For one, Kay's difficulties occurred almost within a day of the first anniversary of the parental separation. In addition, the maternal grandfather had died two years earlier at about this same time of year and was someone with whom Kay described having a special relationship.

I framed Kay's feelings about hurting herself as her continued sadness over old losses. The peer difficulties coming at this time of year, when she was feeling so vulnerable, only added to her unhappiness. I emphasized the fact that the anniversary of an important loss is a period when old feelings of sadness and loss reemerge and when people feel more vulnerable and out-of-sorts than usual. Since it appeared that there were some family confusions and secrets that needed sorting out, I encouraged Kay to draw a genogram of her extended family. Two additional meetings were held over a six-week period. These meetings focused primarily on the children getting clarification from their mother about the family's past history.

In the final meeting, Kay had prepared, with the help of her fourteen-year-old brother, a detailed genogram, and both were asking questions of their mother in their effort to understand old confusions. The mother indicated that Kay was no longer making comments about hurting herself, and Kay reported no significant problems with peers over this period.

In the following clinical situation, I [SF] validate the reality of the presenting complaint and allow the complainant to "save face." In taking a solution-oriented perspective, I build on past parental successes and ask for "more of the same."

A referral was made by a pediatrician regarding an eight-year-old boy with "recurrent abdominal pain." No physical basis for the pain was found. When the family first came for treatment, the child had been reporting somatic complaints for three months. Ben was in the third grade, taking piano lessons, doing well at school, and was described as "sensitive . . . a worrier" like his father. The parents reported that the complaints were most likely on Monday mornings before school. In addition to the somatic complaints, Ben would also cry and "seemed sad."

For the first six weeks or so, the mother, who happened to be the only parent at home at the time Ben was to leave for school, would allow Ben to stay home. But for the last six weeks she was "making him go" to school. I inquired about how she was successful in getting him to school. She told me that she finally decided that unless he had a fever he had to go to school. She reported that on the way to school he would "try to make me feel guilty by telling me what a bad, uncaring mother I was."

I complimented the mother on her ability to bear with this abuse in the service of getting her son to school. Once he got to school, the teacher reported that he settled in quickly and seemed fine. Ben, during this session, described how much his stomach hurt in the morning. In an attempt to empathize with his pain and not discount his discomfort, I talked about the pain as "real" and spoke to him about how he was suffering from a common malady called "growing pains." I talked about how these would come and go as he was getting older and growing up. He seemed to understand.

At the end of the session, I encouraged the mother to continue to do what she had already been doing successfully (that is, getting him to school in the morning) and again reiterated for Ben how painful "growing pains" can be. A follow-up call from his mother indicated that things were steadily improving.

The following is an example of how I [SF] place the mother in the role of primary change agent with her daughter. In addition, drawing on Piagetian principles of development, I join with the child in giving her some "magical" options for dealing with her worries. Giving mother and daughter each an "assignment" serves to increase the involvement of both in the change process.

A six-year-old (Betty) was referred for having trouble sleeping; waking up four to five times a night and needing to be comforted by her mother, who was a single parent. This behavior had worsened recently following the parental separation. In addition, Betty would "go into rages," especially when her mother would try to encourage her to get dressed and ready for school in the morning. This had become a standard morning ritual before leaving the house. It was clear that Betty was an especially sensitive child who was experiencing sadness over the parental split and who worried about each of her parents, both of whom were struggling with their adjustments to the separation.

I suggested that the mother help Betty relax at bedtime (by developing a bedtime ritual) and that mother and Betty plan a time each morning before school to have a fight, with Betty being given the decision about which area they would fight about that day (getting dressed, eating breakfast, and so on). In addition, I gave a ten-minute monologue about Betty's sadness over her parents' separation and how much of a burden that can be for a child. Since Betty had mentioned how close she was to her favorite doll ("Lily"), I asked Betty if she thought it would be possible to put some of her worries into the doll and let "Lily share some of the worry for you." She nodded her head "yes."

At our second meeting, her mother indicated that Betty was sleeping better (the mother was now spending some time with her when she went to bed, which Betty found comforting) and that Betty had let her doll do some of the worrying for her. The usual morning conflict, although still occurring, had decreased in frequency. The mother reported that when she asked "what should we fight about this morning?," Betty laughed. A follow-up meeting was planned and then cancelled. A call from the mother two months after our last meeting indicated that Betty was "usually waking up only one time at night and for only a very brief period," and the mother was spending less and less time with her before she fell asleep. An appointment was set with the mother, at her request, to discuss personal issues related to the divorce process.

In each of these clinical situations, I joined with family members as a "consultant" in creating a context for change. I gave specific tasks and assignments and used the family's own creative energy for change to mobilize them to take action.

Transforming Problems into Possibilities

Language is your most effective tool. The therapy process, at its most basic, is a linguistic event, a dialogue between therapist and client. The client's words are initially organized around a problem. The therapist must be prepared to disturb that organization. You, the therapist, do this by using language in a special way. For example, you talk in terms of "when" the problem will be solved rather than "if" the problem will be solved. In addition, you maintain a focus on those aspects of the client's life (including how he deals with the presenting request) that are going well. These "exceptions" form the basis for the development of an intervention strategy.

Another aspect of language deserves our attention. It is important for you to use jargon-free language that is acceptable and understandable to clients. The use of nonpathological, nondiagnostic, nonpejorative language serves to strengthen the 'treatment alliance' (Harper 1989) and to move the therapy process efficiently and effectively toward solution development.

An orientation that "talks pathology" and uses linguistic labels that emphasize "pathologic" language and terminology fosters a negative and pessimistic view of human capacity for change. We believe that you can be more effective by avoiding "pathological" and "static" diagnostic language. As discussed earlier, our verbal labels and descriptions are capable of taking on a life of their own. By keeping our language focused on resources and strengths (in contrast to limitations and deficits), and on the future (rather than the past), we avoid "reifying" pathology and thus avoid a context that makes reaching the goal that much more difficult (O'Hanlon and Weiner-Davis 1989; O'Hanlon and Wilk 1987).

We take a nondiagnostic approach by defining the original request for service, not as reflecting "illness" (with the need for "cure") but simply as a request for change. By describing requests and goals in behavioral terms, you can maintain a specific focus and clearly assess outcome. The following are clinical illustrations of the advantages of defining the client's request in jargon-free, nonpathological terms.

In the following example, I [SF] frame the situation, not as one of adolescent depression or a "phobia," but as simply the daughter's difficulty in getting to school. This then becomes an issue that a mother (rather than a professional) can resolve. In addition, I use a story, inducing a hypnotic trance in the adolescent, to help her understand the importance of developing increased space from her mother.

A 13-year-old girl was referred by her pediatrician because she was "fearful of leaving the house . . . gets physically sick if she has to go out." No physical basis was found for her symptoms. Dori is the younger of two children living with their single-parent mother separated for eight months from their father, who is described as an alcoholic.

In the initial meeting, the mother described Dori as "sick constantly . . . with nausea, diarrhea, and vomiting (for five months)." Dori had not been to school for the past two weeks and had attended only ten days out of the first two months of school. When at home, Dori listens to music and watches TV. Her mother indicated that right now, she was also at home and not working. According to the mother, the only time Dori is comfortable going out of the house is with her. In addition, she noted that Dori's appetite was diminished and that she was sleeping a great deal. Dori stated that she does have a number of friends but has not had much contact with them recently. Her seventeen-year-old brother, who was at this initial session, mentioned that Dori "was always out of the house before." Now when her mother tries to "push her out," she feels sick.

During this initial meeting, the mother volunteered that a close friend of hers had committed suicide two months earlier and that she continued to feel sad and upset about this. It became clear that Dori was very sensitive to her mother's emotional state and had been worrying about her. This was further made clear by hearing that Dori "helps out at home without being asked." After asking the mother to have the school call me, another appointment was scheduled in four days. My primary goal was to get Dori to return to school and to begin functioning in as normal a manner as possible.

At this second meeting, I spent part of the session with Dori individually, at which time I told her a story about two trees in the forest, with the smaller growing in the shadow of the larger and not getting the sunlight and air it needed to grow and develop. I emphasized how the little tree, when it was able to get more space from the larger tree grew and developed and became free to live its own life. (This story went on for about ten minutes and Dori listened intently as in a trance). I also met individually with the mother and encouraged her to get Dori out of the house in the morning no matter what complaints Dori has, and to tell herself that "this was the best thing she could do for Dori." I also talked with the mother about her returning to work, which she said she was considering. With both present, I gave the mother some ideas for getting Dori to school, such as taking her by the hand and walking with her to the bus stop (which Dori admitted she would find embarrassing). We made a third appointment for five days later.

The day before the appointment I received a call from the mother who indicated that Dori had gone to school for the first time. The school had adjusted her schedule so that she could attend on a half-day basis for a week or so before returning to her normal schedule. The mother reported that Dori had complained some in the morning in her usual way but went off to the bus stop without needing her mother to take her as we had discussed.

At our meeting the following day, Dori reported that she had been in school again (two days in a row) even though she felt sick in the morning. The mother revealed that she was starting a job (the next day!) on a part-time basis and volunteered that "maybe we've been too close." Dori had told her mother about the story of "two trees in the forest," and the mother said Dori found it "very significant." The mother was commended for her efforts, instructed to continue her good work, and to call me in two to three days with an update. Her report at that time indicated that Dori continued to attend school on a half-day basis; the mother had begun working; Dori did some babysitting for a neighbor (which she wanted to avoid but which mother insisted upon). Dori's fourteenth birthday was to be celebrated on the coming weekend. A meeting was set in two weeks.

When I went to the waiting room to look for Dori and her mother I was quite surprised and amazed. Dori had a new hairdo, was wearing makeup and looked more like a young woman than the child she had appeared to be on previous contacts. Dori was attending school on a daily basis. No further contacts were planned. A follow-up call to the mother one year from the last session indicated that although Dori was "struggling" academically she was continuing to attend school.

In the situation above, I dealt with mother and daughter both jointly and individually in working towards a fixed goal—getting the daughter to return to school. By meeting with mother and daughter separately, I set the stage for change (the mother was directly encouraged to look beyond her daughter's complaints and insure that her daughter get off to school; the daughter was indirectly influenced in a hypnotic process in which the idea is seeded that her continued growth requires increased separation from mother). The mother's concern was framed in a manner that allowed her to be successful in helping her daughter move through this developmental process.

In the following clinical situation, I [SF] reframe the parents' description of the daughter as "depressed" to a view of her as "manipulative." By relabeling the daughter's behavior this way, I help the mother to become less reactive and involved in her daughter's activities. My work with this family focused on creating a new "maturity-enhancing" interactional cycle between mother and daughter that would support the daughter's increasing sense of responsibility and independence.

An eleven-year-old girl, Pat, was referred for treatment following a call by her mother to Pat's pediatrician. Concerns focused around Pat's "crying a lot . . . and being afraid of her stepfather" (who had been married to Pat's mother for six years). Pat had received individual psychotherapy (over twenty "play therapy" sessions) in another state for one year approximately two years prior to this referral. Focus at that time was also on "crying at home and . . . occasional outbursts of anger . . . considerable immaturity and confusion."

In the initial meeting, in which Pat and her mother were present, the mother continued to present Pat as a sad and depressed young girl who appeared much younger than her stated age. As the mother spoke of her daughter's sadness and immaturity, Pat seemed to assume her mother's attributions. In our second meeting, two weeks later, the step-father was present. He stated that he expected Pat to carry out certain responsibilities at home and to be more independent (less dependent on others to do things for her). He indicated that his wife tended to "baby" Pat, which the mother acknowledged.

Based on this information I decided to frame Pat's behavior as "manipulative" rather than "depressed"; that is, Pat was "using" her mother as a way to avoid growing up and becoming more responsible. I saw it as the mother's job to begin acting in ways that supported Pat's being less dependent and more responsible. We discussed ways that the mother could "detach" herself when she saw Pat crying about her homework or when she felt the need to try to cheer Pat up. I also suggested that the stepfather assume an increased role in monitoring Pat's responsibilities around the house, to which he agreed. The mother talked about her fear of losing her "special closeness" to Pat by back-ing off. I told her that becoming less reactive to Pat's emotional state would still leave a great deal of time for mutual contact and involve-ment. An appointment was set for one month later.

At the third meeting the mother reported she had "detached herself seventy-five percent"; that Pat was getting her homework done more efficiently (without the mother's involvement); and that her husband had "stepped forward a little more." Pat appeared self-confident, ver-bal, and articulate in a way more consistent with an eleven-year-old. I encouraged the mother to continue to detach herself from Pat's emo-tionality, which was Pat's way of getting her mother to support her immaturity and dependency.

The therapy, in the next example, works to shift the parents' view of their son from that of a "depressed" and "emotionally disturbed" child to an "abusive and manipulative" adolescent. By accepting this latter view, the parents are required to work in concert to assert their executive parental rights. This is not effective, however, until the parents "hit bottom" (feel most defeated). Notice how I [SF] make an attempt to support those actions that the parents have already taken that have been successful and to ask for more of that behavior. I rely on the parents' increasing sense of frustration and desperation to finally "convince" them to take action. By so doing, they are successful in helping their son in his normal socialization process.

Robert (age ten) was referred by his pediatrician for being "verbally abusive towards both parents but especially his mother." He was reportedly doing well at school, with no behavioral problems observed in that setting.

An initial meeting was held with the mother and father and Robert and his younger sister. The parents described a series of "blow-ups" between Robert and his mother in which Robert would make demands on his mother to do something for him. When she did not immediately do what he wished, he would begin to verbally and, on occasion, physically abuse his mother. The father–son relationship was less intense, although the father did express concern about his son's behavior. The father was working at two jobs and left to the mother the responsibility of disciplining Robert. Robert presented himself as a relatively shy, timid, and not especially verbal young man who would sit passively while his parents expressed their distress over his behavior. The mother described her husband as "too easy" on Robert. We discussed some options for dealing with Robert's behavior and scheduled another appointment. The mother called to cancel the appointment, saying that "things are going along ok right now."

Several months later, following another "blow-up" between mother and son, the mother called the emergency service to request that Robert be hospitalized in a psychiatric facility. Robert had kicked a hole in the dining room wall after an altercation with his mother. I told the emergency clinician not to hospitalize Robert but to have the family set up an appointment with me for the next day. At that meeting the mother expressed her frustration by saying "We're losing control. . . . I feel I can never do anything right. . . . I've bent over backwards to make Robert happy." It became clear how both parents "catered" to Robert in trying to meet his needs and avoid conflict.

I asked the parents to think about *what they do that is effective* in limiting Robert's behavior when a "blow-up" occurs. After giving this some thought they mentioned how, on some rare occasions, when the father actively intervened, Robert got himself under control. Also, when his mother could ignore his provocations, he tended to quiet down sooner. Although upset and distressed as both parents appeared to be with Robert's behavior, they still maintained that Robert was "emotionally disturbed and depressed" (sad) rather than "bad." These perceptions led them to treat him oversolicitously, allowing Robert to take advantage of his powerful position and make more demands on them. We discussed the necessity for the parents to work as a team to set appropriate limits on Robert, who had somehow come to the conclusion that he was the center of the universe. The parents agreed that there was a need for setting more limits on Robert, but one or the other would tend to sabotage these efforts by "feeling sorry" for him and bailing him out.

After several more "blow-ups" over a three-month period the parents again returned to therapy. They were both feeling more defeated, frustrated, and upset than in previous sessions. Things had progressively gotten worse, with Robert now provoking fights with both parents and threatening to kill each of them. He had kicked his mother in the leg, and the police had been called. The father was able to get him under control by holding him down on the bed. Although the mother was feeling "tormented" by Robert, she and her husband were still viewing Robert's behavior as reflecting "depression" and pressed me to see him for "individual therapy." Throughout this period Robert continued to doing well at school, was in organized sports, and was described by his father as "a good sport. . . . and a good loser."

I told the parents that I had a different picture of Robert. I dramatically emphasized how I saw both of them as being abused, manipulated, and pushed around by their now eleven-year-old son and that their permitting this to continue would ultimately result in Robert becoming more and more demanding with the potential for one of them to get seriously hurt. Something had to happen soon to reverse this process. I suggested that the parents do more of what had already been shown to work, for father to actively intervene and for mother to ignore and move away from falling prey to Robert's provocations. Since helping Robert would require a significant amount of energy and parental team work, I asked them if they were ready to take this on. Were they prepared to go on the offensive? When both parents had finally agreed that things had gone far enough, I suggested a plan. As a first step they were to stop parenting Robert, they were to refuse to take him to and from sports events, buy him things, make him supper, do his laundry, etc. They agreed to try this, and we scheduled an appointment for one month later.

When they arrived for the next meeting, they seemed pleased with themselves and they described the following: For one week after our last appointment they did absolutely nothing for Robert (he had to walk a mile in the rain to get home after a ball game, had to do his own laundry, and so forth). He threatened to run away from home, did leave, and then two hours later, called his parents for a ride home (although they let him know they wanted him home, they refused to pick him up). He walked home on his own. Later that week he began verbally assualting his father, who immediately grabbed him and held him down on the bed. Robert calmed down. Over the next three weeks the parents eased up some on Robert since they noticed a distinct improvement in his attitude (he was being more cooperative and less provocative). His mother was also able to ignore his provocative behavior more frequently.

A follow-up call six months after treatment ended indicated continued progress. The mother reported that "we're sticking to our guns or walking away from it. Robert is calmer now. Things are better. I meant to write you a note to thank you for your help." (A total of twelve sessions had been held over an eighteen-month period.)

It should be noted that, throughout the therapy, I did not make any attempt to "pathologize" the parents or make the assumption that marital problems were at the root of the son's difficulties. I kept my focus on the parents' request that their son's behavior change. I allied myself with the parents, in a team effort, to help them "socialize" their son to life's realities.

The next section includes several examples of strategies for dealing with developmental issues in the family. Here, I work to both normalize and reframe the original request in ways that create opportunities for change.

Reframing Difficulties in a Developmental Context/Normalizing Developmental Transitions

Difficulties arise as families move through the life cycle, adapting and accommodating to changing developmental needs (Budman and Gurman 1988; Carter and McGoldrick 1988). A "symptom is a signal that a family has difficulty in getting past a stage in the life cycle" (Haley 1973: 42). The goal of therapy becomes assisting the family to get back on track in resuming their normal developmental progression. This requires altering the "symptom" or the family's view of the "symptom" so that normal development can proceed. It is helpful for the therapist to normalize and reframe difficulties in a developmental framework.

Wynne, McDaniel and Weber (1987) suggest establishing a "non-pathologizing frame for the problem." As mentioned earlier, this entails reframing the request in such a way that it falls in the realm of the client system to solve rather than in psychiatric terms. "Intrapsychic" issues can be translated into a systemic (interactional) framework in which the parents can be helped to actively promote the changes they want (Friedman 1990). By so doing, the parents are empowered as change agents for their child. The following clinical situations illustrate the utility of such an approach.

A seven-year-old girl, Karen, oldest of three children from an intact family was referred for "moodiness and . . . fears of separation" especially from her mother. There had been periods when Karen would become very weepy and clingy in anticipation of her mother's leaving the house. Karen was described as "very ritualistic . . . very particular . . . (everything has to be just so)." In addition, she was described as having "strange thoughts" that, according to her mother, affected her fluctuating moods.

After giving the situation some thought between the first and second sessions, I positively reframed Karen's behavior (her fears of leaving her mother, her "mood changes") as reflecting her ambivalence about growing up and becoming more independent. I emphasized to the parents how devoted they seem to be to all of their children, who had come to expect high levels of care and attention. I told them that I thought Karen's behavior indicated that it was time to help the children become more independent by not being so available. I encouraged the parents to continue to follow through on setting appropriate limits with Karen regardless of their perception of her emotional state or mood at the time (the parents had been "dancing around" Karen for fear of upsetting her). I also suggested that they try not to distract her from her "thoughts" or try to pursue her about what was "bothering" her. I reiterated how I saw Karen as confused about issues of independence and dependence and how she needed the parents' help in seeing herself as more independent. A third and final meeting was held one month later. The parents reported that Karen was showing no "mood swings," "odd ideation," or dependent clinging. Her parents were setting limits with her, treating her as a normal rather than as an emotionally disturbed child. The six-year-old middle child had also stopped wetting the bed during this period. No further contacts were initiated.

In the following clinical situation I [SF] suggest a very "drastic" strategy in testing to see how desperate the family is to achieve success in helping the child complete a developmental milestone. Most of the therapy took place by telephone.

A single-mother and her sister came to the mental health department with the mother's four-year-old son, Len, because of a problem with "potty-training." Len was due to begin preschool in two months and needed to be toilet trained to be accepted. Len had learned to use the "potty," according to his mother, about one year earlier and had been successful for about a week. At that point, the babysitter, who was doing the training, left and the pattern was disrupted. Currently, what was happening was that Len would request a diaper from his mother or aunt. They would put it on him and he would then have a bowel movement. The diaper would be removed and he would go back to wearing regular underpants. At night, he wore no diaper and never had a problem.

We discussed how capable a child Len was in all other areas and how this was "one final remnant of his babyhood" to which he was still hanging on. If either the mother or the aunt withheld the diaper, Len would begin to cry, whine, and get very "fidgity." Both would eventually give in and provide the diaper. It was clear that Len had control over his bowels and was ready to engage in normal toileting. I then suggested what I framed as a "very drastic intervention" that I wanted them to think about for a few days before agreeing to. The plan involved removing all diapers from the house and giving Len a choice of either going in the toilet or going in his pants. His mother said she would call me two days later. I told them that if they decided not to go ahead with this, we would consider some other less drastic approaches at our next session.

Two days later, the mother called and said, "Yes", she was ready to put this plan into effect. Both the mother and her sister had agreed that something drastic needed to happen to solve this problem. We set an appointment for four days later. On the morning of this appointment, the mother called to say that Len had not taken a bowel movement for three days and that she was concerned that he would become constipated. I suggested we talk about this later at our appointment.

When the family arrived, it was clear that something had happened. In fact, Len had taken a bowel movement in the toilet about an hour before our session! I complimented the mother and aunt on their perseverance in the face of both Len's crying and upset and his refusal to use the toilet. I also complimented Len on his success in using the toilet. Len was beaming and feeling very proud about his accomplishment. He commented on how he was a "big boy now" and that "the diapers can go to a baby who needs them." I predicted that they would experience continued success and asked mother to call me in a week.

At that time, Len's mother reported that he had been taking bowel movement's in the toilet every day. She described him as "looking forward to beginning preschool." I asked her to phone me one week later for an update. At that time, she reported that Len continued to use the toilet daily and that he had commented that "I'm proud of myself." She expressed surprise at how quickly the change came about, and I complimented her and her sister on their effective efforts in making this happen.

In the following clinical situation, I [SF] reframe the parents' notion that their daughter is "depressed" to one of "acting younger than her age" (Coopersmith 1981). In so doing, the parents are encouraged to help their child move past a developmental hurdle in gaining increased maturity.

A ten-year-old girl, who "mom reports is not eating properly" and whom the pediatrician saw as "anxious and tearful during pediatric exam" was referred for treatment. Her parents reported to the pediatrician that Zelda seems "sad and depressed lately." Zelda was the older of two children. In the initial session with the mother, the father, and Zelda, the parents reported how depressed and sad Zelda seems at home. However, when she's with friends she "enjoys herself." The more they talked about her "underlying sadness" the more unhappy the little girl became. When I pressed the parents for specifics about Zelda's "depression," they did tell me about her occasional nightmares and her need to come into their bedroom to sleep at night.

Rather than a problem of "depression", I framed Zelda's behavior as "acting younger than her age" and viewed her sadness as reflecting her difficulty giving up "the little girl side of herself." I suggested that helping Zelda move out of the parents' bedroom and back to her own room would "encourage that side of her that wants to be older and more independent." Zelda's eleventh birthday was six weeks away, and I emphasized the critical transition point that this birthday symbolized in moving from a young dependent child to a more independent preadolescent. With these messages I encouraged the parents to view Zelda's eleventh birthday as a significant "marker" (Omer 1982) of this change. The parents were instructed, over the next six weeks, to develop a plan to make this transition happen. They indicated that they had some ideas about this that they felt comfortable implementing. I left the details to them.

An appointment was scheduled for after Zelda's eleventh birthday and about eight weeks following the previous session. Zelda's parents reported that she was now sleeping in her own bed, something she had begun to do even before her birthday. However, the parents officially "celebrated" this transition on her eleventh birthday and reported that Zelda was now "more relaxed, not on edge so much." Zelda's mood in this session seemed more upbeat. The parents had also decided to give Zelda more freedom after school rather than having her involved in very structured after-school activities as had been the case for several years. About one year later the parents called requesting contact on a different matter and reported that Zelda was still doing well.

The brief possibility-oriented therapist must be comfortable dealing with issues of loss and death within a framework that is both clinically efficacious and economical. In the following clinical situation, I [SF] deal with a family undergoing a grieving process for their deceased five-month-old infant. Because of the special cultural issues in this situation it was necessary to be sensitive to the established rituals embedded within the family's culture in helping them to deal with the loss and move on in their lives. I suggest several tasks to the family, both inside and outside the therapy room, in helping them actively deal with their grief.

This family was referred to me because of the sudden, unexpected death of their five-month-old son. I met with the family initially about two weeks following the son's death. In the cultural tradition of this family, the parents were not allowed to go to the funeral. However, father did attend the burial the following day. Of the two remaining children, the younger was more vocal and inquisitive about the death, asking numerous questions of the mother and father, who were clearly very distraught over the loss. The mother was having sleep problems, headaches, and "bad dreams"; the father was having "flashbacks" about the death. Since the cause of death was still unknown, the parents had contact with several doctors.

At my request the parents brought several pictures of their baby to the next session. I asked each family member to "talk to———" about their feelings. Both the children and parents were able to verbalize how much they love and miss him. Following this meeting a series of sessions with just the parents was held since they reported feeling increasingly distant from one another in the grieving process. The mother reported feeling "worse now" (two months after the death) than she did initially. Both were obsessed with thoughts of what they could have done to prevent the death.

The couple were provided an opportunity to recount the details of the experience. In addition, the couple was encouraged to attend meetings of a self-help group for grieving parents, which they did on two or three occasions. I also encouraged them to pick up and hold a friend's baby who was about the same age as their son when he died. This was something both had been avoiding, which was creating some tension with the parents of this infant. Although initially uncomfortable, the mother was able to get herself to do this and was pleased with the outcome.

Although the father had visited the grave on two occasions, the mother had refused to go. He tearfully described his most recent visit. After he spoke I suggested that he bring his wife to the cemetery for a brief visit. He indicated his willingness to do this. The mother's headaches increased around what would have been the son's first birthday (culturally, this was perceived as a very special event). We discussed the significance of this event and decided that a special ceremony at the grave would be appropriate. They followed through on this by bringing flowers and saying special prayers.

Since the couple was finding themselves getting into arguments over "trivial things," I suggested that they initiate a discussion about the loss of their infant son "whenever this happens." Discussions moved to the issue of whether to have another child, with the mother in favor and the father more reluctant. The parents agreed to put this on hold. The parents were beginning to return to some level of normalcy at about eight months following the death.

About one year after the death, the mother became pregnant. Although pleased with the prospect of having a baby they were both still grieving the loss of their son. At the anniversary of the son's death another ceremony was conducted at the cemetery. Both parents were pleased and "surprised" that they had done so well in coming through this crisis, and we agreed to terminate our contacts. They were advised to expect to continue to grieve especially around the infant's birthday and the anniversary of his death and were encouraged to allow themselves to acknowledge these events in celebrating their child's memory. The father added, that although their son was with them for so short a period, he was a gift that had very much enriched the family.

As we have seen, both in-session and out-of-session tasks can be a crucial part of the therapy process. In the next section, we look at the effective use of homework assignments and tasks in mobilizing clients to take action in modifying old patterns and routines.

Introducing Novelty (and Change) via Tasks and Assignments

The strategic use of tasks and homework assignments are valuable devices for enlarging clients' perceptions of possible options or solutions and creating a context in which *variety* can be introduced. The therapist can playfully encorporate constructs that shift and modify the family's view of reality and open the door to potential solutions. As discussed above, you can be a very powerful force for change by taking advantage of your new position in the client system in setting the stage for solution development.

In the following clinical situation, I [SF] work to generate a solution by prescribing that the family continue the very behavior they wish to eliminate (having the child sleep in their bed). I framed this, for the parents, as a "temporary sacrifice" they needed to make for the child in allowing him to get his needed rest. Following through on this task not only allowed the child to get some rest, but ended the pattern of conflict and upset that surrounded the nightly attempts to get the child to sleep in his own bed. This task, when carried out, served to interdict the previous ways the parents handled the situation and in so doing destabilized the old unsuccessful patterning. In addition, by decreasing the time they spend being upset and tired, the parents now had additional time and energy to invest in coming up with a novel solution in helping their son sleep in his own bed.

A three-and-a-half-year-old boy, Sam, and his family were referred to me because of Sam's reported "sleep disturbance" and his parents' "limit-setting problems." Sam is the older of two children. The parents reported that, beginning at one year, Sam began sleeping in the parental bed. In fact, when Sam came into their bed, the father would occasionally move to another bed in the same room.

Attempts to get Sam to stay in his own room and sleep in his own bed at night had been unsuccessful. Sam would scream and cry and "get very upset." The psychologist at Sam's preschool encouraged the parents to "make Sam stay in his room." This didn't work, and Sam would be up all night screaming and crying and be exhausted in the morning (as would the parents). The father also spoke of Sam's "clinging to [his] mother" and his difficulty talking to his wife in Sam's presence since Sam would "interfere." If his mother left the room, Sam was described as going into a "frenzy." The two-year-old daughter was described as shy but unproblematic.

My intervention focused on encouraging the parents to "take a break from working so hard at this problem" to which they had been devoting a significant amount of their energies. Both seemed exhausted and out of ideas about what to do next. I instructed them to allow Sam to sleep with them in their bed and in fact for the parents to put him directly into their bed at his normal bedtime. I framed my intervention as a "temporary sacrifice that the two of you need to make right now in putting your son's needs before your own." I also asked them, in this initial meeting, to think about "between now and the next time we meet, what will happen *when* Sam is over this problem." We agreed to meet in two weeks.

At the second session the parents reported that Sam had been sleeping in the parent's bed for the past twelve nights. He was sleeping ten to eleven hours a night and, according to the parental report, was "getting a good night's sleep." There had been no crying or episodes of upset over this period and the parents reported feeling more rested themselves. We then spent some time discussing what the consequences will be when Sam is sleeping in his own bed and not being so "clingy" with his mother. Both agreed that when these problems were resolved they would have more time together as a couple, something each insisted they wanted very much.

The parents had not gone out together for a long period because "baby-sitters can't handle him." When asked to specify a "small but significant step in the right direction," the mother indicated that she would like to be able to take a shower without being interrupted by Sam coming into the bathroom. Sam's father agreed to try to contain him so that this would be possible.

I encouraged the parents, at this second meeting, to (1) find a baby-sitter who could come over during the day and get to know Sam for brief periods before the sitter is asked to stay with Sam in the evening, (2) work out a plan so that the wife could take a shower and "enjoy it" without interruption, and (3) work out a way for the wife to go out for one to two hours one night a week, "so that you could provide an opportunity for your son and husband to have some time together." I again emphasized the need for the parents to continue to make a "temporary sacrifice" by allowing Sam to sleep in their bed. We scheduled a third meeting for two weeks later.

At this meeting, the parents again reported that Sam was sleeping very well at night in their bed. However, the father was beginning to express considerable frustration with this situation and wanted Sam back in his own room. I empathized with his irritation of being deprived of the kind of "togetherness" he wanted with his wife but continued to restrain any move to force the issue of Sam sleeping in his own bed. The mother reported that she was able to take an enjoyable shower without interruption and thanked her husband for his help in making this possible. In addition, the mother had gotten the names of several baby-sitters but had not as yet called any. She did go out one night for a very brief period without significant upset on the part of Sam. The father reported that when his wife was out, Sam responded more positively to him. We scheduled a fourth meeting in one month with parents encouraged to continue to put Sam into their bed at night and for them to pursue the other issues discussed.

Two weeks later I received a call from the father. He told me that he had been getting more and more frustrated and had been thinking about how to get Sam to sleep in his own bed. He had come up with an idea he wanted to share with me. The father told Sam that he had a choice, he could either sleep with his parents or with his "pound puppy" in his own bed, but not with the "puppy" in *their* bed. Sam responded by sleeping in his own bed. He was, however, still awakening occasionally at night. The father decided to cancel our next appointment, although he felt that further service might be needed in the future. I commended him for his creative efforts in solving the problem and encouraged him to call should he wish further contact.

As is evident in the above clinical situation, it is necessary to vary your approach in meeting the needs of a particular family. With some families it is possible to be quite direct about possible steps toward change, while with others, the therapist must take a more strategic stance and indirectly influence the change process. One strategy that I [SF] have found useful, in some situations, is to propose a very drastic intervention. While pushing for the drastic alternative, I encourage the family to use their own initiative to generate other less aversive possibilities. This strategy is related to Haley's (1984) "ordeal therapy."

In one clinical situation, the parents were having difficulty setting limits on their five-year-old daughter who refused to sleep in her own room at night and preferred the parents' bedroom. After some discussion about how to handle this situation I suggested what I termed a "very drastic solution and one which many parents would find abhorrent," that is putting a lock on their bedroom door. I knew from a previous meeting with this family that these parents (being kind and gentle people) would not find this very acceptable. As I had predicted, both parents were visibly uncomfortable with the thought of locking their daughter out of their bedroom. After regaining their composure, the father suggested that maybe they could just keep their door shut at night (they had been leaving the door wide open). While expressing my skepticism that this would be a strong enough message to their daughter, I encouraged them to try their approach for two weeks "but please keep open the possibility that a more drastic approach may be needed."

As it turned out, *their* approach worked. The parents reported (two weeks later) that the daughter had been sleeping in her own room "nine out of ten nights" and had even spent an "overnight" at a friend's house, something she had never done before! I complimented the parents on their successful resolution of the problem.

A slight variation on this approach was used with a ten-year-old boy who had left his mother a very provocative "suicide" note. Having known this youngster and his mother for several years I [SF] knew that, although prone to impulsive behaviors from time to time, he was not a likely candidate for suicide. In a meeting with him and his mother, he refused to discuss the meaning of the note he'd written and continued to hint at "doing something." I dramatized the seriousness of what he had done and discussed the possibility of psychiatric hospitalization "for people who are not able to take care of themselves in a responsible manner." He continued to be withdrawn and nonresponsive. I then picked up the phone in my office, and while he was listening, called a psychiatric hospital, inquiring about an available place. As he listened to my phone conversation, he became more and more upset and finally volunteered that he did not want to hurt himself, but only to "get my mother to love me more." He had a good cry, then calmed down, and his mother brought him back to school. We scheduled a meeting four days later in which both mother and son were in better spirits and had "had a good talk".

Another area in which you can create opportunities for change is through the use of client "experiments." By assigning relevant tasks to the family, an opportunity is created for family members to "try out" various options and strategies. The notion of encouraging experimentation puts the family in a position of learning about their own behavior and opens the door to modifying that behavior. The mere act of observing yourself or others in a specific behavioral context may, in and of itself, create change (see deShazer 1985, 1988, for other illustrations of client "experiments").

In one clinical situation, I [SF] suggested to a mother who was complaining of yelling at her children all the time, that she do an "experiment." On even numbered days she was told to "do what you ordinarily do" and on odd numbered days, to "do something different" from yelling. When the client returned several weeks later she reported significant success in reducing her yelling. She had continued the experiment for only three or four days when she realized that if she could avoid yelling on the "odd" days, she could do so on the "even" ones too. She offered the following: "The task you gave didn't seem so overwhelming to take on. If you had simply said to 'stop yelling,' I never would have been able to do it." Here, framing the task as an "experiment" and giving permission for the problem to continue, served to enable this mother to change her behavior.

At times an assignment doesn't even have to be implemented to serve a useful function. With one family, each parent was prone to viewing their child in a different way. The child (age nine) was referred because of concerns about his demanding and argumentative behavior especially with his mother. The boy had asthma and was wetting the bed. The mother viewed the child as "having a sensitive nervous system and some information processing problems" (and therefore did not hold him fully responsible for his behavior), while father saw him as a "normal and competent boy who could be irresponsible at times." I suggested that the parents do an experiment in testing out which view would lead to more positive change.

I encouraged them to view their son as "sensitive and special" for one week and then as "irresponsible" the following week and to modify their behavior in dealing with him according to this schedule. Just as I had finished proposing this assignment, the mother seemed perplexed. She thought for a moment and then made the profound statement that regardless of how she and her husband viewed their child, "he has to be held accountable for his behavior." With that, our work continued, focusing on the parents' setting firmer limits on their son's behavior.

The following illustrates an "experimental" approach to creating a shift in an entrenched behaviorial pattern.

Paul and Saul are fourteen-year-old identical twin boys who came for help with an issue that concerned their mother very much. Paul would wake up at night and instead of going to the bathroom by himself, would wake up his brother and have his brother go with him to the bathroom. Many times, when they would return from the bathroom, Paul would climb into bed with Saul and fall asleep. Saul expressed his wish to not be awakened at night and for Paul to sleep in his own bed.

After our first meeting, the mother put the twins in bunk beds (with Paul in the lower bunk) in the same room, as a way of trying to help them break the old pattern. This was an idea that Paul suggested as a way of helping him feel comfortable at night and to enable him to go the bathroom by himself. At our next meeting, it became clear that the new sleeping arrangement wasn't having the desired effect. Paul was still waking Saul even though Paul was now only five steps away from the bathroom. I then suggested the following: that Paul flip a coin each day; if "heads" then he must go to the bathroom by himself (and we laboriously discussed and acted out how he could do this); if "tails" it is his choice whether or not to wake up his brother. Saul was to independently make a guess (the next day) about whether Paul had gotten a "head" or "tail" the previous night. Paul and I went out of the room into the hall outside my office and flipped the coin for that night. It came up "tails" and therefore Paul was free to wake his brother up if he chose to. We set another appointment in one month.

At this meeting Paul described using the coin toss system for one week (after which the family took a vacation out of town). During that week Paul went to the bathroom by himself on the two nights he got "heads." He did try to wake his brother up on one of these nights but Saul refused to go with him. However, after the vacation, the twins fell back into the old routine. We then discussed reinstating the coin-toss task with an additional element.

It seems that Paul was also having trouble falling back to sleep in his own bed after going to the bathroom. Borrowing from Haley's (1984) principles of "ordeal therapy" I suggested that Paul try the following: If he finds he cannot fall asleep in his own bed within fifteen minutes he is to sit up and spend a half hour reading a book for school. This would be repeated as often as necessary. Should Paul find that he has fallen asleep before the fifteen minutes has passed, he doesn't have to do the school reading. At no time was he to wake his brother, who agreed not to respond to Paul's requests.

I asked Paul to call me about ten days after this meeting for an update. He did, telling me "the reading at night is not working." We talked briefly about having to revise the plan at our next meeting in one week.

As it turns out, Paul never needed to use the "reading system."

Paul indicated that out of the past twenty days, he went to the bathroom by himself and fell asleep in his own bed on seven occasions—a significant improvement! I then complimented the brothers on their success and encouraged them to continue to work at this. We scheduled a meeting in one month.

Paul reported that the last month had been "good." He was going to the bathroom by himself and then going right back to sleep in his own bed. Although Paul still made an occasional attempt to wake his brother, Saul refused to comply. I congratulated the brothers on their successful efforts. The mother was pleased with the result and felt her sons were acting more maturely. No further appointments were made.

Part of the fun of doing therapy from a constructivist perspective is the potential for generating interesting and clinically efficacious intervention strategies. One approach, which we have found especially effective in working with children and families, developed out of the creative work of Michael White (1984; White and Epston 1990), an Australian psychotherapist. As we have seen, problems can become enmeshed in a vicious cycle or circular pattern. Significant change can occur simply by trying to interrupt the problematic cycle or pattern by introducing a new element or new point of view (O'Hanlon and Wilk 1987).

Michael White has suggested the idea of "externalizing the problem," shifting it from something inside the child to a force or entity separate from the child. For example, in regard to the problem of encopresis, White invented the idea of "Sneaky-Poo," an entity outside of the child "responsible" for the encopresis. Sneaky-Poo, which "has a life of its own" (White 1984: 153) is viewed as victimizing not only the child, but the whole family. The problem becomes defined not as something "bad" inside the child or something that the parents have done wrong, but as how to control (or defeat) Sneaky-Poo. Sneaky-Poo becomes a powerful external agent whom the child and family must work together to defeat. This strategy has the benefit of avoiding elements of blame, guilt, or criticism of either the child or the parents.

It is important for you to introduce Sneaky-Poo as a powerful entity and work to encourage the child, with his parents' help, to develop strategies that will enable the child to prevail over this force. You must find out how badly the child wants to get over the problem and to engage him in a competitive drama in which you and the family are rooting for the child's success. The usefulness and generalizability of White's thinking is illustrated in the following two clinical vignettes offering different initial complaints.

A seven-year-old boy, oldest of four children in an intact family, was referred by his pediatrician for "encopresis . . . which has not responded well to medical management." No physical basis for the problem had been found. For a period of six to seven months, immediately after toilet training (at about age three), Dan used the toilet normally with no soiling problems noted. This was the longest period with no soiling. Dan's usual pattern was to have at least one, and usually two bowel movements each day. For the two-week period prior to coming for treatment, the parents reported that Dan had a bowel movement in his pants on an average six out of seven days. The problem happened both at school and at home, and the parents perceived Dan as not getting particularly upset with having a bowel movement in his pants.

The parents described Dan as "very competitive" both with his siblings and with peers in his sports activities. Dan was reported to be doing well at school and having many friends. The next oldest sibling, a sister, had just recently overcome a similar difficulty. With the above information in mind, the therapist decided to introduce the notion of "Sneaky-poo" (White 1984).

After checking out what the parents had been doing to deal with this problem (which was having Dan sit on the toilet for five minutes after each meal), and finding out that this was not meeting with success, I asked the parents and Dan to develop a chart of Dan's successes over "Sneaky-poo" and of "Sneaky-poo's" successes over Dan. I emphasized both the difficulty and importance of "winning" a victory over "Sneaky-poo." We scheduled another appointment for two weeks later.

At this meeting, they brought in the chart, indicating a sixty-forty split in favor of "Sneaky-poo". We discussed how tricky "Sneaky-poo" can be and talked about how soon Dan thought he could get the edge on "Sneaky-poo." Dan said that he thought he could do it in one more week. I suggested that maybe this was being too optimistic since I knew how sneaky "Sneaky-poo" could be and that he didn't give up very easily. I then talked with the father about how he could help Dan improve the speed with which he can get to the bathroom. Could father time him running from several places around the house to the bathroom and record his times? This the father was willing to do.

The family was planning an extended vacation, and we discussed how this might effect our planning. A meeting was scheduled after the family vacation (which was cancelled). A call to the mother soon after indicated that Dan had made "some improvement." Instead of having bowel movements in his pants six times each week, the problem was now occurring only twice a week. She described Dan as having more control and believed that he would ultimately "grow out of it."

In the following situation, I [SF] generalize the "Sneaky-Poo" framework to a problem of "temper outbursts" in a seven-year-old boy.

Gary was the older of two children in an intact professional family. The parents were concerned with Gary's temper outbursts especially in the mornings before school. If things didn't go exactly as Gary wanted them to, he would get upset, throw things, and become verbally abusive.

After getting more details about Gary's behavior and the parents' attempts to deal with this, I talked with the child in the parents' presence about the Robert Louis Stevenson story of "Dr. Jeykl and Mr. Hyde." I emphasized the ability of Dr. Jeykl to change from being a nice guy to a monster and how awful he felt after the monster side had taken control. I asked Gary if he thought he could defeat the monster since it seemed like the monster was more in control of things in the mornings than Gary was. The parents agreed that they had been seeing more of the monster and less of Gary lately and wished to see more of Gary.

The parents, Gary, and I then developed a plan in which Gary would get a special sticker when "things went well in the morning" and this would be placed on a chart. In this situation, Gary would be declared the winner over the monster. On the other hand, if the morning did not go well (and the details of this were spelled out clearly) it would mean that the monster was the winner and "he" (the monster) would get a special sticker. Although Gary indicated that he was prepared to take on the monster and defeat him, I warned Gary about how powerful the monster can be. We discussed how Gary's parents could help him prepare for the battle. An appointment was then set for two weeks later.

When the family arrived, Gary announced proudly that he had defeated the monster on thirteen of fourteen mornings! The father described his amazement at the change, indicating that he had only hoped for a "fifty-fifty split." Gary indicated that he was now getting to school early rather than late, had more time to play with his friends, and liked leaving home without being angry. Although complimenting Gary on his initial success, I warned him that the monster was very sneaky and unpredictable and could easily reemerge at any time. It was necessary to be vigilant and watchful so that the monster doesn't surprise him when he's least expecting it. The mother reported that Gary had apologized on several occasions during the past two weeks and this was unusual. She told Gary that when he says "I'm sorry" the monster disappears.

Before scheduling our next appointment, I predicted to Gary that the monster might just be resting and that he might resurface more determined than ever over the next several weeks. Gary seemed confident of his power. The parents were very pleased with the progress (especially the "pleasant good-byes" in the morning). We set an appointment for one month later.

At this visit Gary indicated that the monster surfaced only two times (over a four-week period)! The father continued to express his surprise and amazement. A follow-up meeting was scheduled.

Another approach I [SF] have found useful is asking parents to audiotape an episode of interaction with their "problematic" child. In one situation, in which the eleven-year-old daughter was being very demanding and verbally abusive, the parents would prepare tapes of their interaction with their daughter for me to play in the next session. With the whole family present I would play the tape, complimenting the parents in places where their behaviors were particularly effective in getting the daughter to behave appropriately. In addition, I would comment on the daughter's behavior, implying that her behavior did not appear as threatening as I was led to believe and that maybe she was beginning to lose her "acting" abilities. I would criticize her for not being "authentic" enough in portraying a child who really wanted her way. This playful interaction led me to prescribe that the daughter "do a better job next time" of playing the demanding child. Over a relatively brief period of time, the daughter began showing increased control of her behavior and would calm down almost immediately after one or the other parent turned on the tape recorder.

Hypnotherapy

Besides being amenable to therapy utilizing the more straightforward strategies outlined above, many children are especially good candidates for hypnotherapy. My [SF] preferred technique does not involve formal hypnotic induction, but rather draws on the use of metaphor and storytelling to seed ideas and influence behavior. We discussed one clinical situation in which the therapist used storytelling with a twelve-year-old girl who was having trouble separating from her mother. In the situation to be described below, I [SF] use metaphor to seed ideas for change. Notice how I avoid becoming distracted from my primary goal even in the face of family information that might suggest "an underlying problem." This vignette also nicely illustrates the idea of "discontinuous change."

Adam (age 9) and his mother and stepfather were referred for mental health services mainly because of his disruptive behavior in his third-grade class, and his refusal to do any work at school (he would sometimes hand in blank papers). In addition, he was having nightmares almost every night. These problems had begun about a year earlier when Adam was in the second grade. There was a family history of substance abuse, and the mother described going "cold turkey" four years earlier. Adam's biological father, with whom he had no contact for the past four years, was described as having a "drug problem" as well.

Since Adam was not completing his assignments at school, the teacher was sending home, on a daily basis, her report of what work Adam did complete and what he needed to finish at home. She would indicate completed assignments with a C. I suggested that both the mother and stepfather spend more time with Adam around his homework. The parents felt there was "something inside that's bothering him" and pressed me to see Adam individually "for therapy."

I agreed to meet with Adam, and initially we discussed his understanding about his parents' divorce and his mother's remarriage. He seemed to be an especially attentive young fellow, tuned-in to my every word. We then began talking about school and the difficulties he was having completing his work and getting C's from his teacher. I then began talking with him about the "beauty of the sea," about boating, fishing, and swimming. I talked about how I loved to be by the "sea" and how relaxing and warm the sun felt as I was walking along the ocean's edge; how the "sea" had such a marvelous rhythm of its own and how rewarding it was to be near the "sea." I also talked with him about "seeing" beautiful birds by the "sea," each time emphasizing the C. I finally mentioned how satisfying it would be to be closer to the "sea." We ended our talk with my wishing him luck on getting more C's on his daily report. I set up another meeting with Adam and his parents three weeks later.

The next day I received a call from Adam's teacher who described him as a "relatively bright, creative, and imaginative child who was reading at a very high level . . . but who had just about given up doing school work." She said he would rather read than do paperwork and described her new system of sending home daily reports of his work, which I supported.

At our next meeting, Adam's mother reported "a complete turnaround." Adam was now getting C's on all his daily reports! He had also awakened at night with nightmares only four times in the three weeks since we last met, a significant and positive change. His parents both reported that Adam was "more cooperative at home and was listening to directions better." He was completing all of his assignments at school, and his mother and stepfather were both surprised and pleased by the rapid improvement in his performance and behavior.

Although the parents initially refused to accept responsibility for Adam's improvement, I commended their efforts in spending more time with him on his homework. Adam noticed and commented that his parents are "nicer to me now." Rather than schedule another appointment, I suggested that the mother call me with an update in three-weeks time. She called about six weeks later to let me know that Adam was continuing to do his work at school and was not having nightmares.

Listening to Children: Meaning and Metaphor

The potential contribution of the younger child to family treatment has often been overlooked or ignored (Guttman 1975; Korner and Brown 1990; Zilbach 1986). By listening to children and respecting their contribution to the therapy process, the therapist opens himself up to many useful ideas and avenues for intervention. This was brought home very dramatically in a session with a family who were requesting help in managing their four-year-old son. The six-year-old daughter in the family brought with her a drawing she made of her parents in two different poses (smiling/friendly and fighting). She had put a line through the conflictual pose with the title "no yell," and had put the word "yes" over the happy pose. She came up to me [SF] early in the session and handed me the picture. After carefully looking at it, I asked the parents about their relationship. Both acknowledged that they were having marital problems and that these issues deserved priority rather than their original concerns about their son, who was "basically doing okay." Treatment proceeded with a focus on improving the marital situation.

At times, the most direct route to change is via contact with the child. The use of metaphor and storytelling can be especially effective in helping children discuss difficult issues and promote change. Two examples are provided of the usefulness of working directly with the child in therapy. In both situations, changes exhibited in the child's behavior in the therapy room transfer to his world outside of therapy. In both examples, the therapist [Sally Brecher, M.S.W.], although seeing the child individually, also maintains contact with the parent(s).

Nol (age 9), the middle son of three born to an African father and a African–American mother, was referred for treatment after he ran away from school for the third time. He was described by his father as verbally disruptive and defiant in the classroom, teasing other children and getting into verbal fights on the playground. At home, father reported that Nol had become very withdrawn.

When Nol was four years old, his mother died in childbirth. Nol and his older brother were sent to England to live with relatives in order that their father could advance his career in the United States. Visits from the father were limited, and it wasn't until three years later that Nol and his older brother returned to the United States to live permanently with him. Shortly thereafter, the father remarried. The marriage was conflictual and shortlived. When Nol entered treatment, his stepmother had already left the house. Nol was clearly affected by the death of his mother and by the early separation from his father. In addition, Nol felt responsible for the recent departure of his stepmother and the pending divorce. The father was working hard to keep the family together. However, his depression and overwhelmed state made it difficult for him to be emotionally available to his son.

Nol's problematic behavior was seen as reflecting the family's sadness and continued grieving over the multiple losses the family had all experienced. Initially, Nol presented himself as a withdrawn youngster not easily engaged in family sessions. For this reason, the therapist decided to meet with him individually, in addition to family meetings. Therapy extended over an eight-month period with a total of eleven visits.

The approach the therapist took involved having Nol write stories, through which he expressed his feelings of loss, anger, yearning, and resolution. Gradually, he was able to accept those feelings as his own and share them with his father. With encouragement, the father began to hear his son's sadness and speak of his own. The culmination of treatment came in Nol's story of the "Young Boy and the Wizard." In this story, a woodcutter boy comes upon an old man who asks for food. The boy shares his food and the old man offers to grant him a wish should he ever need it. Times goes by, and when the old man becomes ill, the boy takes care of him. When the old man's strength returns, he and the boy travel and become partners. They share the wood money "fifty-fifty." Their fortunes grow, and the boy no longer needs to wish, for he and the old man live happily ever after.

In a family session at the end of treatment, Nol was comfortable sharing his feelings with his father who was able to empathize with his son around the losses they had endured. At the time of termination, Nol's behavior problems were markedly reduced. He was neither running away (the initial reason for treatment) nor getting into trouble at school.

Mark was an intellectually precocious seven-year-old, who was brought to therapy by his parents, at the request of his teacher. The teacher believed that his diminuitive size, caused by a growth hormone deficiency, coupled with problems in fine motor skills, was responsible for Mark's tendency to isolate himself and maintain a noncompliant stance in the classroom.

At an initial family meeting, Mark presented himself as a verbally engaging and highly imaginative child. He made it clear from the outset that he believed his small size meant that he was the weakest student in his class. This thought also troubled him at home, where he was bullied by his older brother. Apart from school, Mark was reluctant to venture far from the safety of his mother and avoided extracurricular programs, cutting himself off from opportunities for social contact. He stated that he felt different from the other kids on the outside, but on the inside he was a "wild and crazy guy" whose social interests and emotional needs were those of a typical seven-year-old.

The challenge for the therapist was to find a tactful way to engage Mark in a process that would lead to greater acceptance of himself as a typical seven-year-old who was simply shorter than his age-mates and to help him overcome his isolation from peers. Since Mark seemed like such an imaginative fellow and had difficulty expressing his feelings directly, the therapist encouraged Mark to tell stories, which she recorded. This storytelling technique allowed the therapist to deal with sensitive issues in displaced form. Mark's "story" consisted of a seven-chapter episodic adventure with accompanying illustrations. Each story ended with the therapist and Mark discussing the theme or lesson of the story.

Mark's story consisted of journey taken by a gang of dwarfs (7) to the Castle of Smog where they were to slay an evil dragon. Along the way, the dwarfs (various representations of himself) engage in perilous adventures resulting in narrow escapes from death. The repetitive theme, the feelings engendered in his characters, and the solutions devised to turn a disadvantage into an advantage were shrewd, inventive, and ultimately provided a means for Mark to gain mastery over his feelings of weakness.

To reinforce Mark's new repertoire of coping skills, two additional sessions were used to adapt his story characters to real life situations. In preparation for a summer program, some distance away from his home, an illustrated map (not unlike the adventure map to the Castle of Smog) was drawn. Plotted along the course were the potential dangers and anticipatory methods of coping. Changing a disadvantage into an advantage remained the central goal.

Following these sessions, Mark demonstrated significant improvement in his social relationships and was less isolated from his peers. The issue of noncompliance at school was no longer a concern. A follow-up visit three months after therapy ended indicated that Mark continued to do well.

These clinical vignettes point up the necessity for the therapist to be attentive to those aspects of a situation that provide the most direct route to reaching the client's goal. The therapist flexibly directs his or her interventions to the parts of the system that are most amenable to change. At times this may involve seeing the whole family, various subsets of family members or only the identified child or adolescent. Since small changes can have significant ripple effects, we need only impact on one link in the system to create opportunities for systemic change.

Conclusions

As you can see from the clinical vignettes presented, the therapist working with children, adolescents, and their families, acts as a consultant who quickly joins the family system by respecting the original request for change. Although the request for change usually comes from a parent in regard to the behavior of a child or adolescent, the therapist's aim is to join with both the child and the parent(s) in a joint effort at solution development. However, as we have seen, sometimes the therapist must work solely with the parent(s), for example, when a child is either too young to actively participate in treatment or when an adolescent refuses to be involved, and sometimes with the child or adolescent, when that seems to be the most effective road to change. Usually, various combinations of family members are seen in a flexible arrangement that allows the therapist maximum leverage in creating a context for change.

The aim of the therapist is to build on already existing strengths and resources in the family as a way to help them reach the agreed-upon goal. By using the families' competencies as leverage points for change, the therapist co-constructs solutions using the language of possibility. By listening closely to the language of the family, the therapist constructs tasks and assignments that provide a pathway toward change. A nondiagnostic approach is taken, which avoids pessimistic language and psychiatric terminology and works instead to empower family members to take responsibility for mastering a developmental issue. Reframing and positive connotation are used as a means of moving the issue out of the pathological arena and into the realm of hope and possibility. While remaining available to the system over time, the possibility-oriented therapist quickly disengages from the system when family members are satisfied that the goal has been reached.

8
The Possibility Frame and Complex Clinical Issues

> Peary relates that on his polar trip he traveled one whole day toward the North, making his sleigh dogs run briskly. At night he checked his bearings to determine his latitude and noticed with great surprise that he was much further South than in the morning. He had been toiling all day toward the North on an immense iceberg drawn southward by an ocean current.
> —Ortega y Gasset in *Meditations on Quixote*.

In this chapter, our attention moves to several complex and thorny issues that are often ignored in brief psychotherapy texts. As with other therapies, there is no magical strategy or technique to "cure" alcoholism or prevent the psychiatric hospitalization of an adolescent, without family supports, who is determined to commit suicide. The approach that we have been discussing, however, does have something to offer in focusing attention on possibilities rather than problems, even in very difficult, multi-problem situations.

By keeping your attention on possibilities and strengths, you can avoid becoming overwhelmed with the apparent chronicity and complexity of the problems you are facing. By emphasizing those things that people do that are good for them and helpful, you can begin to amplify on existing strengths and assets and try to build a foundation for change. By mobilizing significant others in the client's social system, you can build an autonomously functioning social network that will serve as a base of support for the client during times of crisis and stress. By thinking "small," you can develop strategies for the client system to take small steps in the direction of improved functioning. A possibility framework suggests a "primary orientation to the future [with the past viewed] as a reservoir of valuable learnings and potential resources, and the future as the basis for growth and development" (Gilligan & Kennedy 1989:11). Although the approach proposed is no panacea for complex clinical problems, a future orientation, as we will see, can provide a means for opening up options for both you and the client.

In one situation, for example, a mother of four with a fifteen-year history of alcohol and cocaine abuse recently completed a two-week inpatient program. For the past month she had been sober, attending NA and AA regularly. Seeing her and her children (all of whom were doing extremely well at school both academically and behaviorally), I [SF] complimented her, not only on her efforts at sobriety, but on how well she has raised her four children in spite of her drug problem. Focus of the treatment was helping her to do those things that help to maintain her sobriety and support her children's continued positive development. Focus was not placed on her drug history, but rather on supporting those steps that she had already taken which were in the direction of healthy functioning.

Some of issues we will be discussing in this chapter include the abuse of drugs and alcohol, childhood or adolescent problems that occur in families where one or both parents are either abusing substances or show extreme unpredictable and inconsistent behavior, and the problem of anorexia in adolescence. In addition, we will look at the usefulness of psychotropic medication (as an adjunct to treatment with children) as well as the issue of psychiatric hospitalization. Finally, we will explore the value of mobilizing social supports in times of crisis, and the role of the therapist as an agent of social control.

Dealing with Substance Abuse Problems

One of the most difficult issues therapists face in daily clinical practice concerns substance abuse and its ramifications in the individual's family system. Substance abusing systems have a reputation for being especially recalcitrant to all psychotherapeutic methods. While a full discussion of the psychotherapy of substance abuse goes beyond the scope of this book, we share our thinking in applying a possibility-oriented perspective in dealing with this ubiquitous problem. The reader is referred to Elkin (1984), Stanton et al. (1982), and Treadway (1989) for useful ideas in working with substance abusing systems.

In the following clinical vignette, a possibility-oriented approach is used to empower the client to effectively manage her use of alcohol. I [SF] help the client build on her successes rather than allowing her to wallow in self-pity.

A forty-four-year-old woman presented with concerns about her growing dependency on alcohol. She came from a family with significant alcohol and drug related problems. Besides being married to, and subsequently divorced from, an alcoholic man, she worked a second job in a restaurant with a bar. Her usual pattern was to either drink after work at the bar or to come home and start drinking by herself. In addition, she complained about not sleeping very well (getting only about four hours of sleep a night). Her internist had suggested she seek mental health contact since the doctor believed she was "depressed." She presented as very tearful and said that she was feeling sorry for herself.

She described the typical pattern of making herself a drink immediately upon entering her house and how she seemed to go on "automatic pilot" as she walked through the door. We discussed times when she was able to "resist the urge" to take a drink, and she could acknowledge that this did happen on occasion, but couldn't say how she was able to do it. She thought it might be useful to have some kind of "cue" to remind her not to drink, so she could break this troubling pattern she had gotten into. I suggested she think about a convenient cue or signal that would be immediately visible to her when she entered her house. She agreed to try this. Following a strategy developed by deShazer (1985), I also asked her to think about what she does when she is able to overcome the temptation to have a drink (both at home and at her job at the restaurant). In addition, I gave her a copy of the AA meeting schedule and told her to hold onto this since it might be necessary, at some point, for her to attend. We scheduled an appointment for one week later.

At that appointment, the woman reported having had no alcohol for seven days and was sleeping better as well. She did not use my suggestion of developing a cue as a reminder not to drink, but simply shifted into drinking a soft drink rather than alcohol both at home and at the restaurant. While she acknowledged her ability to resist temptation, she could not state exactly how she was able to do this. I encouraged her to continue her successful efforts but also suggested that she "go slow" in making changes since she was now talking about dating and trying to lose weight. We set another appointment for three weeks later.

At that time she reported having had no alcohol for a month and was sleeping even better now. At her restaurant job, someone put a beer in her hand and she decided not to have it. A meeting two weeks later revealed that she had been sober now for six consecutive weeks and was getting eight hours of sleep a night. A meeting three weeks later indicated continued sobriety and comments about "feeling better about myself." We then scheduled a meeting for one month later.

At this meeting the woman indicated that she had drunk alcohol on "three or four occasions" and defined this as an "experiment to see if I would lose control altogether." This didn't happen. She reported that she no longer drank at home after work and had "broken that old pattern." We discussed the potential usefulness of going to AA meetings in order to get support for staying sober. In light of her strong family history of substance abuse, I felt it was important that she consider this option, to which she seemed very open. I told her that if she decided to take another drink she should consider attending an AA meeting. This woman continued making good progress regarding her alcohol use and began attending AA meetings on an "as needed" basis. Several additional sessions were held in dealing with her concerns with her teenage son.

If any clinical issue requires therapist humility, alcohol and drug problems take first place. Just as the alcoholic must give up his willful insistence that he has control over his drinking, so must the therapist accept his powerlessness over his client's use and abuse of substances (Berenson 1987). It is an intriguing paradox (see Bateson 1972) that the alcoholic must admit he is powerless over alcohol (the First Step of AA) and accept defeat, before he can take steps toward change. In fact, "the experience of defeat not only serves to convince the alcoholic that change is necessary, it is the first step in that change" (Bateson 1972:313).

Although a solution-oriented approach, as was described above, can be useful in helping some people effectively manage their alcohol intake, such an approach will not work with many of the clients with whom we deal. Some have been through several detoxification programs only to revert to abusing substances again. Some only call for help when in crisis or inebriated and depressed, and then, when sober, refuse to follow-up.

Although much of what this book is about has to do with developing effective strategies for change, in the area of substance abuse, you must carefully avoid "willful" attempts to direct change. Rather, you are better off maintaining a systemic acceptance of the power of the alcohol or drug in the family system (Berenson 1987; Treadway 1989). By accepting the notion that alcoholism and drug abuse are "addictions," we are able to maintain a nonblaming neutrality in dealing with both the abuser and his family. By taking this posture, we externalize the blame for the development of the behavior, yet still hold the person responsible for changing the pattern. (In line with our constructivist thinking, we accept the notion of "addiction" or "disease" as a useful linguistic distinction, not as an objective truth.) Rather than focusing on "causes," we work to build on previous successes, on sobriety, and on the benefits of sobriety for the individual and his or her family. For someone who has participated in several detox programs and continues to drink, we look to expand periods of sobriety (for example, from two weeks to three months) and view such small triumphs as progress. For those individuals who are trying to maintain sobriety, we encourage participation in "relapse prevention" groups that provide cognitive and behavioral skills in preventing a return to use of the substance. We also encourage involvement in AA and support family member participation both in the recovery process of the substance abuser as well as in Al-Anon and Alateen.

In line with our efforts to use the most economical intervention that will lead to the client's goal, we favor outpatient detoxification over inpatient detoxification. However, there are those individuals whose family and other social supports are such that removal from their natural setting, for a period of time, can be useful in supporting the beginning steps of gaining sobriety.

As possibility-oriented therapists, we try to respect our client's choices, remain nonjudgmental, and work with those family members most motivated for change. The work is neither easy nor quick and requires great patience on the part of the therapist.

In the next section, our attention moves to adolescents and their families who present with concerns about the adolescent's use of illicit substances, and families that present with other concerns about a child or adolescent, and where the issue of substance abuse is evident elsewhere in the nuclear family system.

Adolescent Substance Abuse

As with any other child or adolescent concern, you must engage the family in treatment and begin a process of supporting family members to help the adolescent overcome the problem. By building on family resources and strengths, and supporting parental behaviors that lead to solutions, you create a context for change.

One must obviously differentiate adolescent experimentation with drugs and alcohol and more serious abuse or dependence (see Treadway 1989, for information on assessment). If, in fact, the situation is one in which a clear pattern of alcohol or drug abuse is evident, the therapist, will need to empower the parents as change agents (Piercy and Frankel 1986; Treadway 1989). This involves helping the parents to develop a set of rules, guidelines or expectations for dealing with the adolescent's drug-related behavior. It is important that both parents (if this is not a single-parent household) come to some agreement on how they will deal with violations of the rules. In single-parent families, the absent parent or other adult support persons in the extended family system may need to be involved. Although it may be tempting for you to get involved in marital issues, the family is better served if the focus remains on the adolescent's drug-related behavior and the parents are supported as change agents for their son or daughter.

In contrast to older adolescents or adults, it is less likely that the parents can ask the younger teenager (under 17) to leave the house, although this may be necessary in extreme situations for temporary periods of time (a possibility is having the adolescent stay with a relative). It is very important to help the parents "set reasonable limits with practical consequences and avoid empty threats" (Treadway 1989:146). The adolescent can be involved in this rule-setting process after the parents have developed some agreed-upon behavioral guidelines.

If parents are not able to set limits effectively with their adolescent, Treadway (1989:148) suggests that they "basically acknowledge their powerlessness," letting the adolescent know that it is now up to the adolescent to assume responsibility for his behavior. This is an extreme position. Before reaching this point, parents are encouraged to connect with groups such as Tough Love, which serve as a forum for getting support and as a place in which ideas are shared for dealing effectively with adolescents.

In some situations, the adolescent may need a detoxification and/or rehabilitation program to get sober and maintain sobriety. Unless outside supports (family, or peer) exist that can continue the process begun in the inpatient program, gains are likely to be lost on discharge. On the other hand, where supports exist on discharge, the chances improve for the adolescent to stay off drugs. Therefore, you must devote some time and energy to mobilizing potential support people in the adolescent's network and activating their participation in the aftercare process.

In many situations, you can successfully empower the parents to provide the needed structure in helping their son or daughter overcome a drug or alcohol problem. This is the case in the following clinical situation. Here, I [SF] build on parental actions that have already been successful and redefine the son's "lying" in a way that creates an opportunity for change.

A sixteen-year-old boy was referred by his pediatrician for treatment for marijuana abuse that had been ongoing for two years with concomittant reduction in grades, loss of interest in school, and "lying." He had been smoking every day after school with friends. Doug had a nineteen-year-old sister who was functioning successfully at college. In the initial session with Doug and his parents, it was clear how much the parents cared and worried about their son's behavior. Even before this first meeting, the parents had begun to increase appropriately their level of vigilance (or as Doug saw it their "intrusiveness"). I commended the parents on the excellent job they were already doing in monitoring their son's behavior and suggested they do more of the same.

At the time of this first visit, Doug had not used marijuana in almost two months. An appointment was set for six weeks later, at which time all four family members were in attendance. Doug admitted to one episode of smoking pot over this six-week period and reported "feeling disappointed" in himself. His father had vigilantly picked up on his red eyes and confused speech. Unlike the pot smoking, which had recurred only once, Doug's lying continued over little things (such as his whereabouts). I framed Doug's lying as "Doug's way to keep his parents vigilant." I told Doug that when he felt more confident of his ability to refrain from using pot, he would no longer need to lie and would give up this protective behavior. Another meeting was scheduled for five weeks later. The parents indicated no further indication of drug use, no lying, and significant improvement in Doug's grades at school. Doug felt secure in his ability to say "no" to people at school who offered him pot. The parents and Doug were commended for their dedicated and successful efforts. No further contacts were planned.

At times, parents are "blind" to their son or daughter's drug use, and the adolescent must seek help outside the family in drawing attention to his plight. Such is the case in the family situation to be described.

The therapist [Robert Schneider, Ed.D.], draws on the parents' concern and caring for their children and helps them to help their daughter overcome her abuse of alcohol and drugs. He sets up an initial contract with the daughter, which avoids a confrontation about her parents' involvement in treatment, yet opens the door for their participation. In addition, he uses concerns about the daughter's drug use as a way to open up a more general issue in the family (the parents' unavailability), which then has a positive impact on the other siblings as well. As the parents increase their vigilance, the daughter takes steps to abstain from using alcohol and drugs.

Francine, a fourteen-year-old girl, referred herself to the mental health department, reporting regular use of marijuana, alcohol, and mescaline over a six-month period. She described her drug use as having "helped me to forget and feel better at first, but now I just get rude." She also reported taking fifteen aspirin several months earlier ("not sure why") and that her parents "have no idea" about these problems. Francine insisted on being seen individually, saying, "If you tell my parents, I won't come." The therapist agreed to see her individually only if she kept her appointments and showed improvement (a reduction in her drug use). Francine added, "I don't know how my parents don't know what's going on, every night I come home and fall on the floor." Francine did not keep her next appointment, and the therapist called her parents, who were not surprised to learn about Francine's drug use since she had just been caught purchasing drugs at school.

A meeting was scheduled with Francine and her parents. Both parents were employed full-time in demanding managerial positions and denied any use of drugs or alcohol. They acknowledged that Francine "had not been herself" lately and now understood that this was because of her drug involvement. The therapist set up a meeting with the whole family, including Francine's four teenage siblings. The youngest (age thirteen), created a "family sculpture," placing his parents on one side of the room, facing away from the rest of the family. It seemed that all the siblings were experiencing their parents as distant and disconnected. The therapist, in an attempt to ally with the parents as the primary change agents, discussed the stresses involved in having five teenagers at home and emphasized the hard work involved in overseeing such a large contingent of active adolescents.

The parents were encouraged to increase their vigilance and send their adolescent children a clear message that they (the parents) would do whatever was necessary to continue to supervise them and keep them out of trouble. After this session, the parents began to set limits with curfews as well as by monitoring their outside contacts more closely. Francine "resented" these limits but complied nonetheless. Two additional sessions were held to monitor the parents' progress in helping their daughter. The parents were instructed to display the appointment card prominently on the refrigerator as a reminder to their children that they were serious.

At the second of these sessions, the parents reported that Francine was showing no signs of using drugs. This was verified by urinalysis. In addition, her school performance had improved, she had joined the cheerleading team, was responding to the new rules of the house, and seemed "happier." Francine agreed with her parents' assessment and did not feel the need to return for future sessions. It was decided that Francine would not need to come to any further meetings if she agreed to spend time each week talking with her mother. Meetings with the parents continued on a monthly basis for the next three months At the end of treatment the parents reported that all the children were doing well and that Francine continued to show no signs of alcohol or drug abuse.

Child/Adolescent Problems in a Substance Abusing Family

In addition to adolescents who present with substance abuse issues, we sometimes encounter other situations (a child who daydreams in class; an adolescent who breaks curfews or gets into conflict with peers) that may reflect the impact of substance abuse in the family, even though this is not obvious at the outset.

Our approach here is based on the same principles and strategies outlined in an earlier chapter, taking the original concern seriously and working to engage other family members as allies in this process. Although one or another parent may have a drinking problem, directly confronting this in an initial session has not proven effective in setting the stage for further work. It is essential for the therapist "to maintain a nonjudgmental and empathic response to the family [since] family members are just as dependent on their roles as are abusers" (Treadway 1989:15).

Treadway presents a useful model for treatment when the child or adolescent's behavior is at issue and one parent is abusing drugs or alcohol (1989:113–33). Although we have found this model helpful in guiding our work, it is not always possible to carry it out in its ideal form.

During the initial stage, the parents are encouraged to take responsibilty for helping their son or daughter to manage the original difficulty. You deal with the presenting complaint by assuming that the parents are capable of being effective as change agents with their child or adolescent. You can expect that if one or the other parent is involved with drugs or alcohol, that person will be seen by other family members as ineffectual and progress toward reaching the goal will be stalled. When this happens, you naively ask family members to help you understand why there has not been improvement in the child or adolescent's behavior. In this way, the substance abuse issue is opened up indirectly. By doing so, you allow the family to raise their concerns about the substance abusing parent, rather than you "pulling" for this information. You must continue to empower the substance abusing parent by not turning him into the "identified patient." "[The therapist's] . . . job is to avoid taking sides while validating each person's perception of reality" (Treadway, 1989:119). This is a fine line for the therapist to walk and requires considerable significant training and experience. If the family comes to treatment without the parent who is abusing drugs, you can phone him while meeting with the rest of the family and give him the message that you know he cares about the children and wants to help in the process.

When information about the parental alcohol or drug involvement is revealed, you can reframe the child or adolescent's unwanted behavior as a benevolent response to the parent's substance abuse, that is, a sacrifice he is making to protect the family or to show his love and concern for a family member. By framing the behavior in this way, you begin a process of helping the substance abusing parent come to understand how much his problem is impacting on others in the family (see chapter 3, p. 59 for a clinical example).

In a way, the adolescent's behavior both draws attention to the fact that there is a problem in the family and serves to detour attention onto himself in such a way that the adolescent becomes the recipient of the family's anxiety and tension. The best outcome, is for the substance abusing parent to acknowledge his difficulties with drugs or alcohol and indicate a readiness to take some steps toward his own recovery (for example, by agreeing to see a substance abuse counselor or going to AA).

While gently working to open up the substance abuse issue, you must accept the fact that the person may not be ready to accept help or even willing to acknowledge the seriousness of the problem. In addition, if too much emphasis is placed on this prematurely, the child or adolescent may again engage in behavior that will deflect attention away from the abusing parent and back onto him. One hopes, however, that the abusing parent has developed a sufficiently positive and accepting relationship with you to agree to at least discuss the alcohol or drug use.

Ideally, at this point, you will have gotten acceptance for the fact that the substance abuse is having a significant impact on the family. Continue with reframing future misbehavior by the adolescent as an attempt to "rescue" the family from dealing with change. At this stage, therapeutic efforts are directed to helping family members express their concerns about the substance abuse directly to that parent, stop their "enabling" behavior, and increase their capacity to set limits on the abuser. In the final stage, the abusing parent will ideally seek help. Work then proceeds in helping the family deal with the shift in roles that sobriety brings and to reconnect with each other in reestablishing intimacy and appropriate executive functioning.

When the abusing parent refuses to either acknowledge that he has a substance abuse problem or refuses to participate in treatment, therapeutic efforts are directed towards the nonabusing parent and the children, in helping them to focus on their own lives and "detach" from the behavior of the substance abusing parent. Limit setting is encouraged when the abusing parent's behavior exceeds some acceptable level. We have found both Al-Anon and Alateen to be effective forums for helping people deal on a day-to-day basis with the confusions and traumas of living with a substance abuser.

You may note that we do not use the term "codependent" in referring to the partner of the alcohol or drug abusing family member. We prefer a nonpathological perspective in which the partner is not identified by a pejorative label (Tavris 1990). Our goal in working with the partner of an alcohol or drug abusing family member is to empower him in ways that increase his options and choices. We are always looking for "exceptions" to self-defeating behavior, in order to support and encourge past and present behaviors that are in the direction of healthy functioning.

As most of us are aware, dealing with the issue of substance abuse is a very complex process that requires a great deal of gentle encouragement and patience on the part of the therapist. In many instances, families begin the treatment process and then "drop out" as the parents' substance abuse problem comes to light. With others, the abusing parent continues to deny the seriousness of the problem, and the teenager continues to get into trouble on an intermittent basis. In this latter situation, it is useful to encourage the adolescent to attend Alateen meetings to help him or her develop the capacity to detach from the parental abuser's behavior.

At Harvard Community Health Plan we have experimented with groups limited to eight to ten sessions for children and adolescents living in families with an alcohol or drug abusing parent. A group context is created in which the children and adolescents have an opportunity to discuss and get support and validation for the pain they are experiencing. We have run these groups combining children of different ages to create a "sibling group" in which older members (in their teens) can provide input and ideas to younger members about issues such as what to do if a parent decides to drive while drunk and asks that the child come with him. The group context helps the child or adolescent feel less "alone in their struggles." Some of these children and adolescents are able to move on productively in their lives in spite of the substance abuse issues at home.

Dealing with the issue of substance abuse is a complex therapeutic process in which the therapist must develop the capacity to maintain a "constructivist" stance, nonjudgmentally accepting each family member's view of reality and working within those realities to create change. However, it does seem clear that "if the role of the substance abuse is not addressed, . . . the gains made in . . . therapy do not last and the old pattern reemerges" (Treadway 1989:10). The reader is referred to several useful papers outlining both direct and indirect strategies for dealing with the issue of substance abuse (Ellis 1986; Piercy and Frankel 1986; Potter-Efron and Potter-Efron 1986).

We have included descriptions of several clinical situations that point up the complexities of creating change when a parent or parents are abusing drugs or alcohol. Notice how, even in the face of these difficult issues, the therapist [SF] works to find leverage for creating change.

A sixteen-year-old boy, living with his two alcoholic parents, was referred by the court for "breaking and entering and malicious damage to property." At our initial meeting (which only the mother and son attended) it was clear that this boy was in a very responsible role at home worrying about both of his parents as well as his five-year-old sister. He indicated his wish that his parents would stop drinking and described his frustration and upset at their persistent refusal to listen to him. His mother was drinking a pint of vodka a day and had a seizure disorder. The father refused to come for treatment and was reportedly violent when inebriated.

I spent some time individually with this young man, validating his predicament and acknowledging the reality of his frustration. I framed his "breaking and entering" behavior as a way of expressing his frustration and calling attention to the plight of his family. It was clear to me that this young man was not a "delinquent," but only trying to get someone to take notice of his awful family situation. Unfortunately, he would neither agree to go to Alateen meetings nor to meet with me, since he viewed the drinking as "my parents' problem."

The mother reported that her previous attempts to get sober and attend AA were discouraged by her husband. I decided to use a drastic strategy to try to move the mother to make a commitment to her own sobriety. I told her that since she and her husband were both actively drinking, I would need to notify the Department of Social Services (DSS) that the situation was a potentially neglectful one, especially in terms of the care of the five-year-old girl. I knew how much the mother cared about her daughter and how she would do anything to keep her at home. I told the mother to call me the next day to let me know what her decision would be: either for her to go into an inpatient detoxification program or for me to notify DSS. She did call and agree to the detox program saying, "I don't want my child taken away from me." After discharge from the program she continued on a sporadic basis with therapy and then dropped out. At last contact, the DSS had taken custody of the five-year-old girl, the boy continued living at home and was meeting with a probation officer, and both parents were still drinking.

This family of four (mother, father, fourteen-year-old daughter, sixteen-year-old son, Richard) presented with concerns about Richard's behavior. Richard was "stealing money from the house; smoking pot; acting defiantly to parents; and missing class." After a series of four meetings with the whole family, I had a sense that some important information was missing. After I excused the children from the next meeting, the parents told me that they both were alcoholics. The mother was in recovery, having stopped drinking about two years earlier, and the father was still actively drinking. I then reconvened the whole family and, with the parents' permission, raised the issue of father's drinking and mother's recovery. Seeing the parents alone provided an opportunity for the alcohol issue to come up in a safer context, after which the admonition of "don't talk" was broken, and the stage was set for open discussion of this topic.

The father understood that his leverage in dealing effectively with his son was severely compromised by his drinking, yet he continued to deny the seriousness of his problem. Finally, after several months in which I had no contact with the family, I received a call from mother letting me know that her husband had died suddenly of a heart attack (at age fifty-four). She requested contact in grieving the loss of her twenty-one-year relationship with her husband.

About two months after his father's death, Richard made a suicide attempt by drinking an excessive amount of alcohol. He was admitted to a medical facility for twenty-four hours and then came in for an appointment with his mother. Richard seemed confused and disoriented, not having fully recovered from the binge of the night before. He agreed that he needed to talk with someone to avoid repeating this behavior, and a series of both individual and family meetings were held. Richard's behavior served to activate and mobilize his mother to pull herself out of her depressed state, and I framed it as such. It was clear that Richard was both uncomfortable with his mother's tears and sadness and tended to deny his own feelings of loss for his father. We focused on the importance of Richard sharing the warm, "feelings" side of himself instead of putting up a "macho" front. The alcohol incident so scared Richard that he made significant progress on these issues. Therapy continued with the family for several more months as they dealt with reestablishing roles at home in light of father's death.

In another family with whom I've [SF] had multiple episodes of contact over a three-year period, the now seventeen-year-old daughter is the focus of the family's concerns. Every six months or so, the daughter engages in some dramatic behavior that creates a reason for parents to recontact me and resume therapy. The father has a long-standing history of alcoholism, and the mother has manifold somatic complaints and illnesses. The seventeen-year-old daughter is the most vocal in the family and most able to articulate her worry about her father's drinking. Although I try to frame her dramatic behavior as a "sacrifice she is making in saying she cares and worries about her father," he has, up to this point, refused to get help for his drinking problem.

The mother tends to make compromises to keep the peace (an

example is approving of the father's drinking at home instead of going to a bar). I have directly discussed with the father (without the children present) the impact of his drinking on his daughter's behavior. I have emphasized his caring and concern for his daughter and predicted that her leaving home will be a difficult issue for the family if she continues to worry about him in the way she does. Although he continues to deny the seriousness of his drinking, he is willing to come to sessions with the focus on his daughter's behavior. As a therapist, I must carefully walk the line of keeping the focus on the daughter while also looking for opportunities to connect with father about the relationship of his drinking and his daughter's behavior. The work continues.

At times, the same patterns, as seen in alcoholic or substance abusing families exist in other families in which substance abuse is not an issue. Below, I describe a family in which the father had a history of volatile and unpredicatable mood swings. Treatment efforts went into empowering the mother to take steps to set limits with her husband and helping the children to better understand their father's unpredictable behavior.

In this family of two parents and three children, the father had been diagnosed as having "bi-polar" disorder and displayed significant swings in mood. His unpredictable behavior kept all family members "walking on eggs." He was taking several medications, none of which seemed to be effective in controlling his severe mood fluctuations and occasional violent outbursts. The mother and the three children were referred to me [SF] originally by the father's therapist because they were all experiencing significant stress from living with the father. One of children had been crying at school and all felt intimidated and frightened by their father's unpredictable "moods" and behavior.

The wife was in the position of trying to appease her husband in hopes this would help keep the peace and avoid violent outbursts. This situation was very similar to that which occurs in an alcoholic family system. After several meetings with the mother and the children, I spent some time with the mother individually. The mother had been considering asking her husband to leave the house since she could no longer accept his erratic behavior. She was initially ambivalent about what to do, and my efforts focused on helping her understand her own "enabling" role, accept the fact that she could not change her husband's behavior, and begin to take steps to set limits with her husband.

I held several meetings with the husband and wife during this time to see if they could work out a mutually agreeable plan for him to live at home. This option seemed unworkable for either of them as the wife realized that her husband was unwilling to take responsibility for changing his behavior or agree to become more actively involved as a husband and father in the family.

After the husband left, and then returned home on several occasions, the mother filed for divorce and a permanent separation ensued. The mother felt a great deal of guilt for turning he husband out when he was "sick" but was able to "stick to her guns." The children, as one might expect, were both angry at the mother for "taking away" their father and relieved that she took some steps toward creating a more peaceful life for the family.

As you can see, these clinical situations do not all have happy endings. In many situations, people continue to struggle with the residual effects of living in family situations with high degrees of unpredictability and inconsistency. At times the most therapeutic action the therapist can take is to encourage and facilitate the mobilization of social supports via family and friends or through participation in self-help groups such as Al-Anon or Alateen.

Groups such as Alateen and Al-Anon create a community of peers who can provide a level of acceptance not easily replicated in the therapist's office. In the Ericksonian mold, participants in such groups do not directly provide advice (rule of no "cross-talk"), but instead, through the telling of their own stories create an atmosphere conducive to change and self-exploration. We believe, however, that participation in such groups is best structured as time-limited experiences. As Micheal Elkin (see Collet, 1990:30) points out "If you identify yourself as survivor of . . . abuse, you are making a . . . self-hypnotic statement that defines you by the most destructive thing that's ever happened to you. In the short-term it's important to say it, but you can get stuck there." A self-help group has been described as "like a recovery room. The point is to get better and go out in the world, not live in the hospital forever" (Collet 1990:31).

In the next section, our attention turns to another difficult issue, anorexia nervosa in a teenage girl and how you can effectively apply a possibility-oriented approach to this complex issue.

Anorexia

The problem of anorexia nervosa presents the therapist with a serious, sometimes life-threatening, clinical issue. The therapist must carefully and creatively intervene in a family system in which one member is experiencing significant medical risk. While there are no magic answers to complex clinical situations, a systemic, possibility-oriented framework can be helpful in accessing client resources in moving toward problem mastery.

In the following clinical situation, the therapist [Cynthia Mittelmeier, Ph.D.] maintains an optimistic, flexible, solution-oriented and time-sensitive perspective in successfully resolving a problem of anorexia in a sixteen-year-old girl. The therapist combined brief individual sessions with the teenager with intermittent family meetings, and joined with the teenager and her family in an alliance that fostered movement towards health and improved functioning. Note the necessity for the therapist to be open and ready to take advantage of fortuitous happenings, in this situation, the comments of the girl's pediatrician. Notice how the therapist avoided a pathological perspective and instead framed the problem systemically. The work described took place in twenty-four sessions over a period of thirteen months. Follow-up contacts continue.

Amy (age sixteen) was referred by her pediatrician following one month of inpatient treatment for anorexia nervosa. Amy was a straight "A" student who excelled in track, had many friends, held three part-time jobs and participated on both the student council and swim team. She was the younger of two children living with their single-parent mother. The father had a history of alcoholism and had been physically abusive to his wife in the marriage.

During the initial interview, which included Amy, her mother, and her sister, Amy denied that there were any serious problems and saw no connection between her eating problem and other issues in the family. She also denied feeling depressed. Amy's mother, however, noted that Amy insisted on having complete control over buying and preparing the food she ate, that she would eat only certain foods and would do so separately from the rest of the family. Amy's sister, Clare, remarked that "Amy's abnormal about food and she doesn't deal with what is really bothering her."

Amy's father was invited to a subsequent meeting and presented a position of not quite understanding "why Amy can't just eat." He often tried to buy her favorite foods and would become upset when she refused to eat them. In one family meeting, Amy volunteered that she was the "worrier" in the family. She worried mainly about her mother working too hard and her father's drinking. Amy seemed in tune to her mother's struggles (especially around financial issues) and was very careful not to place demands on her. Clare, on the other hand, was more oblivious to stress in the family.

After several family meetings, the therapist received a call from the pediatrician stating that Amy's weight had dropped and that she might again require hospitalization. An expert on eating disorders was consulted, and recommended a trial of antidepressant medication, group therapy, and attendance at Alateen meetings. Amy refused all of these suggestions. Shortly after this, Amy and her mother had an emergency meeting with the pediatrician who told Amy that she (Amy) was "sad" and needed to focus more on her "feelings" in therapy. Amy told the therapist later, that she was angry with the pediatrician's comments and indicated that she did not agree with the idea that she was "sad." The therapist, accepted Amy's statement, and suggested, that together, they work as detectives and investigate the situation to see if they could prove the pediatrician wrong.

Several additional half-hour individual meetings were scheduled, with family meetings to take place every three weeks. Together, the therapist and Arny generated the idea that Amy was, in some way, acting on her family's behalf, particularly her mother's. They agreed that Amy could be very independent and competent, and yet there was another side of her that was reluctant to "grow up," since it was not clear how her mother would fare if she were to become even more independent and move further from the family. The therapist raised this issue by discussing Amy's expectations of what the consequences would be when her eating problem was resolved. Amy remarked, "I could work more, play sports, wouldn't have to go to the doctors, (and jokingly said), and my mother wouldn't have anything to worry about." This focus was also addressed in family meetings, with the mother able to clearly communicate to Amy that Amy did not need to worry about her and that, in fact, she (mother) was looking forward to the day when she would have less caretaking responsibility. She reminded Amy that she had a network of friends and supports. Amy regained the weight and rehospitalization was avoided.

Over this period, Amy was able to take a stand that differed from that of her mother and sister in voicing her wish to maintain a close connection with the father. Amy and Clare were planning a vacation with their father and they expressed concern about his drinking on this trip. Amy decided she would talk with her father about his drinking and let him know that she would not visit him if he was going to drink in her presence. He agreed that he would not drink while on the vacation.

In working to increase the amount of time the family had for more positive and relaxed contact, the therapist suggested that the mother and her daughters engage in one activity that they could enjoy together that did not involve food. In addition, Amy was asked to spend five minutes each day talking about her worries, with her mother who was instructed not to raise the issue of food during this time.

The vacation with their father went well, and Amy took this as a sign that she was making progress. She reported that, previously, going on a vacation would have been impossible since she would be uncomfortable eating in restaurants. She also reported that the situation at home was less tense and that her mother seemed less focused on her eating. In addition, Amy had been given permission to resume practicing with the track team at school. At this point, less frequent meetings were requested.

In light of how well Amy was doing, she was asked to join the therapist as a "consultant" for another client with a similar eating problem. During this meeting, Amy spoke about the value of not keeping the eating problem a secret and of gaining support from friends. She stated that it was important to express feelings and to try to understand how the eating problem fits into other patterns in her life.

During a family meeting one month later, Amy reported that her father had called her, the previous week, after he had been drinking, and asked her to pick him up from a bar. Amy refused and went out with her friends instead. She noted "I'm like my father, except I took my problems out on food, instead of alcohol." Amy has maintained a stable weight for eight months, eats a variety of foods, and has resumed working. She began practicing with the track team, became a peer counselor at school, and was planning to go to the prom at the end of the school year. She has been sharing her knowledge of substance abuse and eating problems with her peers as part of her role as a peer counselor. Follow-up family meetings continue on an intermittent basis (about every four months) in supporting the "gains" made.

Psychotropic-Medication

> The brain is also part of an individual's ecology.
> —Frank Pittman

Freeman (1988), in presenting a "systems view of the person," includes the "biological self" as one important component. In systems thinking this aspect of self is often overlooked or discounted. Some therapists see a move toward a biological intervention as violating important systemic principles (see Haley 1980). In our view, the prescribing of psychotropic medication, while not our first line of intervention, is one that deserves attention in certain special clinical situations. We do not move rapidly or take lightly the decision to use a biological intervention and are aware and concerned about the potential negative side effects of psychotropic drugs. However, as we will see, in some circumstances, and for brief periods of time, medication can have a significant positive effect both on the individual taking it as well as on the larger family system.

One area in which psychotropic medication can play an important role is with children who have attentional problems in the classroom and for whom many months or even years of environmental intervention have not proved successful. These children are easily distracted,

can be disruptive in class, aggressive with peers, and show a low toler-
ance for frustration. In some of these situations, we have found the
judicious use of medication helpful in creating positive changes in behavior.

Systems therapists "seem prone to view the child's behavior as a
metaphor for a confused interpersonal system and to subtly blame
disturbed systems dynamics for most of the problem. They seem at
times to underplay the importance of biological factors" (Wendorf
1987:295). While it is true that a family becomes organized around a
child who poses a challenge to their usual mode of functioning, it
serves only to "blame the victim" by assuming that the parental behavior "causes" the child's problem.

A valid concern of systems therapists is the potential for stigmatizing the "patient" taking the medication as "sick", releasing other family members from taking responsibility for change. In most of the work
described in this book, we assume that one person wants a change and
then work with that person and/or with others in the family to help
achieve the desired goal. No attempt is made to make all family members "the patient." In addition, by assuming a constructivist stance, we
put little validity into looking for "causes" but rather attend to that
particular "reality" that will provide the most leverage for creating the
requested change. Obviously, however, the perceived "symbolic" and
"transactional" significance to the family of one member taking medication must not be ignored (Freeman 1988). The therapeutic team,
therefore, must be sensitive to the systems implications of prescribing
psychotropic medication. As Haley (1980) says, one must be careful not
to equate the use of medication with "illness" but rather emphasize the
fact that the medicine merely serves to support behavior change on a
temporary basis.

Just as prescribing medication has systems implications, not prescribing does as well. In some cases, not prescribing has negative consequences in the client's system that outweigh the potential consequences
of prescribing. The costs and benefits of taking medication must be
clearly presented by the pediatrician or consulting psychiatrist to the
client/client system, and it is their decision that must be respected.
Although the pediatrician or consulting psychiatrist prescribes and
monitors the medication, it is the therapist who takes primary responsibility for the overall treatment.

We take a multimodal or psychoeducational approach with children who present with significant attentional problems that have not
been susceptible to modification by behavioral methods alone. By inte-
grating psychotherapeutic interventions, school related consulation and
the judicious use of psychopharmacologic agents, the therapist is able
to support rapid and positive change. By accepting the idea of a bio-

logic component, the client/client system allows the removal of blame from both the child for being "bad" and the parents for "managing badly" (Johnson 1987; Wendorf 1987; Zeigler and Holden 1988). Instead, a team approach to problem solving can be set up. You work to amplify the strengths and capacities of the child, the family, and the educational setting in a joint effort with the goal of helping the child increase self-control and reduce impulsiveness. Both the child's and the parents' self-esteem is improved by focusing on their strengths and assets rather than attributing blame and fostering guilt.

"Parents of ADD (Attention-Deficit Disorder) children are often fraught with anxiety and frustration from having tried a gamut of child management techniques . . . and having found that nothing worked. Their children's misbehavior is highly visible and socially embarrassing, subjecting these parents to raised eyebrows or outright condemnation" (Johnson 1987: 342). In line with a psychoeducational approach, we have found parent support groups to be a useful adjunct to direct family work. Such groups serve an educational and support function, with a pediatrician discussing issues regarding medication, and a psychologist helping the parents to develop behavioral strategies for effectively dealing with their child.

Methylphenidate (Ritalin) is the typical stimulant medication used in children with well-documented attentional problems. Research indicates that it produces "desirable . . . changes [which] are often immediate and extensive, dramatically effecting everyday social climates" (Henker and Whalen 1989: 219). In one family, the six-year-old son was showing clear signs of an attentional problem. He was easily distracted, had difficulty focusing on the tasks at hand and was not completing his work at school. An IQ test revealed a very bright and potentially capable student. On the first day, on a low dose of Ritalin (5 mg.), his behavior improved dramatically. He told his mother "God made the medicine for me . . . I'm very happy. . . . Now I wish that things can work out at home, too." Focus shifted to dealing with stresses in this multigenerational family household and helping the parents deal more effectively with their son's behavior at home.

In addition to increasing attention span and decreasing impulsivity, one beneficial "side effect" of using stimulant medication with children with attentional problems is the change that occurs as family members have to shift their usual mode of responding to the child. As Henker and Whalen point out, "studies with parents and teachers have demonstrated that medication-related behavioral improvements in hyperactive children are accompanied by what might almost be called 'normalization' in the adults who interact with these youngsters, reflected most clearly in more positive and less controlling interchanges" (1989:219).

In place of Ritalin or other stimulant medications, the tricylic antidepressants are sometimes used with children showing attentional problems, especially in cases involving sleep disturbances or bed-wetting. The pediatrician or consulting psychiatrist[1] meets with the child and the family, selects a medication, and presents this information to the family for them to decide. In all cases, the medication is prescribed in the lowest dose possible that produces a positive response and for as brief a period as possible. Ritalin is usually prescribed on school days only and not during vacations, except with those children whose attentional problems are so severe that they require more regular support. The usefulness of continuing the medication should be assessed at the beginning of each new school year, if not sooner.

Other circumstances that might necessitate the use of medication include severe mood problems in adolescence and/or as a strategy to prevent hospitalization (Madanes 1981: 143). In these situations, antidepressant medication or lithium carbonate is prescribed, the latter for clearly documented severe mood fluctuations. The following set of general guidelines, adapted from Sargent (1986), are useful when considering psychotropic medication:

1. It is important for the primary therapist and psychiatric consultant or pediatrician to develop a common language and a systemic frame of reference for describing the usefulness of the medication. By using a language that emphasizes the medication as an "aid" to controlling behavior or as a "maturity-enhancing aid" rather than as a medicine for curing "illness," one avoids pathologizing or stigmatizing the client. Even so, the therapist must not lose sight of the interactional implications of one member receiving medication, especially the possibility for stigmatizing that individual as "sick" or "ill."

2. It is important for the consulting psychiatrist to join with the parents and the child or adolescent in a team effort rather than get into power struggles regarding the usefulness or desirability of using medication.

3. The therapist, consulting psychiatrist, school personnel, and family must work in collaboration in developing and maintaining an integrated treatment plan in which the use of medication is only one small part.

4. "[Since] all psychopharmacological agents are powerful drugs, ... side effects ... should be carefully considered [and monitored]" (Sargent 1986:18).

Presented below are several clinical situations demonstrating how one can effectively integrate the use of psychopharmacological agents in the psychotherapy process with children and families. The use of medication is viewed as an adjunctive strategy, targeted at impacting on the presenting difficulty and creating a shift in the interactional process in the family. In this way, options are created for both improved family interaction and an empathic response on the part of both parents and siblings.

A six-year-old boy, Larry, was referred because his teachers felt that this "child has emotional problems due to lack of a father figure." His mother, according to the pediatrician's referral, "disagrees with school findings and would like a second opinion." In the initial session with the mother (a single parent) and Larry (an only child) she reported that Larry had had "behavioral problems" since preschool (age 3) and a "high activity level" since birth. She was feeling blamed by the school for her son's occasional disruptive behavior and tendency to be easily provoked into inappropriate activities. At home, she felt he needed constant reminders to do things. In my [SF] office, Larry appeared to be an exuberant, active little boy with a keen social awareness.

Following the initial meeting, I spoke with Larry's first grade teacher, who described him as unable to stay in his seat, rushing through his work, easily distractible, needing constant attention, and very physically aggressive with the other children. She did, however, say that she liked him. I suggested to the teacher that she call Larry's mother to emphasize that she (the teacher) cares about Larry and sees positive qualities in him, since the mother had a skewed picture of the teacher's attitude about him. I also met with Larry's pediatrician to discuss the potential usefulness of a stimulant medication to be used on school days only. The pediatrician met with Larry and his mother and recommended a trial program of Ritalin.

Two weeks following initiation of medication, I met again with mother and son. Larry's mother reported that she was able to set limits more easily now (even though Larry wasn't taking the medication on weekends), that Larry was doing much better at school, and that she was beginning to date, something she felt unwilling to do when Larry's behavior was so out of control. From this point on, she maintained continued contact with the pediatrician around Larry's behavior.

Billy (age seven), the oldest of three in an intact family was referred because of his "aggressive behavior" with other children at school and with his siblings at home. In addition, he was described as "noncooperative" at home and as "not listening" when his parents told him to do something. The parents described these problems as ongoing for the past two years. A year earlier Billy had seen a counselor who recommended individual psychotherapy. The parents refused. This counselor described Billy as "hyperactive" and "physically aggressive," with a problem in focusing his attention. Both parents were feeling ineffectual in dealing with Billy and reported experiencing a significant amount of tension when Billy was around.

After about four contacts with the family, some improvement was noted in Billy's compliance at home, and a decision was made to discontinue sessions due to mother's hospitalization to give birth to their fourth child. Almost two years later I [SF] received a call from mother again expressing concerns about Billy's behavior. He had just turned nine and continued to be described as "a disruptive force in the family; constantly testing; never satisfied; aggressive with siblings; acts silly and fresh with peers; doesn't compromise with friends and doesn't have any close friends." Billy's parents saw him as having a "poor self-image" and felt badly about their almost constant negative interactions with him. At school he was described as "not showing satisfactory self-control [and] with aggressive behavior easily triggered." His teachers noted that his "moods can easily fluctuate."

At this point I began to take seriously the idea that some kind of medication might be useful for Billy since he was showing all the signs of having a severe attentional problem (Gursky 1985; Henker and Whalen 1989). The parents, however, wanted to delay their decision until the school completed their evaluation on Billy. Although the evaluation was completed in about two months, I did not hear from the family for another year and a half. At which time mother called with similar concerns about Billy, who was now ten years old. This time I began discussing with the parents the potential usefulness of considering medication as an adjunct to our therapy work. The parents agreed and were given an appointment with a consulting psychiatrist who met with Billy and his parents and recommended a trial of an antidepressant medication (Desimpramine). The decision to use a tricylic antidepressant rather than a stimulant was made since Billy, in addition to showing clear attentional problems, cried easily and had difficulties sleeping. The parents agreed to a trial of medication for Billy. I met with the family two weeks later.

At this point the parents were already reporting some improvement in Billy's behavior and in the degree of stress at home. The parents described Billy as getting along better with his siblings; doing chores; and "studying harder and putting more effort into his homework." He was sleeping better, and the parents had begun to respond to him more positively, which he acknowledged. At one point in the session Billy volunteered that he and his parents were talking together in a different and more positive way than he could remember before. I complimented the parents and Billy on their efforts, noting that these changes may in fact have nothing to do with the medication since it sometimes takes up to three weeks for this particular medication to have an impact. I used this as an opportunity to support the parents and Billy and to work with them in building on the positive changes that had already begun.

In subsequent sessions, improvement continued to be noted in his behavior at home, and in his academic work as well. Billy started getting many compliments from relatives about his improved behavior, and he talked about the pressure he felt now to "do well" and to maintain the gains he had made. Both Billy and his parents were encouraged to find ways to allow Billy to "let loose" and not try so hard to do well. Billy was trying "to make up for" his previous academic problems and in so doing was putting himself under enormous pressure.

At our next meeting when Billy's parents mentioned that he had been acting silly, and "fooling around" I supported the need for this kind of behavior and encouraged the parents accept Billy's need to "let off steam." The medication, while making a significant impact on Billy's ability to focus and concentrate, created a new set of expectations for his continued success and this was being experienced as an added pressure. However, the medication did contribute to the development of a new interactional cycle between Billy and his parents, in which the parents were able to be more loving, caring, and involved with him in a new way. Their improved empathic response to him created a new context in which Billy began to feel more like a part of the family.

Twelve-year-old Mitchell was referred by his pediatrician for being "withdrawn in school; doesn't apply himself; fresh to parents." Mitchell is the older of two siblings. Testing at school revealed that Mitchell had a very high IQ and no learning disabilities. At the time of the referral he was "flunking everything." The school described him as "lazy, immature, daydreams, socially withdrawn." Mitchell clearly felt badly about disappointing his parents by not doing his part in helping the situation but couldn't seem to get hirnself motivated and mobilized to do the work. His mother raised the issue of whether Mitchell had an "attention deficit disorder" and I set an appointment for the parents and Mitchell to see our child psychiatrist for a consultation on this question. The consulting psychiatrist did see the usefulness of a trial of stimulant medication and began Mitchell on Ritalin to be taken on school days only.

At our next meeting, about two weeks later, the parents reported some progress in that Mitchell was getting his homework done and seemed more cooperative at home. He had organized his room and done some chores. We discussed some ways that Mitchell could improve his study habits, and he agreed to try them. I encouraged the parents to continue to help structure things for Mitchell who seemed to need some external input in getting himself organized. Mitchell continued making progress, bringing his grades up to C's and B's and feeling motivated to try to make the honor roll by the final marking period. His last report card showed marked improvement and he seemed well on his way to achieving academically at a level commensurate with his abilities. Mitchell's interaction with his parents shifted such that they were able to do less for him and were able to acknowledge his increasing autonomy and good judgment.

A seventeen-year-old girl, Wendy, was referred on an emergency basis following an apparent suicide gesture in which she ingested a small number of aspirin tablets after a conflict with her parents. From the medical record it was learned that Wendy had a longstanding history of developmental (cerebral palsy) and behavioral problems with evidence of impulsivity and poor judgment. The parents described her behavior as generally apathetic and occasionally impulsive with severe shifts of mood. These behavioral problems had been ongoing for many years. The parents were terrified of her running off and getting into "trouble" and had dedicated themselves to caring for and protecting their daughter.

Wendy attended a special day school for adolescents with behavioral problems from which she would occasionally and unpredictably run off, sometimes with a male friend of whom her parents disapproved. After several episodes of running away from school, the school decided to suspend her. Because of the complexity of the situation, a decision was made to briefly hospitalize Wendy in order to obtain a more intensive evaluation and make plans for future treatment.

The evaluation recommended (1) that Wendy be placed in a residential treatment center rather than live at home (she was seen as needing a setting in which she could be closely supervised), (2) that her parents be involved in regular family treatment at the residential center, and (3) that a trial of antidepressant medication be initiated (which was later changed to lithium carbonate).

After several weeks in hospital, Wendy returned home to await placement in a residential center. The lithium served to effectively control her mood fluctuations, and her parents reported her to be less impulsive and with some improvement in judgment. After several month's wait, Wendy was placed in a residential center. The parents continued their involvement in treatment, and Wendy eventually returned home to live with them.

It is important for both the therapist and client/client system to remember that "psychotropic medication does not provide a 'cure' for behavioral or emotional symptoms; the beneficial effects of medication do not provide evidence for organic etiology of the presenting problem; and family therapy, with rare exceptions, will remain the primary agent of change" (Gursky 1985: 72). It is also important that the consulting psychiatrist be familiar and comfortable with a systemic frame of reference and be able to portray the *use of medication as simply one part of an overall treatment strategy*. The therapist, family, school setting, and consultant psychiatrist must work together in a collaborative process in which goals and expectations of treatment are clear and in which treatment outcomes can be measured.

It is worth pointing out that although the use of medication in the clinical situations described here contributed to a positive outcome, there are many instances in which medication is not effective in modifying the child's or the adolescent's behavior. At such times, the therapist needs to look again to the family system to generate new ideas for successful developmental change.

Psychiatric Hospitalization

When I was growing up in Brooklyn, my [SF's] grandfather would often take me on walks to what he called in Yiddish, the *meshuge haus* (crazy house). We would walk through the grounds of the state psychiatric hospital as if taking a Sunday stroll in the country. Occasionally we would meet some of the residents. I often wondered why my grandfather felt so comfortable in this place. He didn't seem to distinguish the *meshuge* from the rest of us and enjoyed his contacts with the people there. When I asked him "why are these people *meshuge*?", he simply shrugged his shoulders as if to say "there's only a fine line between them and us." I began to wonder why we put people in such places if they are so much like us. As I got older it became clearer to me why we put people in such places: Because we have not committed the necessary time, energy, or resources in developing alternatives.

As I moved into the professional domain of psychotherapy, I continued to have great discomfort with the hospital as a treatment facility. Putting someone in the hospital went against everything my systems thinking had said was important. It plucked the individual out of their natural ecology and placed them in an institution cut off from their usual contacts and connections, isolated from friends and relatives, and stigmatized as "sick," in a mode better fitting for someone with a medical condition. It seems easy to lose sight of how intrusive, disruptive, and stressful hospitalization can be both for the individual and for their family system.

Keisler, reviewing studies that compared people randomly assigned to an inpatient facility or who received treatment on an outpatient basis, found the following: "In no case were outcomes of hospitalization more positive than alternative treatment. Typically the alternative care was more effective [on an array of outcome variables] . . . as well as decidely less expensive. Hospitalized patients were more likely to be readmitted to the hospital than were alternative care patients ever to be admitted" (1982: 349). Keisler also found that the alternative treatments that were most effective emphasized "social systems interventions."

Prior to considering hospitalization of the child or adolescent, it is important for the therapist to assess the use of less drastic and stigmatizing alternatives such as, temporary placement of an adolescent with relatives or family friends. The goal is to involve the natural support network in the treatment processs while reducing dependency on institutional resources. Besides being cost-efficient, this approach defines the crisis as one in which the family's role is critical for solution attainment.

Inpatient placement is viewed as an extreme intervention necessitated most frequently by an adolescent making a serious suicide attempt (with a continued high risk for repetition) and in which parents are minimally empathic to the plight of the adolescent or feel themselves unable to provide twenty-four-hour supervision. Suicidal intent is viewed as a serious and powerful statement that should necessitate family involvement (Stanton and Stanton 1985). If possible, a twenty-four-hour "suicide watch" (Bergman 1985; Stanton and Stanton 1985) is arranged in which parents and extended family provide supervision for the adolescent until the adolescent can prove that he doesn't require that level of care. In a way, the family setting becomes the hospital.

In many instances, involving the extended family immediately creates a context that can prevent hospitalization. By encouraging an empathic response on the part of family members to the plight of the adolescent, and by setting up a plan that creates avenues and options for direct communication between the adolescent and significant others in his family system, the need for hospitalization is reduced. In order to do this, the family may need to be seen on a frequent basis in working towards specific goals, the first of which is to impact on those issues that would make hospitalization necessary.

We have not found psychiatric hospitalization of adolescents showing violent or out-of-control behavior as especially useful or effective. With adolescents who present as violent and out-of-control, an attempt can be made to empower the family system to take charge of the adolescent and create the necessary structure to contain the behavior. With Haley (1980), we approach such situations with the idea of supporting parental limit setting and redefining the problem not as a psychiatric one but rather as a discipline problem, reframing "sick" to "bad" (see chapter 7, p. 171, and chapter 9, p. 232 for examples). When the family is unable to deal effectively with the adolescent at home, we prefer to draw on existing community resources such as respite care or home-visitor programs rather than on inpatient placement. As we will see in the next clinical vignette, a family-oriented approach can prevent a psychiatric hospitalization.

Before moving to this example, a few words of introduction are necessary. As we will see, the therapist's [Brian Meyer, Ph.D.] major goal was to prevent the psychiatric hospitalization of a suicidal adolescent living in a volatile family environment. While it was clear that the family system was experiencing multiple problems, the therapist's main focus was on reducing the need for a hospitalization and containing the son's out-of-control behavior, which was both a reaction to, and reflection of, the volatility of the system. The therapist's valiant efforts with this family can be compared to the experience of being on a raft during a storm and trying to maintain one's direction and balance in the face of tremendous turbulence. It took all the strength the therapist could muster to maintain his focus. He begins by developing an alliance with the adolescent and contracting with him for safety. He then makes a stalwart attempt to mobilize the client's extended family network in searching out potential support people to monitor and supervise the adolescent. Finally, he is required to involve a "higher authority" in the form of Departrnent of Social Services in trying to contain both the adolescent and his family. Even in the face of a very high degree of family impulsivity and violence, the therapist does not move to do the "easy thing" by putting the adolescent in a hospital. Instead, he systemically connects with the family in a way that is ultimately successful in reducing the suicidal behavior of the adolescent and preventing a psychiatric hospitalization. The therapist saw this family ten times over a period of three and a half months. Three additional appointments were not kept.

Jerry (age fifteen), oldest of three sons, and his parents came to the mental health department on an emergency basis two days after Jerry's parents found out that he had attempted to overdose on roughly thirty tablets of Fiorinol, Tylenol, and penicillin. He reported being unhappy about waking up after the attempt. He revealed the suicide attempt to a friend, who told his mother, who then informed Jerry's parents. It was learned that Jerry's father had had a bout with cancer a year earlier, had almost died, and had been living at home without work for a year. Jerry's parents rarely spoke except to yell at each other, and they slept in separate beds. The family had few rules and even those were rarely enforced. The parents appeared to have no control over the children, who stayed out late or overnight at will.

In the initial session, Jerry seemed very depressed. He clearly expressed suicidal ideas as well appetite and sleep disturbances. He also had a history of destructive and self—destructive impulsivity, including beating his brothers and mother, getting drunk at least once a week, several attempts (unknown to his parents) to kill himself by cutting his wrists, jumping from high places, and once trying to shoot himself. He was not actively suicidal at the time of the interview. He was able to relate easily and well to the therapist, and reported that talking with the therapist brought some relief. He denied any current plan or intent to kill himself, and he was able to contract for safety and to agree to call if he had the urge to act on his suicidal feelings. In light of Jerry's depressed state, the therapist referred him to a child psychiatrist to assess if a trial of antidepressant medication would be useful. It was understood that any medication prescribed would be given in very small quantities to avoid the potential for an overdose.

In the next two weeks, Jerry's suicidal ideation decreased, as did his fighting with his brothers. The family did not follow the therapist's recommendation of twice-weekly talks, and Jerry was not taking the prescribed medication on any regular basis. It appeared that having someone with whom to discuss his difficulties, relieved some of the immediate self-destructive feelings, but the family situation did not change.

A strategy was then developed to mobilize significant members of Jerry's family network with the hope of involving them in supervising Jerry and providing him with increased structure and accountability. Two meetings with the extended famiily were held, which included Jerry's paternal aunt, his paternal grandparents, and his girl friend. In the first meeting, a great deal of anger was directed towards Jerry for being "selfish" and "attention-seeking," particularly by Jerry's grandfather and mother. The grandfather discussed his schizophrenic son (Jerry's uncle) and the negative experience he had in family therapy around his son's problems. The family was unable to focus on the topic of the meeting, which was to develop a schedule in which they would each spend time with Jerry over the course of each week.

The family missed their next appointment, and the following meeting was another extended-family session. This one was more tightly structured. Family members made commitments to spend time with Jerry over the course of the next two weeks, which included the spring vacation. One suggestion was that Jerry obtain a job, but his mother adamantly refused to permit this.

Following this session, meetings were held separately with the parents and Jerry. While the two weeks of structured time went well, the family was unable to continue providing Jerry with the time and structure he needed. Jerry's suicidal ideation began to increase, and he acted impulsively, breaking windows with his fist and getting drunk. The family pattern emerged more clearly: Jerry wrestled with his father and had screaming fights with his mother. She often threw objects at him, including a hockey puck, a glass ashtray, and her shoes. The therapist also learned that Jerry had several knives hidden around the house.

Concerned by the escalating pattern of violence in the family, the therapist called the parents in for a meeting. He told them that he felt this was a dangerous situation, and that he feared someone was going to be seriously hurt. They denied that there were any risk, other than to themselves. The therapist continued to press the seriousness of the matter, predicting that something bad was going to happen unless they took action, and raised the posssibility of an out-of-home placement for

Jerry. The mother responded, "Over my dead body." The father then raised the possibility of his (father's) leaving. The mother responded that she was moving out. She then began screaming at her husband and suddenly got up and walked out. The possibility of their son leaving home brought the marital issues to the fore.

In the next session, the mother spoke of her bitterness and "hate" towards her husband. Her husband responded sarcastically, and she again said she was moving out. She then turned to the therapist and began screaming, saying that this was all his (the therapist's) fault. She left saying she would not return. The father said that this was how she acted at home. Predictably, when the therapist met with Jerry, he had been thinking more about suicide and about running away. Nonetheless, he was able to continue to contract for safety, and he had not harmed himself under the contract.

The therapist then took a vacation for about ten days. The mother continued to live at home and conflict between the spouses decreased, although they were not speaking to each other. Jerry denied any suicidal ideation, but indicated that he was fighting more with his mother. In addition, he was staying out late, breaking windows, drinking, and not taking the medication.

The day before the next appointment, the father called to say that Jerry had run away. The parents had not called the police. The mother then got on the phone to say that Jerry had "severely beaten" both her and his younger brother a few days before. The therapist advised the parents to call the police and to request help from the court, in the form of a "CHINS" petition (Child in Need of Service). The father agreed to discuss this further at an appointment scheduled for the next day.

The father did not show up for this appointment, and the therapist, calling him, discovered that he had been sleeping. A "CHINS" had not been filed nor the police called. At that point the therapist realized that he needed to file a "51A" with the Department of Social Services (DSS) for neglect of parental duties, to which the father did not object. He told the therapist that he would call when Jerry was found. The mother called a few minutes later and expressed her anger at the therapist, saying that she did not want to talk with him ever again.

The DSS became involved, substantiated the "51A" and the need for services for this family. The therapist remained available to see them but the parents have not called for another appointment. Although the larger, longstanding family and marital problems continue, treatment was effective in keeping Jerry, a very impulsive and depressed adolescent, out of a psychiatric hospital and at home, until the DSS could become involved. By being involved with DSS, the family will be able to access alternative community resources such as intensive home visiting for help in functioning more effectively as a unit.

While some therapist's have developed programs for hospitalizing the whole family (see Abroms, Fellner & Whitaker 1971), and others have developed intensive outpatient models for preventing rehospitalization (Haley 1980; Madanes 1981), it is evident that there are some clinical situations in which it is necessary to hospitalize a child or adolescent in a psychiatric facility. When hospitalization is necessary, the goal is to get the client out of the hospital as quickly as possible. At the outset, we ask "What minimal changes must occur for our patient to be an outpatient?" (Harper 1989:32). In addition, if psychiatric hospitalization is required, it is relatively brief (on the average of two to four weeks) and involves maximal family involvement. Again, the goal of the inpatient stay is to prepare the adolescent and his family for outpatient treatment as rapidly as possible.

An example of the usefulness of a brief hospitalization involves a fourteen-year-old girl who was hospitalized after threatening to kill herself. During the inpatient stay, she revealed that her father had sexually abused her. It appeared that she had been expressing suicidal thoughts while keeping this secret and that the hospital setting provided the safety and protection for the secret to be told. When the secret was revealed her suicidal thoughts diminished. Follow-up work continued on an outpatient basis.

At times, however, the treatment procedures and norms of the hospital differ from those of the referring therapist and a planned brief hospital stay becomes unduly prolonged. The hospital may have rules that their goals can be met only if the adolescent spends six to eight weeks or longer in an inpatient unit. It is therefore, important to negotiate with hospitals in helping them view placement as a short intensive period in which to asses and rapidly stabilize a family situation that has reached crisis proportions. Unless the therapist has a good working relationship with the hospital, difficulties can easily arise that may impede therapeutic progress and turn "acute" problems into potentially "chronic" ones.

In one situation, the hospital colluded with the family's wishes to have their daughter (who made a suicide gesture) out of the house. The message from the hospital to the family was "this girl needs long-term treatment." By doing so the hospital set the expectation for a needlessly long inpatient placement. The hospital fostered a regressive dependency of the adolescent on the institution believing that only longer-term treatment would be useful. After a thirty-day inpatient period the adolescent was discharged at our insistence and against hospital recommendations. In a family meeting following the adolescent's discharge from the hospital, the girl indicated her wish to return to the hospital and the parents talked about their anxieties having her at home. We worked with the parents and their daughter in developing a plan to help alleviate these anxieties.

That evening the daughter made a superficial cut on her wrist. The father called the emergency mental health phone line and told the "on-call" worker that he wanted his daughter rehospitalized at that same hospital. He also called the hospital and informed them of the situation. They readily agreed and encouraged her return. The therapist "on-call", who was not aware of the specifics of the situation, responded by authorizing the hospitalization. The adolescent began a potential "career" of being a psychiatric patient dependent on hospitals for her security and safety. In addition, the parents were relieved of any responsibility for their daughter and were supported in reducing their responsibility to her.

As Combrinck-Graham (1985:101) pointed out, "the hospital may become so much part of the ecological system of the individual and family that return to it may become a way of life." The reader is referred to her chapter for an outline of a number of important considerations in making the hospital a useful therapeutic intervention for the whole family. Of primary importance is family participation and decision making while the adolescent is in the hospital. Lipchik (1988) has emphasized the importance of including parents in treatment planning from the outset and considering family members as allies in the therapeutic process.

Of critical importance is the incorporation of the adolescent's support network in the treatment process, and the building of a support structure such that the adolescent knows clearly who he can go to when feeling upset or "down." With open channels of communication between the adolescent and others in his or her social system, the chances for impulsive behavior are reduced as isolation is diminished and caring demonstrated.

The importance of a well-specified goal in establishing clear criteria for discharge from the hospital cannot be overemphasized. Nurcombe (1989) presents several examples of goal-directed treatment planning that moves away from psychodynamic formulations and emphasizes the defining of goals in clear and measurable behavioral terms. In addition, the therapist is encouraged to notice, incorporate, and build on client strengths to develop a treatment plan.

Too often we decide on hospitalizing someone simply for expediency. However, the implications of these actions have major consequences on the lives of those with whom we work. In addition, hospitals are businesses whose financial stability depends on keeping beds filled. These pressures work against developing short-term constructive interventions when an adolescent must be hospitalized. In addition, applying a "possibility" frame becomes very difficult when the hospital is still working from a "problem" frame. At Harvard Community Health Plan we are working to develop contracts for day treatment and other alternative services that support brief and family-focused interventions.

Many times, we can avoid the need for a psychiatric hospitalization by mobilizing significant social supports from the client's social network. In the next section, we will explore the importance of social supports in creating a context for change.

Mobilizing Social Support Networks in Crisis

> Symptoms of mental illness derive from the alienation of human beings from . . . relationships and resources. . . . A social network . . . has within it the resources to develop creative solutions to the human predicaments of its members.
> —R.V. Speck and C.L. Attneave, in *Family Networks*.

It is of paramount importance in many situations to involve the client network of supports in the treatment process, including professionals from outside agencies (Burns and Friedman 1976). In addition, use of self-help and other available community resources can be vital parts of the overall treatment process.

The larger the unit available for treatment, the more variety of interventions (options) possible (Speck and Attneave 1973). It is useful both for the client and the therapist to get support by developing and mobilizing helping networks that draw on family as well as community resources.

In working with children, it is especially useful to include school personnel in family meetings. When necessary, we will meet at the school, or invite a teacher to join a family meeting in our offices. In addition, we have found it helpful to provide opportunities for children experiencing peer-related difficulties to have the opportunity to participate in a "social skills" group. These groups usually run concurrently with contacts with the family. We have found that mobilizing the combined efforts of the family, the school, and the group leader increases the liklihood of a positive outcome.

By involving outside agency people in treatment planning you increase your support. Getting the client's social system activated is helpful in avoiding use of stigmatizing institutional resources (Hobbs 1966). By using the client's natural network, dependency on the institution is reduced and in some cases a psychiatric hospitalization can be prevented.

We have encountered several clinical situations in which the mere gathering of the whole family, including extended family when available, can produce significant and rapid change. In several cases in which adolescents have presented, with suicidal ideation, this strategy seems to work particularly well, letting the adolescent know that there exists a caring and concerned network of supports. The healing power of social networks has been clearly documented (Pilisuk and Parks 1986; Speck and Attneave 1973). This can be especially useful in dealing with crisis situations, as we will see in the next section.

In any human service agency one encounters crisis situations in which you must deal efficiently and effectively to help resolve the crisis or at least to prevent the crisis from escalating. Two clinical situations are described in which I [SF] engaged the family's significant social supports in leading to resolution of the crisis. In the first case, this prevented psychiatric hospitalization. In both cases, the thinking was "ecological," incorporating people from the family network to provide a context for resolution and support.

A twenty-eight-year-old single mother with a six-year-old daughter contacted the emergency on-call system one evening. She was very upset, tearful, afraid of hurting her daughter, and feeling out of control. She was requesting hospitalization. The woman was a recovering alcoholic who had been sober for one year. A plan was developed for her to spend the night with a friend who agreed to supervise her closely (there was some concern about suicide) until the next day when she would be scheduled for an emergency appointment. The client was also directed to find a place for her daughter temporarily (the maternal grandmother agreed to take care of the child) and to attend a meeting of Alcoholics Anonymous with her friend. The client came for her appointment the next day and a plan was made for continued outpatient work. She was assessed as not needing hospitalization.

Three children (ages 18, 16, and 9) were referred to mental health care on an emergency basis, following the murder of their mother by their father and the father's subsequent suicide. The three children were taken in by the mother's sister who lived nearby. Prior to this event, the children had experienced, over a extended period of time, a household in which there was a significant amount of violence, mainly in the form of father's physical abuse of mother. The oldest child was feeling most responsible for having "missed the signals" that could have prevented his parents' deaths. All three children, after an initial period of being in shock, were overcome with grief and anger.

Rather than try to manage this situation on my own, I decided to draw on significant people in the children's social network who could help them both deal with their ongoing grief as well as support them in getting on with their day-to-day activities (attending school, going to work). While initially seeing the three children on an almost everyday basis, I also involved the mother's sister who was now the primary caregiver, the youngest child's school counselor, the priest who had a connection with the oldest child, a friend of the mother's, and a case-worker from the Department of Social Services. Most of the coordination in this case was done by phone. I encouraged the people mentioned above to take on various aspects of the treatment. The priest, for example, was willing to make periodic visits to talk with the oldest child; the school counselor met with the youngest child on a daily basis.

Over a period of several months my contacts with the children decreased as their social network began functioning more autonomously. The children appeared to be making a satisfactory adjustment considering the severity of the trauma experienced. The HMO permitted the children to continue to receive service even though the insurance (carried through the mother's employer) had been terminated thirty days after her death.

The Therapist Wears Two Hats: Issues of Therapy and Social Control

There are instances in which the therapist needs to differentiate between doing therapy and applying social controls. The latter occurs when you find yourself in a position in which the client reveals information that suggests that the client or someone in the client's family has experienced, or is in danger of, physical or sexual abuse or some other violent behavior. It is at these times that you must switch "hats" and become an agent of social control rather than a therapist. It is our experience that in many instances, reporting child abuse, for example, serves to solidify your relationship with the family when it is clearly understood that you are acting from a legal mandate and when you clearly communicate the necessity for your actions from the outset. Where it is possible, in cases of physical or sexual abuse, we try to encourage family members to request services voluntarily from the Department of Social Services. This puts the family in the responsible position of initiating contact rather than the therapist.

One adult client, with whom I [SF] was working, had a history of violent and impulsive behavior. He had been involved in several violent fights with employees where he worked and with several women friends. One day he came to a session and told me that he suspected that his girl friend was not being faithful to him and that he was going to "take care of her". I asked what he meant by this and he mentioned having a gun at home and intimated that he might use it. After discussing other alternatives for communicating his upset over her apparent unfaithfulness, he left the meeting still considering the use of violence in dealing with his girl friend.

After he left, I consulted with my colleagues who felt strongly that this situation fell in the "duty to warn" category. I then called him at home and told him, that in light of what he had told me, I would need to let his girl friend, and the police, know that he had made these threats. He was upset with me on the phone but indicated that he was planning to come to our next session. I did contact both the police and the girl friend (sending her a registered letter delineating the client's threats). The client did show up for the next session, and in concern for my own safety, I met with him with the office door open. As it turned out, the client never had a gun and, in the session, told me that he "never planned to do it anyway." I told him that, in the future, I would take his comments seriously, and act accordingly as obligated by law. This episode resulted in a level of increased involvement by the client in the therapeutic process, and thereafter, the client made significant gains in developing control over his impulsive behavior.

A family was referred for treatment after suspicion was raised of possible sexual abuse of the three-year-old daughter and her five-year-old sister in a home-based day-care setting. Both parents grew up in alcoholic households and were especially sensitive to their past histories with alcohol. Both had been sober for over five years at the time of the referral. The therapist had to find a way to deal with the presenting issues while respecting the parent's sensitivities and vulnerabilities associated with their own past traumatic histories.

The three-year-old daughter was showing clear signs of being sexually overstimulated. She was masturbating frequently, having nightmares, trying to engage her older sister in sexual play, and so on. The mother, who herself had been sexually abused, was distraught and upset over the possibility that she hadn't protected her own children adequately. The father was concerned that his history of alcoholism would throw suspicion on him as a possible perpetrator. Both parents felt threatened by the fear that their children might be taken away from them by the state.

This issue with their children, raised for both parents, a significant amount of shame and hurt. The therapist [Brian Meyer, Ph.D.] carefully assessed the situation and informed the parents that he was legally mandated to notify the Department of Social Services. He presented this in a way that supported the parent's caring and concern for their daughters and avoided messages that would add to their shame and vulnerability. Throughout his contact with the family, the therapist emphasized the parents love, concern, and caring for their children.

The mother could see how her anxiety about her own sexual abuse was influencing her reactions to her children's behavior. The more distressed she became about past events in her own life, the more the children showed signs of distress. With this in mind, therapy concentrated on helping the mother separate her own abuse and her feelings around this, from the abuse and feelings of her children. For two sessions, the therapist had the mother watch her daughters play, from behind the one-way mirror, while emphasizing how well each was doing in recovering from the trauma. The use of the mirror served to help the mother gain increased perspective on her children's behavior. In addition, the mother was seen individually for three sessions by another therapist, with whom she had had a previous relationship. These sessions focused on helping her separate issues of her own past traumatic history from the situation with her daughters. As the mother became calmer and more in control of her anxiety, the children's sexualized behavior diminished.

Conclusions

As with all of these complex issues, there are no easy answers or magic remedies. We have found, however, that by maintaining an optimistic, flexible and strength-oriented perspective, we are better equipped to deal effectively with whatever issues come our way. As possibility-oriented therapists we search for those client strengths and resources that will allow the client to take steps toward healthy growth and functioning, and in so doing, are less likely ourselves to get bogged down in the mire of pathological thinking. By maintaining flexibility in how we approach each request, and by remaining sensitive and respectful to our client's needs, we enable movement on the client's own pathway toward health and wellness.

Note

1. SF thanks Ethan Kisch, M.D., Senior Child Psychiatrist at the Braintree Center of HCHP, for his expert consultation on issues of psychopharmacology.

9
Generating New Perspectives: Models of Team Consultation

U ntil recently, the therapy process was an activity to be conducted behind closed doors. With the advent of audiotape and then videotape and the use of live observation and supervision (see Berger and Dammann 1982; Montalvo 1973), the therapy process has become more public and less mysterious. Within this context of "observable" therapy, opportunities have been created for looking at the therapy process with increased detail and specificity. In addition, possibilities have been created for collaboration and sharing among professionals. Within the context of live observation and team collaboration, many theoretically interesting and clinically useful ideas have been generated (see Andersen 1987; Furman 1990; Olson and Pegg 1979).

The collaborative therapeutic team has as its goal to tap and amplify existing strengths and resources within the client or client system. Examples will be given here of the usefulness of various consultative models in clinical intervention with particular emphasis on two approaches: the *strategic team* (ST) and the *reflecting team* (RT).

There are many advantages to using a collaborative team in doing therapy. For one, should you find yourself at an impasse, the team can provide a "lifeline" for regaining perspective. By maintaining a primary connection to your team, you are able to move easily in and out of the therapeutic interaction without becoming entangled in the process. In addition, the use of a collaborative team serves to support professional cohesiveness and to provide you with a growth-enhancing support system.

The following case summary illustrates the usefulness of a supportive treatment team in helping me [SF] maintain perspective and avoid induction into the family mythology. The team's consultation provided me with the needed impetus to empower the executive parental unit to manage their son effectively, rather than accept the original request for the son to be hospitalized.

This referral came from a therapist outside the HMO system who had been seeing a fifteen-year-old boy, John, with longstanding behavior problems, weekly and individually for one year. The therapist described John as "depressed, suicidal, homicidal, angry, withdrawn, explosive" and was requesting authorization from us to have the client hospitalized (since the boy was a HMO member). I told the therapist that before authorizing such an arrangement I would need to meet with the family. Only the father and John attended this emergency meeting (John had been living with his mother, stepfather, and a younger sister). John appeared somewhat apathetic and noncommunicative, but did not appear at risk for suicide (or homicide), and it was not clear how he could benefit from an inpatient placement.

Since father and son had a less conflictual relationship than mother and son I recommended that the boy live, on a temporary basis, with his father (who agreed to this) and that the father call me regularly over the next week to report on how things were working out. I also arranged for a meeting, one week later, with mother, father, stepfather, and John. I contacted John's individual therapist and suggested we work together, with me seeing the family and him continuing to see John on an individual basis, before considering hospitalization.

At the following family meeting, John's mother and stepfather reported feeling like they were "at a dead end" in dealing with the boy, who was doing poorly at school and threatening and intimidating family members at home (once with a knife). They all presented a very negative picture of John. The family was trying to put the ball in my court, implying that it was my responsibility to prevent *their* son from "going down the river" and strongly pressed for hospitalization. I felt cornered by the family and set up by the boy's individual therapist, who had "planted" the idea of hospitalization. I suggested that we reconvene in a week so that I could consult with my team. Team members supported me in putting the ball back in the family's court and defining this as family problem that psychiatric hospitalization would not solve.

Coming into the next session fortified against the expected onslaught I began to see clearly that these three adults (mother, father, and stepfather) were "enabling" their son's out-of-control behavior; all had been protecting him, treating him as if he were sick (depressed) rather than treating him as an irresponsible young man; I told the family that what he needed was not a hospital—but for the adults in his life to give John the education he needed in facing the realities of life. Since I saw John, not as "depressed," but as "misguided, confused, and naive about the realities of life," I emphasized John's need for the adults who cared most about him to provide him with consistent, constructive, coordinated limit setting. The family was momentarily silent, until the stepfather looked at me and said "I think you're absolutely right." The mother and father then each acknowledged what I was saying.

In a meeting two weeks later the adults reported significant improvement in John's behavior. He continued living with his father but began visiting his family. He was described as "polite, considerate . . . acting more responsibly." John's father reported that the boy's behavior began to change almost immediately after the last session. All the adults appeared in a surprisingly positive mood (even friendly towards me) and had planned times to get together outside of our meetings to continue their coordinated limit setting with John. The adults had developed a written list of what they expected from him, and, for the most part, he was complying. A total of seven sessions were held. Follow-up calls at six months and two years indicated that John continued doing well.

The use of the one-way mirror for live supervision or consultation has grown significantly in recent years, and has generated many creative approaches (see, Boscolo, et al. 1987; Madanes 1981, 1984; and Papp 1983). Having an observer or observer system provides a "polyocular" perspective (deShazer 1985) with which to view the clinical situation. Multiple perspectives multiply the number of ideas that create increased options or possibilities for change. In addition, the team format, although initially requiring a significant investment of resources, has the potential for creating change in a time-effective and ultimately cost-effective manner (see Green & Herget 1989a, 1989b).

One model that we have found useful employs multiple levels of consultation. Basically, there is a *therapist* (with whom the family has had several contacts), a *consultant* (who is new to the system and joins the therapist in the treatment room) and an *observer* who views the session from behind a one-way mirror and sends in messages or directives encouraging shifts in the therapeutic process. The following is an illustration of the usefulness of this multi-tier consultation process.

This excerpt comes from the second session in which one of us [SF] served as consultant to a therapist [Elinor Stanton, M.S., R.N.] who had been involved with the family for over two years. This is the first session in which the father is in attendance. Usually it is only the mother and her twenty-five-year-old "schizophrenic" son who are present for the meetings. Behind the one-way mirror is a second consultant/observer [Donna Haig Friedman, M.S.] whose role it is to view the ongoing process and to provide ideas and input to keep the therapeutic process moving in a positive and productive direction. In this session, both the therapist and I were inadvertently caught up in repetitive pattern in which the parents (especially the mother) talk for their son Stanley and act to disqualify his personhood. The usual pattern is for either parent to talk for Stanley while he remains passive and noncommunicative. In the session to be described, the observer helps the therapist and me overcome this induction and to shift the focus to Stanley's needs and wishes. It becomes clear at this session that both the parents and the therapist have been pushing for Stanley to change in ways that they each think will be good for him. The therapist and I, with the observer's help, shift the emphasis to empowering Stanley as an individual who is committed to his own change.

> *Therapist [to Stanley]*: What do you think about this conversation that we're [*parents, therapist, and consultant*] having about you?
> *Father [to Stanley]*: Do you think it's a conspiracy?
> *Stanley*: A conspiracy to get me to change.
> *Consultant*: And do you want to change?
> *Stanley*: Slow.
> *Father [to Stanley]*: Do you think it is a good idea . . . to change?
> *Stanley*: Not too much.
> *Consultant*: Just a little change.
> *Therapist [to Stanley]*: If you had your druthers, what would you change first? If you were in charge of the change, what would you change first?
> *Stanley*: I don't know.

[*The mother again takes control of the conversation and tells us how Stanley has continually refused to do things for himself.*]

[*The observer calls the consultant out of the room and tells him to get refocused on what Stanley wants.*]

> *Consultant [reenters]*: We only have a few minutes left, and what I would like to focus on is what *your* ideas are, Stanley. Basically *you* need to be in charge of what happens. We're all talking *about* you, but you're the person who has to make the decisions about what's best for *you*, about change, about what's comfortable to *you*. And one way of saying you want things different is to go out "on strike." [*We previously framed Stanley's refusal to do things as "going out on strike."*] Another is to use words to say "I want things different." So it's very important that Elinor hear from *you* and that your parents hear from *you* about what *you're* looking for. So it's not what your mother wants or your father wants—but what *you* want for yourself, because *you're* the most important person here. Your mother's been working hard to help you, your father's been working hard to help you, Elinor has been working hard as has her whole team to try to help you, And everybody has their own ideas about what is going to be helpful and what is not going to be helpful, what's going to be good for you. But—what it comes down to is what *you* think is going to be good for *you*.

Therapist: And maybe we haven't listened well enough and given *you* a chance to tell us. I'm certainly willing to try listening more to what *you* want.

Consultant [*to Stanley*]: Is there something real small that you can think of that you would want different? Very small.

Stanley: I wish I knew how to handle things better than I can.

Consultant: Handle which things?

Stanley: Handling a check.

Consultant: Do you have a checking account?

Stanley: I'm not talking about that . . . about a restaurant check.

Consultant: A restaurant check?

Father: He has difficulty figuring out what he needs to pay in a restaurant.

Mother: I have him using this lately [*pulls a calculator out of her purse*].

Consultant: [*cuts her off and says*] Let me check with Stanley. What is that you'd like to be doing that you're not doing?

Stanley: To pay the bill.

Consultant: If its $2.69, you want to know how to figure that out and how to figure out the tip? Who does that for you now?

Stanley: My mother usually does.

Consultant: Okay. What I'd like to suggest is that you [*the father*] teach him how to pay the check and how to figure out the tip. You know they sell those cards that tell you what the tip should be. [*The consultant reaches for his wallet and gives the father his "tip" card.*]

Father: Thank you.

Mother: I'm the one in the restaurant most of the time.

Consultant [*to the mother*]: Since you've been working on so many of these other things.

Mother: [*interrupting*] I know you want him [*the father*] to do it, but I'm the one that's there. [*She then describes how she helps Stanley use the calculator.*]

Father [*to his wife*]: If I tell him enough he can approach it when I'm not around.

Consultant: That's right. Or you [*the father*] might need to coach him on the spot. You can decide what's best. But this is an area you [*mother*] will need to stay out of . . . [*to Stanley*] You have to use your dad's directions and figure it out.

[*The observer calls the consultant out of the room and tells him that she thinks the mother is feeling pushed out by this task and that she needs a job to do to make her feel involved and important.*]

Consultant [*reenters*]: One further thought before we stop . . . that you [*mother*] have a role in this too . . . that your husband work with Stanley around the checks and the tip . . . and if he gets it right that you do something special with him. The two of you [*Stanley and his mother*] work out something to do together.

Mother: Okay.

Consultant: And if you're very successful at it, the three of you should go out to a nice restaurant and have dinner. [*laughter*]

As you can see, the ability of the consultant to regain focus was significantly aided by the perspective of the observer. In the next section we will see the additional advantages of expanding the observing role from one person to a whole clinical team.

The Strategic Team

We see significant advantages in creating a context in which a variety of ideas can be generated. As the context of ideas expands, so do the options for both you and the client (family). Trivette (1989) has referred to this process as "tilting the mirror," in providing the client with a new or expanded view of the situation. In *Journey to Ixtlan* (1972) by Carlos Castaneda, the character don Juan talks of the need to "stop the world" in helping someone to see a different view of reality: "If one wants to stop our fellow men one must always be outside the circle that presses them" (xi).

Several methods have been developed using a team structure to "stop the client's world." Peggy Papp (1983) uses a team of consultants, which she refers to as a "Greek Chorus," who observe from behind the one-way mirror and send in messages that strategically generate systems dilemmas for the family. The team may take a position that differs from the therapist's, thus providing another viewpoint or reality that the family is challenged to consider. For example, the therapist might take the position that change is inevitable and needed, while the team makes comments citing the risks of change and emphasizing the need to "go slow."

Using this "therapeutic triangle," the family is placed in a dilemma that dramatizes their natural ambivalence about change. In effect, the family is challenged to prove the "team of experts" wrong and to join with the therapist in victory. In so doing, the family must give up their focus on the presenting complaint and move on in their lives. Papp (1983) categorizes these interventions as either "defiance-based" (paradoxical) or "compliance-based" (examples of which include giving direct suggestions, coaching a parent on dealing with an oppositional child, or reframing behavior). In the examples to follow, both compliance-based and defiance-based approaches were used.

The usefulness of "compliance-based" team interventions is illustrated in the following two clinical examples. A strategic team [ST] was used in the initial meeting, with the therapist [SF] continuing to see the family on his own after this session. The comments of the ST formed the basis for later treatment sessions.

A four-year-old adopted child, Ron, was referred after the parents expressed, to the child's pediatrician, the difficulties they were having in disciplining him. The child was described as "very aggressive, especially toward his mother, responds by kicking or hitting. . . . Parents unsure of how to respond to patient appropriately. Also question of patient's emotional stability due to his background." Ron was adopted at four months from a Central American country where, according to the parents' report, he was "small and undernourished."

The family was interviewed initially in front of the one-way mirror with other team members providing consultation. Observing the interaction of the parents and Ron, the team noticed that Ron was in a very powerful position in the family with both parents trying very hard to meet his needs. He was treated as a very special gift, not an uncommon pattern in families with an adopted child. Listening to the parents, I realized that they were very frustrated with Ron and unsure about how firm to be in dealing with his occasional out-of-control behavior. They could however describe episodes in which a firm response on their parts was successful in getting Ron's behavior under control. After observing for a period of time the team generated a message that I [SF] read to the family. The message said:

> The team is very impressed with the parents' understanding and re-
> sponsiveness to Ron. They have worked hard to strengthen their
> bonds with Ron and have succeeded. The parents, at this point, need
> to move on to the next step, which entails loosening, but not break-
> ing, these bonds. This will occur as the parents experiment with pro-
> viding increased structure and limits with Ron. The team sees the
> parents as competent and creative in developing new strategies for
> dealing with Ron's inappropriate behavior. The team does foresee
> some brief moments of unhappiness as Ron responds to the changes
> the parents are making, but believe that the parents are capable of
> weathering this brief storm.

After the message was read, I instructed the parents to "do some-thing different" over the next two weeks in response to Ron's provocative behavior. I told them that I looked forward to hearing about the creative ideas they come up with in dealing with their son.

At a meeting two weeks later, which only the parents attended, they provided several examples of how they did not give in to Ron's demands and how he had begun to respond to their increased limit setting. The parents were encouraged to continue with this approach and a meeting was set for one month later to follow up on their progress. At that time, the parents reported that Ron had been enrolled in a nursery school and "he loves it." He was described as "less demanding . . . and more in control." No further contacts were requested.

A bright, articulate, boy, Ken (age 10), was referred by his pediatrician when he began to resist taking his stimulant medication, which had been effective in helping him focus and attend at school. A meeting was set up with the therapist [David van Buskirk, M.D.], Ken, and Ken's grandparents, with whom he was living. The therapist interviewed the family in front of a one-way mirror, behind which other team members observed. The child complained that "I'm not fun anymore" and emphasized that he was no longer interacting and playing with his friends in the way he remembered before taking the medication. In addition, he seemed troubled and uncertain about whether he or the pill was responsible for his increased capacity to concentrate at school. The team, observing his animated and spirited play with both the therapist and his grandparents, called the therapist out of the room and suggested that he give Ken the following message:

> The team is impressed with Ken's playfulness and fun-loving spirit and do not believe that the medicine has taken away what Ken prizes so much. The pill that Ken takes serves as nothing more than an aid in helping him concentrate better at school and has not changed his true personality.

The therapist went back into the interview room and read the team's message to Ken and his grandparents. Ken seemed very pleased with hearing this and went off to draw on a piece of paper while the therapist continued to talk with the grandparents. While this interaction was going on Ken turned around and held up to the mirror, for the team to see, a piece of paper that said, in big letters "THANK YOU!"

At the end of the session, Ken was permitted to go behind the mirror. Each team member then told him how much they admired his spirit and fun-loving qualities, to which he responded with obvious delight. Ken continued taking his medication and no further contacts were needed.

In the following clinical situation, an ST approach is used in an initial session with a family, in which an eight-year-old child is experiencing daily vomiting in the morning prior to school. The team develops a "pretend" task (Madanes 1981) as a way of helping the family to help the son overcome this difficulty.

Madanes (1981) discusses the usefulness of placing the problematic behavior in a context of make-believe and play. By so doing the power of the behavior is neutralized and the interaction around the behavior takes on a game-like quality. Basically, the child is encouraged to "pretend" to have the problem, and his family is instructed to "pretend" to help him with it. "In this situation, the child no longer needs to actually have the symptom . . . pretending to have it is enough to become the focus of concern for the parent. But the parent's concern will also be a pretense, and the situation will have changed to a game, to make-believe and play" (Madanes 1981: 73). Since the presenting complaint is being "prescribed," this kind of intervention can be thought of as "paradoxical." In addition to using the "pretend" strategy, the mother in this family is empowered by the therapist as an expert in dealing with her son.

The family consists of mother, father, and their three sons. Dave (age 8), the youngest, had been vomiting each morning before school for about six weeks prior to the initial session. This behavior did not occur on weekends, and the school was not aware of anything in that setting which might account for the behavior. Dave had a number of friends and was doing well in school. There was a sense that he put a lot of pressure on himself to do well at school as well as in his role as a pitcher on his Little League team. What follows is a transcript of the initial session with the family. All family members are present. The reader should note that I [SF] had information from the medical record indicating that the mother had experienced "panic attacks" in the past and had been successful in overcoming this problem.

Therapist: There is a group behind the mirror, and they may be calling me out from time to time, to give me some suggestions or I may decide to go out and talk with them . . . or they may decide to come in here and have a discussion and we would go in the back and listen to them. We'll see how it goes.

[*The therapist makes small talk with the children about school.*]

Therapist: Do all the children see Dr. K. Is he everybody's pediatrician? [*The children nod heads "yes."*] Did one of you [*parents*] talk with him recently?

Mother: I did. I had Dave in for a physical because he was having stomach trouble and I wasn't quite sure where it was coming from— but I thought Dr. K. would be a good place to start. But he didn't seem to think it was anything physical.

Therapist: So he checked Dave out pretty well?

Mother: Yes, he checked him all over and . . . put him on Mylanta for a week for the stomach to help settle him down and he told me if he didn't improve within a week to call him back. I let it go longer than that, and when I called him back he thought the next step would be mental health because he felt it was psychologically based . . . that the root of it was psychological.

Therapist [to the father]: What do you think about this?

Father: Well . . . I think, maybe . . . it's like a phobia.

Therapist: Is this something that anybody else has had any experience with? *[silence]* . . . *[to the other children]*: You've never had days when your stomach is all upset before school . . . and you say, "Hey, I don't think I want to go today?" No?

Father: *[laughing]* They say that every day.

Mother: Not really. Although Mike *[the older brother]* did have some trouble for a brief period, but he outgrew it.

Mike: *[looks at his mother as if to say "I don't remember that"]*

Therapist: *[looking intently at Dave]* And Dave, one day, you won't remember this either. It will all be in the past. . . . So, anyone else who's experienced these kind of feelings or anything like that?

Father: *[turns to the mother and says something about "anxiety"]*

Mother: *[repeats "anxiety"]* Yeah, myself. I was treated . . . I don't remember how long ago that was. . . . I was having panic attacks . . . a panic disorder . . . and I began therapy and did a group type thing. That was part of the reason that I really thought that this would be a good idea. Some of his symptoms reminded me of what I was feeling during the panic attacks. I would rather have him deal with it now than at eighteen or thirty-five. The stomach played a large part in it for me, also. It would be a real tenseness and I would get light-headed and get nauseous and all of that.

Therapist: And how did you get over it?

Mother: Through the group therapy, which was excellent. It made a big difference.

Therapist: That's great.

Mother: And there was a learning technique . . . it was learning how to relax . . . and do breathing exercises. . . . It always originated in my stomach.

Therapist: So you learned some techniques that helped you control it. Have you tried any of those with Dave?

Mother: I have . . . breathing. . . . I just started it a couple of days ago. *[to Dave]* Do you remember what I tried to tell you to do . . . about breathing? You can't remember? Taking deep breaths through your nose and expelling it through your mouth and that relaxes you.

Father: Dave would sometimes get anxious . . . feel pressure when he was playing baseball. . . . He's the pitcher.

Therapist: So you're a pitcher, Dave? That's an important position.

Dave: Yeah.

Father: Sometimes before the games Dave would get anxious . . . tense.

Mother: But sometimes after the games he would vomit . . . not all the time.

Father: The last couple of games.

Therapist: So, how long have these problems been going on?

Mother: They intensified at the beginning of school. . . . What's happening now, that I'm not comfortable with, is the vomiting gives him some sense of relief, it's almost a pattern kind of thing. It seems that once he does it he relaxes. He always goes to school now; at the beginning he didn't.

Therapist: So he's getting to school everyday now?

Mother: He is getting to school. There's been some improvement.

Father: He didn't throw up today.

Therapist [*to Dave*]: You didn't today?

Dave: [*shakes head 'no'*]

Therapist: How many days would you say you haven't thrown up?

Dave: About five days.

Mother: Maybe five.

Therapist: Five days in the past two months?

Mother: Yes.

Therapist: And what makes those days go better . . . those mornings? [*to Dave*] Do you know what's different about those mornings . . . the mornings you don't throw up?

Dave: I feel different.

Therapist: Can you tell me in words what the difference is?

Dave: Not really.

Therapist: It's hard to describe. . . . Is anything happening around you different on those days?

Mother: No. It just seems to vary in intensity.

Therapist: Is it any particular days of the week that things go well?

Mother: Not really. It seems to happen fifteen to twenty minutes before leaving for school. [*She describes how the school work is harder this year.*]

Therapist: Do you have any sense from the school about any specific kinds of things that they can see, that they're concerned about that might relate to this?

Father: No. His marks are all A's.

Mother: He's very serious about his work . . . very intense about doing well.

Father: I think it started in the summer time with the little league . . . and I think that might have carried over to school. It's almost like he has to keep up a certain level.

Mother: He fears making a mistake.

Therapist [*to Dave*]: None of your brothers ever got in trouble in school? Did anything wrong? I see some smiles.

Father: None of them have really been a problem.

Therapist: So Dave doesn't want to be the first . . . uh . . . to get into trouble. What do you [*Dave*] think of your teacher? You can tell me something bad about her, I won't tell, I promise.

[*Dave laughs.*]

Mother: I would rather see him not maintain such a high level.

Therapist [to Dave]: You're pretty tough on yourself . . . yeah?

Therapist [to Dave's brothers]: Do any of you help Dave relax when he's being too tough on himself?

Mike: We probably have. We say things to him.

Therapist: Well, I'm going to take a moment to check in with my team. . . .

[*The team, seeing that Dave tends to keep things to himself and not ask for support, proposes a baseball analogy to help him understand that he can get support from other family members.*]

Therapist: I had a chance to talk with the team, and Dave, it's their sense that you put yourself under a lot of pressure. Do you know what I mean? You're really tough on yourself, and what you haven't understood yet is, just like in baseball, you need to work as a team, so if you're a pitcher you won't do much unless you have a catcher and fielders behind you, otherwise you're going to be all alone out there. And sometimes I think you get into a position where you think you're all alone. And not only do you have a team in baseball but you have a team here, too. You have family who can help you, and you don't have to do it all by yourself, so if you're working on a book report or something you can ask somebody for help. Does he ask? Who does he come to?

Father: To me, when I'm there . . . but my job makes it difficult. [*The father is a firefighter.*]

[*Discussion focuses on who is at home in the morning when Dave is getting ready for school. It is clear that his mother is the primary person during this time. The therapist asks her if she will help Dave work on this problem.*]

Mother: And how would I do that [*help Dave*]? I'm not sure.

[*When the mother pleads helplessness about what do I empower her as the expert.*]

Therapist: Well, you're the expert. You've been through this and have conquered a problem that's somewhat similar to what Dave's experienced.

Mother: I'm not sure of how to handle this. You don't want to feed in too much by giving it more attention than is warranted, but it is a problem for him so you want to help him to deal with it . . . so I kind of drift between. He will always come to me and say "my stomach is starting to hurt."

Therapist: So he gives you some warning.

Mother: Yes, it's very similar every morning, but he didn't throw up on Monday, and I said do you realize that you haven't thrown up for three days now.

Therapist: It sounds like there are days when Dave doesn't throw up . . . like this past Monday and today (Thursday). So, Monday and today you didn't. So how did you [*Dave*] stop yourself? Did you have the same feeling?

Dave: Yes.

Therapist: So the feeling was the same . . . and then what happened after that?

Dave: I just went to school and it settled.

Therapist: But you were used to going and throwing up . . . and then you stopped. Did you talk with your mother? Was there something that helped stop it?

Father: I think he's getting better at dealing with it.

Therapist: What did you [*to the mother*] notice on those two mornings?

Mother: Monday it helped talking about the fact that he didn't have to do that.

Therapist: So you talked with him about how things had gone well.

Mother: Just because he felt those feelings it didn't mean he needed to do that [*throw up*] . . . if he gave it just a little time, it would pass. It seems to be the anticipation of going to school. Once he gets in, he does well.

Therapist: Did you notice anything different Monday and today about how he was able to control things?

[*She isn't sure, although she thinks there are days when Dave wakes up and his stomach feels a little bit better.*]

Therapist: Do you think that's true, Dave, there are days when you wake up and the stomach feels a little better?

Dave: Yes.

Therapist: So it's easier to control then. When you get to school, you feel better?

Dave: Yes.

Therapist: When you're driving to school, do you start to feel better?

Dave: A little.

Therapist: I think I just got signaled by my team. I'll be back.

The team proposes to engage the family in a "pretend" task setting up a situation in which Dave would "pretend" to have his stomachache, and the family would "pretend" to rally around him in demonstrating their care and support. By putting the presenting complaint, and parental responses to the presenting complaint, in a game-like frame, the hope is to neutralize the problem's potency in real life (Madanes 1981). As Jay Haley (in Madanes 1981: xiv) says: "Such interventions can appear deceptively light if one does not understand that reclassifying human behavior is a powerful means of change."

Notice how the therapist prefaces the team's comments in a way that prepares the family to accept the team's message. In addition, the team and the therapist agree to disagree over the speed with which change will occur, with the team giving the message, "go slow," while the therapist encourages rapid improvement.

Therapist: So let me tell you what the team has to say, but I want to warn you that sometimes they come up with some strange kinds of things. Sometimes I agree with them and sometimes I don't. Here's their message [*which I then read aloud*]:

> The team feels strongly that the family should not try to change the problem of vomiting too fast. We think Dave is telling his family that he is feeling under pressure and he needs his family to know this about him. Because his family is not all together in the morning, we would like Dave to pretend, to practice at night, that he has his problem and his family is to help him through it. As his family pulls together behind him everyone in the family will come out a winner.

So that's what the team thinks. My own position is that there's been some improvement in the sense of Monday and Thursday that things have gotten better, and I think things are on their way to getting better . . . and that you [*Dave*] don't need to keep doing this, that the time is coming to really give it up. So in that way I don't agree with the team about not trying to change the problem. On the other hand, I do think that what they're recommending is a good idea in terms of the practicing at night. That means, Dave, that you make believe, pretend, that your stomach is hurting you and then you get people to help you try to feel better. Do you think you can do that?

Dave: Well . . . yeah.

Mother: So . . . as a family . . . how do we do that? What steps do we take? What do we say? Is it just encouragement?

Therapist: Tell me again about your experience in that group. What were they telling you was useful?

Mother: A very big part of that was relaxing the body. I still use this when I'm feeling tense . . . working your way from the head down.

Therapist: And that would be a useful thing to do in this practice in the evening. But, Dave, you have to be able to do a good job of making believe that you're having this problem . . . even though you're not. Do you think you can make believe? What do you say usually? What's the first thing you say in the morning? Do you say "my stomach hurts" or something like that?

Dave: Umm . . . uhm.

Therapist: So you have to do the same thing at night . . . and need to plan a time and just take five minutes. That's all. And then different family members can take turns trying to help.

Father: I think he's starting to improve.

Therapist: I think so.

Father: I think what Joanne [*the mother*] has been doing is the right thing.

Therapist: Yes, but maybe it's just too early for all the benefits to show. Each success is a move in the right direction. I think you're on right track, and the team is suggesting this practice and this pretend task because they think it will help things get better even sooner. So, does that sound okay to you to try this? Dave?

Dave: Yes.

Therapist: So you know you have to pretend. You can't have a smile on your face when you do this [*laughter*]. You really have to have a real morning face . . . and just five minutes. And why don't we set up another appointment when we can meet and follow-up and see how things are going in a couple of weeks or so. Is that okay?

Mother: Do you want to see all of us?

Therapist: For the next meeting it would be good if the two of you [*the parents*] came with Dave. If the others can come that's fine, too.

The day before the next session, Dave's mother called to cancel the appointment due to the illness of one of her other sons. She did report, that for the previous nine school days, Dave had not thrown up, although she described him as still "shaky" in the morning. I asked if they had tried the "pretend" exercise. She indicated that they did try it but Dave started laughing as did other family members and they had to give it up. I asked the mother what she thought helped the most in helping Dave make the progress he had. She mentioned how she spent time with him in the morning telling him about her panic attacks and how she overcame them. In addition, she thought, "it was very useful to have the whole family come together in helping Dave understand how much we care and want to help." We made an appointment for two weeks later. I complimented her on her efforts and expressed my hope that the progress made would continue.

Two weeks later, she and Dave showed up for the appointment. Dave's father was unable to make it due to his work schedule. The following is a brief excerpt from that meeting, which took place one month after the initial session:

Therapist: I wanted to check in and see how things were going with you Dave. Have things been better?

Dave: [nods]

Therapist: Can you say what's been better?

Dave: [shrugs shoulders]

Therapist: Did you try pretending as we talked about?

Dave: Yes.

Therapist: Did you laugh when you did it?

Dave: No.

Mother: Yes . . . we did.

Therapist: You weren't supposed to laugh but you did, I see.

Mother: He tried, but. . . .

Therapist: How did your family help you get over this? What did they do that helped? What did you do that helped?

Dave: [quiet . . . looks to his mother]

Mother [to Dave]: Talking to you.

Therapist: So, since you've been here, have there been any times when you've thrown up in the morning?

Dave: One time.

Therapist: When was that?

Mother: The week before vacation.

Dave: I was sick.

Mother: Yes, he was really sick. and the next day he was fine—and he was really pleased about that, because he was afraid it was the old problem again and he knew that it wasn't.

Therapist: That's good, so the mornings have been easier?

Dave: Yes.

Therapist [to the mother]: Does he still complain to you in the mornings?

Mother: Yes, it's still there. The feelings are still there but he doesn't seem to be as afraid of it.

Therapist: It's a matter of feeling control over it rather than it controlling you. So why don't we make another appointment to follow up.

Mother: He's very proud of himself.

Therapist: He should be, it really is progress. [to Dave] Keep up the good work.

Mother: Each day that goes by is really a bonus—because Dave can remember that yesterday he didn't do it.

Therapist: The successes build on one another.

Mother: Yes.

Another appointment was made for four weeks later. At that meeting, the mother indicated that Dave was neither throwing up in the morning nor experiencing anxiety as had been the case previously. The mother was complimented on her successful efforts with her son. No further contacts were requested.

In addition to using the ST for one-session consultations at the beginning of therapy, we have used this model in working with families over time. Such is the case with the family described below who was seen for nine sessions over a five-month period. The team was present for five of these sessions and offered their commentary as treatment progressed. The process outlined here reflects the use of a "defiance-based" approach.

A middle-income Greek family, consisting of the parents and their twenty-eight-year-old son (Ted) was referred for treatment because of concerns about Ted who had, for the past three months, been having "anxiety attacks" that necessitated that he be taken to a hospital emergency room (ER). Ted was single, unemployed (on disability), and was living with his parents. These "anxiety attacks" consisted of severe and sometimes incapacitating symptoms, including choking, gagging, and hyperventilating. At such times Ted thought he was going to die. His girl friend of fourteen years or his parents would take him to a hospital ER. After several such visits, in which the doctors could find no physical basis for the symptoms, he was referred for psychological help. In this family, the mother worked full-time, and the father was retired due to a physical disability. An older brother was married and living independently.

The following is Ted's description of his problem:

Ted: It's come to the point now where I'm just sick of dragging everybody else into the whole thing. My mother was up all night last night again, and she had to drive me to the hospital, because I thought I was choking. I've had all kinds of tests and they couldn't find anything. Wednesday morning I coughed up a very hard substance—it was about the size of a quarter. It was just like a hard piece of skin. I believe it was physical now. It went away. I thought it was great for two days. It passed—but then last night I had phlegm in my throat and I thought I was gagging again. I've spent over $700 on ER visits, now I just go to the hospital and sit in the waiting room for awhile till I feel better.

[*At one point, in the first session, when the therapist leaves the room to confer with the team, the following brief interaction takes place.*]

Mother: [*whispering*] Are you worried about moving out?

Ted: No, mom, I don't think so. I'm excited about it.

Father: I think it will be good for him because he really wants it.

A team of five clinicians were stationed behind the one-way mirror, observing the family. The team would occasionally call the therapist out of the room to give directives for handling in-the-room interactions. At the end of each session, the team would send in a formal written message commenting on their perceptions, which the therapist would read aloud.

In the initial session the therapist discussed, with the family, the idea of the one-way mirror team, which had originally been introduced in a previous phone contact. Relevant data about Ted's choking behavior and family members' responses to it were gathered.

The therapist and team hypothesized that this family was struggling with the issue of Ted's impending separation from the family. Ted's somatic complaints served to place him in a helpless, dependent position requiring the involvement, care, and concern of his parents and girl friend. Ted's "symptoms" were metaphoric for the process the whole family was experiencing; In essence, they were all "choked-up" over Ted's impending separation. Based on the team's observations, a message was sent that commended the closeness, caring, and commitment of this family. In addition, the statement especially emphasized Ted's loyalty to his parents and described his choking behavior "as a necessary sacrifice he has to make right now."

The therapeutic plan was as follows: The therapist would support Ted's capacity for independence as well as the parents' abilities to function adequately without the benefit of Ted's "help." Whenever the opportunity presented itself, the therapist would comment on how Ted seemed ready to begin a life on his own, something he had been "sacrificing in the best interests of his family." The team would reject this position and instead, emphasize that the costs of Ted's "sacrifice" were less than what the family would suffer if he became independent and more autonomous.

A contract was established for ten sessions on alternate weeks, even though the parents (especially the mother) expressed their wish for weekly meetings. The excerpt below, which occurred at the very end of the first session, illustrates how the therapist [Jennifer Campion, M.S.W., Psy.D.] deals with the mother's requests for more frequent meetings. Notice how she builds on the family's already demonstrated success in handling Ted's somatic complaints.

Therapist: Let's plan to meet in two weeks.

Mother: Why so long? Couldn't Ted just come by himself one day a week?

Therapist: One of the reasons we've decided is partly based on your own sense that things are getting better; that Ted is able to hold off his anxiety by just sitting in the ER; you're rallying around, you're being very supportive and helpful.

Mother: I think that if Ted came sooner it would help. Waiting two weeks—that's a long time.

Therapist: He has managed and managed pretty well.

Mother: What about medication to help him relax?

Therapist: You seem to be doing okay without it, so why don't we just discuss that again next time. Why don't the three of you talk about it between now and then.

Mother: [*as everyone is leaving the office*] If he should have a real problem should we call you?

Therapist: Of course you can call if you need to, but you can probably do what you've been doing, which has been helping.

Mother: That sounds encouraging.

Therapist: We're very optimistic!

This plan to meet every two weeks was an attempt to discourage the family's dependence on therapy, and support their sense of control and competence. Early in the treatment process Ted threatened to go elsewhere if not seen more frequently, and he did initiate one session with another therapist. This therapist was in contact with the team and an agreement was made for us to focus only on the presenting complaint in the family work, and to refer Ted to this therapist for individual treatment after the family sessions ended.

In the second session, two weeks later, it became clear that each parent had his or her own physical problems that alternately received attention from the rest of the family, and that the mother had experienced somatic "symptoms" similar to Ted's. At the end of the session the team sent in the following message:

> The team was surprised to learn that each member of the family has his or her own physical/health problems. It appears that family members have found an efficient way to share attention and care by taking turns having problems. The team is impressed with the way the family has worked this out. At this point, it seems to be Ted's turn to have a problem and to receive the care and attention of other family members. The team believes that it is risky for Ted to give up his symptoms right now—because if he does, the team predicts that someone else will become symptomatic. Some team members especially applaud Ted's dedication and sacrifice, realizing that as unpleasant as the gagging, choking feeling may be, it probably is a small price to pay for keeping other family members healthy.

In subsequent sessions the therapist continued to support Ted as responsible, independent, and ready to move on with his life. When he attempted to dramatize, in a hysterical fashion, the severity of his symptoms (for example, saying "I saw blood in my phlegm"), the therapist would take his comments very seriously, suggesting that the father monitor his phlegm every day and that an appointment be made as soon as possible to see his physician. Each time the therapist responded to Ted's comments in this fashion, Ted would quickly calm down. The team continued to emphasize the risks inherent in Ted becoming more independent and moving out of his parent's house:

> The team agrees with the mother that it will be difficult for Ted to make it on his own, and with the therapist that Ted needs to be more independent. However, the team thinks the timing of such a move toward independence, at this point, is risky. Until Ted's gagging decreases in frequency and his eating and weight increase, the chances for success of such a move are minimal. The team thinks that Ted is right, that ignoring him at times works best. If the mother can prove she can worry less about Ted, he may have a chance to make the move a success.

After eight sessions, Ted's anxiety reactions had decreased both in frequency and intensity. He had moved out of his parents' house and into an apartment (close by) with his girl friend. During the ten days away from home, the therapist received no emergency phone calls, and Ted did not require any trips to the local hospital ER. A session was scheduled three weeks after the eighth meeting. Ted continued to do well in his own apartment. While the therapist praised the parents, girl friend, and Ted for their successful efforts on Ted's behalf, the team sent in the following final message:

> It appears that this family is ready to terminate since Ted, with the help of his parents and Marsha [the girl friend], has made substantial progress. Some team members feel very confident that Ted is on the right track, especially since the father, who has been so available to Ted, and the mother, who is an expert on Ted's condition (having gone through something similar herself), have both been instrumental in helping Ted become more independent. The team is aware of how difficult a task this is for parents. Both parents and Marsha should be applauded for their efforts. Some other team members, however, are a bit skeptical about Ted's progress. These skeptical team members are betting that the symptoms will come back, especially if Ted continues overeating junk food and spending a lot of time alone. The team as a whole did agree that Ted should hold on to some of his symptoms—for example, his fear, since a little caution can be a useful thing.

The team's comments regarding Ted's progress served as a negative opinion against which the family and especially Ted could rebel. A playful quality evolved in the interaction of therapist, team, and family, with the family, but especially Ted, trying to defeat the "team of experts."

The use of this therapeutic triangle, in which the therapist and team take different sides of the family ambivalence, served to dislodge Ted from the parental triangle. Therapy served to provide a structure or frame in which Ted, with the help of his parents, could come to terms with his own needs for independence and autonomy while still remaining connected to his family. In this Greek family with no daughters, it became the responsibility of the youngest son to care for his parents. As a footnote, Ted did not return to see the other therapist after the family therapy ended, as was originally planned. He reported feeling fine and did not see the need for any further therapy.

The Reflecting Team

> Reality happens to be, like a landscape, possessed of an infinite number of perspectives, all equally veracious and authentic.
> —Ortega y Gasset, in *The Modern Theme*.

There is significant debate in the literature on the question of therapist power, and the use of power tactics in therapeutic intervention (see Hoffman 1985). The original strategic models of Jay Haley and the Mental Research Institute take the position that the therapist needs to use his expert position to create change in the family system. The therapy process is viewed as a struggle for control that the therapist needs to "win." Bateson (1978b), on the other hand, was never comfortable with the "manipulative" quality he felt existed in many of the strategic models.

Bateson (1972) believed that the therapist should take a more "neutral" stance in generating a conversation with the client that created multiple options or choices for action. Rather than imposing a task directive or manipulating the client to change (such as through the use of paradoxical interventions), the Batesonian premise was one of respect for the integrity of the client system and its ability to develop new modes of action with minimal facilitation by the therapist.

Current thinking views these perspectives (pragmatic v. aesthetic) as complementary (Atkinson and Heath 1990). Since as therapist, you are always in the position of directing or guiding the actions of the therapy, you cannot avoid an instrumental, goal-oriented position. What you can do, however, is not become too "wedded" to the specific outcome of your interventions. In this way, you respect and accept your client's wishes and autonomy without imposing your own values or needs. As therapists, we provide input and make suggestions, but leave the client to act on those ideas that are the best fit for him.

As we discussed earlier, a constructivist position assumes that hypotheses about behavior are neither true nor false. What is important is that these hypotheses generate new information that open up options for change. The Milan Team of Boscolo and Cecchin (Boscolo et al. 1987) have adopted, in their latest work, the philosophic assumptions of the cybernetic researchers (Maturana and Varela 1987; von Forester 1984) in taking the position "that there can be no 'instructive interaction.' . . . only a perturbation of a system that will then react in terms of its own structure" (Boscolo et al. 1987: 18). The Milan group suggest "that therapists should continually generate alternative hypotheses (or stories) to keep therapists from becoming too wedded to their own ideas or seeking some objective truth" (Epstein and Loos 1989: 411).

The methods of the Milan team have evolved over the years and provide an excellent example of the use of therapeutic teams and "circular questions" (see Penn 1982; Tomm 1987) as a means to enlarge or expand the family perspective and dispel dysfunctional family myths. They emphasize the *observing system* as a means to gather information and develop hypotheses. "The team . . . w[eaves] any response [by family members], even a hostile or challenging one, into an extended hypothesis that [i]s always changing" (Hoffman 1985: 389). Green and Herget (1989a, 1989b) have conducted research indicating the significant positive effects of Milan-style team consultations on treatment outcome.

Where this leads us, is to the notion of the *reflecting team* (RT), an idea developed by Tom Andersen in Norway (Andersen 1987) and based on the Milan approach and its Batesonian philosophy. As we have seen, the ST uses an anonymous group of experts who send in messages that serve to support, confront, challenge, provoke, or disorient the family. The ST arrives at a consensus point of view, which is then communicated to the family via the therapist. In essence, there is a power hierarchy starting with the "expert" team and moving to the therapist and the family.

In contrast, the members of the RT silently view the family's interaction, and then share their thoughts and ideas in front of the mirror while the family observes. These speculations are not meant to be judgments, diagnostic formulations, or interpretations. No attempt is made to arrive at a team consensus or even to come to any agreement. Comments are shared within a positive framework and are presented as tentative offerings.

In contrast to the hierarchal model of the ST, the RT reflects a collaborative process between the therapist, family, and team. This model has been successfully adopted and adapted as an innovative and useful tool in creating a context for change (see, Davidson et al. 1988; Furman 1990; Mittelmeier and Friedman 1991; Roberts et al. 1989).

The RT generates through their discussion in front of the family an array of ideas. These ideas are like seeds, some of which will find fertile soil and others of which will fall on fallow ground. The hope is that the family will find some of the ideas useful in the creation of new perspectives on the family picture. The members of the RT are like "foreigners" . . . who, because of different backgrounds, can add a new and exciting version of the world to the one the system had before" (Andersen 1987: 416).

In one family, the seventeen-year-old daughter, following the conversation of the RT, described the process this way: "We're here to see what they [the team] have to say about their feedback on what we said and our feedback on what they said about what we said." This sums up, in an articulate way, the constructions generated in the evolving dialogue between family and team. The father in this same family described the process like the classic 1951 Japanese film *Rashomon* where perceptions of an event change as a function of who is describing the situation. As this father said: "You have to take all the factors together to get a whole picture" (for details on the RT process with this family see Mittelmeier and Friedman 1991).

The RT model is especially useful and effective when dealing with volatile, emotionally reactive and/or "blaming" couples or families. The RT provides the reactive couple or family with a new perspective and an increased ability for empathy and introspection. Each member of the couple or family becomes better able to focus on his or her own role in the systemic process. One couple, who had been blaming each other for the disappointments and hurts they each experienced for over twelve years, were able to get in touch with the things they loved and admired about each other after an RT experience. These positive feelings, which had gotten lost in the emotional turmoil, formed the basis for the development of a new level of intimacy and understanding. With this couple, the RT helped "translate" their individual styles of relating to the world in a way that the other could understand and acknowledge. While the wife was dealing on a more global, affective level, the husband tended to be more comfortable talking about ideas and "things." The RT discussion moved each member of the couple toward a better understanding of the other's experiential world and helped join them in a common bond of mutual respect and caring.

The RT is most effective when ideas are generated that are different from the family's usual mode of thinking about the problem, yet not so different that they will be rejected. In line with Bateson's notion that information "is a difference which makes a difference" (1972), the therapeutic team must generate ideas novel enough that the family will notice and acknowledge them as different, but not so novel that they will be rejected out of hand. As mentioned in an earlier chapter, humans respond more positively to small changes than to large discrepancies from their levels of expectation (K.E. Weick 1984). It is this principle that is fundamental to the RT approach. Excerpts from a RT session illustrate the usefulness of this approach.

The family consists of the parents and their two children, one of whom (Myra, age 14) had recently been discharged from the hospital after a four-week stay with a diagnosis of anorexia nervosa. Both parents are professionals who work full time. Several segments of the interview are presented as is the RT conversation. Both the therapist and the team are working to expand the focus beyond Myra's "eating problem" into the larger family context. Notice the shift in the focus of the family's comments following the RT discussion.

Therapist [Cynthia Mittelmeier, Ph.D.]: So, why don't we start with . . . what would you like to have happen here today? [*silence, then laughter*]

Mother: Maybe for us to understand a little more what Myra has gone through, and maybe she can understand what we've gone through.

Father: We talk a lot at home, and I think when important issues come up and we're trying to figure out where your [*to Myra*] mood is at. There are lots of times when you don't know why you're angry or why or having certain emotions. It would be nice if we could understand that better; it would be nice if you could understand. I'm not sure a four-way or five-way forum is the best way for you to feel comfortable talking about this. We'd like to be able to be supportive by knowing what's bugging you.

Mother: A lot of that was encouraged at the hospital, because she tended to cover up those emotions . . . and has been a good sport all the time. And the fact that she is allowing the mood swings to happen when they do is a good sign, and when they're done she can still have a smile on her face.

Therapist: So what the hospitalization did, was to open things up, bring things to the surface.

[*The mother talks about the difficulties Myra has had adjusting to being out of the hospital after four weeks.*]

Therapist: There's been a change in the family as a function of the hospitalization?

Mother: We're ready to accept mood swings and not to take them too personally.

Father: My perception was that things were fine as they could be. We're a very imperfect family with a whole host of anxieties, but, to tell the truth, I didn't see there were any problems until we were in the middle of it. I think we have to be more attentive to letting Myra have these feelings. We're all going to have to adjust to change in her character.

Mother: It's made us kind of think about how our children have grown up a little. Having you [*to Myra*] away for a month and thinking about all this and seeing what you've gone through. I realize that both of you [*Myra and her brother*] have grown up a whole lot.

[*The therapist pursues the question of how the issue of Myra's eating relates to other aspects of the family's functioning.*]

Therapist: What is the connection between Myra's eating problem and how the family works things out?

Myra: When I was talking to people at the hospital and letting my feelings show, it came out. I was taking a lot of things seriously at school and I wasn't too happy and stuff, and when this . . . when America went health crazy, I took that a little too seriously.

Therapist: So, your tendency is to take things seriously? Is that like anybody else in the family?

Myra: My parents are serious about some things—but not like that.

Therapist: How would that be connected to the family—your tendency to take things seriously? Your taking school seriously, eating the right food seriously.

Myra: I don't think it had much to do with the family.

Therapist: When you said back in the spring you weren't very happy, did you let people know?

Myra: I kept that inside.

Father: She's good at that. I think about you [*to Myra*] getting home from school, and the dog and I would say hello to you and you'd come in with a big smile and you'd say things were fine and school was terrific. So she's pretty good at putting on a happy face. Maybe there were clues earlier, and I kick myself for not becoming more involved. For example, I remember nights going off to sleep and this one [*referring to Myra*] would still be up doing her homework. In retrospect, that was a mistake, letting her work three or four hours a day, but, on the other hand, she would tell us "I really like studying and doing this." She got great grades and seemed to be content about it, that's my misgiving.

Mother: She was giving up a lot of her free time. We noticed that in the spring and we called the guidance counselor at school because we thought she was studying too hard. She can study half the time and still do well.

[*The therapist emphasizes the risks of change and elicits the feelings of family members in response to anticipated changes.*]

Therapist: The idea of thought-provoking conversations, feeling-oriented conversations, more intensive discussions. . . . It can also be a bit risky because more things can get stirred up. Does anybody have concerns about making these changes? Maybe that could be too much for the family. I'm hearing a lot of "we want to change . . . we want to hear more of Myra's feelings." Does anybody have any feelings on the flip side?

Father: I think it is scarier. We've come to expect behavior from various members of our family. We've gotten comfortable with that, knowing she's a terrific kid relieves you of a fair amount of concern. The kid's got it all put together, all squared away. But now, it's not so simple. She's not squared away and she needs our help. The change is a little scarier. It will remove from us a comfortable perception of her.

Therapist [to the mother]: Is it scary for you, these changes?

Mother: Of course, at some level it is, but I also am realizing that she's reached a different time in her life. All of a sudden I have a young lady at home. Part of it is frightening and part is exciting. I look forward to us doing stuff together at a different level.

[The reflecting team (SF; Sally Brecher, M.S.W.; Brian Meyer, Ph.D.) enters the therapy room while the family and the therapist go behind the one-way mirror to observe their conversation.]

SB: I'm having somewhat of a difficult time understanding what brought this problem on. What's really going on here? I feel that the family's very close. The parents are extremely conscientious and they seem more freed up to express feelings now. It's really an excellent start, and I think Myra's hospitalization . . . she took the ball and ran with it. I wonder whether her fighting with her brother is the beginning, and feelings of anger may come out more and more with the parents. And if that would occur how the parents would feel about it. I think that Myra has also protected her parents, taking the burden for all that's been happening, sparing them anxiety. So I can see this as a difficult shift for the family and one that they are very clear in wanting to take.

SF: The father was talking about the need to be more attentive, worrying that he missed some cues. Myra is in the process of separating herself from the family and there's that sort of conflict between privacy and autonomy and the needs of the family to be vigilant.

BM: And that may be hard to manage since she is growing up and separating, and yet, at the same time, there is some need for the parents to be more attentive to her eating. That may be one of things they can work on in therapy.

SF: What I wonder about is how this family will be functioning when this eating problem, this focus on eating is resolved and no longer a problem. How will things be? What changes will be necessary in the family? Obviously, in making changes there are some risks.

SB: And the sessions here with Dr. Mittelmeier can be an opportunity for them to express what other concerns there are in the family beyond the eating.

SF: It seems like the parents have seriously dealt with this [*the eating problem*] and successfully, I think, in getting Myra past this crisis. In fact, her hospitalization has provided a chance for the whole family to get some perspective on what's happening and what's needed.

SB: They're in the middle of a process. Maybe it's too soon to know what it's all about.

BM: It's kind of like Myra having feelings she doesn't understand. So it's hard for everybody to know what's going on. I think it takes a lot of courage to show her feelings, particularly since there is a risk involved. It does scare some people. I wonder if it will continue to be possible for her to be courageous, to show her feelings . . . and an opportunity for everyone in the family to start showing their feelings and take some risks.

SB: I agree with you. It would be hard for Myra to continue if other family members weren't sharing their feelings in return. There's been a crisis that's occurred and a real opportunity for change. It's really very hopeful.

SF: And Myra's leading the way.

[*The family returns.*]

Therapist: What were people's reactions to what the team had to say? Anything that fit? Anything that didn't fit?

Father: Someone mentioned "process," and that is close to it. We're speaking of it as it's happening. I don't really have a whole lot of perspective on what's going on until more time passes. That rings true for me.

Mother: I think reiterating that the kids have just hit another age. I won't be as protective as I think I have been or we have been of the kids. It's a time to let go a little bit. It will be fun to relax and that's an important issue and one we look forward to.

Father: The other thing about sharing feelings. At this point we're so sick of the word "feeling."

Mother: We sing it. [*laughter*]

Father: In all seriousness, I think our family has always erred on the side of being "the good sport." And *being a good sport is like our "by-word": We all do it.* We've instilled this in our kids. If you want to look at things through that particular filter you can say she's been "too good a sport," denying herself a lot of nasty feelings about another person or a situation.

Mother: Trying to look on the good side all the time . . . we're the youngest children in both our families.

Father: I know I do that role with my family, putting a mask on that keeps everyone happy. Maybe we need to back away from that, and we need to rethink our family credo.

Therapist: Myra, is there anything that made sense to you?

Myra: I followed right along.

The RT conversation appeared to create a shift in the way the family talked about their concerns about Myra's eating, moving it from something "inside" the daughter to a systemic issue in which all family members played some part. At the time of this writing, Myra and her family continue in therapy with the goal of stabilizing Myra's weight and providing an opportunity for the family to "rethink their family credo" of being the "good sport."

Conclusions

As you can see from the examples in this chapter, we use a variety of team approaches in our work. Our philosophy about team models is one of openness and experimentation. Most recently, we have been experimenting with the reflecting team model. However, we have learned that no one model can be generalized to the wide array of clients and families we see. For example, when there are young children involved who might not understand the verbal give-and-take of the reflecting team, we shift to a consulting format in which the team communicates directly with the therapist from behind the one-way mirror and/or sends in written messages, read by the therapist, which are at a level that the young child can understand. In choosing between compliance- versus defiance-based models, we tend to use the former, saving the latter for those systems that have developed more longstanding patterns not amenable to other more direct approaches.

These approaches are also adaptable to situations in which you don't have the benefit of an observing team or a consultant. What we have found useful is giving ourselves permission to take a short break (three to five minutes) during the session (usually towards the end) in which we leave the room and gather our thoughts. Standing outside the intensity of the therapeutic encounter allows us the opportunity to generate new ideas and formulate constructive tasks. In addition, we will sometimes take a "reflecting position" with a client or family, similar to the reflecting team. We this by sharing (within a positive framework) the multiplicity of possibilities inherent in the client's situation. In a sense, we wonder out loud about the family's predicament, offering them "food for thought." Papp (1990) presents other useful ideas for adapting a team format when working alone.

Part IV
Some Rivers
Successfully Run

10
Coaching the Player

To clarify the process of brief psychotherapy as it evolves over time, we have included several longer clinical illustrations of various client constellations. In the clinical examples that follow, we draw on a diverse array of therapeutic approaches in setting the stage for change. What is consistent throughout these examples is our capitalizing on the possibilities inherent in the circumstances that create a context for change. Also, in each situation, we match and tailor the intervention to the needs of each client or client system and utilize the clients' strengths and resources as the means to reach a clearly specified goal.

When we speak of brief psychotherapy, what we are really referring to is a small number of sessions rather than necessarily a short amount of time. Brief therapy can be a few sessions in a short period of time, but it can also be episodes of sessions spanning months and years. For us, *time-effective therapy* is a clearer expression for the therapy we present here, for two of the illustrations (in this chapter and in chapter 12) show the therapeutic relationship continuing over a long period of time, punctuated by episodes of treatment. The relationship is open-ended, while the actual number of treatment sessions, given the elapsed time, are few. The length of each treatment installment is decided by the client and therapist together, while the client has responsibility for recontacting the therapist if and when (in the client's opinion) it is needed.

In the example of therapy presented here there are thirty sessions in all; five couple, nineteen individual and six group sessions over a period of five years. Here you will find examples of well-constructed outcomes, couples' therapy tasks, letter writing, revising personal history, decision-making lists, hypnotic imagery, and storytelling encompassed in a time-effective therapeutic relationship. When Mike (age 31) and Gail (age 29) first turned up in my [MTF] office, they had been living together for five years and were struggling with a decision about further commitment. Mike wanted to just continue the way they were, while Gail was ready to get on with what she saw as the logical next step: to get married, and to start raising kids. She wanted either to get married or break up. Mike was there both because he didn't want to lose Gail, but also because he wondered about what stopped him from going ahead—he did love her, they both had steady jobs, so he wondered what was his problem? As he continued to speak he brought out his worries about "being good enough" to be able to live up to family responsibilities.

It became clear when Mike briefly mentioned a childhood disrupted by his mother's illness, followed by divorce and his father's remarriage to a "cold stepmother," that his critical image of family life was bleak and uninviting. Gail had come from a large and close family centered around her mother who had died two years before. Her unspoken agenda may have been to get started on creating a new version of her family.

In addition to the larger questions of commitment, there were smaller issues they were having difficulty resolving: he didn't like to visit her family so much, she didn't like his going out with his friends to play basketball and drink. They found discussion of these issues got them nowhere and left them more disgruntled than before. They agreed that they would like to learn improved interactional skills in hopes that they would be able to come to some agreement about the next step in their relationship. This was, then, their mutually agreed upon well-constructed outcome. We made a four-session renewable contract, and I assigned them the task of making a list of small behavioral changes that each would like to see in the other to improve the quality of their daily life.

Here are some of the items from their lists:

Gail wants **Mike** to:	Mike wants **Gail** to:
—do laundry more willingly	—stop doing my laundry
—spend less time drinking with his friends, especially Eddie Kelly	—understand that he needs to spend time with his friends without her, especially Eddie Kelly
—dance more with her, especially all the slow dances at parties	—stop turning her back to me during sleep
—listen to her more clearly (pay attention when she's talking)	—laugh more, smile, loosen up, have fun
—put his dirty laundry in the laundry bag	—stop squirreling his clothes into the laundry after they're barely worn
—clean the inside of the car	—stop leaving her bathrobe on the bed

—stop avoiding visits to her family	—stop making visiting her family such a heavy issue
—have people over once in a while	—be willing to see his friends
—take more responsibility for money and household bills	—be willing to let him borrow to buy a motorcyle

These lists offered them specific items for negotiation and further showed areas of mutual concern. Their general critical images and life-stage developments were also highlighted. Here was a woman who wanted to settle down in a tidy house and be a responsible householder paired with a man not yet ready for that stage, who still wanted to go out and play. Their priorities were quite different. So while I got this "instant photo" of their major differences, I chose to continue our contract to help them to develop new negotiating skills. I wanted to use a pair of small items, so that the negotiations wouldn't instantly deterioriate to the level of "if you really loved me, you would want to do that." So I chose first the issue of Gail's leaving her bathrobe on the bed as a starter. This seemed a good choice both because it was a small item and because it was the only one on his list that involved her neatness, while she had several that involved his. I asked Mike to say "I'd like to have you stop leaving your bathrobe on the bed every day, what can *I* do to get you to stop it?" Gail responded by saying "I didn't even know that bothered you! Well, I don't like seeing it there either, but our closet is so small and there are no hooks in it, so that there's no place for me to put it. I'd love it if you would put a hook in the closet, so I *could* hang it up." We were all amazed at this simple solution. The one I chose for her to request, "putting dirty laundry in the laundry bag" seemed similar to his, but turned out to be more complex and to involve their critical images. When Gail asked Mike, "I'd like you to put your dirty clothes in the laundry bag instead of leaving them all over the bedroom, what can I do to get you to do that?" He snorted and exclaimed "I wish you'd stop squirreling my clean clothes into the laundry bag!" Clearly a time to sort out critical images, which we then did. In Gail's house, her mother made it clear that clothes that were worn *once* were dirty, while in Mike's home, the emphasis was on conservation, in other words, wearing something until it *looked* dirty. From his point of view, Gail was snatching up clothes of his that were half-dirty, quarter-dirty, or three-quarters dirty and stuffing them in the laundry bag; he thought this extreme and wasteful. Gail had never known this; she had just thought Mike was careless and sloppy and had never dreamed it was a difference in values. I then emphasized that neither of them really needed to change their views about what constituted dirty clothes, but what was needed was an *appreciation of the other's values as valid*, so that an accommodation could be found. Gail was willing to let Mike have different standards about when his clothes were dirty, but still objected to his leaving them all over the bedroom. He said "But I have to have *someplace* for them," and she agreed, saying "Well, what if you put them all on that chair next to the dresser, then I'll know what they are and the bedroom will be neater." Mike's agreement resolved that issue. They were pleased to have taken care of what had been an ongoing source of friction between them.

The remaining three sessions proceeded in like manner, with some of the hotter issues explored and aired if not fully resolved. In the last session, while their positions were unchanged—she wanted commitment and marriage, he wasn't ready—both of them said they were willing to continue their relationship for the time being, hopeful that they could now better sort out their unresolved issues. They had reached their well-constructed outcome of increased negotiating skills. As is my practice, I encouraged them both to go out and see how they could use their new expertise effectively, at the same time offering to see them again *if* need arose.

Three months later Mike called for another appointment. When he came in, he said that he thought his inability to commit to marriage had to do with his own issues of low confidence and self-esteem. We made a four-session contract to take a look at these topics. He felt inadequate that at thirty-one he wasn't ready to settle down, but quite clearly did not want to. Part of his reluctance stemmed from his relative inexperience with women. He had had two long-term partners with whom he had lived (Gail being the second), but few other experiences; in fact, there had never been a time when he felt he could freely date a number of women if he wanted to. He said that he had been extremely shy and uncertain in high school, even though he had done well in sports, and that he didn't date until after college when he quickly moved in with the first woman who seemed to like and accept him. When they broke up, largely because of his restlessness and resistance to commitment, he had quickly formed a steady relationship with Gail that quickly led to their living together. He rather wistfully said he would like to feel confident enough to date several women to prove that he was a man attractive to more than two women. Recently he had found a couple of women somewhat pursuing him at his work, but out of loyalty to Gail he didn't feel free to respond to them. He also saw his genital herpes and quick ejaculation as drawbacks to getting more experience. He was afraid that other women would not find him acceptable as a sexual partner, so he had better stay with Gail even though it involved a compromise he didn't want. He clarified his unwillingness to settle down before he felt ready and began to see that he was simply at a different stage in his life than Gail was. This reframe helped him to feel better about himself and more confident. He also spoke of his loyalty to his job as a drug counselor and to his colleagues, but that he wasn't satisfied to stay in what he saw as a work situation with no future. He began to see this kind of self-examination as a key to change for him, but decided after the four sessions to continue on his own for the time being.

A year later, Mike called again, still struggling with his ambivalence about settling down before having more diverse sexual experience. He and Gail had begun a trial separation after she pressed him to commit or leave. He felt guilty over his pleasure at having his own place. He reported that he still saw Gail, and their sex life had improved, which he linked to having the courage to live separately. He requested direct sexual therapy for his quick ejaculation. To treat him for this I chose to use storytelling, with a hypnotic trance to intensify the effect. When you create stories for such purposes, you think of metaphors that might represent elements of the patient's current state and then add components that point to changed behavior. For the stories-in-trance work itself I used a version of the three-tiered trance structure described by Stephen and Carol Lankton in their book *The Answer Within* (1983).

The first of the three stories that I used with Mike took him into a relaxed, trance-like state. This consisted of having him attend to his breathing, then to imagine himself in a lovely outdoor space of his own creating, deepening the relaxation by walking through the colors of a rainbow. I used the outdoor setting as a transition to a story about a man who led a very rushed and hectic life, a man who always wanted to get to a destination practically before he started the trip. One day this man was driving to Cape Cod from Boston and he decided to have a different experience. Instead of driving as fast as he could, listening to a professional tape, using his radar detector to elude the police, he decided to go slowly and notice the scenery. He put on some relaxing music, drove at a leisurely pace, and began to notice details of the scenery for the first time. He began to see the subtle shifts in the kind of trees and shrubbery as he got closer to the Cape. He decided to use the several wayside rest stops to examine these changes in more detail. He stopped at each one and got out of the car. One thing he noticed was not only that the greenery changed, but also that some of the same trees, for example the pines, looked quite different in the smaller Cape version. He discovered many new details, it was really like going into an uncharted world where the colors and shapes were much more vivid than he was used to. He got so engrossed in resting and observing the subtle changes in scenery that he almost didn't want the journey to end. He began to realize that the pleasure of the trip far outweighed any time lost in getting to his destination, and when he did finally arrive, it was just at the moment when he could observe a brilliant sunset over the bay. He thought that he had never enjoyed this burst of sunset colors so much because his acute observation of the scenery had heightened his visual awareness immensely.

For some reason this reminded him of another time when he'd had heightened visual acuity, a time when he'd been playing basketball in high school. When he'd first started playing basketball, he had thought that scoring points was the most important thing to do. But as he went along he realized increasingly that the most important thing in basketball was not so much to score points as to be a good team player. He began to focus on his ability to interact with the other players in such a way that he could be instrumental in *their* scoring. He began to have as much fun and excitement as a member of the team as he used to think he would when he made baskets by himself. He began enjoying the team tactics and felt good when others congratulated him on his excellent ability to be an outstanding team player. Along with this, his coach gave them special practice in making free throws, he taught them that besides actual practice on the basketball court, that if they would practice perfect free throws and team plays in their imaginations, that they would improve. As he practiced this in his mind, he became increasingly aware how the mental practice seemed to come to life in his game.

After he recalled this in detail, he found himself once more on a now darkening beach and noticed a slim crescent moon trailed by the evening star, and he could hear the water lapping on the shore. A feeling of peaceful relaxation came over him and he decided to plan more trips in which he would include both rest stops and observation of his surroundings as he headed for his destination. He took a few deep breaths as he looked around at the lovely outdoor scene, and vowed to capture it to store in his memory.

Soon after Mike opened his eyes, he asked me with a broad smile "Did you know that when our high school won the state basketball championship, I was voted Most Valuable Player even though I had never made a basket?" In his next session, two weeks later, he was pleased to report that he had been able to maintain an erection without ejaculation long enough to suit both him and his partner, although, he added "I did start thinking about basketball in the middle of love-making."

As his "world image" changed to that of his being a more competent lover, his confidence increased and when he went on a trip to Tennessee, he met a woman who not only wanted to spend time with him there, but also came and visited him in Boston. One could speculate that this helped him to get unstuck from his adolescent stance, for he soon was ready to deal with his sadness connected to the loss of his parents. Mike was the youngest of three boys, and when he was four, his mother was diagnosed as having amyotrophic lateral sclerosis. Her illness advanced rapidly. Soon she was unable to function adequately as a homemaker and moved back to her parents' home. Mike's father divorced her when Mike was seven, and before long he married an undemonstrative woman who took minimal care of the three boys in what Mike characterized as a very harsh environment. He recalled tearful visits with his debilitated mother, not understanding either her illness or his father's abandonment of her. His father claimed he wanted a real mother for his sons. Mike's father died of lung cancer when Mike was thirteen, leaving him with the distant stepmother. His real mother died from her ALS when he was fourteen, and he recalled reacting to their deaths by "not talking to anyone."

It seemed the perfect moment to get him to write letters to his parents, to tell them about all those feelings he had pent up for so many years. It took him some time to complete these, and when he returned, he reported that after the writing to his mother he had gone on a four-hour bike ride during which he had cried so hard he could hardly see the road. He learned about his parents' difficulties: his mother's anguish at her inability to mother her sons, especially him, her baby; and his father's sadness and struggle to provide for his sons in the best way he knew how. This appeared to be a turning point for Mike, he began to actively pursue a new job that he really wanted, that of baseball coach for a nearby college. Going after this job, one with a future, represented a major change for Mike, who had formerly just "let things happen." When the job was offered to him, at first he was in a quandary, and so I asked him to make lists of the pros and cons. After he put them into priority, and mentally weighed them, he knew clearly that taking the new job was the right step for him. And so he was able to accept the offer despite his close friends at work telling him he was betraying them by leaving them shorthanded.

The following spring, Mike again turned up to examine the issues about commitment and freedom. During these sessions he discovered that he was afraid that if he married, he might die, like his parents did. We then met once a month for four months, again visiting issues about his parents. He had a very somber picture of his early life and realized also that he had no model of a marriage that he would want to be a part of. During these sessions, Mike recalled his maternal grandfather as a man that he could really admire, smart, sensitive, and funny. Mike remembered his grandfather starting to teach Mike the language of his homeland. Mike also recalled his grandparents as being very companionable with each other. We did a version of revising personal history by constructing a number of painful scenes from his childhood where his grandfather came and advised him and so made them better. His grandfather actually died when Mike was fifteen, but with these imagined scenes, Mike was able to make his granfather more of a living presence, and began "carrying him around" with him as an advisor. He also signed up in a class to learn his grandfather's native language.

A few months later Mike called again, this time to take a look at smoking cessation. He was becoming more health conscious and wanted help in adopting more responsible health habits. He worked part-time in a bar where he did most of his smoking and drank "more than he should." He realized that if he wanted to survive marriage, he would need to invest in his health. He was just starting to see a new woman, Terry, steadily. Gail was engaged to someone else. I offered to enroll him in my six-session group program on health and wellness issues. He gladly joined the group. In this group, which uses relaxation meditation and guided imagery, Mike had a chance to discover not only the positive intention behind his smoking (making him feel "grown up") but further discover that he now had other ways to meet this intention. He looked at his fear of getting ALS and lung cancer, and saw his drinking and smoking as habits to avoid his fear of dying by making him feel as though he could "live forever." He realized that his life was more satisfying if he didn't "dope himself up" with alcohol and cigarettes, so he decided to get a different part-time job, drive more carefully, and concentrate on his relationship with Terry.

Two years later we had our last session. He was about to marry Terry and appeared to be surprised at how happy this prospect made him. He was eager to take this step, finding Terry much more relaxed and fun than Gail had been. We discussed a dream he had that involved his parents and Terry in her wedding dress and found that he could accept them all. He said that Terry reminded him of his maternal grandmother, the wife of the grandfather that he had incorporated as his resident advisor.

This case illustrates how an open-ended therapeutic relationship can guide and support a patient over developmental hurdles over a period of years, but in a relatively small number of sessions.

11
The Illusion of a Delusion

In the clinical example to follow, I [SF] describe the application of an Ericksonian paradigm in resolving a marital problem of two years' duration. A rigid behavioral sequence had developed in which the wife would attribute special meaning to her husband's behavior and he would then defend himself in a posture that promoted their disagreement to a furious struggle of competing realities. When an alternative meaning is attributed to the husband's behavior, a new reality is constructed in which the problem is "dis-solved."

Mr. Louis called my office in an extremely agitated and anxious state demanding an appointment as soon as possible for "something very distressing," which he did not want to discuss on the telephone. I had worked, briefly and successfully, with Mr. Louis and his wife (both in their fifties, married two years) four months earlier regarding the wife's concerns about dealing with her adolescent son from her first marriage. During our telephone conversation Mr. Louis kept asking if I would be the right person to deal with this kind of a problem. I told him that before I could answer that question I would need to know more about the problem. All Mr. Louis would say was that he had, over the past two years, dealt with three previous therapists without success, and that one of the therapists laughed when told about the problem. After realizing that he was uncomfortable discussing the situation by phone, I suggested that he and I set up a meeting, at which time Mr. Louis described the following scenario.

At least once a week, especially when Mr. Louis and his wife were eating out in a restaurant, Mrs. Louis would accuse her husband of looking at, and being attracted to, young women sitting at nearby tables. According to Mr. Louis, his wife would say "You seem to find the woman over there very attractive" to which Mr. Louis would voice strong denials, vociferously declaring that he was in fact looking at no one. This interaction would escalate into a full-blown conflict in which the harder Mr. Louis worked to deny the attributions, the angrier Mrs.

Louis would become. In my office Mr. Louis denied that he was looking at other women and defended his love for his wife. During these episodes, Mr. Louis reported that his wife would get "violent" and that they had spent as much as seven to eight hours in continous conflict over this issue. Mr. Louis requested that I help him make his wife understand that he was devoted to her and nobody else. He saw the problem as *hers*. He also stated clearly that he felt there were no other problems in his marriage. In trying to better understand the situation I suggested that he and his wife come in for a joint meeting. He said that she would probably decline since "she sees this as *my* problem." Before agreeing to see him individually in two weeks, I suggested that he think about the consequences of perhaps not denying the behavior his wife was attributing to him. Could he occasionally agree with his wife's attributions to see if this would de-escalate the conflict? To this suggestion he became angry and refused to even consider acknowledging something that was not true. He reiterated how three previous therapists refused to take the problem seriously. I got the message.

Before my next meeting, I decided to seek consultation from another therapist. This therapist told me that she had previously worked with a couple in which the wife had come into treatment with the concern that her husband was being unfaithful to her. After taking the problem at face value, my colleague began to see these concerns as a fixed delusion with no basis in fact. The DSM-III-R describes this as delusional jealousy ("conjugal paranoia"). The wife was eventually convinced by the therapist to take antipsychotic medication, which did not abolish the wife's concerns, but did serve to reduce her distress *about* the concerns. As I listened to this therapist, I began to wonder if this is what I was encountering in my situation. However, before moving in this direction, I decided to consider some other (less medical) approaches.

I began to generate systemic hypnotheses about the function of the pattern Mr. Louis described. It served to modulate intimacy; it permitted the husband an opportunity to declare his love and devotion to his wife, and so on. All of these hypotheses were interesting but seemed miles away from a useful and efficient resolution of the problem. I thought of a comment made by O'Hanlon and Wilk (1987:98) that "every now and then . . . a hypothesis might accidentally enter the therapist's head, and the best remedy for it, is to lie down until it goes away." Would it be possible to simply bypass the presuppositions inherent in generating systemic hypotheses and focus instead on directly intervening in ways that shifted or altered the context or meaning system in which the problem was embedded?

I began to think about ways that would trigger a change in the couple's interactional *pattern* and in each partner's *perceptions* of the other's behavior.

After my second meeting with the husband in which he reiterated his love for his wife and reviewed the two most recent incidents of conflict, I suggested he ask his wife to call me for an individual appointment. Mrs. Louis called a few days later, indicated her worry about her husband's behavior and readily agreed to come in to discuss *his* problem. At this meeting Mrs. Louis reported that she was most annoyed by her husband's denial of, what was to her, his very obvious looking behavior. She also described other behaviors that she called "nervous mannerisms" (such as fidgeting in his seat and talking inappropriately loudly at times). Besides staring at young women, these other behaviors distressed Mrs. Louis as well.

I listened closely as she talked of these "nervous mannerisms," where she thought they came from, how long she'd noticed them, and so forth. I realized that she had just provided me with an *alternative reality* in which to view her husband's behavior. I told her that I thought her husband had developed, long before he met her, a set of nervous behaviors, which may have had meaning at some other earlier time, but which now had lost their meaning. I talked about her husband's looking behavior as one such nervous mannerism that was a vestige of times past. I framed his behavior as both unconscious (a reflex) and content free, he was looking but not seeing. I described this as similar to a knee-jerk response, where a whole class of stimuli applied to a certain spot elicit a similar reaction. We discussed how such behaviors could easily be taken personally but how they could also be viewed as merely idiosyncratic mannerisms which bore no relationship to the wife. I set up an appointment with Mrs. Louis for three weeks later and with her husband for the following week.

When Mr. Louis arrived for this appointment, he began by telling me that his wife had talked with him after her meeting with me the previous week. He said that my understanding of his behavior, as I communicated it to his wife, had made a lot of sense to him since he never *intended* to look or show interest in other women. He was also able to acknowledge that he noticed himself "doing it" at certain times during the past week. I then suggested that he "consciously try to make the looking reflex happen" in order to gain increased control over this behavior. At first he appeared upset with the idea of making something happen that he didn't want to happen and that had contributed to so much marital turmoil. I tried to "explain" to him that if he could make the "looking" happen it would mean that he could exercise some control over making it not happen. I suggested he "practice" the looking behavior when his wife was not around. He said he needed to think about this since he wasn't sure he could do it. I also told him that I admired his willingness to accept his wife's assertion that he was looking at other women, with the understanding that the looking had no intent or meaning.

Two weeks later I met with Mrs. Louis who reported that her husband seemed "more aware' of his "nervous habit," that *she* was "noticing it less" and had not been getting upset after noticing it. I met with Mr. Louis two weeks later. He noted that, although his wife would at times still comment on his "nervous behavior," these comments did not lead to any conflict as in the past. No further contacts were requested.

About six months following this last meeting with Mr. Louis, Mrs. Louis called because of a concern about "being caught in the middle" of increased conflict between her husband and her son. Two meetings held with Mrs. Louis, her son, and Mr. Louis focused on this issue. The family communicated their satisfaction with these meetings and agreed to call should they wish further contact. No mention was made of our previous meetings.

About nine months after this contact I received a call, regarding Mr. Louis, from a therapist at another center. The couple had transferred their HMO membership to this new center. The therapist reported that Mr. Louis had presented with very similar concerns (that his wife was "suspicious" again). I discussed my therapeutic strategy with this new therapist. I encouraged him to view the problem as a "relapse" and to reiterate my original strategic frame. To this he agreed. After a contact with Mrs. Louis individually, the new therapist held two meetings with the couple. At this point, the presenting complaint was no longer viewed as a problem and other relationship issues were briefly discussed. The therapist has reported no contact with the couple in the past twelve months.

The success of the interventions used may be attributed to several factors: (1) each spouse's perceptions were positively affirmed without pathologizing either spouse as "sick"; (2) the original request was taken seriously; (3) a reframe was introduced that evolved out of the wife's perceptions of her husband's behavior; (4) a new and acceptable meaning for the husband's behavior was proposed such that neither spouse "lost face"; and (5) more cumbersome presuppositions about the "function of the symptom" were avoided and a solution-oriented approach taken in directly "utilizing" the information provided by the clients.

12
A Family in Transition

The family presented here was seen by one of us [SF] over a three-year period and illustrates how the family itself regulates professional contact. In addition, it emphasizes the importance of using a flexible theoretical framework in creating a context for change. Some of the twenty-one sessions were held with various combinations of family members, but most of the sessions involved only the parents. The therapy process included three distinct therapy "episodes" with the final episode resulting in successful resolution of the original complaint. In the first episode, the family was seen for seven sessions over a six-month period. After a ten-month break in treatment, the family returned for six more sessions over a four-month period. Finally, after another ten-month hiatus, they returned, and eight additional sessions were held over a period of three months. On each occasion, the decisions to interrupt therapy, as well as the decisions to return to treatment, were made by the family. I had no contact with any family members during the intervals between episodes.

The family consisted of two parents, Harry and Joan, and their adolescent offspring, Mike (age fifteen) and Dorothy (age eighteen). Both parents worked full time and had been married twenty years at the time of initial contact. The original concern was the behavior of their son Mike, who was described as getting into increasingly unpleasant confrontations with his parents. Mike would become verbally abusive to his mother and father and at times physically abusive with his father. In addition, Mike's grades had dropped off recently, and he was doing poorly in school, which also upset the parents. In my initial meeting with the whole family, I learned that Dorothy was planning to go to college in about two months and that she was worried about how her parents and brother were going to get along after she left. The parents described her as the "peacemaker."

Dorothy's view of the situation was that her brother was more a typical teenager than she was in that he had a rebellious side, which she didn't. She described her brother as having a "quick temper" like his father and saw her mother as "overreacting" to Mike's provocations. Mike, an articulate and clearly intelligent young man, talked about himself as "determined to rebel" and believed that his parents' rules were unfair. In the initial session it became clear that Dorothy's impending separation from the family was the reason they sought help now in dealing with Mike's behavior. In addition, the mother was experiencing several health problems (bleeding ulcers) and felt a heavy burden of responsibility for things at home. Her physical problems suggested that she was under extreme stress and looking for increased support from her husband, who was described as "the impractical one." A number of unresolved issues relating to each parent's family of origin also came to light.

A further issue raised had to do with Joan's reaction to Harry's occasional out-of-town work assignments. It appeared that she would become very anxious and upset on those nights her husband was away. Both parents requested help setting "realistic expectations" for Mike and were committed to improving the situation at home. My sense after this initial meeting was that Mike was in a special position of drawing focus and attention onto himself as a way of deflecting or detouring a significant amount of anxiety in the family, anxiety which originated in issues with parents' families of origin as well as the loss of the family peacemaker.

These initial meetings with the family focused on helping the parents set appropriate limits with Mike and developing a set of mutually agreed upon guidelines for Mike's behavior at home. The therapist took a solution-oriented approach in attempting to build on the parents' past successes in dealing with Mike. As we continued on this track, however, it became obvious that other issues were getting in the way of moving in this direction. Joan appeared more and more depressed and expressed increasing worry about her own mental health. She described feeling "like a failure" and as isolated and lonely. By this time Dorothy had left for college, and the conflicts between Mike and his parents had intensified. Joan also began describing anxiety and "panic" at night when Harry was away and when Mike was out of the house. She described how she felt more comfortable and less anxious when Mike was around.

Now that Dorothy was at college, the mother, in many ways, depending on Mike to be there at those times father was away on trips. Mike's special role in the family prevented her from being able to set firm limits with him. He could abuse her at will knowing that she needed him. Both parents were, to some extent, cut off from their extended families and were especially sensitive to the behavior of members of their nuclear family. The family's anxiety was intensified within the small network of the nuclear family. Mike provided a focus for this anxiety and his "reward" for serving in this role was to "be his own person" without parental intrusion.

At the end of our first episode of therapy, Joan was more openly acknowledging her anxiety about being alone, about which she felt great shame. The parents continued to be concerned about Mike's behavior. The father described Mike as a "lightning rod" who deflects anxiety for everyone. I suggested to the family that Mike's failing grades and provocative attitude at home might be a small price for Mike to pay in helping his parents deal with their anxieties. The parents agreed about the need to come back without Mike to discuss the issues that were getting in the way of their success in setting limits with Mike. I told them to think about this and call me when they were ready to move ahead. Ten months later I got the call.

In the six sessions of the second episode of contact, I saw Mike once and then only briefly. My primary contact was with the parents. Although describing some positive events (for example, Mike had worked during the intervening summer and had obeyed his curfew), concerns focused on the fact that he failed two subjects and had been "nasty, abusive, and physical with us." Joan described feeling like a "prisoner to my son." Other concerns centered around Mike's alleged drug use.

Mike, in my brief individual contact with him, admitted to being "obnoxious" to his parents, but indicated that "[I'm] trying to change my attitude." He saw his parents as the problem and believed that "their pressure gets directed at me." He denied regular use of drugs or alcohol and told me he was meeting with the school guidance counselor on a weekly basis. The parents, while acknowledging that Mike was "trying to be better," continued to express concerns about his behavior.

Since the parents were able to describe some times when they had positive interactions with their son, I again began to taking a solution-oriented approach in helping them build on these past positive contacts. For example, they described how they prevented escalation of conflict by walking away or keeping their attention on the issue and not the person. I complimented them on these positive steps. Joan described herself as "not being so overprotective; I've backed off some" and viewed herself and her husband as more united in how they handled situations with Mike. At this point, she again raised the issue of her anxiety when Harry is away on business trips saying: "This is one area where I'm a nut case." I suggested we move slowly on this since there was still much work to do in helping Mike.

We ended this episode of contacts with the parents working more cooperatively and being effective in diffusing tense situations with Mike by using humor and staying calm. The parents were pleased with the progress and suggested moving our attention to the other issues such as their relationships with their families of origin and Joan's "panic attacks." A meeting was scheduled and then cancelled. I had no contact with the family for another ten months, at which time I received an urgent call from the father who was concerned about his son's drug use and wanted to schedule a meeting as soon as possible.

In this session (number 14), it was apparent that both parents had returned to being supervigilant about Mike's behavior and had been involved in several intense conflicts with him. Mike, although acknowledging some drug (cocaine, pot, LSD) and alcohol use, denied that he was physically dependent. However, he did admit that he might be "psychologically dependent" and agreed to meet with a substance abuse counselor.

It became clear to me that Mike's drug use was yet another way for him to be both rebellious yet dependent on his parents (and they on him). After complimenting the family for coming in to deal with this problem, I scheduled an appointment with the parents for one week later. I realized that at our next meeting I would need to review for the parents my perception of the events of the past two and a half years. I needed to put these perceptions in a form that would allow some movement in breaking a longstanding cycle that was preventing Mike (who was now almost eighteen years old) from making an important developmental transition towards increased independence and autonomy. Portions of transcript from the next two sessions with the parents, are presented below:

In the fifteenth session the parents and I discuss Mike's follow-through on his appointment with the substance abuse counselor; I review the past two therapy episodes and frame Mike as a caring, sensitive young man who has taken on the burden of worrying about his parents; I then raise the issue of the mother's fear of being alone.

Therapist: I think Mike is an unusual boy in the sense of how much he cares about the two of you. He's not a delinquent kind of kid or a "druggie" turned off on the world. I think he's concerned about himself. I think he's concerned about his family, which is unusual for an eighteen-year-old.

Mother: He doesn't show it.

Therapist: He doesn't show that side—but I really think it's there. We've met over a period of time now, maybe two years. Let me see, you came originally in June of '87 and we met till November. You came back in September of '88 and we met till the beginning of December. Now you're back—and it's September again.

Father: I've been thinking about that pattern. I think it has something to do with Dorothy being gone. She's kind of like the moderator, the buffer. She served that function, and I think when she left there was the strain of her approaching departure and then she wasn't there to deflect. . . .

Mother: Do we just ignore it? I think I've ignored it. I've been afraid of it. I think I've just tried to pretend there wasn't a problem.

Therapist: What's "it"?

Mother: My fear of my son. I'm afraid of him.

[*The therapist, drawing on his previous contacts with the family, takes this opportunity to make reference to mother's other fear, of being alone.*]

Therapist: There are other fears too that have come up and it's at those points that we've stopped meeting. You know what I'm talking about? We've talked about Mike and handling him and then we've talked about you [*the mother*] and we've stopped meeting. I think that happened the previous two times. When we stopped last time, we were talking about you being alone when your husband was gone and how frightening that was. I'm bringing it up because we've been through these cycles before, and Mike has a lot to do with all this. He's aware of your worries and your anxieties; he's playing some part in worrying about you, I think. And now he's by himself because Dorothy is out of the house. She's not there to mediate. We talked about Mike as a "lightning rod" in deflecting things that were going on and he's still in that role. And drugs are an interesting way of asserting your independence and autonomy but at the same time being dependent on your parents—in getting your parents to worry about you.

Mother: I can't handle that fear [*being alone*]. I cannot, I can't, I can't, I can't.

Therapist: If you got some help around that. . . .

Mother: What? Nothing works.

Therapist: I wonder if you got some help around that if you'd be in a better position to help your son. That's the question I have; I don't know the answer to it.

Mother: Last year he hardly traveled and it wasn't an issue. This year he's traveling again.

Father: Not excessively.

Mother: To you, not excessively.

Father: To you one night is excessive.

[*When I try to shift the focus away from her fear, she continues to pursue it.*]

Therapist: I don't want to get off into this now. I'm just bringing it up.

Mother: It's the one area that I cannot handle, and it drives me crazy. I don't know what I'm going to do. This is one issue . . . I've tried to hide this fear from Mike, but I can't hide it from him anymore.

Therapist: I'm sure he knows.

Mother: It's totally irrational . . . awful.

Therapist: What's awful? That you can't control it?

Mother: I'm not like that. I'm not the type of person who is hysterical. I'm usually the one in the family who handles things rationally . . . handles the affairs of the family rationally. [*sighs*]

Therapist: Everyone's entitled to some irrational part of themselves.

Father: My feeling is that she's achieved a certain amount of comfort with this fear and that . . . we talked about this, we sat on the beach this summer and talked. It almost seems to me that she doesn't want to let go of it. As much as it torments her, and it does, she holds onto it . . . won't let go of it.

[*I then bring the issue back to Mike's role in the family.*]

Therapist: Tell me something. I wonder how you would envision things when your son is off and on his own, functioning well, working or going to school, living independently. How would that be? What changes would you envision for the two of you?

Father: For myself I see no change, except that a source of my controversy will be gone. We had a big clash on Sunday night. [*gives details*] I asked the wrong questions at the wrong time and from that a major explosion occurred, obscenities, violence. He took a swing at me. So in my case, I see my life would be easier. In her case, truthfully, I would worry about her. I think she would become—I don't know how she would handle being alone. This is an issue that existed when we were first married and I see the same terror in her now, about being alone, that I saw in her then—twenty years ago.

Therapist [*to the father*]: Well, don't you have an irrational side to yourself and sometimes that gets directed to your son?

Father: Right. I have a great need to control. I'll actually look for things to set right. If the house is all locked and the cars are all locked up, and everyone is snug as a bug, I will look around and say "you left this laying here, pick it up and put it away." I do that and I know it's wrong.

[*Joan then "ups the ante" by suggesting that she is "suicidal." Rather than pursuing her suicidal words, I look for ways to move her out of the self-pitying posture she has accepted and toward taking action for change. I also try again to bring the focus back to Mike's role in the family.*]

Mother: I can be so rational about all this [*handling an issue with Mike*] and yet I'm the one who goes absolutely bananas. I'm afraid one day I will overdose when I'm alone. [*She was taking over-the-counter sleeping medication and drinking wine when her husband wasn't home.*]

Father: Is that a real fear?

Mother: Yes. It's a real fear. I cannot believe me! How can anyone be like that? I don't understand that fear, I don't. I've had to confront it this past month, and I said to myself "I'll handle it" Uh-uh, I didn't handle it.

Therapist: Are there times when you handle it better than others?

Mother: No. I can't say that. All right, if someone's in the house. Doesn't that sounds stupid? What do I do, put an ad in the paper for someone to come and stay with me?

Therapist: What happens when Mike is out of the house? That's what I'm asking. What changes is that going to make?

Father: It's going to push her to a point of crisis with this.

Mother: With this one issue. It'll give me peace of mind in so many other ways. It will totally make me face this one issue. I can't tell you why this fear is there. I take sleeping pills when you're gone and it doesn't help.

Therapist: What I haven't heard you say is that you're willing to see someone who knows about these kinds of problems and can help you overcome them.

[*She then becomes quite tearful and upset and shares her feelings of shame about what she views as an "irrational" fear that has plagued her since childhood. Her shame about this issue is tied to her belief that she is like, or will turn out to be like, her mother who was described as "mentally ill" and "crazy." I take an empathic position in normalizing her fears and presenting the possibility (the hope) for change.*]

Mother: [*silence*] Because I'm embarrassed and ashamed of it . . . [*begins to cry*], so much so, I'm about to die. The person who's supposed to solve everybody else's problems. [*I offer the husband tissues to give to his wife.*] It's been such a long time, I don't know how I can get any help. I'm not looking forward to anything in life anymore because of this horrible thing just hanging over my head.

Therapist: I wonder what things would look like without this hanging over your head. You've had this for so long. How would your world be different?

Mother: I don't know.

Therapist: What would that mean to you?

Mother: I'd have to face for the first time that he was gone and that there wasn't anybody.

Therapist: Just you.

Mother: Just me. And there wasn't anybody who cared or who was there, not Dorothy, not Mike, not a sister or brother—or anybody. If anything was the matter, there wasn't anybody I could pick up the phone and say "help me." And there's never been anybody—there just never was. When I have to go to sleep and I know there isn't anybody that cares, that's there, that I can reach out and touch . . . wow [*crying*]. It's so stupid.

Therapist: It's not stupid. You're not alone in having that kind of fear.

Mother: It's so strong . . . panic. You can't imagine . . . panic . . . so uncontrollable. I feel, as if, maybe I'm just going insane.

Therapist: There's a sense you'll turn out like your mother.

Mother: [*nods*] You have no idea of how many years I've fought that. No idea.

Therapist: But you seem to be holding on to this one piece of irrationality that's like her, that says "I'm like her."

Mother: My mother slept in my room till I was older. She didn't leave my room till I was a sophomore in high school. Nobody ever knew that. Why did she do this to me? And you can say why am I doing this to Mike.

Therapist: You've made a very different life for yourself than your mother did.

Mother: But I haven't succeeded.

Therapist: You're a very tough judge of yourself. The question is how your going to feel comfortable, how is your son going to feel comfortable, how is your husband going to feel comfortable—with you being alone?

Mother: I don't know, Dr. F. And you know I would do anything for Mike, anything in the world to help him. This is the one area I can't control. What do I do to help him?

[*After getting the Mother to agree to do something about her problem, I raise the issue of the risks of change.*]

Therapist: To help yourself, that's the most important thing. What you've already done—confronting him about the drugs is important—and being vigilant about that is important—but he's got to be able to be comfortable going off and leaving the two of you—and leaving his worries about both of you. And it's not just you [*to the Mother*] because I think he worries about you [*to the Father*] also. You come home in a bad mood, and Mike gets the brunt of that. Where's that going to go? Is his mother going to bear the brunt of that—your moods? So there's some real risks in having a independent young man who is functioning well.

Father: [*head down listening*]. So he's doing some of these activities . . . so to speak. . . .

Therapist: He's making a costly sacrifice. That may not be something he's consciously thinking about, but it's there.

Father: He's giving up his freedom and independence?

Therapist: Yes.

Father: Wow.

Mother: All right. I want to help. So where do I go from here? What do I do?

Therapist: What I would suggest is that you [*to the mother*] see someone here who can be helpful, personally for you, about overcoming this problem.

Mother: Are you saying that it's possible to overcome?

Therapist: Yes.

Mother: [*crying*] I would do anything not to have this. Oh, I would.

Therapist: I would say this, that your dealing with this problem will have repercussions. There will be changes that I can't even delineate, but I would guess there would be lots of changes, maybe ones which wouldn't be so pleasant. Maybe your husband would think he could travel more.

Father: Any action has potential risks, but you have to weigh the benefits. If I were you it's worth the risks.

Mother: What if I find out I can live without you? Without your moods and your anger?

Father: Is that a potential risk?

Therapist: yes, that's right.

Father: Then I damn sure better shape up, because I don't want to lose you. We're talking about potentially going into a new dimension in our relationship.

Mother: You might have to be nice.

Father: I'm willing to do whatever it takes.

Therapist: It's like dominoes. Something changes and then the next person down the line has to make some changes—so that's what might happen . . .

Father: I'll do whatever it takes because I love her.

Mother: I love you too.

Father: I would be very upset if she went through this and then ended up saying "I'm going to divorce you." I wouldn't want that to happen.

Therapist: That's where it's important that things don't change too quickly. [*to the mother*] Think about the idea to see someone and then call me, instead of telling me now.

Mother: I want to.

Therapist: Think about it and call me because it's a big decision.

Mother: You really do think it can go away?

Therapist: I do think so.

Mother: [*sigh of relief*]

[*The parents and I end the session discussing parenting issues and the difficulty of "letting go"; the parents describe several instances in which Mike displayed good judgment. We schedule another session in two weeks.*]

In the next session also with the parents, a significant shift is evident, with mother (Joan) becoming more assertive and sure of herself in confronting her husband about their relationship. Joan did call to request an appointment to deal with her "anxiety problem". She was given an appointment two weeks later with a behavioral psychologist.

[*The parents begin this meeting with some concerns about Mike's behavior but also some evidence of positive change, as reflected in Mike's decision to move out of the house and take a job away from home, and in the reduction in conflict between the parents and Mike.*]

Therapist: How are things?

Father: Maybe you just adapt to your environment. It's like a family cold war. It's the issue of Mike. It's still the immaturity continuing. Although he's "on his own" working and has his own car, he is spending more than he brings in. He's writing checks to cover traffic fines for some friends and the checks are bouncing. District courts are sending letters to home for him. He lost his license, lost his wallet last week with one of my credit cards. Took off to the mountains without a driver's license.

Therapist: When did he leave?

Father: Yesterday morning.

Mother: He went to the mountains [*about three hours away*] to find a job at a ski resort.

Therapist: I see. So he's thinking of moving out.

Mother: He went with a friend to apply for this job. He was very depressed last week. He was home every night before twelve. On the weekend he was home before twelve. We couldn't figure out what was going on.

Therapist: He wasn't going out with his friends in the way he had been.

Mother: He made us breakfast in bed on Saturday! We've had no confrontations since the last time [*we were here*].

[*The parents and I then discuss the different ways each of them deal with their son. In the next segment, I pick up on the fact that father gave Mike a hug, rather than on the details of their "minor skirmish". In this way, I support the father as a nurturant figure for his increasingly independent and self-reliant son.*]

Father: When he got home [*from the trip*] I wanted to ask him about where he lost the wallet, and he got very angry and sarcastic with me. We had a minor skirmish. He left the house, then came back, and we talked. Then I wound up giving him a hug before he left. We also had some words about my concerns [*about his drug use*] [*Joan stayed out of this incident.*]

Therapist: So you gave him a hug. What inspired you to do that?

Father: Because I love him and I said I was worrying about him.

Therapist: You wanted to give him that message before he left.

Father: I also told him if he needed us while he was away to call. He saved $80 to cover one of the bounced checks but I didn't have the money to mail the letter. So I gave him five dollars. I hope he mailed it.

Mother: He owes about five hundred dollars.

Therapist: That's a lot of money.

Mother: It sure is. I have not given him any money. What I have done is made him sandwiches for lunch—to help him out. That's it.

[*She describes offering to help him figure out a payment plan. He told her "it's my responsibility."*]

Therapist: It looks like he's trying to make it on his own. It's going to be difficult and there's going to be the temptation to jump in, and there's going to be the temptation he's going to throw up for you to jump in.

Father: I don't want to jump in.

Therapist: You're at a very critical point—a very difficult point for parents.

Mother: How do you know how much to do and how much not to do.

Therapist: Yes. It sounds like you're finding a balance—to let him know you care about him and that you're there for him but that you're not going to pick up the pieces after him.

Mother: If he's using drugs and driving without a license and gets picked up, he's in trouble, and we can't do anything about that. It's so strange. He always keeps in contact. He called me yesterday. He may not leave notes for us but he gets absolutely crazed when we don't leave notes for him. [*her to husband*] I just realized I didn't leave a note.

Father: I don't think we owe him a note.

Mother: I asked if he was going to continue counseling and he said [*abruptly*] "only a couple more times." He did go back to see his old counselor at the high school.

Father: He did?

Mother: He went to speak with him.

Therapist: He's got a relationship with him over time. Good.

Mother: The question is what happens now. I don't know what to do anymore. What if he doesn't show up for that [*counseling*] appointment? What's the right thing to do?

[*I raise the issue of the need for parental teamwork in dealing successfully with Mike, and Harry wonders out loud if he and his wife are, in fact, working as a team; Joan then begins to assert herself with her husband around several marital issues that had not, up to this point, been discussed.*]

Therapist: One of the ways that you know is what the two of you can feel comfortable with and agree on. That's the most important thing, that the two of you are working in concert.

Father: I'm not sure we are.

Mother: I feel you [*to Harry*] get really angry at times, and Mike is easy to get angry at. I'm a mild person but he can have me a raving idiot. He can have me right off the wall. So I understand. But everything is so delicate right now, if you would only just stop the nit-picking the little stuff. That's his [*Harry's*] nature, I know. But he's [*Mike*] at a point where he can't handle the nit-picking.

Father: I don't think I've been nit-picking.

Mother: You always nit-pick—that's just you. You nit-pick so much for so long that when you're really right nobody listens.

[*She then brings up her concerns about her husband's irrational behavior, his nit-picking and general criticalness. She tells him he "walked all over" her for twenty years and that she allowed it. "I'm being honest. I've thought a lot about this. You treated me very badly." Her husband is initially tearful, then angry with her remarks, and then seems to become more open and understanding.*]

Mother: If you were a complete shit, I would have left you. I think I have enough guts to do that.

[*She describes that fact that she sees a positive side to Harry, "a compassionate, loving, good, kind" side; she actively takes the initiative in directly bringing up some uncomfortable material*]

Mother: I've changed so much. I always believed it was my fault when you got into a bad mood, that I did something wrong.

Father: Am I an abusive husband?

Mother: You were a very bad abusive husband. Mentally you were horrible. It's my fault too. I always protected the kids. The children would say I was a really stupid person for putting up with things, being a martyr. *I don't want to be a martyr anymore.* Do you know that I had a meeting the other night until 9 pm, and you said "Well, I'll be home after that then."

Father: Why should I be home alone, if you're not there?

Mother: But, it's all right for me to be home alone, isn't it?

Therapist: [*to Harry*]: You can appreciate her honesty in doing what she just did.

Father: My initial reaction was to brood and feel sorry for myself, but right now I'm proud that she's being so open, letting her true feelings out.

Therapist: Joan is changing right in front of your eyes.

Father: I can see that.

Mother: I was always afraid, afraid of being disliked, that everybody would hate me. This year I said "Look, you're forty-four years old. You might be dead soon. Why not just stop worrying if they hate you?" [*turns to Harry and says "I love you. There's so much that is so good about you."*]

Therapist: Joan's changing, and last time we were talking about taking care of this other problem [*her anxiety*] and how that's going to create changes also.

Father: Do I need to change?

Therapist: Well, I think you're going to be dragged along in this.

Mother: Maybe since the last time I was here and you said "You can conquer that fear" and I thought about it, and I made the appointment. And I'm going next week. Maybe I am a worthwhile person, and if so, I don't want to live the way I have for the last twenty years or so. I want to start again.

Father: You're going to leave me?

Mother: No, but I want you to change—even if it takes a knockdown, drag-out fight.

Father: I'll change.

Mother: It's easy to say, but you are. You're not going to be nasty for no reason. [*said in an animated tone of voice*] I did something I never do the other night. He [*Harry*] brought me this book which I've really gotten into. I really love this book. He is into another book. The other night he said "I'm going to read to you in bed." [*from his book*]. I didn't want to hear it that night. I was into a good part of my book, and for the first time in my life, instead of putting my book down and listening, what I usually do is shut up, I said "Honey, I don't want to do this tonight but would you read it to me tomorrow night or another night?" He got furious.

Therapist: It's going to take some practice. You both are very dependent on one another. It's very clear. And some of that is breaking loose a little bit, and it's not going to be pleasant, I don't think. It's not going to be easy.

Father: But I want to be dependent on her in the sense I always want her to be there.

Mother: I just wish once in a while you could really just give in. [*silence*] And I got off the track of Mike, didn't it?

Father: Maybe Mike's behavior reflect us. I feel very guilty about that.

Mother: Mike has to realize that we're not Donna Reed's family.

Therapist: The two of you have done the best you can and these kinds of problems arise in all families.

Mother: I'm very concerned about Mike, but today I realize that I'm also concerned that we have a life, that there's life after Mike.

The next session number (number 17) is held about one month later. The parents report that Mike stayed with his mother while Harry was away on business. Joan was pleased with this and expresses her surprise, since she never asked him to be there. She talks about Mike as a sensitive, caring young man. Joan also tells me, that for the first time, while her husband was away, she took a four-hour drive to visit her brother and spent two days with him. Harry got home before she did and expressed his surprise at not finding her at home. Joan persisted in saying that Harry was "angry" while he denied this and said he was simply "surprised." I comment on how this was very different from past behavior and reflects the continued changes the couple is making. Some time was spent discussing Harry's difficulties dealing with the anticipated holiday period. No altercations with Mike were reported. Joan appeared much more confident and assertive and had met twice with a behavioral psychologist about her anxiety reactions.

Two weeks later I met with the couple again (session 18). Mike had just turned eighteen and was expected to leave two days later for a job at a ski resort about three hours from home. He had gotten an apartment with a friend and had straightened out his financial situation. He was described by his parents as having undergone a "remarkable change", being more "goal-directed" and "acting more responsibly." The parents reported that he was showing increased respect for them and was more cooperative at home. There had been no angry confrontations or altercations between Mike and either parent, and the parents were seeing themselves as having "let go" from worrying so much about him. The father expressed his surprise and pleasure that Mike was not responding negatively to limits. Mike had repeatedly invited the parents to visit him on a "regular basis." A meeting was scheduled in three weeks. The following are excerpts from the transcript of session 19 with the parents.

The parents begin by describing how Mike and his friend, on their way up to the mountains, experienced problems with their car, which required several hundred dollars worth of repairs. When Mike called his father, Harry told him "We're here, but you need to find a way to solve your own problems."

Mother: And he did. He borrowed from many people, but not us.

Father: Very creative financing!

Therapist: These are experiences he will always remember. [*laughter*]

[*The parents did make a visit to Mike and bought him about "two weeks of groceries."*]

Father: We went up there Christmas night, and we were late. He was very concerned and upset by it. He worried that something happened to us.

Mother: All of a sudden it's like the roles have suddenly changed.

Father: We were amazed, I think, at how well he and his roomate were doing up there. They had everything under control. The place was clean, picked-up.

Mother: Mike was doing dishes.

Therapist: How long had they been up there before you got up there?

Father: A little more than a week, but they're really functioning. He seems, I guess, to have matured more in the last couple of weeks than in last couple of years. He's talking about budgeting.

Therapist: Has he started earning money?

Mother: Yes. Not very much, but some.

Father: You could see how they were budgeting the food, I guess, rationing the food. He seemed to be, it was more like talking to an adult, he was no longer a kid.

[*The parents describe how Mike made dinner for them and refrained from smoking in the house while they were there.*]

Mother: It was a whole different ball game.

Father: All the things that I would remind him about at home—he was now doing it to me. [*such as keeping the door shut so the cold wouldn't come in*]

Therapist: He's really picked up and internalized a lot of things you've taught him.

Father: He kept telling us, when we were about to leave, to drive carefully, watch these roads. Apparently he's doing well on the job. And we feel good about him. Dorothy is planning to visit him this coming weekend.

Mother: I miss him more now, having spent time with him in a pleasant way. It's been years since I've spent time with him like that.

Father: But I feel good knowing that he's doing well. I would like him to come back and visit.

Mother: But you know I don't think I'll ever treat him the same again, I don't think, I think, I might treat him more like I do Dorothy now. Dorothy has no rules.

Therapist: The two of you seem relieved and relaxed.

Mother: I think he will be all right, eventually. I can go to sleep now and not worry every minute about where he is, what he's doing.

Father: I think he's going to set his own agenda. I think he's going to go to college.

[*The parents and I spend about twenty minutes here discussing the holidays and how the couple can manage, and deal with, continuing issues with their extended families.*]

Therapist: So you're going away this weekend, just the two of you? Is this something you've been planning?

Father: No, it's pretty much spur of the moment. We going to do some cross-country skiing.

Mother: I'm really looking forward to it.

Therapist: So, it sounds to me like the two of you are really doing well. You've really turned the corner.

Mother: In many ways.

Therapist: It's very impressive.

Mother: We've learned a lot.

Father: Do we need more sessions?

Therapist: What do you think? Do you want to set up some kind of follow-up meeting in two months, three months, six months?

[*A follow-up meeting is scheduled for two months later.*]

At the beginning of the next session (number 20), Joan hands me a Valentine card written by Mike and sent to his parents, which humorously expresses how much fun he had skiing with his parents several weeks earlier. On that visit he spent a considerable amount of time teaching each of them how to ski. He ends the letter by saying "I love you both." Joan tells me that Mike is planning to move back home in about a month, after the ski season and his ski instructor's job end. We spend some time discussing the implications of his return home. The parents express appropriate concerns about Mike's "reentry", although Joan believes that "it will never be as bad as it was." She then goes on to tell me that "he's grown an awful lot. I think we've grown in our attitude towards him."

Therapist: Have you seen some changes in Mike over the time he's been away?

Mother: Consideration. Maybe a realization that we're people. Remembering things that he would never have given thought to, like the Valentine card . . .

[*Joan described how Mike made a birthday cake for father for his birthday. She goes on to emphasize "how we've changed. He's not the only one changing." She then gives me an example of how she and her husband have changed. A bill came, registered mail, for an old debt that Mike had incurred a year earlier. The parents were upset with this but knew that directly confronting Mike about this issue would interfere with their having a pleasant day with him on their planned visit. Rather than confront him, they put the issue aside.]*

Mother: And we went cross-country skiing, and I will remember it forever. It was one of the nicest times I've spent with my son. So then we went home . . . This is something we would have never done . . . I would have yelled and screamed and said "How can you do this?" but I didn't do it. When we got home I decided to write him about it. He wrote back saying he was upset about it and would send us money to cover the debt. [*which he did*]

Father: He [*Mike*] was very caring in teaching us to ski.

Mother: I like my son again, and I can see growth in us as well.

One additional meeting was held with the parents following Mike's return home. Both parents described Mike's reentry as uneventful and expressed their surprise and delight at the ease they felt in dealing with him now. Mike found a job within one week of returning home and was viewed as a contributing and involved member of the household. In reviewing the course of the therapy, Joan offered the idea that "Mike was a catalyst for my own emotions." Joan participated in five sessions with a behavioral psychologist. At these meetings, the therapist introduced her to the usefulness of self-hypnosis. With the psychologist's help, Joan successfully mastered her anxiety about being alone.

Conclusion

The process of treatment illustrated here demonstrates several important ideas. Rather than pathologizing members of the system, the therapist builds his interventions around the caring, love, and attachment of family members. All of his reframings are one that emphasize how much family members worry about each in a loving way. For example, the mother's agreeing to get help for her fears is reframed as a way of helping her son. As a woman used to making sacrifices, this frame fit for her, and she is able to take the necessary steps to master the fears that held her captive for over twenty years. The son's "irresponsible" behavior is also reframed as useful in forcing both mother and father to look at and resolve mother's fears and to reassess their marriage. The therapist saw his role as helping the parents through a developmental transition as they struggled to let go of each of their children and refocus on their marital relationship.

As this family demonstrated, clients are capable of regulating their professional therapeutic contacts. Although the parents in this family decided on two different occasions to discontinue treatment, the therapist remained available to them. He respected their wishes to take a respite from treatment, understanding that external events outside his office would continue to impact on the focal issues. By emphasizing the love, caring, and commitment in this family, the therapist facilitated a process of change in a time-effective manner (about twenty one hours over a three-year period).

13
At River's End: Conclusions

Doing effective brief therapy requires more than just learning a
set of techniques or strategies. It is a mode of thinking, a
posture or attitude, integrated into the individual therapist,
who then creates the context necessary for change-promoting therapeutic interventions.

Learning to do therapy is like "that required of the Samurai
swordsman who must initially spend great amounts of time learning
skills and techniques. After much rigorous training, the pupil is instructed to go meditate in the mountains. When he forgets all that he
has learned, he can return and Be the sword" (Minuchin in Keeney
1979, 126–27).

We have adopted a possibility orientation as the guiding framework
for our therapeutic work. We have described our understanding about
how this framework can be applied in everyday clinical practice. As we
mentioned earlier in the book, our approach is not the only road to the
effective discovery of human possibilities. It is one approach, one mode
of thinking that provides opportunities for mutual client–therapist negotiation and construction of action possibilities in overcoming life
difficulties. Our principles and philosophies differ from other more
traditional approaches and represent a "paradigm shift" in moving
therapy out of the realm of the mystical and mysterious and into the
realm of the practical and possible.

The view outlined here contrasts with one that sees past experience
as *determining* present behavior. That approach focuses on understanding negative past influences on current behavior, aiming to remove
pathology and "cure the patient." This linear, cause-and-effect thinking
is based on a medical model or paradigm that postulates that the
precondition for change is an understanding of the origins of problems.
Rather than using this deterministic thinking, the possibility-oriented
therapist takes a constructivist posture and avoids speculating about
past causes. He or she is not wedded to one particular point of view

and does not believe in the "Truth" of any one hypothesis. Rather, attention is focused on enabling the client to take action now, within the context of his or her own current reality, and so change that reality.

As Haley (1987) so articulately points out, the way we talk about ideas influences the way that we think. Historically, we have constructed metaphors describing psychological processes, which then exert an arbitrary influence on our belief systems. To quote Haley (1987: 25):

> [In] an old tradition . . . the important entities for therapy within the human being were vertically spaced . . . the conscious was up at the top, and the unconscious was down below. . . . It was . . . possible to give *deep* interpretations because one knew that the important area was *down there* in the roots, not up here in the superficial surface. One could . . . say that the other person's therapy was *shallow*, while one's own therapy was *deep*. This was often said about those of us who did brief therapy by people who did endless therapy and called it deep.

He goes on to speak of the limitations of such a construct by asking what if "it had been agreed that the unconscious was to be left, not down below, and the conscious was to the right? [Then] one could say, "My therapy is more leftist than yours." An objection to brief therapy could be that it was *rightest* rather than shallow."

Some therapists assume that clients are not capable of communicating their "real problem" and that solution-oriented methods ignore this possiblity. We say that each request the client makes needs to be received respectfully and taken seriously. By tackling requests, one at a time, you not only show respect for the client's issues that are meaningful to him or her but you also avoid hypothesizing needlessly about psychodynamic etiology. In addition, a possibility-oriented approach avoids dumping "interpretations" on the client and then "blaming the victim" by calling the client "resistant" when he doesn't accept that point of view. The possibility-oriented approach also avoids insisting that the client join the therapist's world. Instead, we join the client's world. When the client says he is satisfied with the outcome, our criterion for success is met. Clients are capable of telling us what they need. We therapists must be appropriately responsive to those communications.

As you have already seen, in some situations, the client returns for treatment later on with another issue. That does not mean that the therapy has "failed." Just as one goes to the dentist to have a cavity filled, the fact that one gets another cavity two years later, doesn't mean the original procedure was unsuccessful (Cummings 1979). As possibility-oriented therapists we see ourselves as available to clients over time as they move through the developmental cycle, and we respect their judgment of need and their requests for treatment.

In contrast to psychodynamic therapies, solution-oriented approaches have been criticized as being "manipulative" (see Okin 1990). We are reminded of a comment made about Carl Rogers' non-directive, client-centered approach, that "Rogers was as nondirective as a sledgehammer." All psychotherapy involves persuasion. *All communication has as its goal to influence others.* Bateson (Ruesch and Bateson 1951) talked about the "demand" characteristics inherent in any communication: "One cannot not communicate" (Watzlawick, Beavin and Jackson 1967: 49). As Franz Alexander pointed out almost fifty years ago, "methodical psychotherapy is, to a large degree, nothing more than the systematic, conscious application of those methods by which we influence our fellow men" (in Alexander and French 1946: viii). By consciously and methodically employing the language of possibility, we influence people to find options that liberate them from the problem and increase their sense of effectiveness and autonomy.

Our work is significantly based on a bedrock of hopefulness, laced with optimism about our client's capacities for growth and change. We have profound respect for their self-healing capabilities and are sensitive to their wishes and their requests about the conduct of therapy.

Basic to our philosophy is the creation of a context for the generation of hope. You can see the power of hope at work in the film *My Left Foot*, which focuses on the life of Christy Brown, a man born with cerebral palsy. Christy Brown shows us that even with severe disabilities a person is better served by developing his assets (in this case, his left foot) than by dwelling on his limitations. Brown's intense eagerness to embrace life shows the kind of hopefulness that potentiates human growth and change.

The importance of hope appears dramatically in special care settings such as nursing homes (Rodin 1986). One of us [SF] served as a consultant to several nursing homes in which some of the residents were viewed by staff as "uncooperative," "combative," "oppositional" (refusing to take their medication or to eat), or "depressed" and "withdrawn." The pervasive feeling in these nursing homes was an overwhelming sense of hopelessness, helplessness, and loss of control.

I began to see how the behaviors that so concerned the staff were natural outcomes of institutional policies and procedures. Rather than reflecting "pathology" in the resident, they reflected "healthy coping strategies on the part of the elderly person to regain a sense of control and autonomy" (Friedman and Ryan 1986: 267). The "dysfunctional" behaviors of the elderly residents developed out of a loss of hope and a sense of futility about the future. As we mentioned in an earlier chapter, several research studies (Langer and Rodin 1976); Rodin and Langer 1977; Schulz 1976) have found that when elderly nursing home residents are given increased choice and autonomy in making decisions about their lives, positive effects are noted in both their psychological and physiological (physical) well-being.

> In one [situation], the staff expressed much concern about an eighty-one-year-old woman, [Katherine], who packed her bags every day and insisted to the staff that she was leaving. The staff were encouraged to ignore her packing and invite her to assist them with simple tasks, such as delivering the mail. Katherine later said: 'After all, where would I have gone? I packed my bags so that I could keep track of my belongings. But I'd still like to see my home town again, you know.' She had no intention of leaving but used this behavior as a way of dealing with her sense of loss of the home and community in which she lived most of her life . . . [The consultants] found it useful to view [her] behavior as a useful activity in *anticipation* of the day . . . she will leave. [She] did not actually attempt to leave, . . . but found some *hope, value and dignity* in believing that [she] has a *choice* about the decision to leave. (Friedman & Ryan 1986: 270)

That is what our therapy is about. Providing a context in which the client's hopes, values, and dignity are respected, and choices, options, and pathways for transforming "problems" into possibilities are created. An optimistic perspective, a positive outlook on life, an ability to make fun of yourself as part of the human condition—all are prerequisites for doing effective possibility-oriented therapy.

This book presents a paradigm change—a new mental set—one captured in the deceptively simple phrase "from problem to possibility" and summarized in figure 13–1. This profound change leads not only to a new conception of the process and practice of therapy, but also elicits and supports positive psychophysiological health in both client and therapist. The basic tools of psychotherapy—words—take on new force and meaning when specifically linked to this enhancement of health.

We have compared and contrasted the difference between cause-and-effect and cybernetic thinking. As you have seen, we are not interested in *why*, but only in *what* and *how*. We do not want to enlarge the client's view of his "problem" by exploring it in detail, and thus intensify his distress. Nor do we believe that you need to find past causes to help clients achieve their desired goals. We immediately direct clients' attention to future possibilities and help them shift their limiting visions to expanded views of reality that allow for new effective actions. As we have illustrated, in many instances such changes need not take a long time.

Epilogue

We have come to the end of this journey. We stop in an eddy on the side of the river. A bald eagle looms above the canyon, its expanding

Theory about Change

Cause-and-effect ⟶ Cybernetic or feedback

First order change or more of ⟶ Second order change or
the same   something entirely different

Objective reality ⟶ Constructed reality

The Treatment Process and How It Works

One best treatment ⟶ As many treatments as clients

Therapist is expert/analyst ⟶ Therapist is partner/catalyst

Generalize patient categories ⟶ Each client unique

Teach the patient the therapist's ⟶ Learn the client's assumptions,
assumptions and language   use client's language

Try to overcome resistance ⟶ Utilize individuality

Ask what is wrong and why ⟶ Ask what is wanted and how

Explore historical causes, who ⟶ Construct future actions, look
or what is to blame   for solutions tried, patterns to
                                      interrupt

Use left-brain digital language to ⟶ Use right-brain imagistic
interpret past   language to challenge
                                      assumptions

Use free association and ⟶ Use reframing and task-setting
reflective listening

Good therapy is hard work, ⟶ Effective therapy can be easy,
painful, and long   playful, and brief

Goal

Character change through insight ⟶ Behavior change through seeing
                                      the possibility of new actions

Result

Cure or failure ⟶ Feedback: goal attained or
                                  recycle

Physiology and Mood

Reinforce anxiety, stress ⟶ Shift to hope, challenge

Depressed immune function ⟶ Inhanced immune function

Figure 13–1. Paradigm Shift: From Problem to Possibility

wings drifting on the thermal currents above us. No one speaks, and a sense of accomplishment is evident. The sun is low in the sky now, and we must float a short distance more till we reach the beach area where we will disembark. The group is quiet, partly from the good feeling of muscles well used and partly out of a sheer joy and exhiliration, which is shared in the beauty and silence around us. We look forward with keen anticipation to our next adventure on the river, and we feel more confident of our abilities to negotiate the rapids in the journeys to come.

References

Abroms, G.M., and C.H. Fellner, C.A. Whitaker, (1971). The family enters the hospital. *American Journal of Psychiatry* 127: 1363–70.

"Advances." (1990). *Ongoing Research News* 7, no. 1: 6.

Alexander, F., and T.M. French, (1946). *Psychoanalytic therapy: Principles and applications.* New York: Ronald Press.

Andersen, T. (1987). The reflecting team: Dialogue and metadialogue in clinical work. *Family Process* 26:415–28.

Anderson, H., and H.A. Goolishian, (1988). Human systems as linguistic systems: Preliminary and evolving ideas about the implications for clinical theory. *Family Process* 27:371–93.

Andolfi, M. (1979). *Family therapy: An interactional approach.* New York: Plenum.

Atkinson, B.J., and A.W. Heath. (1990). Further thoughts on second-order family therapy—This time it's personal. *Family Process* 29:145–55.

Bandler, R. (1985). *Using your brain—for a change.* Moab, Utah: Real People Press.

Bandler, R., and J. Grinder. (1979). *Frogs into princes.* Moab, Utah: Real People Press.

———. (1982). *Reframing: NLP and the transformation of meaning.* Moab, Utah: Real People Press.

Bandler, R., J. Grinder, and V. Satir. (1976). *Changing with families.* Palo Alto: Science and Behavior Books.

Barker, P. (1985). *Using metaphors in psychotherapy.* New York: Brunner-Mazel.

Bateson, G. (1972). *Steps to an ecology of mind.* New York: Ballantine Books.

———. (1978a). Addendum: Bateson's workshop. In M.M. Berger (Ed.), *Beyond the double-bind,* 197–229. New York: Brunner-Mazel.

———. (1978b). The birth of a matrix or double-bind and epistemology. In M.M. Berger (Ed.), *Beyond the double-bind,* 39–64. New York: Brunner-Mazel.

Bennett, M.J. (1983). Focal psychotherapy: Terminable and interminable. *American Journal of Psychotherapy* 37:365–75.

———. (1984). Brief psychotherapy and adult development. *Psychotherapy: Theory, research, and practice* 21:171–77.

———. (1985). Focal behavioral psychotherapy for acute narcissistic injury: "De Mopes"—report of a case. *American Journal of Psychotherapy* 39:126–33.

———. (1989). The catalytic function in psychotherapy. *Psychiatry* 52:351–64.

Berenson, D. (1987, July/August). Alcoholics anonymous: From surrender to transformation. *The Family Networker*:25–31.

Berger, M., and C. Dammann. (1982). Live supervision as context, treatment, and training. *Family Process* 21:337–44.

Berger, P.L., and T. Luckmann. (1966). *The social construction of reality.* New York: Doubleday.

Bergman, J. (1985). *Fishing for barracuda: Pragmatics of brief systemic therapy.* New York: W.W. Norton.

Berk, L.S. (1990). What are the physiological effects of laughter? *Mind-Body-Health Digest* 4:6.

Berlyne, D.E. (1960). *Conflict, arousal, and curiosity.* New York: McGraw-Hill.

Berwick, D.M. (1989). Continuous improvement as an ideal in health care. *New England Journal of Medicine* 320:53–56.

Boscolo, L., G. Cecchin, L. Hoffman, and P. Penn. (1987). *Milan systemic family therapy.* New York: Basic Books.

Bowen, M. (1978). *Family therapy in clinical practice.* New York: Jason Aronson. Used with permission.

Bresler, D.E. (1981). *Free yourself from pain.* New York: Simon & Schuster, Wallaby Books.

Budman, S.H. (1990). The myth of termination in brief therapy: It ain't over til it's over. In J.K. Zeig, and S.G. Gilligan (Eds.), *Brief therapy: Myths, methods and metaphors,* 206–18. New York: Brunner-Mazel.

Budman, S.H., and A. Gurman. (1988). *Theory and practice of brief therapy.* New York: Guilford.

Burns, K., and S. Friedman. (1976). In support of families under stress: A community-based approach. *The Family Coordinator* 26:41–46.

Cameron-Bandler, L. (1985). *Solutions: Practical and effective antidotes for sexual and relationship problems.* San Rafael, CA: FuturePace Inc.

Carpenter, G.C., J. Tecce, G. Stechler, and S. Friedman. (1970). Differential visual behavior to human and humanoid faces in early infancy. *Merrill-Palmer Quarterly* 16:91–108.

Carter, B., and M. McGoldrick (Eds.). (1988). *The changing family life cycle.* New York: Gardner.

Castaneda, C. (1972). *The journey to Ixtlan.* New York: Pocket Books.

———. (1974). *Tales of power.* New York: Pocket Books.

Chase, R.A. (1969). Biologic aspects of environmental design. *Clinical Pediatrics* 8:268–74.

Chasin, R., S.A. Roth, and M. Bograd. (1989). Action methods in systemic therapy: Dramatizing ideal futures and reformed pasts with couples. *Family Process* 28:121–36.

Coale, H. (1989). Common dilemmas in relationships and suggestions for therapeutic interventions. *Journal of Strategic and Systemic Therapies* 8:10–15.

Collet, L. (1990, January/February). After the anger, what then? *The Family Therapy Networker*:22–31.

Combrinck-Graham, L. (1985). Hospitalization as a therapeutic intervention in the family. In R.L. Ziffer (Ed.), *Adjunctive techniques in family therapy*, 99–124. New York: Grune & Stratton.

Coopersmith, E.I. (1981). Developmental reframing: He's not bad, he's not mad, he's just young! *Journal of Strategic and Systemic Therapies* 1:1–8.

Corrales, R.G. (1989, January/February). Drawing out the best. *Family Therapy Networker*:45–49.

Cousins, N. (1989). *Head first: The biology of hope*. New York: E.P. Dutton.

Cummings, N. (1979, January). The general practice of psychology. *APA Monitor*.

Davidson, J., W. Lax, D.J. Lussardi, D. Miller, and M. Ratheau. (1988, September/October). The reflecting team. *The Family Therapy Networker*:44–46, 76–77.

Davis, M., S. deShazer, and W.J. Gingerich, (1987). Building on pretreatment change to construct the therapeutic solution: An exploratory study. *Journal of Marital and Family Therapy* 13:359–63.

de Shazer, S. (1985). *Keys to solution in brief therapy*. New York: W.W. Norton.

———. (1988). *Clues: Investigating solutions in brief therapy*. New York: W.W. Norton.

Diagnostic and Statistical Manual of Mental Disorders (DSM-III-R). (1987). Washington, D.C.: American Psychiatric Association.

Dunst, C.J., C.M. Trivette, and A.G. Deal. (1988). *Enabling and empowering families: Principles and guidelines for practice*. Cambridge, MA: Brookline Books.

Ekman, P., R.W. Levenson, and W.V. Friesen. (1983). Autonomic nervous system activity distinguishes among emotions. *Science* 221:1208–10.

Elkin, M. (1984). *Families under the influence*. New York: W.W. Norton.

Ellis, D.C. (1986). When strategies fail: The chemically dependent family system. *Journal of Strategic and Systemic Therapies* 5:50–58.

English, O.S., and S.M. Finch. (1954). *Introduction to Psychiatry*. New York: W.W. Norton.

Epstein, E.S., and V.E. Loos. (1989). Some irreverent thoughts on the limits of family therapy: Towards a language-based explanation of human systems. *Journal of Family Psychology* 2:405–21.

Erickson, M., and E.L. Rossi. (1979). *Hypnotherapy: An exploratory casebook*. New York: Irvington.

Farrelly, F., and J. Brandsma. (1974). *Provocative therapy*. Cupertino, CA: Meta.

Fenichel, H., and D. Rapaport. (1954). *The collected papers of Otto Fenichel*. 2d ser., New York: W.W. Norton.

Fisch, R., J.H. Weakland, and L. Segal. (1982). *The tactics of change: Doing therapy briefly*. San Francisco: Jossey-Bass.

Fisher, G. (1968). Ambiguity of form: Old and new. *Perception and Psychophysics* 3:189–92. Used with permission.

Fisher, S.G. (1980). The use of time limits in brief psychotherapy. *Family Process* 19:377–92.

_____. (1984). Time-limited brief therapy with families: A one year follow-up study. *Family Process* 23:101–6.

Fiske, D.W., and S.R. Maddi. (1961). *Functions of varied experience.* Homewood, Ill: Dorsey Press.

Foerster, H. von. (1984). On constructing a reality. In P. Watzlawick (Ed.), *The invented reality*, 41–61. New York: W.W. Norton.

Fogarty, T. (1983). Personal communication.

Frank, J.D. (1968, May). The Role of Hope in Psychotherapy. *International Journal of Psychiatry*:383–95.

_____. (1973). *Persuasion and healing.* Baltimore: The Johns Hopkins University Press.

Freeman, L. (1988, June). *Existential family psychopharmacology.* Paper presented an annual meeting of the American Family Therapy Association, Montreal.

Freud, S. (1909). Analysis of a phobia in a five-year-old boy. In J. Strachey (Ed.), *The standard edition of the complete psychological works of Sigmund Freud.* Vol. 10, 5–149. London: Hogarth Press.

Friedman, D.H., and S. Friedman. (1982). Day care as a setting for intervention in family systems. *Social Casework* 63:291–95.

Friedman, S. (1972). Habituation and recovery of visual response in the human newborn. *Journal of Experimental Child Psychology* 13:339–49.

_____. (1975). Infant habituation: Process problems and possibilities. In N. Ellis (Ed.), *Aberrant development in infancy: Human and animal studies*, 217–39. Hillsdale, N.J.: Erlbaum Associates.

_____. (1984). When the woman presents herself as 'the patient': A systems view. *Women and Therapy* 3:19–35.

_____. (1989a). Brief systemic psychotherapy in a health maintenance organization. *Family Therapy* 16:133–44. Used with permission.

_____. (1989b). Child mental health in a HMO: A family systems approach. *HMO Practice* 3:52–59. Used with permission.

_____. (1989c). Strategic reframing in a case of delusional jealousy. *Journal of Strategic and Systemic Therapies* 8:1–4. Used with permission.

_____. (1990). Towards a model of time-effective family psychotherapy: A view from a Health Maintenance Organization (HMO). *Journal of Family Psychotherapy* 1(2):1–28. Used with permission.

Friedman, S., L. Bruno, and P. Vietze. (1974). Newborn habituation to visual stimuli: A sex difference in novelty detection. *Journal of Experimental Child Psychology* 18:242–51.

Friedman, S., and S. Pettus, (1985) Brief strategic interventions with families of adolescents. *Family Therapy* 12:197–210. Used with permission.

Friedman, S., and L.S. Ryan. (1986). A system perspective on problematic behaviors in the nursing home. *Family Therapy* 13:265–73. Used with permission.

Friedman, S., and P. Vietze. (1975). The competent infant. *Peabody Journal of Education* 49:314–23.

Fry, W.F. (1990). What are the physiological effects of laughter? *Mind-Body-Health Digest* 4:6.

Furman, B. (1990, May/June). Glasnost therapy. *The Family Networker*:61–63, 70.

Furman, B., and T. Ahola. (1988). The return of the question 'why': Advantages of exploring pre-existing explanations. *Family Process* 27:395–409.

Gallop, R., W.J. Lancee, and P. Garfinkel. (1989). How nursing staff respond to the label "borderline personality disorder." *Hospital and Community Psychiatry* 40:815–19.

Gilligan, S.G., and C.M. Kennedy. (1989). Solutions and resolutions: Ericksonian hypnotherapy with incest survivor groups. *Journal of Strategic and Systemic Therapies* 8:9–17.

Glaserfeld, E. von. (1984). An introduction to radical constructivism. In P. Waltzlawick (Ed.), *The invented reality*, 17–40. New York: W.W. Norton.

Gleick, J. (1987). *Chaos*. New York: Penguin.

Gordon, D. (1978). *Therapeutic metaphors*. Cupertino, CA: Meta Publications.

Gordon, D., and M. Meyers-Anderson. (1981). *Phoenix: Therapeutic patterns of Milton H. Erickson*. Cupertino, CA: Meta Publications. Used with permission.

Green, E., and A. Green. (1977). *Beyond biofeedback*. Ft. Wayne, IN: Knoll Publishing Co.

Green, R.J., and M. Herget. (1989a). Outcomes of systemic/strategic team consultations: I. Overview and one-month results. *Family Process* 28:37–58.

———. (1989b). Outcomes of systemic/strategic team consultations: II. Three-year follow-up and a theory of emergent design. *Family Process* 28:419–37.

Greenson, R.R. (1972). Beyond transference and interpretation. *International Journal of Psychoanalysis* 53:213–17.

Grinder J., & R. Bandler. (1981). *Transformations*. Moab, Utah: Real People Press.

Gursky, E. (1985). Psychotropic medication: Its role in family therapy. In R.L. Ziffer (Ed.), *Adjunctive techniques in family therapy*, 67–98. New York: Grune & Stratton.

Guttman, H.A. (1975). The child's participation in conjoint family therapy. *Journal of the American Academy of Child Psychiatry* 14:490–99.

Haith, M. (1976, July). *The organization of visual behavior at birth*. Paper presented at 21st International Congress of Psychology, Paris.

Haley, J. (1969). The art of being a failure as a therapist. *American Journal of Orthopsychiatry* 39:691–95.

———. (1973). *Uncommon therapy: The psychiatric techniques of Milton H. Erickson, M.D.* New York: W.W. Norton.

———. (1976). *Problem-solving therapy*. San Francisco: Jossey-Bass.

———. (1980). *Leaving home*. New York: McGraw-Hill.

———. (1984). *Ordeal therapy*. San Francisco: Jossey-Bass.

———. (1985). *Conversations with Milton H. Erickson*. 3 vols. New York: Triangle Press.

———. (1987). Therapy—A new phenomenon. In J.K. Zeig (Ed.), *The evolution of psychotherapy*, 17–28. New York: Brunner-Mazel.

———. (1989). Interview. *Milton H. Erickson Foundation Newsletter* 9(3): 11.

Harper, G. (1989). Focal inpatient treatment planning. *Journal of the American Academy of Child and Adolescent Psychiatry* 28:31–37.

Hebb, D.O. (1946). On the nature of fear. *Psychological Review* 53:259–76.

Held, R., and A. Hein. (1963) Movement-produced stimulation in the development of visually guided behavior. *Journal of Comparative and Physiological Psychology* 56:872–76.

Henker, B., and C.K. Whalen. (1989). Hyperactivity and attention deficits. *American Psychologist* 44:216–23.

Henry, J.P. (1989). The arousal of emotions: Hormones, behavior, and health. *Advances* 6 (2):58–61.

Hill, P. (1986, November). Personal communication

Hobbs, N. (1966). Helping disturbed children: Psychological and ecological strategies. *American Psychologist* 21:1105–15. Reprinted in O. Milton and R.G. Wahler (Eds.). (1973). *Behavior disorders: Perspectives and trends.* 3d ed., 238–59. Philadelphia: Lippincott. Used with permission.

Hoffman, L. (1985). Beyond power and control: Toward a "second order" family systems therapy. *Family Systems Medicine* 3:381–96.

———. (1990). Constucting realities: An art of lenses. *Family Process* 29:1–12.

Hubel, D., and T. Weisel. (1962) Receptive fields, binocular interaction, and functional architecture of the cat's visual cortex. *Journal of Physiology* 160:106–54.

Hunt, J.M. (1965). Intrinsic motivation and its role in psychological development. In D. Levine (ed.), *Nebraska Symposium of Motivation.* Vol. 13. Lincoln: University of Nebraska Press.

Isen, A.M., K.A. Daubman, and G.P. Nowicki. (1987). Positive affect facilitates creative problem solving. *Journal of Personality and Social Psychology* 52:1122–31.

Jacobs, M.K., and G. Goodman. (1989). Psychology and self-help groups: Predictions on a partnership. *American Psychologist* 44:536–45.

Johnson, H. (1987). Biologically based deficit in the identified patient: Indications for psychoeducational strategies. *Journal of Marital and Family Therapy.* 13:337–48.

Jung, C.G. (1966). *The practice of psychotherapy.* Vol. 16 of *The collected works.* Princeton, NJ: Princeton University Press, Bollingen Editions.

Kantor, D.(1980). Critical identity image: A concept linking individual, couple, and family development. In J.K. Pearce and L.K. Friedman (Eds.), *Family therapy: Combining psychodynamic and family systems approaches.* New York: Grune & Stratton.

Kaplan, H.S. (1975). *The illustrated manual of sex therapy.* New York: Quadrangle, New York Times Book Co.

Katz, S.N. (1975). *Creativity in social work: The selected writings of Lydia Rapoport.* Philadelphia: Temple University Press.

Keisler, C.A. (1982). Mental hospitals and alternative care. *American Psychologist* 37:349–60.

Kelman, H. (1969). Kairos: The auspicious moment. *American Journal of Psychoanalysis* 29:59–82.

Keeney, B.P. (1979). Ecosystemic epistemology: An alternative paradigm for diagnosis. *Family Process* 18:117–29.

Keeney, B.P. and D.H. Sprenkle. (1982). Ecosystemic epistemology: Critical implications for the aesthetics and pragmatics of family therapy. *Family Process* 21:1–19.

Kent, J., T.J. Coates, K.R. Pelletier, and B. O'Regan. (1989). Unexpected recoveries: Spontaneous remission and immune functioning. *Advances* 6(2):66–73.

Kerr, M., and M. Bowen. (1988). *Family evaluation.* New York: W.W. Norton.

Kiecolt-Glaser, J. W. Garner, C. Speicher, G.M. Penn, J.E. Holliday, and R. Glaser. (1984). Psychosocial modifiers of immunocompetencies in medical students. *Psychosomatic Medicine* 46:7–14.

Kiecolt-Glaser, J., R. Glaser, E.C. Strain, J.C. Stout, K.L. Tarr, J.E. Holliday, and C.E. Speicher. (1985). Psychosocial enhancement of immunocompetence in a geriatric population. *Health Psychology* 4:25–41.

Klein, A. (1989). *The healing power of humor.* Los Angeles: Jeremy P. Tarcher.

Kobasa, S.C.O. (1990). Stress-resistant personality. In R. Ornstein and C. Swencionis (Eds.), *The healing brain: A scientific reader.* New York: Guilford.

Korner, S., and G. Brown. (1990). Exclusion of children from family psychotherapy: Family therapists' beliefs and practices. *Journal of Family Psychology* 3:420–30.

Kreilkamp, T. (1989). *Time-limited, intermittent therapy with children and families.* New York: Brunner-Mazel.

Langer, E.J. (1989). *Mindfulness.* New York: Addison-Wesley.

Langer, E.J., and J. Rodin. (1976). The effects of choice and enhanced personal responsibility for the aged: A field experiment in an institutional setting. *Journal of Personality and Social Psychology* 34:191–98.

Lankton, C.H., and S.R. Lankton. (1989). *Tales of enchantment.* New York: Brunner-Mazel.

Lankton, S. (1980). *Practical Magic.* Cupertino, Calif.: Meta Publication.

Lankton, S.R., and C.H. Lankton. (1983). *The answer within: A clinical framework of Ericksonian hypnotherapy.* New York: Brunner-Mazel.

———. (1986). *Enchantment and intervention in family therapy.* New York: Brunner-Mazel.

Lipchik, E. (1988, June). *Brief solution-focused therapy in inpatient settings.* Paper presented at annual meeting of the American Family Therapy Association, Montreal.

Lipchik, E., and S. deShazer. (1986). The purposeful interview. *Journal of Strategic and Systemic Therapies* 5:88–99.

Locke, S., and D. Colligan. (1987). *The healer within: The new medicine of mind and body.* New York: New American Library, Mentor.

Madanes, C. (1981). *Strategic family therapy.* San Francisco: Jossey-Bass.

———. (1984). *Behind the one-way mirror.* San Francisco: Jossey-Bass.

Malan, D.H. (1975). *A study of brief psychotherapy.* New York: Plenum.

Mann, J. (1973). *Time-limited psychotherapy.* Cambridge: Harvard University Press.

Martin, R.A., and H.M. Lefcourt. (1983). Sense of humor as a moderator of the relation between stressors and moods. *Journal of Personality and Social Psychology* 45:1313–24.

Masterpaqua, F. (1989). A competence of paradigm for psychological practice. *American Psychologist* 44:1366–71.

Maturana, H.R., and F.J. Varela. (1987). *The tree of knowledge: The biological roots of human understanding*. Boston: New Science Library.

McClelland, D.C. (1989). Motivational factors in health and disease. *American Psychologist* 44:675–83.

McEwen, B.S. (1990). Hormones and the nervous system. *Advances* 7:50–54.

McGoldrick, M., and R. Gerson. (1985). *Genograms in family assessment*. New York: W.W. Norton.

Menninger, K. (1959, December). Hope. *American Journal of Psychiatry*: 481–91.

Milne, A.A. (1924). *When we were very young*. New York: E.P. Dutton. Used with permission.

Minuchin, S. (1974). *Families and family therapy*. Cambridge: Harvard University Press. Used with permission.

Minuchin, S., and H.C. Fishman. (1981). *Family therapy techniques*. Cambridge: Harvard University Press.

Mittelmeier, C., and S. Friedman. (1991). The Rashomon effect: A study in constructivist conversation. *Family Therapy*, in press.

Molnar, A., and S. deShazer. (1987). Solution-focused therapy: Toward the identification of therapeutic tasks. *Journal of Marital and Family Therapy* 13:349–58.

Montalvo, B. (1973). Aspects of live supervision. *Family Process* 12:343–59.

Napier, A., and C. Whitaker. (1978). *The family crucible*. New York: Harper & Row.

Nhat Hanh, T. (1987). *The miracle of mindfulness*. Boston: Beacon Press.

Norris, P.A. (1988). Clinical psychoneuroimmunology: Strategies for self-regulation or immune system responding. In J.V. Basmajian (Ed.), *Biofeedback: Principles and practice for clinicians*. 3d ed. Baltimore: Williams & Wilkins.

Noyes, A.P. and L.C. Kolb. (1963). *Modern Clinical Psychiatry*. Philadelphia: W.B. Saunders Co.

Nurcombe, B. (1989). Goal-directed treatment planning and the principles of brief hospitalization. *Journal of the American Academy of Child and Adolescent Psychiatry*. 28:26–30.

O'Hanlon, W.H. (1987). *Taproots: Underlying principles of Milton Erickson's therapy and hypnosis*. New York: W.W. Norton.

———. (1990, March/April) Debriefing myself: When a brief therapist does long-term work. *The Family Therapy Networker*: 48–49, 68–69.

O'Hanlon, W.H., and M. Weiner-Davis. (1989). *In search of solutions: A new direction in psychotherapy*. New York: W.W. Norton.

O'Hanlon, W.H., and J. Wilk. (1987). *Shifting contexts: The generation of effective psychotherapy*. New York: Guilford.

Okin, R.(1990). Review of "In search of solutions: A new direction in psychotherapy." *International Journal of Short-term Psychotherapy* 5:75–78.

Olson, U.J., and P.F. Pegg. (1979). Direct open supervision: A team approach. *Family Process* 18:463–69.

Omer, H. (1982). The macrodynamics of Ericksonian therapy. *Journal of Strategic and Systemic Therapies* 1:34–44.

Ortega y Gasset, J. (1961a). *The modern theme.* New York: Harper Torchbooks.

Ortega y Gasset, J. (1961b). *Meditations on Quixote.* New York: W.W. Norton.

Papp, P. (1983). *The process of change.* New York: Guilford.

———. (1990). The therapeutic debate. In J.K. Zeig and S.G. Gilligan (Eds.), *Brief therapy: Myths, methods and metaphors,* 111–19. New York: Brunner-Mazel.

Patterson, R.B. (1987). Becoming a strategic therapist. *Journal of Family Psychology* 1:241–55.

Penn, P. (1982). Circular questioning. *Family Process* 21:267–80.

"Performance anxiety: A mind-body approach." (1990). *Mind-Body-Health Digest* 4, no.1:30.

Piaget, J. (1952). *The origins of intelligence in children.* New York: International Universities Press.

Piercy, F.P., and B.R. Frankel. (1986). Establishing appropriate parental influence in families with a drug-abusing adolescent: Direct and indirect methods. *Journal of Strategic & Systemic Therapies* 5:30–39.

Pilisuk, M., and S.H. Parks. (1986). *The healing web: Social networks and human survival.* Hanover, NH: University Press of New England.

Pittman, F. (1988, June). Personal communication.

Potter-Efron, P.S., and E.T. Potter-Efron. (1986). Promoting second-order change in alcoholic systems. *Journal of Strategic & Systemic Therapies* 5:20–29.

Rako, S., and H. Mazer. (Eds.). (1983). *Semrad: The heart of a therapist.* New York: Jason Aronson.

Real, T. (1990). The therapeutic use of self in constructionist/systemic therapy. *Family Process* 29:255–72.

Ritterman, M. (1983). *Using hypnosis in family therapy.* San Francisco: Jossey-Bass.

Roberts, M., L. Caeser, B. Perryclear, and D. Phillips. (1989). Reflecting team consultations. *Journal of Strategic and Systemic Therapies* 8:38–46.

Rodin, J. (1986). Aging and health: Effects of the sense of control. *Science* 223:1271–76.

Rodin, J., and E.J. Langer. (1977). Long-term effects of a control-relevant intervention with the institutionalized aged. *Journal of Personality and Social Psychology* 35:897–902.

Rosen, S. (1982). *My voice will go with you.* New York: W.W. Norton.

Rosenhan, D.L. (1973). On being sane in insane places. *Science* 179:250–58.

Rosenthal, R., and L. Jacobson. (1968). *Pygmalion in the classroom: Teacher expectation and pupils' intellectual development.* New York: Holt, Rinehart, and Winston.

Rossi, E.L. (1986). *The psychobiology of mind-body healing.* New York: W.W. Norton.

———. (1987). Mind/body communication and the new language of human facilitation. In J.K. Zeig (ed.), *The Evolution of Psychotherapy,* 369–87. New York: Brunner-Mazel.

Ruesch, J., and G. Bateson. (1951). *Communication: The social matrix of psychiatry.* New York: W.W. Norton.

Sabin, J.E. (1978). Research findings on chronic mental illness: A model for continuing care in the health maintenance organization. *Comprehensive Psychiatry* 19:83–95.

Salapatek, P., and W. Kessen. (1966). Visual scanning of triangles by the human newborn. *Journal of Experimental Child Psychology* 3:155–67.

Sargent, J. (1986, May/June). Psychopharmacology and family therapy. *The Family Therapy Networker*: 17–18.

Satir, V., and M. Baldwin. (1983). *Satir step by step*. Palo Alto, Ca: Science and Behavior Books.

Schulz, R. (1976). Effects of control and predictability on the physical and psychological well-being of the institutionalized aged. *Journal of Personality and Social Psychology* 33:563–73.

Schwartz, G., D. Weinberger, and J. Singer. (1981). Cardiovascular differentiation of happiness, sadness, anger, and fear following imagery exercise. *Psychosomatic Medicine* 43:343–64.

Seeman, J. (1989). Toward a model of positive health. *American Psychologist* 44:1099–1109.

Seeman, L., B.I. Tittler, and S. Friedman. (1985). Early interactional change and its relationship to family therapy outcome. *Family Process* 24:59–68.

Shainberg, L. (April 9, 1989). Finding the "zone." *New York Times Magazine*. Used with permission.

Sherrod, K., P. Vietze, and S. Friedman. (1978). *Infancy*. Monterey, CA: Brooks-Cole.

Shulem, B. (1988). The introduction of humor in supervision and therapy—Work is depressing enough without being too serious. *Journal of Strategic and Systemic Therapies* 7:49–58.

Sifneos, P. (1972). *Short-term psychotherapy and emotional crisis*. Cambridge, MA: Harvard University Press.

Solomon G.F. (1990). Emotions, stress, and immunity. In R. Ornstein and C. Swencionis (Eds.), *The healing brain: A scientific reader*. New York: Guilford.

Speck, R.V., and C.L. Attneave. (1973). *Family networks*. New York: Vintage.

Stanton, J.L., and M.D. Stanton. (1985). Treating suicidal adolescents and their families. In M.P. Mirkin and S.L. Koman (Eds.), *Handbook of adolescents and family therapy*, 309–28. New York: Gardner Press.

Stanton, J.L., and T.C. Todd, Associates. (1982). *The family therapy of drug abuse and addiction*. New York: Guilford.

Stechler, G., and E. Latz. (1966). Some observations on attention and arousal in the human infant. *Journal of the American Academy of Child Psychiatry* 5:517–25.

Tavris, C. (1990, January/February.) The politics of codependency. *Family Networker*, 43.

Tomm, K. (1987). Interventive interviewing: Part II. Reflexive questioning as a means to enable self-healing. *Family Process* 26:167–83.

———. (1989, October). *Pips, tips, hips and slips: A heuristic alternative to DSM-III?* Paper presented at annual meeting of American Association for Marriage and Family Therapy, San Francisco.

Treadway, D.C. (1989). *Before its too late: Working with substance abuse in the family*. New York: W.W. Norton.

Trivette, C. (1989). Personal communication.

Vaillant, G.E. (1977). *Adaption to Life*. Boston: Little, Brown and Co.

Varela, F.J. (1989). Reflections on the circulation of concepts between a biology of cognition and systemic family therapy. *Family Process* 28: 15–24.

Watzlawick, P. (1978). *The language of change*. New York: Basic Books.

———. (Ed.). (1984). *The invented reality*. New York: W.W. Norton.

———. (1987). If you desire to see, learn how to act. In J.K. Zeig (Ed.), *The evolution of psychotherapy*, 91–100. New York: Brunner-Mazel.

———. (1990). *Munchausen's pigtail or psychotherapy and "reality."* New York: W.W. Norton.

Watzlawick, P., J.H. Beavin, and D.D. Jackson. (1967). *Pragmatics of human communication*. New York: W.W. Norton.

Watzlawick, P., and J.C. Coyne. (1980). Depression following stroke: Brief problem-focused family treatment. *Family Process* 19:13–18. Used with permission.

Watzlawick, P., and J. Weakland, and R. Fisch. (1974). *Change: Principles of problem formation and problem resolution*. New York: W.W. Norton.

Weakland, J., R. Fisch, P. Watzlawick, and A. Bodin. (1974). Brief therapy: Focused problem resolution. *Family Process* 13:141–68.

Weick, A. (1984). The concept of responsibility in health model of social work. *Social Work in Health Care* 10(2):13–25.

Weick, K.E. (1984). Small wins: Redefining the scale of social problems. *American Psychologist* 39:40–49. Used with permission.

Wells, R.A. (1980). Engagement techniques in family therapy. *International Journal of Family Therapy* 2:75–94.

Wendorf, B. (1987). Attention deficit disorder: Addressing the biological issues in behavioral disorders. *Family Systems Medicine* 5:293–303.

Whitaker, C.A. (1976). The hindrance of theory in clinical work. In P. Guerin (Ed.), *Family therapy: Theory and practice*, 154–64. New York: Gardner.

Whitaker, C.A., and W.M. Bumberry. (1988). *Dancing with the family: A symbolic-experiential approach*. New York: Brunner-Mazel.

White, M. (1984). Pseudo-encopresis: From avalance to victory, from vicious to virtuous cycles. *Family Systems Medicine* 2:150–60.

White, M., and D. Epston. (1990). *Narrative means to therapeutic ends*. New York: W.W. Norton.

White, R. (1959). Motivation reconsidered: The concept of competence. *Psychological Review* 66:297–333.

Woodworth, R.S., and H. Schlossberg. (1954). *Experimental Psychology*. New York: Holt, Rinehart & Winston.

Wynne, L.C., S.H. McDaniel, and T.T. Weber. (1986). *Systems consultation: A new perspective for family therapy*. New York: Guilford.

———. (1987). Professional politics and the concepts of family therapy, family consultations, and systems consultation. *Family Process* 26: 153–66.

Zeig, J.K. (1985). *Experiencing Erickson: An introduction to the man and his work*. New York: Brunner-Mazel.

Zeigler, R., and L. Holden. (1988). Family therapy for learning disabled and attention-deficit disordered children. *American Journal of Orthopsychiatry* 58:196–210.

Zilbach, J. (1986). *Young children in family therapy*. New York: Brunner-Mazel.

Index

About the Authors

Steven Friedman, Ph.D., is a psychologist and coordinator of Child and Family Mental Health at the Braintree (Mass.) Center of the Harvard Community Health Plan and senior lecturer in the graduate school at Lesley College in Cambridge, Mass. He teaches courses in family therapy and brief psychotherapy and consults to human service agencies on the practice of brief psychotherapy. Dr. Friedman is the author (or co-author) of over fifty clinical and research publications, including the book *Infancy* (1978) and is listed in *American Men and Women of Science*. Dr. Friedman is co-editor, with doctors Budman and Hoyt, of *A Casebook of Brief Therapy*, to be published in 1992.

A native of Brooklyn, New York, Dr. Friedman received his A.B. degree from Long Island University, and his A.M. and Ph.D. degrees from Boston University. He received postdoctoral training in clinical psychology at George Peabody College of Vanderbilt University and at the South Shore Mental Health Center in Quincy, Mass. His current interests center on teaching and consulting in the area of brief systemic psychotherapy and in further development of possibility-oriented approaches for effective clinical intervention.

Margot Taylor Fanger, ACSW, LICSW, is a clinician in Adult Mental Health at the Harvard Community Health Plan (HCHP) in Cambridge, Massachusetts; an associate of the HCHP Teaching Center; and co-developer of the Ways to Wellness Program in the Behavioral Medicine Department. She is lecturer on psychiatry at the Cambridge Hospital, Harvard Medical School; and offers diverse workshops on possibility-oriented therapy in the Greater Boston area and nationally.

A native Californian, she was trained as a psychiatric social worker at the University of California (Berkeley). Trained as well in Neurolinguistic Programming, she holds the title of Master Programmer and a certificate in hypnosis.

Margot Taylor Fanger has taught in the schools of social work at Simmons College, Smith College, Boston College, and Boston University. Her current interests center on teaching the principles of the possibility-orientation to all health-care providers, as well as to further develop mind/body treatment approaches for clients.